Dinosaurs in Fantastic Fiction

Dinosaurs in Fantastic Fiction

A Thematic Survey

Allen A. Debus

WITH FOREWORDS BY
DONALD F. GLUT *and* MARK F. BERRY

McFarland & Company, Inc., Publishers
Jefferson, North Carolina, and London

ALSO BY ALLEN A. DEBUS

Prehistoric Monsters: The Real and Imagined
Creatures of the Past That We Love to Fear (2010)

BY ALLEN A. DEBUS, BOB MORALES AND DIANE E. DEBUS
Dinosaur Sculpting: A Complete Guide, 2d ed. (2013)

BY ALLEN A. DEBUS AND DIANE E. DEBUS
Paleoimagery: The Evolution of Dinosaurs
in Art (2002; paperback 2011)

ALL FROM MCFARLAND

The present work is a reprint of the illustrated case bound
edition of Dinosaurs in Fantastic Fiction: A Thematic
Survey, *first published in 2006 by McFarland.*

Frontispiece: This illustration reveals how dinosaurs had already
influenced popular imagination by the 1880s. Here a monstrously-sized
bipedal *Iguanodon* strikes a decidedly modern pose often repeated in science
fiction and horror dino-fiction (and film) a century later. (From Camille Flammarion's *Le*
Monde avant la creation de l'homme: Origines de la terre, Origines de la vie,
Origines de l'humanité. Paris: C. Marpon and E. Flammarion, 1886.)

LIBRARY OF CONGRESS CATALOGUING-IN-PUBLICATION DATA

Debus, Allen A.
Dinosaurs in fantastic fiction : a thematic survey / Allen A. Debus ;
with forewords by Donald F. Glut and Mark F. Berry.
p.   cm.
Includes bibliographical references and index.

ISBN 978-0-7864-7510-0
softcover : acid free paper ∞

1. Fantasy fiction, American—History and criticism.   2. Fantasy fiction,
English—History and criticism.   3. Science fiction, American—History
and criticism.   4. Science fiction, English—History and criticism.
5. Dinosaurs in literature.   I. Title.
PS374.F27D45   2013   823'.0876609—dc22   2006025700

BRITISH LIBRARY CATALOGUING DATA ARE AVAILABLE

Cover art: "A Gun for Dinosaur," Bob Eggleton, 2004

Manufactured in the United States of America

McFarland & Company, Inc., Publishers
Box 611, Jefferson, North Carolina 28640
www.mcfarlandpub.com

To my loving wife,
Diane

Acknowledgments

I would like to thank the following individuals who in some way inspired or otherwise aided this effort: Diane E. Debus; Dr. Allen G. and Brunilda Debus; Kristen L. Debus; Lisa R. Debus; Sara Debus; Juanita Ball, Mike Fredericks; Jack Arata; Bob Eggleton; Lynne Clos; Dennis Druktenis; J.D. Lees; Dr. Thomas P. Hopp; Jean Reynolds; Mark F. Berry; Donald F. Glut; James Gurney; Robert J. Sawyer; Rick Debus; Karl Debus; Tanner Wray; Steve Brusatte; Masaaki Inoue; Dee DiIacova; Gary Williams; John R. Lavas; Dr. Arthur B. Evans; Abby Brown; Terrie Poly; Ray Bradbury; James J.J. Wilson; A.C. Farley; Donald Heller; and Monty.

Contents

Foreword

by Donald F. Glut

The only book I ever read twice was *The Lost World*, Arthur Conan Doyle's 1912 adventure novel about the discovery in South America of a plateau where dinosaurs and other extinct forms of life, including early versions of Man, had somehow survived long passages of time.

My first reading of that popular classic was in 1963 during a summer vacation spent in Hollywood, California. I found myself spending much of that vacation in a small rented apartment with no phone or TV and, consequently, having a considerable amount of extra time on my hands. *The Lost World*—the 1962 Pyramid Books paperback edition of the story— filled in some of that time. I loved not only the dinosaur-related scenes, but also the story's characters, particularly Professor George Edward Challenger, the bombastic scientist who led the expedition to that plateau.

During the 1980s I read that same paperbound edition, by then in poor shape, with cover loose and pages falling out as I turned them, when the independent company First Comics hired me to adapt a comic-book version of Conan Doyle's tale for their revived *Classics Illustrated* series. The story was to have been illustrated by popular comic-book artist Arthur Adams. Alas, both that series and the company went "extinct" before my adaptation could be issued. Unfortunately, at the time optimistically believing that the project would see print, I'd already put my original (and only) copy of the script up for auction at a meeting of the Society of Vertebrate Paleontology, where someone quickly acquired it.

In a way, I sort of read *The Lost World* three times, if you also count my mother reading it to me during the late 1950s while I was bedridden with some childhood illness, having long been intrigued by a reference to it—or, rather, to the original movie adaptation—in Roy Chapman Andrews' very popular young readers' book *All About Dinosaurs*. I'd found a copy of the story at a Chicago Public Library branch in a hardbound collection of Conan Doyle's Professor Challenger stories. At the time I had still not seen the silent movie version of the story, although I had—via television—been exposed to several movies, like *Two Lost Worlds* and *Lost Continent*, having similar (i.e., "lost world") themes.

Discounting such earlier tales as Jules Verne's *Voyage au centre de la terre*, Conan Doyle's novel established the basic "lost world" theme in popular literature. Indeed, since the publication of *The Lost World*—as will be made evident by Allen A. Debus in the present book—

three story premises have traditionally served as templates for most subsequent novels and short stories involving prehistoric life: (1) The aforementioned "lost world" plot, wherein people from the modern world journey to some isolated "prehistoric place" (e.g., plateau, island, jungle, hollow earth, another planet, etc.) that has been forgotten by time; (2) the "time travel" plot, such as L. Sprague de Camp's "A Gun for Dinosaur," in which people journey, usually via some kind of time machine, back to an earlier era (although this theme can have the same kinds of incidents and characters found in the "lost world" theme); and (3) the "prehistoric era" plot, as in Jack London's *Before Adam*, wherein the story is actually set in some bygone era.

Yet a fourth premise—that of a (usually gigantic) prehistoric creature creating havoc in a modern city, a staple of Hollywood movies established in the first *Lost World* movie—is more rare in prose fiction. Obviously scenes of dinosaurs and other extinct monsters stepping on automobiles and knocking down buildings are better suited for the motion-picture screen than the printed page. Most published stories based upon this theme have been adaptations of screenplays, e.g., novelizations of the movies *Gorgo* and *Reptilicus*, both of which featured added sex scenes—not seen in the movies themselves—to supplement the scenes of mass destruction.

Of all the above plot premises, the "lost world" theme seems to have been the most popular, especially in earlier and less sophisticated decades when the real world was less explored and mapped, and when it might not have seemed that far fetched to imagine that such "pocket worlds" as plateaus and islands populated by prehistoric beasts could really exist.

Like the author of this book, I've long been a fan of fiction with prehistoric themes. In fact, I've tapped the "lost world" theme myself in three novels—*Spawn!* (1976), inspired by Conan Doyle's and Burroughs' tales, but also by Michael Crichton's *Westworld*, about a theme park where the main attraction is alien dinosaurs, and where things go terribly wrong (I've heard that Crichton later authored his own novel about a dinosaur theme park); *Frankenstein in the Lost World* (2002), including story elements borrowed from Sir Arthur as well as Mary Wollstonecraft Shelley, Edgar Rice Burroughs and the movie *King Kong*; and *Dinosaur Valley Girls: The Novel* (in press, at the time of this writing), based on the screenplay for a motion picture I directed a decade ago.

Novels and short stories featuring dinosaurs and other forms of ancient life have long provided readers with an escapist means of experiencing the primitive thrills and romance found in exotic, far-off localities and remote periods of "deep time." Through such tales the reader could live vicariously the adventures of Professor Challenger, David Innes, Tarzan, Jongor and other protagonists whose exploits often brought them into contact with such erstwhile creatures. Many of these tales are no longer in print or are not easily obtainable.

Thanks to Allen A. Debus, however, equally a fan and a scholar of such fiction, many of those "lost worlds" have been rediscovered, preserved between the covers of this excellent book.

Donald F. Glut is a prolific book and article writer and movie producer-director. Among his many works are *Dinosaurs: The Encyclopedia* (1997; paperback, 2013) and its seven *Supplements* (1999 through 2012), *Carbon Dates* (1999), *Jurassic Classics* (2001), *The Frankenstein Archive* (2002), *I Was a Teenage Movie Maker* (2007) and *Shock Theatre Chicago Style* (2012)—all published by McFarland.

Foreword

by Mark F. Berry

For a book entitled *Dinosaurs in Fantastic Fiction*, trying to think of a potential author more ideally qualified than Allen A. Debus would be like trying to think of a dinosaur cooler than *Tyrannosaurus Rex*. Mr. Debus' expertise spanning the worlds of dinosaur science and dinosaur fiction is equaled only by his love and enthusiasm for same, and the variety of titles found on his paleo-authorial résumé offers a clue to the diversity of his interests. Whether exploring the possibilities of prehistoric giant squid in "Monster Teuthoid from the Tethys" or looking at the history of lizards portraying movie dinosaurs in "Get Real! Dinosaur Masquerade," whether surveying the fantasy dinosaurs of alien planets in "Exo-Dinosaurs Attack!" or discussing the real-life ceratopsians in "In Praise of Mesozoic Buffalo," there is always this constant and unmistakable vein of affection, enjoyment, thoroughness, and pure dinosaur fun running through everything Debus writes. It is, I believe, impossible for anyone who enjoys the classic works of dinosaur fiction not to also relish the nonfiction paleo-writings of that self-described "dinosaur groupie," Allen A. Debus.

Although dinosaur fiction predated dinosaur cinema by several decades, the two are intimately connected. What is possibly the first moving picture ever to include dinosaurs, 1905's *Prehistoric Peeps*, born from the printed media, in this case a popular cartoon series of the same name that ran in England's *Punch* magazine. In the years to follow, many of the major works of dino-fiction have been pressed into duty as ready-made starter kits for filmmakers to adapt—with, it should be noted, widely varying degrees of success. Some of the best-known dinosaur movies in history would not exist if authors like Jules Verne, Sir Arthur Conan Doyle, and Edgar Rice Burroughs had never penned their imaginative sagas. Conan Doyle's seminal *The Lost World* was the first to be filmed, of course, with First National's groundbreaking silent epic in 1925 ... or was it? Pioneering Spanish filmmaker Segundo de Chomon made a version of Verne's *Journey to the Center of the Earth* way back in 1909, three years before Conan Doyle's book was published. Verne's adventure was successfully given the big-budget treatment a half century later by 20th Century–Fox, with an excellent James Mason as the estimable Professor Lindenbrook. Dinosaurs have even been arbitrarily added by filmmakers to not one but two different move versions of Verne's *Hector Servadac!*

The dinosaurian stories of Edgar Rice Burroughs, most notably his trilogy of the prehistoric continent of "Caprona" (of "Caspak"), were neglected by moviemakers for decades. Though Johnny Weissmuller's Tarzan encountered a few dinosaurs—for no particular reason—in 1943's RKO quickie *Tarzan's Desert Mystery*, Burroughs' beloved dinosaur fantasies had to wait until 1975's frugally budgeted yet enjoyable *The Land That Time Forgot* for their big-screen debut. The even less opulent *The People That Time Forgot* followed two years later, with an unremarkable filming of *At the Earth's Core* sandwiched in between. The same core production team spoke of completing Burroughs' Caspak trilogy with the final installment, *Out of Time's Abyss*, but the project was never filmed. On the other hand, Conan Doyle's *The Lost World* has been tapped time and time again, with no fewer than half a dozen examples having been produced as of this writing. In 1960, thirty-five years after the silent classic, the first *Lost World* remake appeared, an ambitious but flawed spectacle directed by Irwin Allen and greenlighted as a direct result of the success of Fox's *Journey to the Center of the Earth*. The novel was filmed four more times—none of them for theatrical release—between 1992 and 2001, the latest example being a very handsome and entertaining effort from the BBC.

Considered as a whole, the dino-fiction of Jules Verne, Arthur Conan Doyle, and Edgar Rice Burroughs spanned the years from the mid–nineteenth century through the first quarter of the twentieth, and all of the stories in question share the basic notion of prehistoric creatures' being discovered in some hidden corner of the globe—or even *inside* the globe. By the time Michael Crichton put fictional dinosaurs back on the bestseller lists in 1990, satellite imagery and other modern wonders had rendered the "lost world" plot obsolete. Yes, there still remains the option of *setting* your story in an earlier time and relying on the willing suspension of disbelief (as did director Peter Jackson with his affectionate *King Kong* remake), or envisioning an "alternate history" (like Greg Bear's novel *Dinosaur Summer*), but Crichton decided that, by gum, if technology could take away the traditional "lost world," it could darn well usher in a new type of dinosaur fiction to replace it. His techno-thriller *Jurassic Park* not only sparked an even greater interest in dinosaurs in general, it all but forced the renewal of the grand tradition of dinosaur sagas' moving from page to screen. I mean, when a bestselling novelist writes a book about scientifically reincarnated dinosaurs running amok in a tropical theme park, just at the time when a filmmaker named Steven Spielberg is itching to return to the fantasy/creature realms of his early career, *and* some of the top special effects artist of the day have been raised on and inspired by the classic dino-magic of Willis O'Brien and Ray Harryhausen ... how could a blockbuster knock-your-socks-off dinosaur movie *not* be the result? Filmmakers—at least, those with imagination—have never needed much coaxing to put dinosaurs on the screen, and a popular piece of dino-fiction sitting available on a bookshelf, whether by Verne or Burroughs or Conan Doyle or Crichton, has often been all that was needed to get the cameras rolling.

If dinosaur fiction has always been an obvious and ready source for dinosaur screenplays, the filmmakers faced one big problem that the writers did not. Talented authors can create whatever dinosaur or other prehistoric creature they desire, and place it in the most magnificent of primordial milieus, all with the proverbial stroke of a pen, while the moviemakers must try to bring the beasts into physical being. Where the novelist could utilize the reader's mind as a canvas, the movie people had to rely on special effects artists and technicians, art directors, cinematographers and others, who in turn often had very little to rely on other than their own intrepidity. Sometimes, when stop-motion animation or skill-fully crafted animatronics or—in recent years—expert computer graphics were employed, the results were outstanding and beloved classics of fantasy film genre were born. Other times, inevitably, the outcomes were less than sufficient, especially when modern-day rep-tiles with rubber appliances or modern-day stuntmen in rubber suits were asked to portray the wondrous creatures. Still, dinosaur movie fans tend to be a forgiving lot, and even the less authentic dinos have inspired much enjoyment and affection. But the fact remains that dinosaurs in film are limited by such things as technological capabilities, inadequate budg-ets, and inflexible schedules, while the dinosaurs of fiction are limited only by the author's talent, and the reader's capacity for visualizing the fantastic. The techniques for putting dinosaurs on the screen have repeatedly changed, and will continue to change even until someday the word "screen" itself becomes meaningless. But an inspired writer, armed only with a love of dinosaurs and words on a page, will always be able to bring the magnificent beasts back to roaring, thundering, earth-shaking life. And thanks to Allen Debus, we now have a wonderful companion and guide to that world of dinosaur fiction that has given us all so much prehistoric pleasure.

Mark F. Berry is the author of *The Dinosaur Filmography* (McFarland, 2002) and has written on prehistoric animals in pop culture for *Film Fax, Prehistoric Times, CreatureScape,* and *Horror Biz.*

Preface

Why should we care about what science fiction writers have to say about dinosaurs? It's because those who have written such stories care a great deal about dinosaurs. And through their talents and our collective imaginations, we are taken to an exotic Neverland, on to vivid encounters with living dinosaurs. Can one dream up any animals more appropriate for science fiction story-telling? Such tales help us rein in the possibilities and probabilities of a fascinating science, which is itself woven in the abyss of time and remote (paleo-ecological) space. Dinosaur bones and what we know about them *are* the essence of science fiction—a great race of beings that survived for an incomprehensible 160 *million* years! Yet they all disappeared in the aftermath of an unimaginably horrific, and era-ending event.

Or did they?

Let me offer a personalized twist in reply to that time-honored question, "Why do I so love dinosaurs?" In the spring of 2003, during a downturn in my father's health, I had occasion to drive us back to our roots, old local neighborhoods dimly recalled through dusty family photo albums dating back to the early 1950s. One of these places, my first residence after leaving the hospital, beginning in August 1954, was at a Roger's Court street address in Waukegan, Illinois. There, my family lived in a small second story apartment overlooking a ravine. During my visit there in 2003, it was revealed to me for the first time that this was the very ravine which fired author Ray Bradbury's creative instincts three decades earlier. References to Waukegan's ravine are recurrent in Bradbury's books like *Dandelion Wine* through fictional settings such as his mythical Green Town. Perhaps it's no coincidence that two of my favorite fantasy tales involving dinosaurs happen to be his "A Sound of Thunder" and "The Fog Horn." It was just really cool, after so many years, to be able to make this somewhat tenuous, slightly extrasensory connection to my favorite author of fantastic fiction!

I was raised on Syd Hoff's magical children's story *Danny and the Dinosaur* (1958). My parents used to read that story to me at bedtime in the late 1950s, and whenever they finished I'd beg them to reread it. *Danny and the Dinosaur* blends elements of outrageous dinosaur fantasy (a talking dinosaur having the personality of a friendly puppy) with Hoff's wonderful cartoon paleoimagery, even borrowing from dinosaur monster-on-the-loose-in-the-big-city lore. Danny's toothless dinosaur at first appears as a life-sized museum restoration that comes to life in the form of a polite, friendly plateosaur-ish sort of creature. Carrying Danny about on his neck, he takes the boy on a tour of the city. Instead of fleeing in terror, people come flocking to see Danny's dinosaur. The only time anyone runs from the dinosaur is when Danny's friends play hide and seek, after the dinosaur covers his eyes without peeking. In the end, after having a "wonderful day" together, the best his dinosaur pal has had in a hundred million years, Danny and the dinosaur part ways. Danny goes home alone, reflecting, "We don't have room for a pet that size." Was it all a dream? The dinosaur must return to his museum display setting, perhaps tragically never to live this way again, ever ... that is, until the next evening, when the tale would be read to me once more.

Several years later, I read *The Anytime Rings* (1963) by R. Faraday, a now obscure chapter book intended for young adults, in which kids are whisked magically back to a prehistoric realm with their pet *Cynognathus*, which rescues them from a tribe of menacing cavemen. And how many of you realized there was even a dinosaur in the land of Oz—yes, the land of Dorothy, the Wicked Witch and the Scarecrow? Dinosaurs were extremely popular in the early 1930s, perhaps inspiring Ruth Plumley Thompson to create a dinosaur character, illustrated by John R. Neill, for *Speedy in Oz* (1934). We had it on the bookshelf at home.

As you may suspect, reliance on dinosaurs to charm younger readers is an elderly ploy. But while the uninitiated may have been deluded into believing that Michael Crichton's *Jurassic Park* (1990) was the one and only dinosaur science fiction story written for adults, they would be surprised to learn that dinosaurs and other prehistoria of science fiction and fantasy literature intended for adult readership have haunted us for nearly two centuries!

How did prehistoric animals get into fictional settings of literature, and why are they featured? Are there patterns established within the early genre of dinosaur fiction writing?

Stimulated by the Darwinian controversy, paleo-fiction of the early twentieth century is characteristically laden with evolutionary messages. During this time, writers plotted stories in which prehistoric animals inhabited the subterranean realm because there was some science supporting the idea of a hollow earth. Alternatively, nineteenth-century paleontologists had sufficient cause to believe that some prehistoric life forms would be found living in the world's isolated corners and oceanic recesses, based on Thomas Henry Huxley's conclusions concerning the primordial ooze described as *Bathybius*. Dredging up organisms from the sea floor stimulated a "romantic trek: a quest in the uncharted depths for lost empires. Here might be living fossils, 'survivors of a world passed away,' creatures from the dinosaurian Chalk Era. And why not? Wasn't the chalky *Globigerina* mud made up of microscopic shells like those in our Cretaceous rocks? This hunt for past forms would become endlessly enmeshed in the science fiction notion of prehistoric monsters dredged from the deep, but for a moment it seemed real."[1]

Later, prehistoric animals were forced into hidden places—misty plateaus or uncharted islands—until the time that geographers had almost everything mapped, without sighting prehistoric animals. In fact, the first *adult* dinosaur fiction novel I ever read, in 1968, was an Ace Books 1960s reprint of Edgar Rice Burroughs' *The Land That Time Forgot* (1918). Burroughs combined elements of a strange "alternate evolution" with deadly dinosaur encounters on a lost island setting.

Next, writers turned to physics and chemistry for inspiration. In the mid–twentieth century, radioactive dinosaurs out of the atomic age threatened civilization. Or sometimes Man went out of his way to encounter living dinosaurs, enlisting time machines and technological devices designed to flip us into parallel universes. Michael Crichton deserves credit for sustaining interest in dinosaurs during the 1990s, although his novel *Jurassic Park* (1990), with its bio-engineered beasties, probably wouldn't have been written had dinosaur popularity not escalated to unprecedented levels during the preceding decade. Following the dinosaur discoveries of the late 1970s, however, science fiction writers were refreshed and writing about dinosaurs again. Increasingly, since description of the real hadrosaur genus *Maiasaura* in 1979, fictional dinosaurs of literature such as those inhabiting James Gurney's imaginary *Dinotopia* seem less monstrous.

Because dinosaurs were no longer regarded as sluggish, cold-blooded brutes, evolutionary mistakes destined for extinction, dinosaurs of 1980s and 1990s fantasy literature had shifted remarkably. The new dinosaurs were quick and lively and smart, warm-blooded, sufficiently cold and calculating to be like humans. Yet, in many ways they were superior to Man. The real danger was that if we let them get a clawed foot in the door, human civilization would be history. They would own a future that should rightfully be ours.

Prehistoric life has inspired science fiction writings since the Romantic period in England. A gentlemanly, traditional form of geological sermonizing was through poetry or, more effectively, blending verses with visuals. If the idea of paleo-poetry sounds quaint or even foreign to you, how many dino-philes would recall the most famous dinosaur poem of all, written by Bert L. Taylor in 1912 for the *Chicago Tribune*? This is the poem about *Stegosaurus'* supposed two brains, beginning with these familiar words, "Behold the mighty dinosaur,/ Famous in prehistoric lore...."

Dinosaur speculations begin with language, often a visual language, perhaps because of the alien aspect of prehistoric landscapes. We want to see as much as possible into the remote past, far beyond what words can convey. Charles Dickens was in the vanguard of those who welcomed dinosaur imagery as literary devices. Dickens contemplated dinosaurs in this metaphorical opening passage, setting the mood for his 1853 novel *Bleak House*: "Implacable weather. As much mud in the streets as if the waters had but newly retired from the face of the earth, and it would not have been wonderful to meet a Megalosaurus, forty feet long or so, waddling like an elephantine lizard up Holburn Hill." In his reference to retreating flood waters, Dickens, who was most surely aware of the construction of Benjamin Waterhouse Hawkins' dinosaurian sculptures for the Crystal Palace exhibition—first displayed in 1854 on the prehistoric island at Sydenham—reflected on the reversibility of nature. Can we bring back dinosaurs and other Mesozoic life simply by altering planetary ecology? Over a century later, in his 1962 novel *The Drowned World*, J.G. Ballard foretold of how the Triassic saurian environment would reestablish itself when flood waters encroached in the aftermath of natural disaster. We'd be wise not to harm Mother Nature.

The present work, *Dinosaurs in Fantastic Fiction*, primarily covers the subject of dinosaurs in literature. In fact, perhaps *the* overlooked category of "paleoartists" are the master writers who weave uncanny tales from prehistoric lands with words. Accordingly, this book is devoted to classic dinosaur writers viewed as paleoartists who recreate prehistory and restore dinosaurs and other prehistoria to life through classic and pulp literature. Their influences and the impact of their words are closely examined in historical and pop-cultural contexts. I am very selective about dinosaur fiction intended for younger readers (e.g., Oliver Butterworth's 1956 *The Enormous Egg*); I don't treat "cave romances" (e.g., Jean Auel's *Clan of the Cave Bear*) unless dinosaurs are involved; and I de-emphasize comics (e.g., *Turok—Son of Stone*). To me, cave romances of the late nineteenth and early twentieth centuries (involving cavemen in contemporary settings) seem inherently apart from fiction involving other pre-historic animals that existed before mankind's arrival. The former are prehistorical stone-age-themed novels with some evolutionary sound bites often thrown in for good measure, while the latter have a more cryptozoological flavor. Where in the modern world, or how—using scientific devices including time machines—can one find the exotic dinosaur, and what does it represent to a contemporary audience? That's the ticket.

This book considers historical trends in the crafting of classic dinosaur stories. It explores the enlivened figurative and metaphoric meaning of fictional dinosaurs and related prehistoria (a term introduced in my 2002 book, *Paleoimagery*). Contemporary ideas about geology, the Cold War, environmentalism, the space race, time travel, evolution, bioengi-neering, geopolitics, and the time-honored Frankenstein myth are mirrored in fantastic fiction. Everything from the significance of imagetext in the 1867 edition of Jules Verne's *Journey to the Center of the Earth*, through Ray Bradbury's beloved dinosaurians to the iconic *Tyrannosaurus rex*, the twentieth century's most popular dino-monster, are assessed. Select novelizations of movie scripts such as Delos W. Lovelace's *King Kong* (Grosset & Dunlap, 1932) are also examined.

Dinosaurs are emphasized throughout, although other favored pseudo-dinosaurs such as pterodactyls, finbacked reptiles and other famous prehistoria—including primeval mam-malian and avian forms—are discussed. Rather than actually prehistoric in nature, many so-called prehistoric animals of fantastic fiction (excluding tales where prehistoric life is encountered by humans in earth's past through use of time-travel, or on alien planets) would appear to be cryptozoological species instead. After all, if they're prehistoric, they shouldn't be interacting with modern humans at all, at least in our present. Many of the creatures loosely named "dinosaurs" in the movies, such as the *Rhedosaurus* from *The Beast from 20,000 Fathoms* (Warner Bros., 1953), as well as its literary antecedent appearing in Bradbury's "The Fog Horn," aren't truly dinosaurs; for the purposes of this book, however, I regard them as sufficiently prehistoric-looking pseudo-dinosaurs. Here, I follow Mark F. Berry's formula as expressed in the preface to his fascinating book, *The Dinosaur Filmography* (McFarland, 2002), where his criteria for inclusion specified, "The movie must show on screen one or more creatures represented as *prehistoric, reptilian,* and *non-humanoid*...." Inaccurate portrayals such as magnified live reptiles are included, as long as the intent is to represent a real or fictional "dinosaur." However, whereas Berry disqualified films featuring "only prehistoric mammals," instead, in the present work, I cover literature involving a wider variety of prehistoric ani-mals, but not stories featuring only cavemen in their natural paleoecological settings.

Now a word about the Appendix. There is insufficient space to discuss the hundreds of stories that could be covered in a book of this nature. Each chapter outlines a problem or theme placed in historical context naturally emphasizing more than a handful of stories for illustration. However, in cases where significant tales only received short shrift in chap-ter contents, or where personal favorites couldn't be otherwise incorporated, I've included a short summary of that particular story in the Appendix, which for practical reasons has been abbreviated as much as possible. Admittedly, selections were made with a nod to sub-jectivity. I'll omit my own "Frankenstein vs. the Creature from Another World," destined for a future *Scary Monsters* issue, in which the fabled Frankenstein monster assists a NASA team in destroying a cruel alien from Altair—a member of the Krell race found frozen, along with a cache of Ice Age mammals inside a spaceship which crashed in Antarctica millennia ago. One of these, a *Megatherium*, is revivified with the alien. (There—I sneaked in a reference to my story anyway!) There's just no end to the madness, is there?

This first-of-its-kind book addresses prehistoria in fiction and fantasy like never before. While there have been a handful of articles covering "standards" such as Conan Doyle's *The Lost World*, Burroughs's prehistoric fauna, Godzilla's significance and the relevance of Crichton's recombinant dinosaurs, no book has been devoted to the topic of dinosaurs, emphasizing the literature, until now.

The book is regrettably chauvinistic, as the emphasis must be on stories available in English. Thus, I don't comment further on Russian paleontologist Ivan Antanovich Efremov (1907–1972), who wrote dinosaur fiction with (translated) titles like *Star Ships* (1948), and *The Shadow of the Past* (1953),[2] or Japanese writer Shigeru Kayama's novelization *Gojira* from the original movie script. However, I run the gamut of things dinosaur without neglecting several superb examples of dinosaur literature reflecting Cold War angst.

In their 1986 outline of the history of science fiction, *Trillion Year Spree*, Brian Aldiss and David Wingrove refer to the escapist literature subgenre of tales of prehistory. I would propose a related subgenre, loosely termed "dinosaur fiction," encompassing stories about prehistoric life, whether encountered in man's past, present or future. I clarify this definition as the book proceeds. But first, let's explore the roots of this genre, shall we?

Allen A. Debus
Fall 2006
Hanover Park, IL

Introduction

"Where the scientist must speculate reservedly from known fact and make a small leap into the unknown, the writer is free to soar high on the wings of fancy."[1]

Perhaps unwittingly, I began this book more than two decades ago with a short amateurish article titled "The Lost Worlds of Science Fiction" printed in the October 1983 issue of an extinct fanzine named *Cosmic Landscapes.*[2] Then, more than ten years ago, I reexplored the topic for the *Earth Science News* (bulletin of the Earth Science Club of Northern Illinois)[3]; these excursions were mere summaries of a vast and growing literature. After an even longer hiatus, during the fall of 2004, I decided to pursue a topic of particular interest, the meaning of "imagetext" as conveyed collectively by artist and writer in the 1867 edition of Jules Verne's *Journey to the Center of the Earth.* With my intentions being to elaborate further how Verne's classic can be interpreted as a life-through-time museum tour, the work simply, naturally expanded into this volume.

Imagetext is relevant to any discussion of science fiction literature. After all, fantasy writers succeed by seeding dark visions in our minds, each reader then conjuring his or her own unique scene visualization. Books and stories are sometimes transformed into film and televised broadcasts with varying success. Often, sadly, the book is relegated to secondary importance, if the show is successful. Is this simply because reading is harder to do than watching a screen? Maybe, but also perhaps because for many of us images prove longer lasting than words. Words convey more exact meaning and emotion. Yet a well-orchestrated *combination* of words and visuals can be ... truly *awesome!*

Jules Verne and Edouard Riou started a tradition that just won't quit. Since the early twentieth century, most magazines offering dino-fiction fare, as well as later science fiction pulps and graphic novels, have included their share of startling visuals used for story promotion and illustration. Today, paperback novels and sci-fi magazines often have dinosaurs emblazoned on their covers as "come-ons," advertising incredible tales to be found therein. Artistry within and on the jacket covers of James Gurney's *Dinotopia* volumes exceptionally exemplifies how dinosaur imagetext is employed in the modern day. And front cover artistry of Bob Eggleton, William Stout and Bob Walters merits mention in the modern day as well.

I've wrestled with what this book was supposed to be a companion to. Early on, because of an emphasis on the "text" part of the imagetext formula, the idea of *Dinosaurs in Fantastic Fiction* nicely complemented my recent writings on "paleoimagery," focusing more on visual images than textual content. But *Dinosaurs in Fantastic Fiction* may also be considered the dinosaur equivalent to Charles De Paolo's 2003 book, *Human Prehistory in Fiction*, which dealt with stories that Charles G.D. Roberts, author of *In the Morning of Time*, referred to in 1919 as "a kind of historical romance—about Prehistoric men." And yet ties could be made to Mark F. Berry's *The Dinosaur Filmography* as well.

Besides my own scattered explorations of dino-fiction, there have been few attempts to tackle this subject matter. In his *The Dinosaur Scrapbook* (1980), Donald F. Glut included two landmark chapters titled "The Lost Worlds of Edgar Rice Burroughs" and "The Pulp Dinosaurs." Three months following publication of my *Dinosaur Memories* (June, 2002)—which included a section titled "Fantasy Dinosaurs"—paleontologist Jose Luis Sanz's *Starring T. Rex! Dinosaur Mythology and Popular Culture* was released, with its emphasis on dinosaur films. So in a way, all of these precursors are intellectually related to the present volume.

A website purporting to list author and publishing information for every dinosaur novel, short story and novella ever published offers perspective on how prevalent dino-fiction has become in recent years. When I tack on a few stories I'm aware of that were omitted from a 2003 listing, the total number of tales is nearly 300. I find it interesting that nearly 60 percent of the stories were published since 1990, right on the heels of *Jurassic Park*. For over a century, from the genre's beginning in 1854, through 1965—a year representing the beginning of America's dinosaur renaissance movement—only about 25 percent of dino-fiction had seen publication.

As the stories themselves offer escapist possibilities, *writing* this book has been an escape of sorts from worry and the trappings of modern culture. Rereading old absorbing favorites such as Bradbury's dino-tales, Crichton's *Jurassic Park* duo, Verne's *Journey*, Burroughs' "Caspak" trilogy, as well as a host of fresh examples, has uplifted me from middle-age doldrums. Vicariously, I've enjoyed and overcome many impossible or often fearful episodes through the unforgettable and often heroic experiences of Afsan, Toroca, Edward Malone, Reginald Rivers, Axel, Captain Kirk and Raptor Red. I've juxtaposed "serious" classic literature such as Verne's *Journey to the Center of the Earth* and Conan Doyle's *The Lost World* with pulp novels like Carson Bingham's *Gorgo* or David Gerrold's *Deathbeast*. You see, it's never been my purpose to critique literature here, but rather to paint broad brush strokes of how this time-honored legacy of fantastic literature originated, developed and matured especially within a pop-cultural, speculative scientific framework. I've striven to tell a story from the stories themselves and each tale forms a piece of the puzzle. And yet this book isn't intended as a complete compilation of all stories tied to the genre that have ever been printed or published. Rather, this is a survey of the field. Toward that endeavor, older works are potentially more significant than later, possibly derivative writings because the former, which are far fewer in number, may represent pivotal ground-breaking undertakings or launching points.[4]

Does it matter where human contact with prehistoric life occurs, whether in outer space, prehistory or even more surreptitiously in our own city streets and backyards? In a universal sense, aren't all the fictional realms inhabited by prehistoric animals unequivocal "lost worlds"? That may well be. However, we require further sub-classification of these fictional places and environments—comprising the lost worlds of science fiction and horror—because, intriguingly, use of such devices is tied to human history and industry.

Just as trends may be identified in the history of paleoart and paleoimagery,[5] broad brush strokes may also made in what has been defined here as "dino-fiction." Here, my emphasis is on non-human prehistoric life, while recognizing that it's impossible to consider the genre unless ape-men, Neanderthals and Cro-Magnon cave peoples also are admitted into the discussion.

I note in this work how prehistoric animals—dinosaurs in particular—matured from paleontological infancy. At first, they were cast as curiosities to be gazed upon as one would a specimen in a museum case. Later they were viewed as brutish monstrosities, or as "paleo-props" symbolizing prehistory, extinction, or, more intriguingly, evolution. Dinosaurs waged war with man, represented the Bomb, and traveled through space and time, as writers comprehended modern physics while mysteries of the cosmos unfolded. Dinosaurs then became smarter than we, as we learned more about genuine dinosaur societies of the past and dwelled upon their horrific extinction. In this fictional realm, arguably the grandest invention of all has been the intelligent "dinosauroid." However, I recognize that this view may be too Procrustean for some; others may tell the tale of the dinosaur tale differently.

A vital first step toward infiltration within human society would be for dinosaurs to attain human-like intelligence and to adopt customs that are human-like. Ultimately, dinosaur intelligence coupled with humanoid attributes leads to or facilitates integration/infiltration into human society. Increasingly, and reflecting our comprehension of rising dinosaurian savvy, dino-fiction has been told from a personified first-hand dinosaurian perspective. In short, an uncanny resonance between science and paleontological pop-culture has shaped this remarkable, previously uncharted pathway through the annals of fictional dinosaurs. Over the course of fifteen decades, while mankind has striven to think of, or to think like, dinosaurs, we've seen dinosaurs gradually evolve into people, a classic case of Dressler's Syndrome, the fictional illness invented by Eric Garcia in *Anonymous Rex* (2000) and *Casual Rex* (2001)!

And what's the reader's role? Wouldn't we aspire to become the omniscient "Watcher" of Sawyer's *Quintaglio* trilogy, or the "Outsider" of Landis's short classic "Embracing the Alien," or even view earthly doings from on high as did the wise old pterosaur in Bakker's *Raptor Red?*

Well, you can! *If* you read on the "wings of fancy."

CHAPTER 1

Verne's Subterranean
"Museum"

BACKGROUND

To most of us, the title *Journey to the Center of the Earth* (20th Century–Fox, 1959) conjures images of James Mason, singer Pat Boone and actress Arlene Dahl cavorting through a Hollywood forest of giant fiberglass mushrooms prior to being threatened on the shore of the Central Sea by Hollywood's best gagged-up, costumed lizards ever, that much-larger-than-life herd of *Dimetrodons*. Special effects master L.B. Abbott's rhinoceros iguanas outfitted with realistic looking sails, framed to look absolutely enormous on-screen, vaulted pseudo-dinosaurs onto the pantheon of mainstream Hollywood monsters. Few realized, however, that Jules Verne never incorporated the species *Dimetrodon* in his novel, a masterpiece which until now has been misinterpreted. (For the purists, *Dimetrodon* was a pelycosaur, not a dinosaur.)

Although the 1959 film is one of my favorites, it cannot surpass the novel itself. True, Verne was intrigued by prehistoric life, a fascination conveyed in his epic novel. And Verne did allow readers to sample a living prehistory in *Journey to the Center of the Earth* (1864, 1867), providing vivid confrontations with the most awful extinct prehistoria then known to science. However, in order to comprehend the greatest dinosaurs and other speculative prehistoric monsters which followed in a science fiction tradition, we must appreciate literary inspirations leading to Verne's remarkable *Journey*, while understanding their forceful impact and persistence.[1]

Long regarded as a geological epic, the 1867 edition of Jules Verne's (1828–1905) *Journey to the Center of the Earth* should instead be viewed as a *paleontological* opus. First, artistic use of imagetext (a melding of artistic visuals with written text) is presented in a life-through-time sequence. Secondly, the apex (or climax) of the story occurs on the shores and waters of the Lidenbrock Sea (e.g., the Central Sea as referred to in the 1959 film), where living prehistoria are encountered, and also where Axel has his waking dream, brilliantly reinforcing the life-through-time motif. Furthermore, Verne entertained questions central to the Darwinian controversy. Principal scientific problems explored in the novel are (a) controversy over central heat/fire, a matter related to cooling earth theory, and (b) how did antediluvian men and animals get inside the earth? Resolution of these interrelated points under-scores how *Journey's* 1867 edition is predominantly a fictionalized paleontological treatise, or odyssey through life's history.

Journey is a mystical grand tour through a cavernous "museum" where fossil exhibits are encountered *in situ*, where prehistoric monsters come alive literally and imaginatively, and where signage offers explanations to each display framed in contemporary paleontolog-ical knowledge (i.e., through Axel's written commentary). Verne's Lidenbrock Sea environ-ment represents a Romantic culmination of the oracular cave setting, a popular paleo-fiction metaphor persisting into the twentieth century.

IMAGETEXT, PALEOART, AND CAVE METAPHOR

In fiction, dinosaurs and other prehistoric animals reflect our aspirations, human ten-dencies, contemporary understanding of nature, earth history and, perhaps especially, our fears. Yet favored prehistoria have been traditionally projected into modernity through time portals, allowing us to witness the remote past alive. The earliest available window into pre-history was the cave setting where, in fact, fossil vertebrate deposits were often encountered. Poets and geologists alike established the iconic cave as a literary device by the early nine-teenth century. According to University of Chicago cultural historian William J.T. Mitchell, dinosaurs and other prehistoric animals are constructed images because their fossilized remains must be reassembled in one form or another for modern man to visualize and com-prehend. Thus, full comprehension reflecting contemporary scientific understanding, often culturally founded, is supplemented by words, "descriptive terms, narratives, and statements. We never *see* a dinosaur without *saying* something about it, naming it, describing it, or telling its story. The dinosaur is thus a composite 'imagetext,' a combination of verbal and visual signs."[2] Imagetext is then a mixed medium of messages; dinosaur imagery is established through artistic use of imaginative time-portals.

The practice of fossil vertebrate reconstruction matured considerably during the late eighteenth century. By the 1810s, in-the-flesh, lifelike restorations of fossil creatures were being attempted by artists who increasingly speculated about missing, non-preserved soft tissue anatomy such as integument, musculature and hair. At the time, the only sort of writ-ten text considered appropriate for accompanying such images were technical, scientific descriptions. As Martin J. S. Rudwick noted in his *Scenes from Deep Time* (1992), speculative imagetext (or imagery) was avoided at all costs to "safeguard ... scientific prestige and author-ity..." of practicing scientists' careers and to uphold credibility in the relatively new scientific discipline of geology.[3] By the 1830s, however, images associated with prehistoric vertebrates had daringly developed in complexity, reflecting a divergence in the field of 'paleoart.'[4] Rud-wick suggests that by then, "'geology' emerged as a self-conscious new discipline with clearly defined intellectual goals ... there was thus a comparable emergence of ... a *visual language* for the science...," exemplified by increasing reliance on and complexity in published depic-tions such as geological maps and diagrams representing geological time, for which conven-tions had been devised to clarify understanding.[5] Specialized imagetext—scenes from deep time, idealized landscapes of remote ages incorporating life recreations of extinct animals and flora—formed a conventional part of this visual language.

Recognizing that even most *scientific* descriptions of prehistoric organisms introduce elements of speculation, the roots of a *literary* paleo-*fiction* become noticeable during the 1820s and early 1830s, when two artistic British scientists, William Conybeare (1787–1857) and Henry De la Beche (1796–1855), merged verse or text deftly with illustration. They illustrated remote prehistory, drawing inspiration from fossils found in caves. In time caves, subterranean cavernous spaces penetrating into an abyss of time became a principal metaphor. One accessed the earth's deep interior through a cave mouth, an oft-used poetic metaphor. Thus, as contemporary gentleman scientists and Romantic poets alike comprehended, for those possessing special sensibilities, the Earth would 'speak,' yielding secrets of its past or future.

During Britain's Golden Age of geology and Romanticism (circa 1770 to 1830), writers perceived a mystic union between man and nature fully accentuated by the cave environment. As noted by Marianne Sommer, in the hands of 1820s diluvial geologists, caves had become windows into the past: "...the descent into the cave was styled in the manner of a quest in poetry as well as in geology, and the scientific and poetic personae were constructed as the equivalent of the hero or knight, equipped with peculiar faculties to overcome the obstacles of caving and eventually to read the 'annals of the cave.'"[6] For many, the experience of caving evoked awe and terror, feelings of sublimity associated with an immensity of time.[7] According to Sommer, who doesn't discuss Verne in her thesis, "The task of making sense of the contents of caves was sometimes perceived as demanding a kind of gift that allowed the conjurer to evoke the deep past. This notion as well as the visions themselves ... often came close to poetry. Although the hammer and pickaxe of the early explorers cannot be said to correspond to any Romantic ideal of man's interaction with nature, the pioneers again and again gave way to expressions of awe, to emotions of fear mixed with pleasure, timidity mixed with curiosity."[8]

While those held spellbound by such awful majesty were conjurers known to create verses inspired by the oracular cave setting, science was the key to unearthing secrets from caves. So, the cave's special language—often geology—must be comprehended. Or, as in Jules Verne's *Journey*, for example, a metaphoric "code" (i.e., Arne Saknussemm's) must be deciphered before the nature of prehistoric life will unfold for two geologists deep within the bowels of the earth. Saknussemm's runic code is entirely analogous to another (i.e., the DNA code) utilized by Michael Crichton in *Jurassic Park* (1990).

Here, the cave researches of British diluvial geologist William Buckland (1784–1856) merit special attention, as well as the whimsy and artistic sense of fellow geologist, William Conybeare. Romanticism was often associated with history, and in fact, geologists were sensitized to notions about the age of the earth and its progression through time. Rudwick claims that "The heightened sense of the drama of human history associated with the Romantic movement was the context for a renewal, in the 1820s, of the pictorial tradition of depicting scenes from at least the deepest *human* time imaginable. Although initially this had *no obvious connection with the new science of geology*, it can be seen in retrospect to have provided an important precedent for some of the earliest scenes from even deeper, *prehuman*, time."[9] In a sense, caves permitted geologists to witness prehistory by peering through windows into the past. Furthermore, fossil evidence found in cave deposits, ordinarily considered objectively by scientists, could be "reexplored" speculatively in illustrations and poetry.

Perhaps more than other contemporary geologists, Buckland gained notoriety as an explorer of British caves and of remains found in cave deposits, allowing him to reconstruct remote history. Ancient bones were often at the heart of such intrigue, in particular those of antediluvian hyenas, long extinct in Britain. Buckland affirmed his widely known interpretations of the geological history of caves in a landmark volume, *Reliquiae diluvianae; or, observations on the organic remains contained in caves, fissures, and diluvial gravel, and on other geological phenomena attesting the action of a universal deluge* (London: John Murray, 1823). In 1822, Conybeare poked fun at the gregarious Buckland in a cartoon as well as in verse. While Buckland's cave descriptions, especially the inspirational cave at Kirkdale, were written in scientific prose, Conybeare borrowed the Romantic poetic style to caricature Buckland, offering a fictionalized account of the ancient hyena den documented as imagetext.

EARLY EXAMPLES OF PALEO-FICTION

Conybeare's lithographed cartoon wove illustration with verses. In this unusual, humorous drawing we see Buckland holding a lit candle, entering a cave chamber through a tunnel. The candle may be thought of symbolically as shedding light on mysteries posed by cave deposits (i.e., fossilized hyena bones). The eminent Buckland is seen crawling on his hands and knees, a rock hammer in his belt—not the usual station for an esteemed scientist exiting a shaft into a cave chamber. Inside the chamber extinct hyenas are witnessed yet alive, feasting on prey, a purely fanciful scene! Conybeare's anonymously published 1822 poem, titled "On the Hyaena's Den at Kirkdale, near Kirby Moorside in Yorkshire, discovered A. D. 1821," described the circumstances of this speculative encounter, which for our purposes may be considered time travel, a journey permitted by the miraculous cave portal.[10] Here, Conybeare described the restored hyenas, based on Buckland's researches, while marveling at time's remoteness as proven by relics found in the mystic cavern. Thus, Conybeare's poem may be considered a rudimentary tale of time travel, embellished by illustration—his own. Such melding of poetry with illustration is highly analogous to the nineteenth century's most magnificent tale mirroring life's history, written by Jules Verne over four decades later— *Journey to the Center of the Earth*, lavishly embellished by Edouard Riou's stylistic illustrations.

Contemporary artists illustrated the earth's deep past, outlining geological history through projection of life through time. While Conybeare's 1822 entry offered a vignette from deep time (the Recent Ice Age), other artists found themselves occupied with depictions of time's deeper recesses based on paleontological remains. As the practice of restoring individual scenes from deep time became increasingly accepted through the 1830s and on into the 1850s, artists centered on the nineteenth century's most popular paleoart metaphor, imagery conveying the *progression* of life through the Earth's geological ages, as known to contemporary science. However, with one exception—one of Henry De la Beche's caricatures (undated, yet circa 1830)—none of the visual representations combined prehistoric life with cave imagery.

Whimsically titled "A Coprolitic Vision," De la Beche's work provided one of the earliest life-through-time portrayals. This illustration shows Buckland gazing into the inner recesses of a cave chamber, backward through time. Holding a rock hammer and adorned in professorial robe, he sees the panorama of geological history beckoning to him. Nearest to the entrance we see familiar Ice Age forms (a cave bear, hyenas, Irish Elk), while further inside swim ichthyosauri; a dinosaur rests on a ledge. Pterodactyls flit about above. From the rear ends of the animals which are visible, we see dung dropping to the cave floor—hence the title of this curious illustration.[11] Sommer notes that this paradisiacal vision resembles an 1830 time travel Romantic description of the Eldon Hole at Derbyshire written by William Ainsworth and Henry H. Cheek. It should be mentioned that another of De la Beche's caricatures, "Awful Changes," offered a humorous, speculative (science fiction) vision based on Scottish geologist Charles Lyell's theoretical claims, whereby the great aquatic saurians of the Mesozoic era reappear, superceding Man in a far-off *future* age. Furthermore, De la Beche is credited with another depiction, titled *Durior antiquior* (1830), which Rudwick regards as the "first true scene from deep time."[12]

Another early geologist, the American Rev. Edward Hitchcock (1793–1864), found the poetic style sufficient for literary endeavor, in (facetiously) defending his views concerning a mysterious fossilized three-toed footprint trackway found in Massachusetts. While Hitchcock's poem, "The Sandstone Bird," was a product of his "long dormant muse," the verses were published anonymously in *The Knickerbocker* (January 1836).[13] His brief tale concerns the conjuring of an extinct "sandstone bird" (now known to have been a genus of Triassic dinosaur).

The enormous "Praeadamic" bird is recreated in Romantically inspired verse. This verbal recreation is permitted by the shining light of science, viewed as a sorceress. The mighty sandstone bird, once creation's head, eyes the puny, humbled geologist scornfully, and relates how in its heyday it ruled over the greatest saurians of the past (*Megalosaurus*, *Hylaeosaurus*, *Ignanodon* and *Plesiosaurus*). Then after lamenting the earth's current, dismal and degenerate state, the bird sinks into the earth, vanishing from sight, leaving only its tracks impressed upon the sand. No illustrations accompanied Hitchcock's piece, and cave metaphor isn't as apparent, although ultimately the bird vanishes *into* the earth: "Strangely and suddenly the monster sunk; Earth oped and closed her jaws—and all was still."[14] However, it would seem that in the years leading to Richard Owen's invention of the "Dinosauria" (1841–1842), before the art of crafting dinosaur fiction had matured, geologists (as opposed to Victorian novelists and other contemporary writers) were gaining confidence in crafting paleo-fiction, poetically.

By the 1830s, when geology's visual language had matured, the picture frame itself or borders of a restoration on the printed page, rather than an actual cave setting, proved sufficient for transporting viewers to remote ages so as to witness scenes from prehistory. Early timid efforts at writing speculatively about the earth's prehistory and its former inhabitants could indeed be coupled with or inspired by visual prehistoric animal restoration, particularly life-through-time representations of past geological ages. Thereafter, while restorations and reconstructions appeared with ever-increasing frequency in popular geology books through the 1850s, there were few literary examples of dinosaur fiction.[15]

VERNE'S PALEONTOLOGICAL JOURNEY

While during the early nineteenth century, Mary Shelley (1797–1851), Edgar Allan Poe (1809–1849), and a handful of other practitioners reveled in horror and speculative themes, beginning in 1863, Jules Verne captivated the reading public through his many beloved *Les Voyages Extraordinaires*. And perhaps his greatest, *Journey to the Center of the Earth* (1864), not only borrowed extensively from contemporary life-through-time geological accounts, but through incorporation of visual paleoimagery in the 1867 edition became in itself one of the nineteenth century's finest examples of speculative prehistoric animal imagetext. While, previously, authors have stressed the hard rock/geological inspirations behind Verne's masterpiece, as well as the writings of Poe and John Cleaves Symmes (1780–1829),[16] the novel remains foremost a carefully plotted life-through-time characterization, influenced greatly by contemporary prehistoric animal imagetext. Furthermore, the exploring party's penetration into cavernous spaces deep within the earth revives influences from Britain's Romantic period. As the Romantic poets and geologists had sensed decades before, remote history and prehistory's real monsters were to be revealed, prophetically, surrealistically, *inside* the Earth.

Verne wasn't by any means a writer of the Romantic period, per se, although Butcher in the 1998 Introduction to *Journey's* Oxford University Press edition claimed he was "influenced by late Romanticism."[17] Much has been written about the probable geological and literary influences leading to Verne's *Journey*. However, the importance of Verne's life-through-time contribution of 1867 has been overlooked. Verne's emphasis was on *organic* transformation of the planet, framed within a secondary, disbelief-suspending geological debate over central heat.

In their 2003 *Earth Sciences History* study, William Butcher, who recently re-translated the 1867 French edition, and John Breyer contend that a critical source of inspiration, the "direct source," for Verne's 1864 edition was French historian Louis Figuier's (1819–1984) *La Terre avant le deluge* (*Earth Before the Deluge*, 1863), without which "*Journey* could hardly have been written. The parallelism is remarkable both in the scientific details presented and the general geologic and scientific attitudes espoused. The *piece de conviction* is the multitude of figures, proper names and scientific terms shared in the two works."[18] They view *Journey's* paleontological elements as "less central, but more controversial" when compared to the "central question" explored in the novel: the "condition of the earth's interior. Was it molten or was it solid?"[19] However, Verne's *central* theme explored in the 1867 edition of *Journey* was *paleontological*, conveyed as a blending of life-through-time elements, written passages and visual messages—imagetext. The fact that major revisions added to Verne's 1867 edition (which was the first illustrated edition) involved paleontological themes underscores the primary intention. Rather than a geological epic, more specifically, Verne's *Journey* was organized as an extraordinary life-through-time voyage, or paleontological opus, modeled after Figuier.[20]

In Verne's tale, Earth's mysterious interior, not unlike the iconic cave of the Romantic period, was in essence speaking of or revealing prehistoric, former inhabitants of the globe to our intrepid protagonists and even hinting at organic degenerative processes which gave rise to such fauna. Through Axel's and Lidenbrock's banter and dialogue, Verne took pains to weave his instructional plot temporally, yet artistically. Lidenbrock, imbued with scientific knowledge vastly beyond his predecessor Buckland, makes astute interpretations in this rich, enlivened, sublime setting concerning the extinct creatures found both in fossilized form as well as, later, alive. But Verne, through Figuier and other documented geological sources, possessed additional knowledge about how such caverns in the earth formed volcanically and mineralogically, deftly employed to accentuate the story. The earth's labyrinthine interior framed in Verne's *Journey* may be regarded as the most magnificent and sublime cave environment of all, one which could be pondered from a contemporary scientific, rather than poetic, perspective.

Breyer and Butcher note that "the density of borrowing is greater in the parts added in the 1867 version. Why ... did he [i.e., Verne] wait three years before adding the three chapters? One answer may reside in the surge of interest in prehistory in France during the intervening period.... But in absence of any documentation about the additions, answers will remain largely speculative."[21] Authors have recently offered speculations as to what factors and events may have inspired Verne to add paleontological elements to the 1867 edition, although the basic contemporary ingredients were already in place by 1864.[22] Citing the French translation of Charles Darwin's *The Origin of Species* (1863), Costello suggests that "Verne, it seems, was on the side of the apes."[23] Besides Figuier's and Darwin's influences, there were perhaps a number of additional contemporary factors, including the Paris Exhibition of 1867, which Verne may have attended, and recent dramatic paleontological discoveries such as news of the first two fossils attributed to "missing link" *Archaeopteryx* (1860 and 1861). Although not documented in his *Backwards to Britain* (1992), it's plausible that Verne was aware of the life-size prehistoric animal sculptures on the Crystal Palace grounds at Sydenham—the world's first outdoor life-through-time display—which he missed an opportunity to visit during his 1859 tour of London.[24]

Also, during the early 1860s, at least two other French writers, George Sand (1804–1876) and Pierre Boitard (1789–1859), published novels about fictional encounters with prehistoric animals, titled *Laura: Voyage dans le cristal* (1864) and *Paris avant les hommes* (1861), respectively.[25] Verne and Sand worked with the same editor, Jules Hetzel (1814–1886); Boitard characterized man's interaction with prehistoric animals including a fossil human. It is not my intention, however, to discuss details of how Verne's *Journey* was textually modified relative to the 1864 edition for the 1867 edition, because here the emphasis is on life-through-time *imagetext*, best viewed through examination of the 1867 illustrated edition.

EDOUARD RIOU AS PALEOARTIST

Riou's pictorial style has been described as "romantic realism." Of Riou's fifty-six illustrations for *Journey*, ten feature scenes of the prehistoric animals and flora encountered either as fossils or creatures living inside the earth, whereas Figuier's book featured Riou's twenty-five ideal views of landscapes of the ancient world. By the 1860s, paleoartists had become adept at depicting scenes from a number of geological periods, ordinarily focusing on restorations of organisms alive during those periods. But few efforts had been made to restore the entire panoramic history of the globe, visually. Martin J.S. Rudwick[26] mentions two important precedents, Joseph Kuwasseg's (1799–1859) illustrations for Franz Xaver Unger's (1800–1870) book *The Primitive World in Its Different Periods of Formation* (1851), and the previously mentioned outdoor display of life-sized prehistoric animal sculptures, sculpted by Benjamin Waterhouse Hawkins (1807–1889) under Richard Owen's (1804–1892) tutelage, completed by 1854. New idealized landscapes were printed in Figuier's 1863 volume, including modern geological landscapes, pictures of fossil specimens and life restorations of individual extinct animals and plants, as well as diagrams divulging geological processes within the earth's interior. Such a wealth of extra depictions exemplifies how devices (i.e., visual language) cleverly conveying geological and paleontological information had matured by this period.

While the Romantic period in British literature transformed during the 1830s into the Victorian era in writing, visual artists from John Martin (1789–1854), who gained fame beginning in 1819 for a number of remarkable paintings showing scenes from biblical history, to Frederic Church (1826–1900) and Albert Bierstadt (1830–1902), renowned for their majestic landscape paintings of the New World, continued to capture nature's sublimity on canvas through the 1860s. Their artistic visions reflected a persisting Romantic, if not heroic, progress of scientific exploration in the era Verne and Riou belonged to. Edouard Riou was a landscape painter of the 1850s through 1870s, of whom space artist Ron Miller has stated, "I believe [Riou's] work stylistically spans the transition between the illustrators of the early nineteenth century and those of the latter half—when the profession of professional illustrators became established."[27] Through his artistry, Riou expertly conveyed the gist of Verne's dialogue in *Journey*, speeches which Michael Dirda has stated "are deliberately couched in the language of the sublime—that mixture of awe and fear one feels in the presence of natural magnificence."[28]

Besides Riou's portrayals of the mysterious chambers traversed by the adventurers and the Lidenbrock Sea deep within the earth, of particular interest are ten illustrations representing life deep within the earth's interior. Clearly, in the case of Figuier's lavishly illustrated volume, Riou's 1863 depictions of prehistoric life were more voluminous, pronounced and detailed. Yet Riou's 1867 figures for *Journey* carry considerable charm too.

The exploring party spies Arne Saknussemm's runic signature engraved on a rock face inside the volcanic crater, an eerie occurrence. Following thereafter are a number of episodes depicting mysterious caverns, tunnels and other settings within the earth, including the Lava Gallery, the dimly lit Cross Roads, the Coal Mine, the Diamond Mine, the Boiling Jet of Water, the Guiding Stream, a Vertical Descent, the Grotto, and then ultimately the Lidenbrock Sea. Riou's forebears, Conybeare and De la Beche, provided only single scenes, intending humor while adding an organic component to their cave scenes. However, Riou provided an entire *sequence* of scenes revealing the Earth's imaginary interior (several of which seem derived from figures in Figuier's book) which seem all the more factual due to Verne's mastery. By then, also, readers in the know would have been more familiar with geological visual language—diagrams showing bedrock cross sections and idealized hypothetical scenes showing earth's interior, or even restorations of prehistoric life, such as published in Figuier's 1863 volume.

SUSPENDING DISBELIEF GEOLOGICALLY

Having temporarily suspended disbelief through Arne Saknussemm's cryptogram (although it's ultimately inconclusive whether Saknussemm truly penetrated deeper toward the earth's "very center" than did Lidenbrock's party), Verne deftly melds science about the formation of the earth in various geological ages with general safety issues. For if Lidenbrock's theory about the earth is correct, they'll survive the plutonic fire from below and be able to relate their adventures later after emerging to the surface. Axel fatalistically believes in a theory of central fire, founded on the nebular hypothesis; after all, they've just descended into a *volcano*. Verne would have been familiar with the nebular hypothesis, volcanoes and the concept of a central fire through his reading of Figuier. However, my British edition of *Earth Before the Deluge*, based on the fourth French edition (1867), doesn't mention an important individual from the Romantic period connected with a key ingredient in the story's *geological* controversy, British chemist Humphry Davy (1778–1829), whose volcanic theory is mentioned very briefly therein (on page 15).

Verne employed an extraordinary geological diversion, as readers weigh the validity of Lidenbrock's arguments, founded in Humphry Davy's 1828 theory of volcanic eruptions.[29] With readers focused on this sleight-of-hand, the fear of dying inside the earth as projected through Axel's anxieties, it's easy to neglect that their predecessor, Arne Saknussemm, somehow survived the remarkable journey. While the astronomical nebular hypothesis implies an earth still molten within, Davy's theoretical alternative suggests the earth's honeycombed interior should be sufficiently moderate to continue inward on their extraordinary voyage. Their debate surfaces repeatedly throughout the novel until its final resolution, an implication being that Davy, who was deeply interested in remains of fossilized saurians from the Secondary Era (Mesozoic), is right after all.

Davy claimed on chemical grounds that springs or seawater penetrating the earth would percolate into deposits of metal substances therein, consequently triggering vigorous chemical reactions which would be visible at the earth's surface. In other words, volcanic eruptions were not caused through the episodic dissipation of internal heat from the earth's primordial core. Davy's 1828 chemical oxidation theory for volcanic eruption was well antiquated by the 1860s, although most enchanted readers wouldn't have known this. Yet Verne needed a convincing geological device to make it seem plausible, on pseudo-scientific grounds, that his protagonists could indeed penetrate eighty-seven miles down inside the earth, through a volcanic shaft no less, in relative safety. Beyond this geological motif, however, most of the "geological" dialogue taking place between Lidenbrock and Axel is inherently paleontological, organized in a life-through-time format.

Figuier discusses Pierre Simon Laplace's (1749–1827) astronomy in an early chapter of *Earth Before the Deluge*. According to Laplace's theory of the solar system's nebular origin, the earth should be steadily cooling through time, even though the temperature at its center was then estimated to be 195,000 degrees Celsius. Furthermore, Figuier suggested that "the process of contraction ... was another cause of dislocation at the surface, producing either considerable ruptures or simple fissures in the continuity of the crust ... eruptions of granitic or metallic matter—these vast discharges of mineral waters through the fractured surface—would be of frequent occurrence during the primitive epoch we are contemplating."[30] In other words, *directional* cooling of the Earth's crust would cause buckling, faulting and fissures through which flood waters penetrated from the planetary surface. Furthermore, through time, as the Earth cooled, such catastrophic (volcanic) episodes would have lessened in frequency and intensity. Verne relied on this plausible mechanism to introduce prehistoric fauna and flora, several of which survived into modernity, which would have episodically fallen through fissures into his vast subterranean realm. Thus, resting on plausible scientific grounds, Verne's fauna (fossilized, living or imagined) inhabited or otherwise occupied the most iconic cave setting ever conceived in science fiction history.

Journey's Life-Through-Time Imagetext

Verne's and Riou's artistic effect is rather like my early 1960s reminiscences of visiting Hall 38 in Chicago's Field Museum of Natural History, also known as the dinosaur hall, which was arranged as a triumphant life-through-time display. Therein my classmates and I would spy fossil exhibits, signage, diagrams, mounted skeletons, sculpted restorations and, framing the walls above, guiding us along, Charles R. Knight's (1874–1953) twenty-eight enchanting murals showing (idealized) restorations from prehistory. We entered the hall at the primordial end of the exhibit, our wide eyes darting from one display case to another while strolling forward through the Age of Fishes, the Coal Age, an Age of Reptiles and on toward Ice Age displays. Although we advanced steadily through a representation of geological time, our roving eyes feasted on certain paleontological displays in a sequence often slightly out of order with respect to the established geological time scale. In Verne's *Journey*, largely patterned after Figuier's 1863 book, there is broad movement forward in time as well, with visuals and signage temporally ordered within the many winding corridors of Verne's subterranean "museum." Axel may be regarded, perhaps, as the museum's "curator" or guide, who through his written commentary "introduces" each exhibit.

How do Riou's depictions of fauna and flora appearing in *Journey* accentuate perception of a life-through-time movement? Admittedly, Riou's portrayals in *Journey* convey the life-through-time theme less effectively than do his more detailed depictions published in Figuier's volume. It is mainly through Verne's plotting that we perceive broad movement through stages in the progression of life on earth. Riou's images, coupled to Verne's text, are not presented in quite an obvious journey-through-time format, as in Figuier's volume. However, the combination of story plus art (as imagetext) conveys the principal paleontological theme subtly and effectively.

A general rule of thumb followed by Verne in *Journey* is his tendency to introduce organisms through their remains—bones or fossils—effectively foreshadowing animals that will later make fleshed-out appearances. (Furthermore, through expression of his anxieties, Axel foreshadows things to come.) Juxtaposition of living creatures with skeletons in certain scenes may seem curiously coincidental or even Flintstones-like, yet *Journey* generally leapfrogs forward in time from the Primordial era through the early Paleozoic to the Quaternary. And yet the center of the earth also *is* a Flintstones-like environment because living flora and fauna do exist contemporaneously. It's just that the exploring party conveniently seems to encounter the various forms (fossilized, living, and imaginary), introducing and describing them in a generalized life-through-time pattern or sequence.

Having deciphered Saknussemm's code, the explorers know which tunnel to enter within the volcanic vent of Snaefells, where the life-through-time adventure soon begins. Within the context of his marvelous story, Verne first takes us down one dimly lit "museum" hallway into the middle of the Transition era, or the Silurian Period. Following scientific discussion concerning life in the Silurian, Axel notes fossilized impressions of seaweeds, club-mosses and a trilobite imprint on the tunnel wall. Next Verne shows us fossils of Ganoid fish and reptilian life preserved in strata correlated to the Devonian Period, forcing Axel to muse, "It became plain that we were moving back up the scale of animal life, of which man forms the peak."[31] Then Axel and Lidenbrock tread through a coal deposit, prompting discussion of life in the Carboniferous. After realizing from their knowledge of life through time that they've taken the wrong shaft—the one leading upward through time instead of downward into the Earth's center—they backtrack to the correct passage.

After the explorers reach Port Grauben (along the shore of the Lidenbrock Sea), they enter the Transition Forest, depicted by Riou as a forest of forty-foot-high mushrooms. While the immense mushrooms don't appear in Figuier's book, there are several illustrations of restored vegetation in his chapter on the Old Red Sandstone: "cryptograms ... of which our mushrooms convey some idea...."[32] appear in Riou's Ideal Landscape of the Devonian Period. Verne further embellishes his fictional setting, borrowing from Figuier's written description and Riou's detailed scientific restorations. In addition to the mushrooms, Verne mentions, in relative geological order, enormous lycopods from the Devonian, and Coal Age *Sigillarias*, tree-sized ferns visible in the distance. Lidenbrock refers to the assemblage as a "menagerie," while Axel exclaims it is a "hothouse" of "all the antediluvian plants which have been reconstructed by the scholars."[33] The ancient plants Verne describes date from the Devonian and Carboniferous while, next, strewn about before them are skeletons of Cenozoic mammals, *Deinotherium* and *Megatherium*. Lastly, the explorers find an accumulation of *recently* lignitized logs, "all sorts of northern conifers, petrified by the sea water."[34] No *living animals* are yet in sight, although master storyteller Verne—through Axel—has us already dreading such a fateful encounter.

Riou's next image shows the explorers' raft made of petrified wood timbers approaching algae of the Lidenbrock Sea, a scene which at first glance bears no significance to the prehistorical theme. However, Axel muses, "What natural force could have produced such plants? What must the Earth have looked like during the first centuries of its formation when, acted upon by heat and humidity, the vegetable kingdom was developing solitarily on its surface?"[35] In other words, the algae, like the mushrooms before, are also representative of earth's primordial flora, life which may have flourished before animals. Figuier suggests, for example, "Did plants precede animals? ... such would appear to have been the order of creation."[36] Algae are also discussed in *Earth Before the Deluge*, and are seen commingling with trilobites in Riou's restoration of the Silurian Period.[37] Verne's use of soft marine algae, which wouldn't be as prone to fossilization as shelly marine fauna, must be borrowed from Figuier's suggestion that life first developed in the sea. As Figuier claimed, algae slightly antedate the lycopods and other flora just witnessed on the shore, so the sequence of scenes—Transition Forest followed by marine Algae—would seem inverted. However, the exploring party logistically had to get their raft launched *before* the marine form of ancient algae could be encountered. Having provided imagetext of living plants, thought scientifically to have come before animal forms, living animals now appear.

The life of this invigorating subterranean cavern, lit ethereally from above, occurs along and within the spacious sea, reflecting Verne's preoccupation with fluvial and marine settings. Here, the first living vertebrates are encountered, first a blind variety of *Pterichthys*, followed by an eyeless *Dipterides*, both hooked by Hans. These fossil fish, "more perfect the longer ago they were created,"[38] date from the Devonian Period; a restoration of *Pterichthys* appears in Figuier's volume.[39]

The novel's central vision follows, Axel's waking dream, an epiphany described by Costello as uniting "the scientific outlook with romantic feeling into one great prose poem."[40] Here, Verne relates the entire transformation of the earth from its primordial beginning, in reverse order beginning with the biblical ages before man's birth. Axel's dream serves a central purpose, underscoring the quest's paleontological theme. For only here, in this ethereal, Romantic setting, Axel's exalted reverie courses through the panorama of life's history, majestically foreshadowing fauna of his foreseeable future.[41]

In reverse order, Verne condenses extended contents of Figuier's 1863 volume, focusing on the beginning through the Asiatic deluge, into one remarkable passage. Many of the animals specifically mentioned in the passage were illustrated by Riou in Figuier, either individually or included in the idealized restorations of time periods. However, for *Journey*, Riou prepared only two similar images corresponding to Axel's remarkable waking dream, both of which recall De la Beche's life-through-time theme cartoon, "A Coprolitic Vision." At first glance, Riou's more elaborate portrait of the antediluvian world may appear as an anachronistically posed (Flintstones-like), in-the-present agglomeration of prehistoric animals. Two geological time eras are represented. We see the *Megatherium*, a *Mastodon* and an *Anoplotherium* in the foreground, all dating from the Cenozoic Era. Further into the illustration, extinct birds and pterodactyls haunt higher vistas, while furthest in the distance, swimming on the Lidenbrock Sea we see a plesiosaur and an ichthyosaur spouting a twin jet column of water from its blowholes.[42]

Thus, relying on this delimited sense of time-depth perception, Riou's visual array *approximates* the grand movement of life's transformation through time described by Verne, with the oldest organisms in the distance—furthest inside, under the vault of the Lidenbrock Sea—and, generally speaking, the more recent fauna posed closest to the keyhole through which readers experience the magnificent panorama. Certainly Riou couldn't condense the entire extent of Axel's waking dream, including the geological and astronomical elements, into a single illustration. So Riou visually projected the most intriguing elements of Axel's epiphany—a segment showing the *temporal* succession of vertebrate life in a pivotal *imagined* sequence.

Then Axel's worst fears become realized through their first encounter with living prehistoric reptiles. Verne masterfully builds suspense, as a crowbar used for sea soundings comes up roughened by fresh tooth imprints, foreshadowing what is to come. Next, we read Verne's descriptions of awful, extinct reptiles which may still swim in the Lidenbrock Sea. Then—horrors!—a pair of marine saurians is spotted near the raft, one a *Plesiosaurus*, the other an *Ichthyosaurus*, described as:

> ...the most frightful of all the antediluvian reptiles.... Only two monsters are disturbing the surface of the sea. I have before me two reptiles from the Primitive oceans. I can see the bloody eye of the ichthyosaurus, as big as a man's head. Nature has given it an extremely powerful optical apparatus, able to resist the pressure of the water in the depths where it lives. It has been called the saurian whale, for it is just as big and just as quick. This one is not less than 100 feet long, and I can get some idea of its girth where it lifts its vertical tailfins out of the water. Its jaws are enormous and according to the naturalists contain as many as 182 teeth.
>
> The plesiosaurus, a serpent with a cylindrical trunk and a short tail, has legs shaped into paddles. Its whole body is covered with a hard shell, and its neck, as flexible as a swan's, rises more than 30 feet above the waves.

Opposite: **Four of Riou's images for the 1867 edition of Verne's *Journey to the Center of the Earth*. Here are shown (top left) the Transition Forest; (top right) algae of the Lidenbrock Sea; (bottom left) antediluvian life of the Lidenbrock Sea corresponding to Axel's waking dream; and the frontispiece to the 1867 edition. (Author's collection.)**

These animals attack one another with indescribable fury. They raise mountains of water, which surge as far as the raft. Twenty times we are on the point of capsizing. Hisses of a frightening volume reach our ears. The two animals are tightly embraced. I cannot distinguish one from the other. Everything is to be feared from the rage of the victor.

One hour, two hours pass. The struggle continues unabated. The two foes now approach the raft, now move away from it. We remain motionless, ready to fire.

Suddenly the ichthyosaurus and plesiosaurus disappear, hollowing out a veritable maelstrom in the open sea.... Will this combat finish in the ocean depths? Suddenly, an enormous head surges out—the head of the great plesiosaurus. The monster is mortally wounded. I can no longer see his enormous shell. Only his long neck stands up, beats down, rises, bends over again, lashes at the waters like a gigantic whip.... As for the ichthyosaurus, has it gone down to rest in its mighty underwater cavern; or will it reappear on the surface of the sea?[43]

Riou lavishly complements Verne's vivid description of the sea battle with two illustrations, the more impressive of which shows the pair of colossal beasts, their toothy jaws sunk into one another's scaly flesh, while the raft tosses to and fro on the angry waves. Verne's passage is the first science fiction description of battling "prehistoria," presaging ever-popular dino-monsters exploited in paleoart scenes scripted by twentieth century writers, visual artists and 1950s movie producers.[44]

Riou had also completed far less dramatically posed illustrations of these animals for Figuier as well, notably in his idealized depictions of the Lias and Lower Oolite. Rudwick[45] noted how by the 1860s, portrayals of ichthyosaurs fighting plesiosaurs would have seemed a visual cliche, perhaps much like restorations of *Tyrannosaurus* fighting *Triceratops*, which have been done since Charles R. Knight's groundbreaking depiction of 1906, would be regarded today. Interestingly, Verne includes no dinosaurs in his novel, species which then carried no more psychological or emotional impact than their pop-cultural cousins—Mesozoic aquatic saurians, mighty Ice Age mammals such as the *Mastodon*, or dragon-like pterodactyls.

Next, Verne guides us into the most controversial portion of his 1867 opus—that dealing with the possibility of prehistoric man. First, readers contemplate a field of fossilized bones characterized by the enormous shells of Pliocene glyptodonts and, farther on, other mammalian fauna. Axel notes how in one three-square-mile area "was accumulated the whole history of animal life.... A thousand Cuviers would not have been enough to reconstruct the skeletons of all the once-living creatures which now rested in that magnificent graveyard."[46] Here the party spies an "assortment" of "every monster from before the Flood, all in a pile...."[47] Axel theorizes the bone deposit got there through sedimentary action of flood waters which first penetrated from ocean basins on the surface of the globe through fissures inside the earth. While it isn't entirely clear or proven whether at least some of the remains may represent species which formerly *inhabited* the earth's interior, Axel theorizes that the bone deposit evidently formed as flood waters receded into the Lidenbrock atmosphere/ sea system. The fossils include Secondary era pterodactyls as well as several of the other creatures Axel conjured during his waking dream. However, Riou's first image showing the field of fossilized bones reveals skulls and tusks of elephants; remains of geologically older pterodactyls aren't apparent in this illustration. Therefore, one has a distinct impression that we have progressed successively into more recent representations of life history, well beyond the saurian stages of life, through the Pliocene when *Mastodon* thrived, and beyond. The imagetext has prepared us for Man's arrival.

In the field of bones Lidenbrock spies a human fossil, illustrated by Riou as an articulated, mummified corpse, a "perfectly recognizable human body" from the Quaternary era.[48] A rather deranged looking Lidenbrock is shown pontificating on the ghoulish specimen, identified as caucasian and less than six feet tall. Verne refers to this individual, found beside Stone Age flints and hand-axes, as a "contemporary of the mastodons,"[49] although Figuier had assigned *Mastodon* to the Tertiary Period (appearing in Riou's idealized landscapes of the Miocene and Pliocene epochs). While in the ossuary there is intermingling of fossils from different ages of life history, *Journey's* imagetext introduces key species in a *relative* life-through-time sequence. Additional remains belonging to the human race are found in the graveyard, fueling Lidenbrock's sense of wonder. Then, in a bit of foreshadowing, Axel is worried whether "some man of the abyss (was) also still wandering along these lonely shores."[50]

Having set the table with *fossil* remains dating from the Tertiary and Quarternary, Verne and Riou progress to *living* organisms once more, although this time representing the Tertiary and Quaternary. Tramping inland from the Lidenbrock Sea, the explorers enter a Tertiary forest with its peculiar admixture of vegetation, inspired by Figuier's descriptions. Riou conjures another pair of illustrations, the first showing vegetation of the Tertiary world, and another, fueled by Axel's premonition, regarding a possible encounter with beasts. In this second illustration, we spy a shadowy silhouette of a twelve-foot-high anthropoid, a "shepherd from *before* the Flood,"[51] wielding an enormous bough, driving a herd of *Mastodon* through a forest trail. Axel muses, "So the dream world where I had seen the rebirth of this complete world from prehistoric times, *combining* the Tertiary and Quaternary Periods, had finally become reality! And we were there, alone in the bowels of the Earth, at the mercy of its fierce inhabitants."[52] And yet, despite the reality of the moment, Axel can scarcely believe his eyes, his skepticism reflecting the state of contemporary, 1860s paleoanthropology. Understandably at the sight of this horrific apparition, Axel, Lidenbrock and assistant Hans run for their lives.

In *Journey*, Riou's Quaternary images stylistically depart from figures appearing in 1863 and 1867 editions of Figuier's work. Rudwick[53] discusses factors leading to Riou's creation of an additional Ice Age scene published in Figuier's 1867 edition. While the original edition offered an Arcadian perspective of the "Appearance of Man," between 1863 and 1867, Boucher de Perthes (1788–1868) offered controversial evidence that ancient (Quaternary) humans had *coexisted* with extinct mammoths, cave bears, European rhinos and hyena, and *Mastodon*. Figuier incorporated latest findings concerning the creation of man, antediluvian stages of life history, and Boucher de Perthes' discoveries in the 1865 and 1867 editions of *Earth Before the Deluge*. Besides relying on Figuier's revision, Costello further suggests that Verne may have met Boucher de Perthes and "that part of the inspiration behind his ideas derived from this great man who had laboured all his life against prejudice to prove the antiquity of man."[54]

While during the Victorian era the depiction of life through geological time was becoming traditionalized, especially in France through Riou's images published in Figuier's popular book, not every scientist accepted the concept. British geologist Charles Lyell (1797–1875), for example, believed in a steady-state, pseudo-cyclical model for generating organic inhabitants of earth's past, present and future. De la Beche's aforementioned cartoon "Awful Changes" was intended to caricature Lyell's constricting view. Rudwick noted how Lyell suggested that extinct animals of the past, such as ichthyosaurs and other reptilians of the Secondary Period, would reappear in future geological ages, albeit not as the exact species from before, but very similar.[55] Thus, life-through-time would lose significance as a true record of planetary history. Lyell's strict 1830s views opposed French savant and paleontologist Jean-Baptiste de Lamarck's (1744–1829) evolutionary—progressionist organic theories. By the 1860s, life-through-time imagetext proved a popular, edifying, and widely understood means for characterizing planetary prehistory, supplanting Lyell's steady-state ideology (which, save for De la Beche's facetious cartoon, lacked reinforcing imagetext). It should be noted, however, that artistic luminaries who were able to perceive and recreate earth's succession of ages—such as Verne's contemporaries, Charles R. Knight, Benjamin Waterhouse Hawkins, and Jules Verne himself—certainly weren't "evolutionists," at least not in any Darwinian sense.

PERSISTENCE OF THE ICONIC CAVE IN DINOSAUR FICTION

Dinosaur fiction's distinctive origins can be traced from incipience during the Romantic age, through imagetext featuring the fanciful, iconic cave. I am not proposing an alternate origin for the science fiction sub-genre here referred to as "dinosaur fiction" (or, alternatively, "prehistoric-land fiction"). However, dinosaur fiction's roots lie entangled with the traditional view. While the term "scientifiction" didn't appear until the 1920s, Brian Aldiss and David Wingrove stress in *Trillion Year Spree* that the Gothic origins of science fiction stem from Mary Shelley's 1818 novel *Frankenstein: or, The Modern Promotheus*, published during the early Industrial Revolution. This is also an early period of evolutionary revolution. For example, noted Aldiss, Erasmus Darwin, who "qualifies as a part-time science fiction writer" on the strength of his epic poem *Zoonomia*, published in two volumes in 1794 and 1796, speculated freely about the age of the earth and evolutionary processes.[56] As Sommer stated, *Frankenstein* is a byproduct of this fascinating age, and Mary Shelley, Percy Bysshe Shelley's (1792–1822) wife and confidant, herself was a product of her times—the age of Romanticism, coinciding with "the poetic, geological, and public '(re-)discovery' of the cave."[57] Victor Frankenstein's fictional monster, for example, shrinks from humanity in caves, and the opening scene in her novel *The Last Man* (1826) takes place in a cave Mary had visited on December 8, 1818.[58]

Due to its inherent life-through-time imagetext, the 1867 edition of Verne's *Journey* is rather like time travel, *sans* technology. While modern writers frame stories on awe-inspiring temporal concepts such as deep time—past or future—and Einsteinian cosmological spacetime, the edifying life-through-time paleontological motif, central to Verne's *Journey*, lost significance through passing decades.[59] However, symbolic use of the cave as portal into prehistory was often inventively retained. In *Journey*, Jules Verne infused his subterranean cavern with Romantic spirit, employing both an oracular cave as well as life-through-time

Oppposite: **Four more of Riou's images for the 1867 edition of Verne's** *Journey to the Center of the Earth*. **Here are shown (top left) a plesiosaur tossing the raft made of petrified wood; (top right) marine saurian combat in the Lidenbrock Sea; (bottom left) a field of bones; and a "human" fossil in the field of bones. (Author's collection.)**

Two of Riou's images for the 1867 edition of Verne's *Journey to the Center of the Earth*. Here are shown (left) the Tertiary Forest; and a shadowy anthropoid driving *Mastodonts*. (Author's collection.)

imagery founded on contemporary science. With the groundwork laid, other writers would follow Verne's tradition, fully relying on the cave setting to conjure prehistoric fauna.

Between the time of Verne's tour de force *Journey*, and publication of Arthur Conan Doyle's 1912 classic *The Lost World*, only a handful of stories involving prehistoric animals were published, several of which relied on cave or underground settings. Afterward, oracular caves and other portals into prehistory remained a favored theme through the early 1930s.[60] Some examples will illustrate this point.

C.J. Cutcliffe Hyne's (1866–1944) short story "The Lizard" (1898), involved a suspenseful encounter between a Yorkshire native and an ancient crocodilian which is resurrected from a fossil cast within a mysterious cave. Conan Doyle's (1859–1930) short story "The Terror of Blue John Gap" (*The Strand* 1910) pitted a doctor against an enormous beast, an evolutionary descendant of the cave bear (or possibly a saber-tooth cat), in a foreboding cave setting. At the climax of Conan Doyle's *The Lost World*, Professor Challenger's intrepid exploring party flee to safety through a *tunnel* leading downward from "Maple White land," or the prehistoric lost world plateau. Earlier, in order to reach the plateau, they must penetrate a river segment: "The thick vegetation met overhead, interlacing into a natural pergola, and through this *tunnel* of verdure ... this *tunnel* of hazy green sunshine"[61] (emphasis added).

In Wardon Allan Curtis' (1867–1940) short story "The Monster of Lake LaMetrie" (*Pearson's Magazine*, September 1899), a plesiosaur emerges from a lake which seemingly extends deep into the very bowels of the planet. Climactic scenes in novels such as Frank Saville's *Beyond the Great South Wall* (1901), Eric Temple Bell's (i.e., John Taine's) (1883–1960) *The Greatest Adventure* (1929), and H.P. Lovecraft's (1890–1937) *At the Mountains of Madness* (1931, which incorporated prehistoric elements including pterosaurs), involved caverns.[62] Russian geologist Vladimir A. Obruchev (1863–1956) and Erazm Majewski (1858–1922) published novels involving man's encounter with prehistoric animals inside the earth, respectively titled *Plutonia* (1924), and *Professor Antediluvius* (1898).[63] Besides Edgar Rice Burroughs' (1875–1950) series of popular novels involving a hollow Earth (beginning in 1914 with *At the Earth's Core*), Tarzan's inventor also wrote an intriguing Caspak trilogy. Here, in order to access plesiosaur—infested fresh waters within the prehistoric isle, a torpedo U-boat pilot must sail through a treacherous undersea tunnel. Even in *Kong Kong* (RKO, 1933), the prehistoric life-through-time array of stop-motion animated visuals can only be witnessed once Ann Darrow's rescuers penetrate a great barricade made of logs, serving in lieu of a cave as a metaphoric portal into prehistory.[64] In a film sequel, *Son of Kong* (RKO, 1933), and in the silent movie *The Lost World* (First National Pictures, 1925), volcanic eruptions signal the end of the prehistoric journey, perhaps in homage to Verne's concluding action scene in *Journey*. We'll further explore these ideas and tales in subsequent chapters.

Relying on his profound "waking dream," Verne painted a remarkable portrait of earth history, emulating the entire body of illustrations Riou had completed for Figuier's 1863 volume. How effective paleontological life-through-time imagetext can be when talented visual and verbal artists perform their magic concertedly! And nobody did it better than Verne, acting in concert with Riou.[65]

CHAPTER 2

Lost and Found:
The Mystique of Lost Worlds

BACKGROUND

A century ago, prehistoric animals, especially dinosaurs and other Mesozoic saurians, were still regarded as scientific and pop-cultural novelties. This was also a time when controversy stirred the biological sciences, centering on the matter of organic evolution. Reflecting this scientific intrigue, writers of fantastic fiction contrived astounding stories set in primeval landscapes where fictional scientist heroes and other characters encountered prehistoric animals, creatures that were extinct everywhere else and became emblematic of the mysteries of evolution.

Although a fictional editor in Conan Doyle's *The Lost World* (1912) frets over where to send his reporter Edward Malone for a good news story, remarking, "The big blank spaces in the map are all being filled in, there's no room for romance anywhere," in actuality the earth's "lost" places are all around us. When it comes to dinosaur fiction, frozen places of the globe (i.e., the Arctic and Antarctica), uncharted volcanic islands, primeval jungles unravaged by modernity, the ocean deeps, Atlantis, the earth's hidden interior, and even North America's western wildernesses have all qualified in this context as "lost" places where dinosaurs and other prehistoric forms still lurk and roam. But what sets lost-world dinosaur fiction—which is inherently cryptozoological in nature—apart from the other forms discussed in this book? In the most remarkable examples, we note inherent evolutionary or paleoanthropological themes.

As stated by cultural historian W.J.T. Mitchell, "Like beast fables of any kind, dinosaur stories are really about human beings. Either the dinosaurs must be treated as if they were human, or they must be brought into some kind of encounter with human beings as an alien, hostile life-form. Dinosaurs, in short, are "us," or they are "not us.""[1] Literary "lost worlds" aren't about dinosaurs but, in more ways than one, about *us* instead. Themes principally explored in such tales are evolutionary biology, paleoanthropology and the aura of lost races and civilizations. Dinosaurs and those intriguing other prehistoric animals are often cast as elaborate paleo-props accentuating the main themes.

Lost-world tales became popular at a time when the means and purpose of organic evolution proved highly controversial both among scientists and at a pop-cultural level.[2] So, quite naturally, writers seized the opportunity to dazzle readers' minds with mystery and fear through revelation of man's dark, hidden past. Often too, the quest into prehistory to find the *object*, ostensibly ancient life but—more significantly—scientific *knowledge*, destroyed the very object being sought. Inclusion of symbolic dinosaurs was often a sleight-of-hand diverting readers' attention from ominous, perhaps even objectionable (Darwinian) ideas explored in lost-worlds fiction of the early twentieth century.

Few realize that cryptozoological dinosaur fiction is derived from a cave romance tradition or prehistoric fiction ancestry. The earliest definitive examples of prehistoric fiction appeared circa 1860, remaining popular today, as in Jean Auel's writings. The genre seems to have originated in France, with Verne fueling the fire especially in *Journey's* 1867 edition (even though, here, Verne's seminal entry is categorized as dinosaur fiction due to its anachronistic, cryptozoological flavor), leading a few decades later to *Quest for Fire*.[3]

By the late nineteenth century, the Frenchman J.H. Rosny the Elder (1866–1940) became a prominent prehistoric fiction writer. He wrote some of the earliest lost-world dinosaur fiction as well, although none of his tales involved dinosaurs, per se. Four of Rosny's lost-world tales involved strange primates or anthropoids discovered in regions of the globe isolated from civilization. For example, in his 1896 tale "In the Depths of Kyamo," an explorer named Alglave finds a race of giant gorillas considered ancestral to man. In 1975, J.P. Vernier commented that "Rosny was fascinated by the notion of an a historical era, of a time when the complexities of modern society were unknown, and in which brute strength determined evolution ... prehistoric times ... provided him with a setting in which he could outline the concept of a fundamental link uniting men and animals." Through Rosny's writings and his contemporaries this was clearly a literary period when prehistoric nature was thought stained through savagery, red in tooth and claw.[4]

Let's now consider the most exemplary cases of lost-world dinosaur tales from the early twentieth century through the onset of the Second World War, particularly the works of Arthur Conan Doyle, Edgar Rice Burroughs and John Taine (pseudonym for mathematician Eric Temple Bell). And no discussion of literary dinosaurs in lost-world settings would be complete without addressing *King Kong*, or rather, Delos W. Lovelace's (1894–1967) highly competent 1932 novelization of the movie script.

LOST WORLDS OF SCIENCE FICTION

What is the purpose of lost worlds and why do they persist? According to Brian Aldiss, lost-world tales, heightening in popularity between the 1890s and 1920s, offered fanciful escapes from "claustrophobic urban culture."[5] Romantic interest in primitive lost worlds superseded fantastic literature's "utopian society" heyday; stories concerning the latter were most appealing during the late nineteenth century. Writers such as Arthur Conan Doyle and Edgar Rice Burroughs may have used H. Rider Haggard's (1856–1925) novels as a springboard to their own imaginative recesses. For although he didn't write science fiction, Haggard perfected the *historical* lost-race novel. In his popular *She* (1887), when the immortal lady Ayesha—a descendant of the ancient Egyptian race surviving in a hidden African valley—dies after bathing in a life-prolonging flame that fails to provide nourishment, her corpse shrivels into that of an ape, a "little hideous monkey frame." It wasn't long before writers sensed dramatic connections that were possible between primeval forgotten places of the globe and *prehistoric* life somehow mysteriously surviving into modernity.

Cave settings, a source of inspiration and intrigue for writers of the Romantic period and early nineteenth century geologists, served as prototypical lost worlds of literature, as we've already seen in the case of Verne's classic *Journey*. Eventually, however, writers restructured the romantic, exotic nature of the cave, placing terrors of the remote past right in our own back yards, so to speak. As writer Lin Carter noted in 1972, C.J. Cutcliffe Hyne (1866–1944) was an imaginative British writer with a predilection for "plesiosaurs and other anachronistic Mesozoic reptiles." Hyne's best-regarded short story, "The Lizard" (1898), incorporated prehistoric fauna in a cave environment.

Hyne builds suspense in "The Lizard" as the protagonist, a spelunker named Chesney investigates an ancient cave in Yorkshire. Wading waist deep in water, Chesney notes a fossil mold in the cave wall having the form of a crocodile, which "had been lost to the world's knowledge for so many millions of years."[6] Then he spies a penknife nearby, having been lost by a previous explorer. The animal with the crocodile shape seems to have been recently disinterred by the action of water and an earth tremor. Chesney continues his investigation, noting a musky stench and then a *second* mold in which yet another crocodilian lies entombed. After Chesney kicks the limestone, the matrix covering cracks and begins to flake off. Chesney rejoices, "Here was I the discoverer of the body of a prehistoric beast, preserved in the limestone down through all the ages just as mammoths have been preserved in Siberian ice.... I wondered whether they would make me a baronet for the discovery."[7] Unfortunately, Chesney's visions of grandeur suddenly dissolve into sheer terror as the "ten million" year old, *living* beast, about the size of two horses, gives chase. Tripping, he frantically stabs the creature with the penknife, and the wounded monster flees back into the depths of the dark cave.

Perhaps buoyed by Thomas Huxley's 1873 announcement of *Bathybius* (see the Preface), undersea ocean depths proved another kind of viable, subaqueous lost-world realm. Increasingly, however, writers were associating lost places with exotic lost civilizations, of any kind or species. Hyne's most famous tale, *The Lost Continent* (1899), involved another prehistoric setting. *The Lost Continent*, a tale of Atlantis, was originally serialized by *Pearson's Magazine* in 1899 and was republished as a novel in 1900. Mammoths are beasts of burden in Atlantis, and there are "greater lizards" lurking about too. One kind, "whose hugeness no human force can battle against ... made the wet land shake and pulse as it trod. It could have taken Phorenice's mammoth into its belly and even a mammoth in full charge could not have harmed it. Great horny plates covered its head and body, and on the ridge of its back and tail and limbs were spines that tore great slivers from the black trees as it passed amongst them."[8] Of course, the paradoxically ancient, yet advanced civilization became "lost" when the continent of Atlantis plunged catastrophically into the sea.[9]

And in H.G. Wells' short story "In the Abyss" (1896), readers encountered another kind of ancient civilization. Here, a deep-sea explorer observes the underwater cities of an intelligent deep-sea race, "descendants, like ourselves, of the great Theriomorpha of the New Red Sandstone age" (i.e., Permian Period) from a diving bell. Wells describes the creatures, disturbingly too close for comfort on the evolutionary scale, as aquatic *anthropoids*.[10] As we shall see in the next chapter, Wells' tale presaged Karel Capek's important *War With the Newts* (1936).

Writers gradually took prehistoric monsters and paleoanthropological themes entirely out of the cave and the ocean deeps into other lost-world settings, such as the world's coldest imaginable polar environments, which were actually being trekked by intrepid explorers of the time. For instance, in Frank Mackenzie Savile's 1901 novel *Beyond the Great South Wall*, a monstrous brontosaur—named the god "Cay," inhabiting Antarctica—terrifies a shipload of explorers intent on rediscovering the ancient Mayan race, who fled there centuries before with treasure.[11] The archaeologists find Mayan remains and mummies before Cay, the avenging brontosaur, the "last dinosaur alive," expires in a climactic volcanic eruption.[12] Certainly, as of late 1898, hugeness of dinosaurian giants such as brontosaurs could be equated to "horrific."

Perhaps it's no coincidence that the popularity of the *idea* of prehistoric life forms populating lost-world settings escalated during the early twentieth century, as that was a period of growth for America's natural history museums featuring paleontological displays.[13] In the form of erected skeletal reconstructions, museum murals and art, and through other entertaining media and exhibits, dinosaurs and other prehistoric animals were enjoying an unprecedented blaze of pop-cultural attention. So it's no surprise that soon individuals were actually on the hunt for living prehistoric beasts, or, conversely and allegedly, became wary of dinosaurs out hunting for them, although in real lost-world settings. Indeed, during this period, in the matter of cryptozoological lost worlds, the line between reality and fiction became increasingly blurred.

The Sunday, January 11, 1911, issue of the *New York Herald* carried a sensational headline: "Prehistoric Monsters in Jungles of the Amazon," reporting a 1907 encounter in the Amazon jungle. According to the article's author, Franz Herrmann Schmidt encountered a thirty-five-foot-long "bullet proof monster" resembling a plesiosaur.[14] Another German, exotic animal collector and zoologist Carl Hagenbeck (1844–1913), had learned of rumors concerning unknown dinosaur-like animals, "half elephant, half dragon," living in the swamps of Central Africa and Rhodesia. In 1909, news began to spread through England and the United States after an English translation of Hagenbeck's autobiography, *Beasts and Men*, appeared. When stories began circulating in 1910 issues of *London Sphere, The American Weekly* and *New York Herald*, Hagenbeck's "dinosaur controversy" had reached its peak. "Although other explorers had entertained ideas about mysterious African beasts, it was Hagenbeck who imprinted the idea of a living dinosaur upon the public."[15]

During a 1909 Mediterranean voyage, Arthur Conan Doyle himself claimed to have witnessed a four-foot-long ichthyosaur swimming alongside their ship. Years later, Doyle remarked, "This old world has got some surprises for us yet!"[16] And intriguingly, in 1912, shortly following publication of Conan Doyle's *The Lost World*, huge carnivorous reptiles had been discovered in the primeval Pacific island setting of Komodo. Following American Museum of Natural History naturalist W. Douglas Burden's capture of living Komodo Dragon specimens, delivered to the Bronx Zoo, Merian C. Cooper became inspired to do something similar, however fictionally, involving a giant gorilla.[17]

LOST WORLDS "THEORY"

Writers and critics refer to any literary setting involving *prehistoric* life as a "lost world," when instead the term should only apply to settings on present-day earth. Rather than prehistoric in nature, many such animals of fantastic fiction (excluding tales where prehistoric life is encountered by humans in earth's past through use of time-travel, or on alien planets), would appear to be cryptozoological species instead. After all, if they're prehistoric, they shouldn't be interacting with *modern* humans *at all*. The problem for the writer then becomes: how can animals known to be extinct everywhere plausibly penetrate the barrier of time into the present? Some rules must be broken, and as paleontologist Dougal Dixon noted, lost worlds "suffer from ... rather obvious faults."[18] First, the indigenous fauna includes an admixture of prehistoric animals which in fact were separated in geological time by many tens of millions of years. Dixon blames the "originators" of the genre—Verne and Arthur Conan Doyle—for this problem, although I suspect that Verne's progressive life-through-time theme may have been misunderstood by latter-day writers.[19]

Secondly, Dixon notes that if the lost-world setting is to be unnoticed by modern explorers well into any historical period, then its surface area must necessarily be small relative to other known islands and continents (unless it plunged into the sea). But a diminished habitat area couldn't support large populations of gigantic dinosaurs which thrived on ancient continents such as Gondwanaland and Laurasia. So one would anticipate the evolution of *dwarf* species instead. But hold off launching an expedition in search of a dog-sized stegosaur pet![20] For if dinosaurs had really survived somewhere into modernity, then they would have evolved from their familiar Mesozoic forms into new species (such as birds)—that is unless, on these special settings, *time stands still*. How could this be possible, unless most unusual *anti*-evolutionary forces are at work in these places?

Most readers are probably familiar with lost worlds of science fiction *film*, such as in movies like *The Lost World* (1925), *King Kong* (1933), *Unknown Island* (1948), *Lost Continent* (1951), *The Creature From the Black Lagoon* (1954), and *The Land Unknown* (1957).[21] Themes projected in such film fare are often derived from classic novels and literature, this chapter's emphasis. Paleontologist Jose Luis Sanz claims that a fictionalized lost world is a "prohibited and damned place.... It is a place where humans are not the dominant species and in which mankind is scarcely able to survive against the enormous beasts of the past."[22] Another aspect to this is the sense of brooding evil lurking within the lost world. "The myth of the lost world is ... in some way linked with that of Paradise after the departure of Adam and Eve. The lost world is a morally and physically dangerous place. Dinosaurs ... [are] the fundamental evil that has existed since the beginning of time."[23] Consider the sense of evil associated with *The Lost World*'s mysterious "spirit of the woods," called "curupuri," or the allosaur Gwangi's demise in *The Valley of Gwangi* (1969), for example, where the titular beast is extinguished—actually *and* symbolically—in a burning cathedral.

In the movies, there's usually no clue as to how the extinct beasts have survived all those millions of years. Usually, however, directors incorporate dinosaurs for their "cool" special effects potential, thereby elevating them from their lowly paleo-prop status as originally conveyed in the literature, from which their on-screen appearances have been derived. And, rather ironically, the evolutionary messages so central to the written story become lost in translation with projection onto the silver screen.

But unlike lost places ruled by the "time stands still" principle, evolutionary forces can also operate in lost-world settings.

Who published the earliest tale concerning a prehistoric beast which also incorporated distinctive evolutionary messages? The answer may be Arthur Conan Doyle, although for a less celebrated tale relying on the familiar cave device, "The Terror of Blue John Gap" (1910). Here, a cave bear-like being terrorizes the British countryside. Through his diary, we learn that a since-deceased Dr. Hardcastle, who was convalescing near a limestone cave system, learned of the legend of the Blue John Gap (an old Roman mining cave) from a neighbor.

The climactic scene—confronting a cave bear horror—from Arthur Conan Doyle's 1910 short story "The Terror of Blue John Gap," figured by Harry Rountree. See text for further details. (From *The Strand Magazine*, 1910, author's collection.)

Hardcastle then visited this particular cave himself. Soon a ponderous monster shuffles by in the awful darkness, leaving huge footprints in the mud. After escaping this ordeal, Hardcastle is reluctant to tell anyone of the encounter for fear of asylum. When his neighbor disappears mysteriously, he resolves to confront the creature by the cave entrance, where he plans to shoot it. Flashing on his lamp as it strides past on a moonless night, he spies the hideous creature which was "something bear-like ... [but] ten-fold the bulk of any bear seen upon earth ... in his pose and attitude...." From this brief glimpse, Hardcastle recognizes that the creature is also sightless. Knocked unconscious by a swing of its heavy paw, Hardcastle recovers, later offering his theory as to the apparition's origin.

> ... in this part of England there is a vast subterranean lake or sea, which is fed by the great number of streams which pass down through the limestone. Where there is a large collection of water there must be some evaporation, mists or rain, and a possibility of vegetation. This in turn suggests that there may be animal life, arising, as the vegetable life would also do, from those seeds and types which had been introduced at an early period of the world's history, when communication with the outer air was more easy. This place had then developed a fauna and flora of its own, including such monsters as the one which I had seen, which may well have been the old cave-bear, enormously enlarged and modified by its new environment. For countless aeons the internal and external creation had kept apart, growing steadily away from each other. Then there had come some rift in the depths of the mountain that had enabled one creature to wander up and, by means of the Roman tunnel, to reach the open air. Like all subterranean life, it had lost the power of sight....[24]

The subject of blind cave-animals was under scientific scrutiny during the late nineteenth century.[25] Zoologists were fascinated by how such species could have evolved, and the "degeneration theory" of evolution many ascribed to their origin—through an "inherited effect of disuse"—had already been seized by H.G. Wells in *The Time Machine* (1895) for his fictional, underground Morlocks species.[26] "The Terror of Blue John Gap" stems from a period in Conan Doyle's life when the distinguished author evidently took an interest in evolution and paleontology, an odd preoccupation then escalating in popularity. This wouldn't be the last time Conan Doyle would tinker with an evolutionary theme.

As noted by historian of science Peter J. Bowler, "The historian of evolution theory who seeks to deal with the debates around 1900 enters a world of bewildering complexity."[27] Nevertheless, the most prominent evolution themes may be recognized in contemporary lost-world fantastic fiction. Verne's *Journey* was a progressive life-through-time tale instead of a time-stands-still story, much like Conan Doyle's *The Lost World* and the 1933 feature film *King Kong*. Two other theoretical lost-world frameworks explored in acclaimed science fiction dating from this literary period which we'll consider later in this chapter will be the Biogenetic Law and Orthogenesis.

TIME STANDS STILL

In 1998, W.J.T. Mitchell noted how "Lost worlds fictions typically reinforce the neo–Darwinist, Osbornian mythology of Anglo-Saxon superiority."[28] We see this exemplified in Conan Doyle's *The Lost World*, first serialized in *The Strand Magazine*, beginning with the April 1912 issue.

By *The Lost World*'s opening, intrepid and hot-tempered Professor Challenger has made

John Lavas's "topographic depiction of Maple White Land and the Central Lake, with main features and animals enlarged." This schematic diagram is reproduced with permission from his 2002 volume, *The Lost World of Arthur Conan Doyle— Collector's Anniversary Edition*, which includes in-depth introductory sections by Lavas.

a reconnaissance of the base of a South American volcanic plateau, already accessed by American explorer Maple White. However, Challenger's claims of living prehistoric fauna are ridiculed by colleagues. He convinces reporter—protagonist Ed Malone of his utter sincerity in the matter, and following a raucous London meeting, an expedition (including, principally, Malone; Challenger's scientific colleague Dr. Summerlee, a professor of anatomy; and a curious sporting champion, Lord Roxton) is launched to judge the veracity of Challenger's contentious conclusions. The year is, presumably, 1908.

Malone, Challenger and company scale the plateau, where they discover prehistoric fauna. Encounters with pterodactyls, an *Iguanodont* herd, plated *Stegosaurus*, and a giant carnivorous bird *Phororhacos*, prove that Challenger isn't a madman after all. Malone unwisely takes a walk in the dark down to the plateau's central lake, only to be pursued by a carnivorous dinosaur pouncing relentlessly after him. He falls unconscious into a pit manufactured by ape-men for catching wild animals, thereby escaping the cruel jaws of the menacing, kangaroo-like carnivore.

However, the expedition's chief menace aren't dinosaurs, but a lost race of savage red-haired "missing links" (debated to be akin either to *Dryopithecus* or *Pithecanthropus* by Challenger and Summerlee). Malone's comrades are captured by these missing links. Roxton escapes and finds Malone, and they rescue the professors. Then, reunited, they join a modern yet lost Indian tribe who also inhabit the plateau, battling the more primitive ape-men. With rifles blazing, the company of Indians and Europeans nearly exterminate the missing links. Expressing a decidedly politically incorrect tone, Challenger justifies their decisive

Edward Malone chased by a bounding, bipedal dinosaur, possibly *Megalosaurus*, as depicted by Harry Rountree for *The Strand Magazine* (1912). (From *The Strand Magazine*, 1912, author's collection.)

military maneuver: "Now upon this plateau the future must ever be for man."[29] Back in London they prove their case dramatically when Challenger releases a living pterodactyl into the night sky. In the end, crackpot science emerges victorious and boisterous Professor Challenger is its champion.

Does time truly stand still in Challenger's Maple White Land? The assortment of primitive animals represents the Jurassic, Cretaceous, Tertiary, and Recent geological time periods. How can this be? At first, evolutionist Challenger claims the Jurassic fauna is a result of volcanic upheaval, lifting the plateau and effectively isolating the summit from lower elevations. Consequently, "the ordinary laws of Nature are suspended. The various checks which influence the struggle for existence in the world at large are all neutralized or altered. Creatures survive which would otherwise disappear ... both the pterodactyl and the stegosaurus ... have been artificially conserved by those strange accidental conditions."[30] Later, Summerlee proposes that a herd of *Iguanodon* still inhabits the plateau because environmental conditions haven't changed on Maple White Land since the time of their extinction elsewhere.[31] But *Iguanodon* lived at a later time than *Stegosaurus*, and so, as the professors eventually realize, more recent animals from lower elevations ascend the plateau sometimes, presumably through natural tunnels in the rock. This seems to be the only plausible explanation for the presence of the anatomically recent Indian tribe. "On no possible supposition can we explain the evolution of such a race in this place. For that matter, so great a gap separates these ape-men from the primitive animals which have survived upon this plateau, that it is inadmissible to think that they could have developed where we find them."[32]

So it seems as if the plateau's steep cliffs have filtered the passage of animals onto its summit. Through the ages select forms have ascended to the top—through tunnels, presumably—only to become suspended in an evolutionary stasis. So, it's not time which truly stands still here. Time marches on, while instead, evolutionary forces, natural selection—specifically in the sense of climatic conditions—don't operate on Maple White Land. Regardless, here as elsewhere, "Man was always the master."[33] However, Conan Doyle admits a possibility that after gaining access to the plateau, "anthropoid apes" may have "developed into the creatures [i.e., ape-men] we have seen...."[34] Reading between the lines, perhaps at a subliminal level, the fact that a lost race of ape-men have been spawned through *evolutionary* processes would have made them seem even more reprehensible to some contemporary readers.

To his credit, Conan Doyle was certainly supportive of abolitionist causes, yet he was also a child of his time. While *The Lost World* was aimed at a younger audience, it proved immensely popular across generations of readers. To the casual reader, Conan Doyle's fantasy science seems anti–Darwinian, because the evolutionary force has been silenced on Maple White Land. And yet *The Lost World* is cryptically laden with evolutionary and even subtle racial commentary.

Conan Doyle had befriended British paleontologist E. Ray Lankester (1846–1929), who in his retirement years published *Extinct Animals* (1905), based on his popular lecture series.[35] In fact, Lankester coached Conan Doyle during his preparation of *The Lost World*'s manuscript. Descriptions of Maple White Land's prehistoric menagerie were highly influenced by *Extinct Animals*. Lankester has been hailed as something of an evolutionary hero for merging Charles Darwin's and Alfred Russell Wallace's (1823–1913) natural selection concept with August Weismann's (1834–1914) theory of inheritance caused by a "germ plasm"—

thought to be unalterable by the environment.[36] Yet, during the 1910s, Lankester was also duped by fraudulent fossils considered by many as proof of the Anglo-Saxon race's origin and superiority in ancient Great Britain, or the infamous Piltdown Man hoax. In a *Science 83* article Conan Doyle was even charged as Piltdown's perpetrator, a fascinating case the details of which we haven't the space for here.[37] While I personally do not support Conan Doyle's implication in this unscrupulous affair, his inclusion in *The Lost World* of a society of smaller-brained, primitive missing links, discussions of modern man's racial superiority, and lost civilizations surviving in a world where natural selection failed, mirror contemporary angst concerning man's alleged ape-like origins and a godless, randomly operating natural selection "law."

Edgar Rice Burroughs' Odd Evolutionary Ideas

Native Chicagoan writer Edgar Rice Burroughs (1875–1950) is most highly revered as the creator, in 1912, of Tarzan, a heroic character who "represented in embryo the whole course of evolution, from ape to man."[38] Perhaps inspired by Conan Doyle's and Verne's tales, Burroughs' first venture into mainstream dinosaur fiction, however, was *At the Earth's Core*, serialized in 1914. By then the "hollow earth" idea was already tired. Yet Burroughs was a master at suspending disbelief with scientific romance, the key to *Earth's Core*'s success. Here, American explorers David Innes and Abner Perry bore through 500 miles of the earth's crust in a mechanical "iron mole." Emerging on the inner surface anti-world of Pellucidar, the explorers discover (1) that the earth is hollow, (2) that its spherical shell rotates about a tiny radiant star with an orbiting satellite, (3) that its seas exist where continents lie on the outer crust and vice versa, and (4) that primitive and bizarre life forms, long extinct on the outer crust, share this world of a "million years ago" with primitive human inhabitants.

In this Vernian environment, Stone Age Cro-Magnon–like people known as Gilaks coexist with an exotic "lost" civilization known as "Mahar." The bloodthirsty Mahars are a late-surviving "Saurozoic" species, six-to-eight-foot-tall pterodactyls—descendants of "Rhamphorhynchoids"—who have subjugated the Gilaks and other gorilla-like anthropoids known as Sagoths. Anticipating a key gender-related element of Michael Crichton's *Jurassic Park* (1990), all Mahars are *female* because, ages ago, the winged race learned how to procreate artificially so as to prevent their overpopulation, using a closely guarded chemical formula termed the "Great Secret" (i.e., parthenogenesis).[39] Through the course of the Pellucidar series, the humans eventually defeat the fiendish reptilian Mahars, a predictable outcome of manifest destiny.

Pellucidar's fauna may seem for the most part frozen in time, with Late Paleozoic, Mesozoic and Pleistocene forms represented. However, the evolutionary process *did* formerly produce a Mahar species which remained in stasis due to "Great Secret" technology. The explorers reason that the ancient fauna also developed in Pellucidar through a *stunted* evolutionary process.

> This inner world must have cooled sufficiently to support animal life long ages after life appeared upon the outer crust, but that the same agencies were at work here is evident from the similar forms of both animal and vegetable creation which we have already seen.[40]

Burroughs' literary experimentation with evolutionary processes would escalate in his most imaginative novel, *The Land That Time Forgot* (1918), a brilliant life-through-time saga published serially in *Blue Book Magazine*.[41]

A reader accused Burroughs of plagiarism, referring to similarities between Conan Doyle's *The Lost World* and *The Land That Time Forgot*. According to Burroughs expert John Taliaferro, Burroughs "deflected the charge by saying that he had started Conan Doyle's novel but had never finished it. Yet in a letter to one Bob Davis three years earlier, Burroughs hinted he had read *The Lost World*, "and very carefully at that."[42] Whereas on Maple White Land time—meaning evolution—stands still, on Burroughs' imaginary isle "Caspak," evolutionary forces are vibrant and incessant. As opposed to Conan Doyle, Burroughs wove dinosaurs and prehistoric men more fully into a science fiction tale about the majesty of evolution. So, to me, Burroughs' contribution was highly original, representing a marvelous extrapolation on the lost-worlds theme.[43]

Land That Time Forgot's protagonist, Bowen J. Tyler, Jr., son of a wealthy Santa Monica ship builder, relates in a diary his capture at sea following an attack by a German World War I torpedo boat, the U-33. Tyler, his dog Nobs, and a female companion named Lys La Rue are rescued by an English vessel, only to be attacked again by the U-33, although this time they subdue the Germans, commandeering the submarine. The captured Germans sabotage the communications system and navigation, thwarting all efforts to reach friendly shores. So Tyler, Lys and company sail through uncharted waters toward south polar seas, uncertain of their position. Icebergs encountered at sea and sighting of distant cliffs suggests they may have sailed toward the coastline of a mysterious continent named Caprona, first discovered 200 years before by an Italian navigator. By now the U-33 crew are in need of a fresh water supply lest they perish. After spying the corpse of a primitive human on the sandy shore, Tyler urges the men to find a way past the rugged coastline barrier at all costs.

The lofty cliffs appear forbidding and the land's interior impenetrable, until the explorers spot a fluvial channel issuing to the sea through an underwater opening in the rocky coastline. Tyler steers the U-33 through the submarine fissure. They surface in a broad, primeval river system, "the banks of which were lined by giant, arboraceous ferns, raising their mighty fronds fifty, one hundred, two hundred feet into the quiet air." Well, not so quiet after all, as huge insects buzz about and pterodactyls soar in skies above. Paradoxically, in spite of their southerly latitudinal position, the air is muggy and warm here. But horrors lurk in this pristine, Lower Jurassic setting. Soon, the U-boat's deck is swarming with eighteen-foot-long, long-necked plesiosaurs, which one sailor refers to as "giraffes." In one gripping passage an aquatic monster seizes a German, one of the first such scenes in literature in which a creature from the Mesozoic devours a human. "Shrieking and screaming, the German was dragged from the deck, and the moment the reptile was clear of the boat, it dived beneath the surface of the water with its terrified prey." Together, German and Allied crew forces fend off the aquatic saurians, fleeing to safety aboard the U-33.

Tyler theorizes that, like the 1883 Krakatoa explosion,

> ... in a far distant era Caprona was a mighty mountain—perhaps the world's mightiest mountain—and that in some titanic eruption volcanic action blew off the entire crest, blew thousands of feet of the mountain upward ... leaving a great crater; and then, possibly, the continent sank ... leaving only the summit of Caprona above the sea. The encircling walls, the

central lake, the hot springs which feed the lake, all point to such a conclusion, and the fauna and the flora bear indisputable evidence that Caprona was once part of some great land-mass.[44]

After surviving ordeals with various dinosaur props encountered along their route, including an allosaur and later a tyrannosaur, the U-33 is attacked by a band of stocky Neanderthal-like anthropoids. Listening to the screaming and hissing saurians at night, through Lys, Burroughs tips his hand about Caprona's secular condition when Lys remarks to Tyler, "I am depressed by the awfulness of it all. I feel of so little consequence—so small and helpless in the face of all these myriad manifestations of life stripped to the bone of its savagery and brutality. I realize as never before how cheap and valueless a thing is life ... we take ourselves too seriously; but Caprona should be a sure cure for that."[45] And in a sequel, Burroughs' *The People That Time Forgot* (1918), we learn through protagonist Tom Billings, who intends to rescue Tyler, that "Life is the cheapest thing in Caspak, as it is the cheapest thing on earth and, doubtless, the cheapest cosmic production." During the tragic First World War period, prehistoric savagery coupled to odd Darwinian principles must have seemed both socially "relevant" as well as soul-stirring.

So far this all seems like another typical lost-world setting, until, rather cryptically, a Neanderthal whom they've captured, named "Ahm," divulges that he eventually will *become* a "Galu," like his captors. Further, Tyler notes that the farther north they travel, the fewer dinosaurs there are. Also, "though we had seen many of the lesser developed wild people of Caspak [as Caprona is known to indigenous tribes], we had never yet seen a child or old man or woman." Eventually, after he's learned the *truth* about Caspak, reflecting incendiary public debates between evolution and religion, Tyler remarks in his diary, "If I should return to civilization, I should have meat for the clergy and the laymen to chew upon for years—and for the evolutionists too."

At *Land That Time Forgot*'s conclusion the truth about Caspak's mystical evolutionary forces remains rather mysterious. Caspak's evolutionary forces are more fully revealed in *The People That Time Forgot*.[46] Here, it is apparent that various human species coexist in time yet are situated geographically according to their scale on the evolutionary "ladder." Thus the most primitive hominids live farthest south, while the advanced forms live farther north. Also, "the farther north one traveled in Caspak, the fewer the terrible reptiles which rendered human life impossible at the southern of the island." Horse evolution is also mirrored in Burroughs' story, with the diminutive "ecca," a *Hyracotherium*, appearing in the south regions, grading to more advanced forms in the north.

Eventually the "Caspakian scheme of evolution" is revealed, "which partly accounted for the lack of young among the races I had so far seen. Coming up from the beginning, the Caspakian passes, during a single existence, through the various stages of evolution, or at least many of them, through which the human race has passed during the countless ages since life first stirred upon a new world...."[47] In other words, evolution on Caspak mirrors German paleontologist Ernst Haeckel's (1834–1919) long-since-disproved Biogenetic Law, namely that "ontogeny recapitulates phylogeny," allegedly founded in Darwinian principles. Haeckel believed much of this recapitulation took place during embryonic development. On Caspak, however, the process normally operates externally, or outside of the womb, during the lifetimes of *individual* organisms. Individual "cor sva jo" organisms usually undergo seven cycles of evolution, taking place within a 700-year period, to come up "from the beginning" to become Galus.[48]

EVOLUTION AT LARGE: ORTHOGENESIS IN LOST WORLDS

The brilliant naturalist and geologist Charles Darwin never resolved two pressing matters in his landmark volume, *The Origin of Species*.[49] First, he never elucidated the mystery of life's origins. Darwin implied that the earliest organisms known to contemporary science must have had progenitors in the mysterious Precambrian era, unrecorded in the fossil record, but avoided the touchy issue of how life itself *originated*. Secondly, although implying that *Homo sapiens* was a product of evolution, he stated rather cryptically, "Much light will be thrown on the origin of man and his history."[50] Darwin took up the matter of man's evolutionary past more fully in his *The Descent of Man and Selection in Relation to Sex* (1871), where he addressed our ape-like ancestry, reasoning (correctly) that Africa was the cradle of mankind.[51] Darwin considered differences in skin pigmentation—evident in the various races of mankind—merely resultant of sexual selection. By the early twentieth century, evolutionary science unfolded and diverged into many fascinating and sometimes misguided scholarly undertakings, far too many to fully consider in this book. However, besides Haeckel's Biogenetic Law—illustrated through Burroughs' Caspak trilogy—another popular evolutionary delusion derived from Darwin's (and Wallace's) theory surfaced, the principle of *orthogenesis*.

Orthogenesis held that evolution sometimes was directed along mysterious trend-like paths, building momentum through many generations toward the production of enlarged features such as horns, antlers and fangs, so oversized as to no longer be favored organic adaptations. The affected organism's genetic machinery misfired, producing aberrant forms; features seen in extinct species, such as *Titanothere* horns, the Irish Elk's antlers, or the fangs of sabertoothed cats, were oft-cited cases. But, theoretically, orthogenesis could also produce *degenerative* trends, resulting in diminution of anatomical parts and an inevitable decline in species through geological history. So, orthogenesis was an internally programmed, *anti–Darwinian* process leading to an inevitable outcome: extinction. Certainly, there were more successful contemporary theories explaining the evolutionary mechanism. However, the orthogenetic principle—often referred to as "racial senility"—retained pop-cultural status on into the 1930s as writers applied the concept to human evolution and paleoanthropology.

One early example was cast in Wells' 1892 essay, "Man of the Year Million," where we learn that in the penultimate evolutionary stage, due to progressive trends in man's cranial capacities, man will evolve into bizarre creatures with "hopping heads, great unemotional intelligences, and little hearts...."[52] On another front, writers grappled with our evolutionary cousins, the great apes, primates which instilled fear and loathing.

Wells's contemporary John Taine was mathematician Eric Temple Bell's pseudonym. As a boy, for a short time Bell had lived on a hill near Sydenham overlooking the Crystal Palace grounds where he could see Benjamin Waterhouse Hawkins' large sculptures of dinosaurs and other prehistoric animals. Later in life he recalled how this experience had instilled a "life-long fascination" for the "great amoral brutes."[53] In his spare time, Taine wrote several science fiction stories, some embracing evolutionary themes, the two most prominent of which are *The Greatest Adventure* (1929) and *The Iron Star* (1930).[54] The Iron Star is a great meteor containing a fictional radioactive element named "asterium" which is brought to the attention of a physician by a villain who intends to disprove Darwin's theory of evolution. Asterium causes humans to undergo evolutionary regression, backward through primitive forms we evolved from, cascading backward down the evolutionary "ladder of progress," or inverse to the biogenetic law. The closer native populations happen to reside to the largest African meteor deposit, the more they regress, increasingly acquiring ape-like characteristics. Therefore, *Iron Star* is a bit like Burrough's Caspak in the sense that evolutionary status is geographically dependent, and progress is measured along a ladder of time.[55]

Alternate saurians are featured in Taine's *The Greatest Adventure*, concerning Dr. Eric Lane's expedition to an intensely volcanic Antarctica where living gigantic dinosaurians thrive. Also there are great untapped oil reserves there. Intense flaring from volcanic vents menaces the expedition periodically. The combination of dinosaurs with oil would have seemed natural at the time, as companies like Sinclair were using dinosaur symbolism to

In Taine's *The Greatest Adventure* (1929), explorers discover gigantic dinosaurians in Antarctica's lost-world landscape. Here is one of the odd dinosaurs as figured by Jack Arata, modeled after Lawrence Sterne Steven's cover illustration for a June 1944 reprint of Taine's classic story appearing in *Famous Fantastic Mysteries*. See text for further details about this story. (With permission of the artist, Jack Arata.)

advertise gasoline and petroleum products because the carcasses of prehistoric animals were thought to have formed petroleum within the earth. Also, the discovery of oil on a southern continent recalls one scene in Burroughs' *Land That Time Forgot* where a discovered oil reserve allows the Germans to escape Caprona in the U-33.

But *Greatest Adventure* is primarily about determining life's origins and comprehending a peculiar, preordained course of (orthogenetic) evolution. The "prehistoric" beasts—Frankensteinian abominations—encountered by Dr. Lane's party turn out to be artificial, having gradually evolved from spores created by an intelligent prehistoric race who experimented with bioengineering eons before man. Therefore the Godzilla-sized dinosaurians found there are not evolutionarily related to Mesozoic life, real dinosaurs found on other continents. For as Lane observes, "They are like bad copies, botched imitations if you like, of those huge brutes whose bones we chisel out of the rocks from Wyoming to Patagonia. Nature must have been drunk, drugged, or asleep when she allowed these aborted beasts to mature. Every last one of them is a freak."[56] Once the awful, predestined evolutionary course was forecasted, the ancient technological race wisely concealed the evolving spores and recorded their scientific knowledge as inscriptions carved onto the wall of a great cave, a warning to future intelligent life to prevent the repeated mistake of creating artificial life. The spores have potential to infect the rest of our luxuriant planet, so it is imperative that they remain confined to Antarctica.

> That is why they made those pits, three miles deep, with perpendicular walls as smooth as glass. Whatever bred in those mines and galleries would live and die there. Soil and heat alike eventually becoming exhausted, the last vestiges of life in the mines and tunnels would perish. We happen to have arrived before the natural end, which may not come for millions of years yet. These monsters have been living, evolving, multiplying, and dying in the galleries and uncemented mines for millions of years, literally for ages of geologic time.[57]

Such thrilling tales of "alternate" evolutionary processes uncovered in foreboding, lost places of our planet anticipated the greatest prehistoric monster of the early twentieth century, once hailed as the "eighth wonder of the world"!

After the London Zoo received its first gorilla specimen in 1858, Thomas Huxley proclaimed that differences ("intervals") between man and gorilla were relatively few. Shortly thereafter, French artist Emmanuel Fremiet (1824–1910) captured the essence of the emotional dilemma—Darwin's sexual selection carried to an extreme—in his 1859 sculpture, *Gorilla Carrying off a Native Woman*.[58] While hairy-armed vestiges from our savage past might not rape our women, certainly they proved haunting, formidable foes, at least in fiction. Then, for the 1871 through 1873 English editions of Verne's *Journey*, an unknown writer furnished Verne's text with the unlikely "Ape Gigans," described as an "antediluvian gorilla," or "the progenitor of the hideous monster of Africa." Ape Gigans was "Fourteen feet high, covered with coarse hair, of a blackish brown, the hair on the arms, from the shoulder to the elbow joints, pointing downwards, while that from the wrist to the elbow pointed upwards.... Its arms were as long as its body, while its legs were prodigious. It had thick, long, and sharply pointed teeth—like a mammoth saw."[59] When approaching the frightened explorers, Ape Gigans groaned, sounding like "fifty bears in a fight."

Through the nineteenth century, gorillas retained their ferocious mien, viewed as creatures "from a hellish nightmare."[60] Then, the largest primate, a gorilla species—the Mountain Gorilla, males of which can weigh up to 550 pounds—was discovered in 1901. And if

Perhaps the most imposing (psychological) horror evident in early samples of dino-fiction wasn't dinosaurs, but, rather, the prospect that modern civilized man evolved from primitive ape-like creatures. Salacious fears that more (evolutionarily) advanced females might be carried off and raped by ape-like primitives were often played upon in early dino-fiction, as in this illustration from Charles G. D. Roberts's *In the Morning of Time* (1919 ed.). (See Appendix and note 58 for more on this title.)

gigantic gorillas represented a primeval stage in evolution, so were their worlds considered somehow "lost" in time.

Perhaps the most famous lost-world island of all became Skull Island, home to a huge ape named Kong as well as native saurians, featured in the 1933 RKO film *King Kong*. The film was co-directed by Merian C. Cooper (1893–1973) who was greatly interested in contemporary popularizations of evolution and primate natural history. Cooper even wrote an 85,000-word manuscript about baboons from firsthand observations, and later conceived the idea of a giant gorilla under attack in New York City after learning the plight of Komodo Dragons exhibited at the Bronx Zoo. Few know, however, that Ruth Rose and James Creelman's screenplay for *King Kong* was novelized by Delos W. Lovelace in 1932. Book differed in many details from film.[61] Significantly, in the novel Kong dispatches the two most majestic forms of prehistoric savagery known to early twentieth-century science, the mighty icon *Tyrannosaurus*, and its ancient nemesis *Triceratops*. With Rex and Tops defeated on Skull Island, modern man's puny arsenal cannot stop the rampaging Kong either, who symbolically mounts the Empire State Building. For, climactically, as fictional film director and Kong promoter Carl Denham exclaims, "The aviators didn't get him.... It was Beauty. As always. Beauty killed the Beast."

Mitchell stated dinosaur stories of fantastic fiction are about us. My premise here it that classical *lost-world* tales are principally about human evolution or lost races of man where dinosaurs serve simply as outlandish props, symbolizing prehistoric savagery or exploitation of nature. This is entirely the case in the "beauty and the beast" tale, *King Kong*. Here, not only do explorers find a lost civilization on Skull Island, but the remnant of a huge and nearly extinct primate, which by its huge appearance would seem to be a product of orthogenesis. In fact, prehistoric Kong, a "beast-god" of "some prehistoric survival," is considered one of nature's grand "mistakes" in Lovelace's 1932 novel, much like the prehistoric reptiles which co-exist in a place where time stands still. Before she ever lays eyes on Kong, Ann Darrow clarifies Kong's status for us by commenting, "But there was never such a beast! ... At least not since prehistoric times." This foreshadows the expedition's fate because while attempting to rescue Ann from Kong's clutches, after they've killed a huge charging *Stegosaurus*, Carl Denham remarks, "But if this thing we've killed means anything, the plateau is alive with all sorts of creatures that have survived along with Kong." Nearly all the intrepid sailors and explorers who pass through Skull Island's great wooden gate suffer and die.

Distinctly human attributes could of course be conveyed through the majestic Kong, both in Lovelace's novel and projected visually on film. Rather than any of Skull Island's saurians, beast-god Kong symbolizes humanity, even falling for "beauty" —Ann Darrow.

In Lovelace's novel, dinosaurs are merely props foreshadowing the climax to come in New York City. Metropolis then becomes itself a symbolic lost-world setting. For, lurking beneath or within an urban culture, much as savage nature lies hidden beneath the light pigmentation of "civilized" man, resides a heart so savage that even a heroic Kong, endowed with human-like attributes, can't survive ... that is, without Beauty. Since frontier times it has been traditional to regard our fabled American west—home to the *Mastodon, Brontosaurus,* and *Tyrannosaurus*—as another kind of lost-world setting (akin to Skull Island). Now we can add Metropolis to the growing list of lost-world places.

CONCLUSION

Verne's interior-world setting in *Journey* is the oldest kind of *prehistoric* lost world imagined, invented and published. Yet Verne wasn't entirely original in his selection of a subterranean setting for a fictional work. Verne did, however, utilize his prehistoric menagerie purposefully, conveying an impression of geological time while framing controversial ideas concerning human antiquity and evolution in his epical 1867 edition. For in the subterranean world, questions concerning the mysteries of evolution and the races of mankind could be subjected safely to speculative commentary. In the decades following Verne's masterpiece, other, non-human prehistoric animals became increasingly carried along for the ride in lost-world tales involving or otherwise invoking prehistory.[62]

Ironically then, prehistoric paleo-props—the dinosaurs and such—are usually the focus of discussion surrounding lost worlds, because most people associate such places with classic or cult movies. After all, those dinosaurs (e.g., the *T. rex* that battles King Kong to the death on Skull Island, or the brontosaur that tramples London in the 1925 silent film *The Lost World*) rank highly in popular consciousness for inherent "coolness," especially in classic films relying on revered special effects. Consequently, evolutionary messages—often conveyed through paradoxical theories explaining *why* time has seemingly stood still in lost world settings, or through the introduction of missing-link hominoids into lost-world settings—are often abbreviated and relegated to subsidiary significance in fanzine "lost-worlds" critique and commentary or popular dinosaur books. In fact it is only through exploration of the original published stories from which films are derived that these evolutionary messages can be exposed and understood.

The early twentieth century represented a revolutionary period in the biological sciences. Evolution, especially its theoretical basis, paleo-history and meaning with respect to man's place in nature, resoundingly seized the day entering mainstream pop-culture like a firestorm. Burroughs was intrigued by Piltdown Man's discovery and the implications of this species for placing white Europeans at evolution's pinnacle. Such attitudes are reflected in his dinosaur fiction, including, for example, *Tarzan the Terrible* (1921).[63] Burroughs, who was proud of his Anglo-Saxon heritage, became fascinated by evolution, perhaps as best exemplified through Tarzan—born to British aristocracy yet raised by apes—a fictional character inspired by "the idea of a contest between heredity and environment."[64] So, perhaps understandably, Burroughs' stories are "Darwinized," infused with ideas concerning human evolution and a conviction that nature's savagery, or "call of the wild" (as Jack London referred to it), lurked closely, underlying civilization's threadbare surface. To Burroughs, God and Nature—meaning natural selection—were as one and the universe was a secular "work in progress."[65] Or as Jack London—a great admirer of Darwin—put it, to "Kill or be killed, eat or be eaten, was the law."[66]

Throughout his steady stream of novels, Burroughs, who had carefully researched contemporary paleontology and paleoanthropology, often portrayed a fictional cast of primitives interacting with white representatives from more advanced societies. From our twenty-first century vantage, Burroughs would appear to be, "if not overtly racist, certainly very patronizing."[67] Mirroring the contemporary racial mythology, savage Nature—blood-red in tooth and claw—and sexual selection were driving forces in these prehistoric settings, and when time turned the tables on modern man, only the fittest—usually those endowed with Anglo-Saxon heritage (like Tarzan)—would survive.[68] The symbolic presence of hungry, savage dinosaurs, pterodactyls, mammoths, saber-tooth cats and their ilk underscored the primeval nature of the newly discovered, unspoiled territory—to be conquered and plundered by civilized men.

CHAPTER 3

At War with Dinosaurs

BACKGROUND

Man and living dinosaurs are separated by sixty-five million years, except of course when intermingled through the grim imaginations of science fiction and horror writers. For in fiction, dinosaurs and other prehistoric animals reflect man's folly, our aspirations, contemporary understanding of nature, and, especially perhaps, our fears. Yet ours has been a love-hate relationship with dinosaurs. Prior to 1900, fictional human heroes or adventurers were awestruck by living remnants of prehistoric life, although without the need for aggression against them. By the 1910s, 1920s, and through the 1940s, however, humans used weapons and war engines increasingly against dinosaurs and their brethren. Ever since, both in the pulps and movie-land, we've killed them shamelessly whenever or wherever they were encountered or appeared, but especially when they invaded our cities and shores.

Why such bloodshed? Can't we just, well, get along with science fiction dinosaurs and other prehistoria? What are the origins of man's apparent militaristic conflict with dinosaurs in literature, and hence film? While our eternal conflict with dinosaurs was preceded by startling images projecting prehistoric savagery, dinosaurs and other prehistoric animals of fantastic fiction increasingly became targets of man's wrath during the first half of the twentieth century during global wars. First we exploited prehistoria, and then they came after *us*, vengefully!

By the early twentieth century, more so than any other scientific principle, Darwinism had gained hold on popular consciousness through a complex known as "Social Darwinism."[1] While striving to further objective science, biologists of the time often distorted evolutionary principles. Political diversions and extrapolations of Darwinism with pop-cultural overtones led to belief in a "master race." In Great Britain and later the United States, paranoia ruled the day, then as now.[2]

Dinosaurs being at war with man seems allied to H.G. Wells's 1898 novel *The War of*

Opposite: At the conclusion of Wardon Allan Curtis's 1899 story "The Monster of Lake LaMetrie," a U.S. military unit kills an elasmosaur which swam up from the bowels of the earth to the shore of Lake LaMetrie in the American west. The saurian, in which a human brain has been planted, is thus a very early and tragic victim of man's brutality. See Appendix for more on this title. (From *Pearson's Magazine*.)

the Worlds, a highly appropriate title for the dinosaur war as well. After all, in the former case, the modern world of man anachronistically clashes with the Mesozoic world, while in the latter, rulers of the fourth planet Mars launch an all out assault against fertile Earth. The horror of Wells's tale is that the Martians are in some mystical way related to us, although possibly representing a later or otherwise degenerative state in our evolutionary development.[3] Also, as Brian Aldiss noted, "Wells is saying, in effect to his fellow English, 'Look, this is how it feels to be a primitive tribe, and to have a Western nation arriving to civilize you with Maxim guns."[4]

During the waning years of the nineteenth century, Great Britain wielded the world's most formidable military and naval power and operated the most advanced technology. It may have seemed silly at the time for anyone to have speculated that Britain could ever be defeated in battle, yet in *War of the Worlds* Wells forecasted Germany's growing war machine in the decades leading to the First World War. Forty years later, on Halloween Eve, 1938, another "Welles," Orson, broadcast a version of Wells's classic tale on public radio. On the verge of a second global conflict, "America's gullibility seemed to result from its shaky mental condition on the eve of World War II."[5] The Nazis' ascent to power was fueled by a belief in a supremacist Aryan race, a myth which sadly had many followers in the United States, especially during the pre-war years. Furthermore, German Ernst Haeckel's (inventor of the biogenetic law) treatment of *Darwinismus* preached "masses of his countrymen ... must accept their evolutionary destiny as a "master race" and "outcompete" inferior peoples, since it was right and natural that only the "fittest" should survive.[6] The title of Adolf Hitler's 1925 autobiography, *Mein Kampf* (i.e., "My Struggle"), was borrowed from a translation of Haeckel's term for "struggle for existence."

Why did savagery become associated with dinosaurs, and how was this phenomenon first manifested? From the 1910s on until James Gurney's *Dinotopia*,[7] concerning a land somehow *apart* from time, was published in 1992, we held no truce with dinosaurs and their prehistoric brethren. In this and the next chapter we'll review the great dinosaur war, emphasizing how it was triggered, how it unfolded and who survived. What do war dinosaurs symbolize, and why must they be slain? Here, we'll address, among others, Alexander M. Phillips's "The Death of the Moon" (1929), Karel Capek's *War With the Newts* (1936), and Isaac Asimov's "Big Game" (1974, written in 1936).

"VERSUS": T. REX AS A NATIONAL SYMBOL

If the physicists are correct, then the deep geological past may not be fixed until we look at it. Does this mean, paradoxically, that the Mesozoic era did not begin to unfold until its fossils were discovered and interpreted by scientists and artists? Could it be that *T. rex* never existed as a flesh and blood animal until Charles Knight painted its visage? In

Opposite: **Robert Nason's vision of (at right) a rampaging sauropod dinosaur, the evil "god" Cay, menacing explorers in search of the lost Mayan civilization in Antarctica. With two characters (Jack and Gwen) trapped inside a labyrinthine cave, Cay—the last dinosaur alive—threatens the lives of expedition members and must be destroyed in order to ensure their escape. (From Frank Saville's *Beyond the Great South Wall*, 1901.) Also see Chapter 2 for further details.**

restoring prehistory are paleoartists themselves creating alternate dimensions of reality? Well, in a sense, yes, they are. For our comprehension of prehistoric landscapes is dependent upon literary and visual paleoartists who so often turn inwardly to their own nightmares and dreamscapes for inspiration.

In two 1892 restorations, artist Carl Dahlgren depicted a band of spear-wielding humans confronting *Hypsirophus* (i.e., *Stegosaurus*) and *Amphicoelias*. Such restorations captured the popular belief that prehistoric (antediluvian) men coexisted with dinosaurs and other prehistoric animals in a primeval, savage state. Then, for an 1897 issue of *McClure's Magazine*, Charles R. Knight painted a Neanderthal hunting party attacking a woolly mammoth.[8] If prehistoric man couldn't manage to coexist peacefully in art with dinosaurs and other prehistoric animals during the prehistoric age when savagery was the natural order, then how could dinosaurs, however science-fictionally resurrected, manage to get along with *modern* man, in our present?

Artists depict prehistory's violent nature by drawing, painting, sculpting, animating, or otherwise suggesting a "nature red in tooth and claw" struggle for survival between titanic combatants, especially those judged under contemporary standards to be the most worthy adversaries—e.g., *Tyrannosaurus* versus *Triceratops* in the early twentieth century, or *Ichthyosaurus* versus *Plesiosaurus*, etc., in the mid–nineteenth century. However, the origin of the most popular prehistoric life imagery and restorations, depicting savagery and violence in the prehistoric world, is often misunderstood. Generations of paleontology aficionados have delighted in the universal appeal of such paleontological restorations and reconstructions.[9] It would be understatement to declare that we have become simply obsessed with paleoimagery signifying prehistory perceived as untamed and feral.

The thematic, metaphoric nature of many of the most famous "versus" restorations and imagery exerts a visceral impact. It is also often derivative. Depicted figures and ideas are borrowed, tweaked, or even swiped from previous portrayals. Paleoimagery cliché? Well, it's sort of like a comical cartoon everybody's seen, Xeroxed onto a page that's already been Xeroxed half a zillion times, sequentially, to the point of extreme graphical distortion. (But you need your own copy, and so you press the copy button too.)

In this vein, let's consider *T. rex* vs. *Triceratops* imagery introduced by Charles R. Knight.[10] His beautiful 1906 American Museum painting shows a three-fingered *T. rex* striding in an anatomically incorrect, upright fashion (although this is how Knight's mentor, Henry F. Osborn, thought it looked and moved), toward a family of *Triceratops*. The beasts are strikingly huge (except for the juvenile *Triceratops* protected by its presumed parents), and are poised ultimately for primeval bloodshed merely suggested, yet imagined and subconsciously experienced by entranced viewers. For over a century, "Rex & Tops" have symbolized the most violent confrontation imaginable in America's vast prehistoric landscape. Now artists had been painting dinosaurs and other prehistoric life engaged in deadly combat for decades by the time of Knight's painting. But never before had two such impressive dinosaurs from their most illustrious age—the Late Cretaceous—been restored in the flesh and with such photographic skill.

Two decades later, Knight revisited his most inspirational theme, this time in a Field Museum of Natural History mural. This second Rex vs. Tops face-off has become, arguably, the most famous and beloved dinosaur painting of all time. The painting triggered a wave of "versus"-themed restorations, films and other engaging imagery reflecting a persistent,

Riou's 1863 restoration of two fighting, quadrupedal dinosaurs, *Iguanodon* (left) vs. *Megalosaurus* (right), projecting the idea of savagery in the prehistoric world—perhaps the key paleontological notion about prehistory handed down to twentieth century science fiction writers and film producers, who often dramatized struggles between *Tyrannosaurus* and *Triceratops* instead. (Author's collection.)

militaristic metaphor—the struggle for existence in prehistory. Knight's design has been redone numerous times by scores of amateur, professional and "copycat" artists.

Would it then be blasphemous to suggest that Knight's exemplary mural was itself, in a sense, derivative—that even Rex vs. Tops entered mainstream pop-culture only at a mid-point in the history of paleo-image-making? But it's true. Long before Rex vs. Tops joined in their twentieth century death throes, even before their bones had been discovered, paleo-image precursors portrayed perceptions of a prehistory gone savage![11]

Artistic portrayal of the theme of violence-as-depicted-in-prehistory predates the cultural history of dinosaurs. Savagery in nature was a prevalent theme prior to the Darwinian movement (i.e., biological evolution through natural selection acting on inherited variation). Historian Paul Semonin notes the origin of the "savage nature" theme in art, as envisioned by eighteenth century painter George Stubbs (1724–1806).[12] Stubbs' painting *Horse attacked by a Lion* (ca. 1762), portraying conflict in nature and symbolizing "the extinction of species," foreshadowed the Darwinian movement of the following century, beginning in 1859.[13]

Semonin argues persuasively in *American Monster* (2000) that for decades prior to the discovery of dinosaurs, and well into the mid–nineteenth century, the American Mastodon, perceived by many as carnivorous, represented primeval ferocity and a national virility. That perception of prehistory became wedded to the Founding Fathers' agenda during a romantic age of westward expansion—justifying the eradication of native populations, then perceived as "primitive" and therefore unfit. Anglo-Saxon fears of low culture became mirrored, or instilled through such imagery as Dahlgren's, or in contemporary fiction.[14]

Knight's dramatic 1906 painting captured more than just a scene of perceived prehistoric savagery in nature. For, oddly, *Tyrannosaurus* became a new national symbol of prehistoric heritage, here supplanting the former "Incognitum"—our American Mastodon.[15] For America's most formidable and fabled prehistoria—*T. rex* and *Triceratops*—restored from the most illustrious prehistoric age, represented our industry, might, valor and even "just" ascendancy to power over primitive humans indigenous to North America, in a cultural "war of the worlds."

In providing a national symbol of heritage and racial "virility," *T. rex* perhaps represented to early twentieth-century America what the Piltdown Man represented for Great Britain (in either case without dispelling notions of the Aryan myth). One of *T. rex's* earliest appearances as a formidable beast of fiction, referred to as the "conquerer," was in Chapter XI of paleontologist Charles H. Sternberg's (1850–1943) *Hunting Dinosaurs* (1917).[16] (See the Appendix for further description of this remarkable, originally self-published account.) Following Sternberg's spirited precedent, *Tyrannosaurus* soon ruled the day in dinosaur fiction, as exemplified in two late–1920s short stories, Harley S. Aldinger's "The Way of a Dinosaur" (1928) and Alexander M. Phillips' (1907–1991) "The Death of the Moon" (1929).[17]

Pulp fiction magazines of the time seized opportunities to print artistic images of our favorite cult dinosaur violently combating imagined prehistoric nemeses, much as Knight had done. Every picture tells a story, in these cases each worth more than a thousand words. Aldinger's story was printed under a depiction of Rex chomping into the neck of a brontosaur. For "Death of the Moon," artist Frank R. Paul (1884–1963) portrayed Rex heroically fending off a laser ray attack from insect-like "Lunarians."

Aldinger opens a window into prehistory with his tale about a day in the life of *T. rex*, the "King of the Jungle," or the "most destructive living thing that ever existed." Rex leaps and stomps about, first dispatching a "Plated Lizard"—*Stegosaurus*. Next, reprising Knight's most famous paintings, *T. rex* engages the mighty "three-horn," described in gory detail. Following a terrific battle, ending with *Triceratops*' demise, wounded *T. rex* now stalks a seventy-five-foot-long brontosaur. Inflicting a bite wound that would surely be fatal, nonetheless, *T. rex* is fended off by lashes from the brontosaur's whip-like tail. Swimming out to sea, cunning Rex is ravaged by an entire school of hungry ichthyosaurs. Aldinger's ichthyosaurs—a species prominently featured six decades earlier in Verne's *Journey*—are relegated to a cameo. This is a relatively simple story, underscoring the brutality of the Mesozoic world with its admixture of Jurassic and Cretaceous fauna.[18]

Alexander Phillips's story "Death of the Moon," most likely inspired by H.G. Wells's *War of the Worlds*, appeared in the February 1929 *Amazing Stories*. On the surface, this story concerns a paradoxical pairing of philosophies—the mystery of Life's chance contingency coupled with man's (inevitable) ascent. While the featured dinosaur was a *T. rex*, this heroic beast, "the mightiest ... most terrible engine of destruction known to the history of the world," wards off an attack of Lunarians from the dying Moon during the Cretaceous period, eventually permitting the evolution of man in future ages. For "the fate of humanity to come hung upon his ability to reach and wipe out his enemies. If [*Tyrannosaurus*] failed, if he were killed, and the Lunarians escaped, they would overrun the world and preclude forever the development of man...." But it's not just man's fate at stake, for at one crucial moment when the Lunarians first spy Rex, "the *whole universe* [my italics] seemed held in breathless suspense." *T. rex* expires, but only after defeating the Lunarians on earth, which will lead inevitably to their extinction, hence the story's title.

The last *T. rex* alive on earth suffers a mortal wound, yet triumphs majestically while Phillips ponders, "Why had life originated upon the moon, why had it struggled up from simplicity to complexity, from ignorance to brilliant knowledge, if it were only to be destroyed in the end by a giant inhabitant of the earth?" Phillips posed deep philosophical, evolutionary questions which he was ill-equipped to resolve. The dying, heroic beast then gazes for the last time toward the sun sinking in the sublime west, "over the unbroken plains to the western sky. The great, tawny sun was just sinking behind the wavering grasslands and its level rays reached far across the plain's floor and up the canyon, bathing all in a solemn, ethereal glow." With Rex's "purpose" accomplished, the world will be safe for future ordained life, liberty, justice and eventually the American way.[19]

By the 1930s, writers saw how prehistoric shape-shifters, an assortment of dinosaurs and other prehistoria, could be cast in a variety of roles underscoring the Darwinian savagenature theme. Aryan survival-of-the-fittest war propaganda wasn't ignored.

Early Skirmishes

In 1932, a far more malevolent Rex battled Kong, the human race personified; Kong heroically sacrificed himself to defend beauty on Skull Island in Lovelace's novel. Interestingly, as I've argued elsewhere, one of the earliest children's books featuring a dinosaur character was evidently inspired by *King Kong*.[20] This was a story about the original "lost world"—the land of Oz! For a dinosaur named Terrybubble, a distortion of the word "terrible," is a central figure in Ruth Plumly Thompson's (1891–1976) *Speedy in Oz* (1934).[21] Terrybubble becomes an inhabitant of Umbrella Island, which floats in the sky.

Terrybubble is a sauropod-looking dinosaur skeleton that walks like a bipedal plateosaur but chases cats on all fours. Terrybubble's bones were excavated by a dinosaur hunter and a young boy named Speedy. Speedy and the skeleton are hurled up into the sky by a volcanic geyser, and the skeleton comes alive upon its arrival on the flying magical Umbrella Island. Terrybubble, whose bones are "thousands of years old," recalls being slain in his 400th year by a "Mogerith" (a *Megalosaurus*). Following several adventures, Terrybubble rescues Speedy and a young Umbrella Island princess from a giant who is even larger than the enormous dinosaur.

During a 1930s New York City parade, the Messmore and Damon mechanical brontosaur—bedecked with a Nazi swastika—occupied a float, symbolizing the Axis war monster Hitler. *Speedy In Oz* was conceived during the dawning of World War II and, accordingly, woven into the plot are elements of political strife and war in Oz. Thompson explores the nature of war in Chapter 12 and even discusses a secret weapon of mass destruction: a water cannon bearing potential to flood and sink the intervening Umbrella Island. Umbrella Island itself may represent United States air force capability of the time, and the Island's intervention in the ongoing war between neighboring Roaraway Island, controlled by "Radj the Red," and Norroway Island presages the USA's later war declaration following Pearl Harbor. In one passage, protagonist Speedy expresses his desire to join the Navy and develop a water cannon for the United States—a most peculiar confession for a character in a children's book. Friendly Terrybubble wasn't in conflict with humans in Thompson's book. However, by the 1940s, humankind would find itself increasingly "at war" with fictional dinosaurs and other prehistoria, now emblems of prehistoric savagery in nature and metaphors of contemporary geopolitical circumstances.

Consider.

In today's culture, Conan Doyle's *The Lost World* would be politically incorrect. Doyle's heroes eradicate a crypto-species of primitive hominid and theropod dinosaurs as if they have no right to live. They also bag dinosaurs and pterodactyls with elephant guns, casting the message that the only good dinosaur is a dead dinosaur. At the climax scene of the 1925 silent movie *The Lost World*, a brontosaur tramples London. A contemporary movie advertisement for the classic film preys visually on our minds, revealing an enormous, four-fingered theropod dinosaur clutching a train car with its right foot talons as it rages at fleeing people below. In the background we see city lights. The dinosaur invasion had begun!

While many might regard Doyle's "first strikes" on Maple White Land as mere (racist) skirmishes against ancient natural fauna, during the World War I era, two other writers,

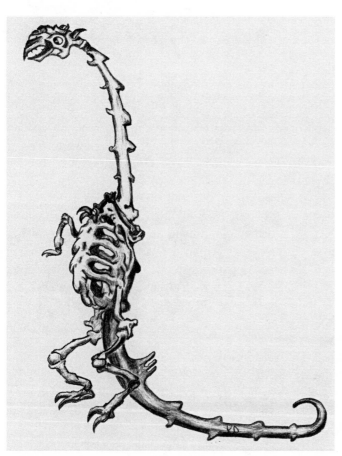

Edgar Rice Burroughs and Vladimir Obruchev, waged an all-out assault on prehistoria found in other lost world settings, respectively, in Caspak and Plutonia. In *The Land That Time Forgot* and its two sequels, first published in 1918, Burroughs' adventurers slaughtered Caspak's dinosaurs and other indigenous prehistoric fauna with reckless abandon. Furthermore, Burroughs' heroes waged war on the mighty pterodactyl race, the Mahars, and a host of other prehistoria deep within the earth, at its hollowed core named Pellucidar. And when Obruchev's adventurers penetrate into the Arctic's inner hollowed cavity, a setting named Plutonia, they leave a trail of bloodshed, as if they own the place. Terrorist actions such as these could only prompt vengeful retaliation ... eventually!

Also, as we noted in the previous chapter, in his 1929 novel *The Greatest Adventure*, John Taine's explorers obliter-

"Terrybubble" from Ruth Plumly Thompson's 1934 novel *Speedy in Oz*, as figured by microbiologist/chemist Kristen L. Debus. (With permission.)

Professors Challenger, Summerlee and company shoot up the pterodactyl nesting ground atop the Maple White Land lost plateau in Conan Doyle's 1912 novel *The Lost World.* (With permission of zoologist and artist John R. Lavas.)

ated a prehistoric pseudo-dinosaurian fauna thriving in Antarctica. True, the scientist-led expedition was ostensibly on a noble scientific quest to discover the mystery of life's origins there, but along the way they wiped out as many of the great beasts as they were able. And so, with each passing fictional encounter, man seemed to slay increasing numbers of prehistoria dead in their tracks, and in *their* natural habitat, no less. But in 1933, during the time of Nazi oppression, matters went too far when man killed the majestic, prehistoric ape named Kong, whom we carried triumphantly and yet so ignorantly to our hallowed shores! Forevermore, the "parade of life through the ages" would march to the steady, pounding beat of war drums.

A FOOT-"NEWT" IN HISTORY

Few are aware of what is perhaps the most significant novel about a fictitious amphibian monster directly based on one of the eighteenth century's most significant fossil discoveries, *Andrias scheuchzeri*, or the *Homo diluvii testis* ("human witness of the deluge"), as it was known for over a century.[22] ("Andrias" means man-image.) Today this extraordinary fossil is rarely mentioned in popular books on paleontology. *Andrias* spawned a fantastic novel two centuries later, Czech writer Karel Capek's (1890–1938) *Valka S Mloky* (1936), or in English, *War with the Newts* (1937). Here, Capek transformed an old fossil into a highly relevant species of fantastic fiction.

Capek's novel paid homage to Johann Scheuchzer throughout. Who was Scheuchzer? Johann Jakob Scheuchzer was born in Zurich, Switzerland, on August 2, 1673, and began accumulating his fabulous fossil collection in 1690. Scheuchzer earned a doctorate, specializing in medicine, mathematics and geological studies. Some historians of science consider Scheuchzer, who died in 1733, as the founder of European paleontology. Most importantly for our purposes here, he became *the* authority of his time on fossils, a century before Cuvier, and the first investigator to have claimed discovery of a fossil man.

Scheuchzer's major claim to lasting fame, if not immortal infamy, came in a short publication of a fossil later described in the *Philosophical Transactions of the Royal Society of London* in 1726. For in 1715, Scheuchzer obtained a stone slab from the Ohningen (sometimes spelled Oeningen, or Oensingen) quarry, containing the supposed remains of one of the multitude of humans who expired in the Flood. Scheuchzer seemed hellbent on proving the validity of the biblical Deluge using fossils as evidence.[23]

Naturalist Scheuchzer had been trained as a physician, although "moderns" have whimsically remarked how he wasn't much of an anatomist. During his student days, he misidentified fossil vertebrae found in Altdorf as human bones. Author Herbert Wendt suggests that because these had been found near a macabre site, the town gallows, it is understandable how his friend Langhans decided the remains must be human. It was Scheuchzer, however, who claimed they were ancient, dating to biblical times. Subsequently, after he published an illustration of the Altdorf vertebrae, Scheuchzer vigorously debated their nature, and that of other fossil vertebrae found along the shore of Lake Constance, through correspondence with Johann Jakob Baier (1677–1789). Baier claimed they were the remains of fish, not humans. As it turned out, both Baier and Scheuchzer, who was already wedded to the Deluge theory, were wrong, for these vertebrae were ichthyosaurian.[24]

Scheuchzer had collected at a fossiliferous site on the left bank of the Rhine near Lake Constance in Switzerland at a village named Ohningen since 1706, this being the source of fossil inspiration for his books, *Piscium querelae* and *Herbarium*. The most notable fossil ever extracted from the Ohningen limestone quarry was the *Homo diluvii testis*, described in a special dissertation published in 1731, the "Flood witness" who, Scheuchzer calculated, must have drowned in 2306 B.C. Scheuchzer even claimed there were still soft parts of flesh visible in the schist and that the specimen represented the "rarest relics which we have of that accursed race which was buried under the waters." The original specimen which caused the sensation resides at Harlem's Teyler Museum, while a second specimen, found in 1728 and never figured for publication, is missing.[25]

Scheuchzer's peculiar fossils might appear a curious source of inspiration for twentieth-century monsters from the abyss, yet Capek wove his tale expertly!

I became introduced to *War with the Newts* through two books, Brian Aldiss' *Trillion Year Spree: The History of Science Fiction* (1986), and W.J.T. Mitchell's *The Last Dinosaur Book: The Life and Times of a Cultural Icon* (1998).[26] Capek, who coined the term "robot" in 1921, stated that *War with the Newts* was "not a speculation about the future, but a mirroring of what exists."[27] Mitchell refers to *Newts* as an allegory of mass society. But beyond its dark side, *Newts* is also an amusing satire about everything that seemed wrong with the world then—science, "runaway capitalism," civil rights, environmental pollution, geopolitics, militarism, religion and even the 1930s Hollywood scene.

A small relict population of anthropoid salamanders ("newts") surviving from the Miocene epoch is discovered on the coast of a Pacific island. They are soon exploited by an unscrupulous man, one Captain von Toch, who offers them knives to defend themselves against the sharks which prey on them, in exchange for pearls for which they dive adeptly. Von Toch realizes the commercial possibilities of this new slave-labor "resource" and becomes filthy rich by exploiting the newts. The newts perform efficiently and prove a sensation, and soon scientists are in a mad scramble to describe the crypto-species, which is found identical to Scheuchzer's "antediluvian man." Surprisingly, the highly adaptable newts are capable of speech.

Rescued from their isolated habitat, the newts begin to flourish around the globe, as the "coiled spring of evolution within" is released. Based on their breeding vitality, projections of newt populations made by the newly formed Salamander Syndicate place their total numbers at fifteen billion within three years' time! Rather than viewing that astonishing figure as alarming, the Syndicate instead relishes opportunities for harvesting the seas and coastlines using the economical newt labor force.

Next we learn that countries are providing "their" newts—the ones living along *their* coastlines—with explosives and other devices for mining and burrowing into the ocean shelf. Newts are bred in farms where they receive instruction from humans. Of course the newts are mistreated by their human "superiors"; newts are restricted from performing rituals such as their traditional moonlight dance.

Newts rise to scholarly positions and gain political clout. Newt delegates address the League of Nations. They press for equal rights and freedom of religion, finding faith in the Great Salamander or the temple of the salamander cult. Newts are becoming increasingly affiliated with the nations whose coastlines their habitats border. Their progress knows no bounds. Soon, secure in their underwater spaces, newts have become technologically advanced and as civilized as humans. However, one variety of newt, the Baltic Newt, is considered the most evolutionarily advanced, a swipe at Hitler's Aryan Race concept. Soon newts are being trained for combat.

War erupts between man and newt, with the newts quickly gaining control. They have the capacity to sink any ship, and to drill under continental masses extensively. Detonation of explosives, discharged under tunneled coastlines, sinks land masses. Humans drown by the millions in terrorist attacks as great cities of the world flood. The newts quickly change the map of the world, flooding continental areas to accommodate their numbers (twenty billion and swelling) along coastal waters. Most ironically, the doomed human race becomes "witness" to a great deluge, caused by the descendants of an "old flood witness"—*Andrias scheuhzeri*. Humans lose their will to fight, ultimately praising the newts for their industry, perfection and ability to rule the world.

In the end, however, remains a twist, the possibility that newts may end up fighting other newts for ultimate supremacy. Then, the newts will become "an extinct race. All that's left of them is that ancient Oeningen imprint of *Andrias Scheuchzeri*." Presumably, humans will regain their prominence and "A new legend will arise of a Great Flood sent by God upon a sinful humanity. And there will be stories of drowned mythical lands said to have been the cradle of human culture; there will perhaps be legends about some country called England or France or Germany...."

Scheuchzer's *Homo diluvii testis* is perhaps the first iconic vertebrate fossil—known centuries before *T. rex* or modern examination of the *Mastodon*—as its popularity stemmed from its celebrated proof of the biblical Deluge. Subsequently, other discoveries of fossils of "antediluvian" men were made by a fresh wave of diluvial geologists. As Louis Figuier remarked

By the late nineteenth century, before the onset of modern man's strife with dinosaurs, people found themselves associating prehistoric men with dinosaurs situated in lost-world settings. In this imaginary "old west" scene, artist Carl Dahlgren projects the idea of savagery in a prehistoric nature, where war is waged between spear-wielding Native Americans and sauropod *Amphicoelias*. (From the *California Illustrated Magazine*, 1892.)

in 1867, few "dared to dispute the opinion of the Swiss naturalist, under his double authority of theologian and savant."[28] By the late eighteenth century, however, other naturalists questioned Scheuchzer's analysis of the original *Homo diluvii testis* specimen. Some now regarded the fossil as a catfish instead of a human, while in 1787, Peter Camper (1722–1789) claimed that *Homo diluvii testis* was a lizard fossil. This collection of odd interpretations seems all the more curious today, considering that Andreas Vesalius' (1514–1564) detailed treatise on human anatomy, *De fabrica*, had appeared in 1543.[29]

Capek, who earned a Ph.D. in philosophy in 1915 from Charles University, was a deeply thoughtful, talented and troubled man who pondered the meaning of human life. Centuries apart, both Scheuchzer and Capek were inspired by the very same fossil, the first "iconic" fossil, relying on an "old sinner" to prove and expose the "wickedness" of mankind. Through his brilliant exploitation of *Andrias*, Capek not only associated fictional prehistoria bearing man-like attributes with modern warfare, but ingeniously mirrored human foibles and flaws on every level.

BIGGEST GAME

After the newts have defeated the humans in Capek's brilliant tale, they direct their arms against one another, repeating mankind's folly, a theme Isaac Asimov (1920–1992) turned to prior to Pearl Harbor in his 1941 short story "Big Game" (1974).[30] Asimov proudly showed his 1,000-word tale to John Campbell, *Astounding*'s editor, on November 24, 1941, but: "He glanced over it and, rather to my astonishment, handed it back. It wasn't what he wanted." Much later, in a 1972 volume, Asimov lamented, "I wish I could remember what 'Big Game' was about, for I thought enough of it to try submitting it to *Collier's* magazine (an over-awing *slick*) in 1944—and it was, of course, rejected. The title, however, recalls nothing to my mind, and the story now no longer exists." But indeed the story still existed and in 1974, "Big Game" was finally published! For one of Asimov's fans found the manuscript archived at Boston University's library; he mailed a Xerox to Asimov, thereby restoring to the world a most precocious tale, perhaps the best piece of very short dinosaur fiction ever written.[31]

In "Big Game" an inventor named Hornby divulges to colleagues at a bar that he'd built a time machine, using it to travel to the late Mesozoic era. Hornby observed what happened to the dinosaurs, debunking the theory that deteriorating, drying climate caused their extinction. When pressed as to what did them in, Hornby replies, "Same thing that knocked off the bison. Intelligent life! ... Those reptiles had kitten brains, but they used it *all*."

That is, intelligent *dinosaurs*. After all, dinosaurs had millions of years to evolve into intelligent species, yet the fossil record didn't preserve their kind because, as Hornby explains, "You don't find many fossils of intelligent animals. They don't fall into mudholes, you know, as a general rule." Moreover, these dinosaurs could communicate using telepathy. Curiously, the "brainy little reptiles" killed wild saurian game with reckless abandon, "with all the enthusiasm of a big-game hunter bagging lions." Asimov concluded sardonically, "The only fun they got out of life was this big-game hunting.... So when they ran out of brontosauri and diplodoci, they turned to the very biggest: themselves! ... Why not? Aren't men doing the same thing?"

Had Campbell accepted Asimov's "Big Game," it would have been the first published story merging the ideas of time travel to the Mesozoic with (dinosaurs' self-inflicted) safaris. The extermination of species on a global scale, genocide caused by Asimov's dinosaurs through out-of-control "safaris" or otherwise, must be regarded as a final war waged against nature itself, a holocaust. Dinosaur versus dinosaur. Newt versus newt. Brother against brother. The dinosaurs' folly is of course mankind's dilemma. Asimov reworked the essence of "Big Game" into "Day of the Hunters," a tale which was further inspired by the dawning Cold War (1950).

J. Allen St. John's (1872–1957) magnificent artistry graced many pulp magazine pages and covers during the first half of the twentieth century, including two curious stories which must be mentioned here, John York Cabot's "Blitzkrieg in the Past" (1942) and Robert Moore Williams' "The Lost Warship" (1943).[32]

By today's standards, Cabot's "Blitzkrieg in the Past" would seem a trite little story invoking a *T. rex* that is merely incidental to the plot. J. Allen St. John's magazine cover promises much more than what Cabot delivered, a Charles R. Knight—inspired Rex charging toward a tank firing on the bloodthirsty dinosaur. Man's military might versus dinosaurian savagery, a fairly novel theme for the time. A very cool picture indeed and one with which readers of the time could presumably identify. Prehistoric species in Cabot's story are associated with Nazi brutality. After a "short, dumpy bald-headed guy in civvies" installs an invention—a time transfer device—in a tank that proceeds into the Georgia wilderness on maneuvers, a lightning bolt sends the tank and its three operators backward in time. Shortly afterward they notice a single three-toed dinosaur footprint and disturbingly they hear the bloodthirsty scream of a very strange "bird."

The soldier trio are captured by hairy and smelly primitives referred to as Neanderthal men, who bind the time travelers inside a cave, where they are introduced to a beautiful woman who controls the Neanderthals. The "dame" is intrigued by the soldier's tommyguns and ruthlessly orders the execution of another modern-looking human cave dweller, one of her own kind. Or as "Leeds," the tank crew's brainy member observes,

> This dame on the throne is a female Hitler, Neanderthal style. She's a renegade from the primitive tribe that I stumbled on trying to find you lads. A tribe much more advanced than these Neanderthal ape-men with whom she's trying to start a blood-rule. This young Tarzan beside me is a member of the tribe that threw her out. We were caught by a raiding party of your female Hitler's bunch.[33]

The ending is predictable. Leeds leaps to a snap judgment based on appearance: "... if we've got to stay around this neck of time from now on, I think it'd be a good idea to see to it that we'll be living with primitives who have a slant on things a little closer to our own." So after escaping, the soldiers use their tank to exterminate the "flatheads," or the Neanderthal race. Then a *T. rex* suddenly attacks the tank, seemingly vengeful for the Neanderthal race's extinction, and is quickly extinguished. Having secured a bright past for man's apparent future, another well-timed lightning bolt sends the tank spinning through time back to present-day Georgia.

For "The Lost Warship," pterodactyls resembling Burroughs' Mahars are seen attacking a World War II navy vessel, the *Idaho*, on the cover, and also a loincloth-clad human on the story's title page. A synopsis under the byline explains "Jap bombs rained down, there was a tremendous blast—and a weird thing happened to the *Idaho*." The weird thing that happens is caused by a "Michaelson space-time Fault," or a time-slip. Wielding a bit of mumbo jumbo, Williams's conveniently cast on-board civilian physicist theorizes that Japanese aircraft bomb explosions caused the destroyer to "cause a momentary dislodgment of the space-time balance in this area, with the result that we were precipitated through the fault."[34] Furthermore, a space-time fault can only be past-directed; it's impossible to move forward in time through a time-slip.[35] Essentially, man's cruelty toward fellow man—modern savagery, barbarism and war-like nature—become projected into the savage Mesozoic era, where the crew is marooned forever. However, this suits two of the characters, Craig and Margy Sharp, both "misfits" in the modern world who welcome this primitive time as their natural "frontier."

Astonishingly, soon they find themselves under attack by an air force squadron equipped with advanced technology and chemical weaponry such as poison gas which the *Idaho*'s planes and guns are no match for. After the crippled *Idaho* is beached, Craig and some navy men cross a jungle terrain where they're attacked by a pterodactyl which is quickly dispatched by machine-gun fire. Craig befriends a primitive pre-stone age "dawn man" (perhaps akin to Britain's dawn man, Piltdown Man) named "Guru," from whom they learn of their oppressors, the feared Ogrum, who've crippled the *Idaho* and captured its remaining crew. The Ogrum have a nasty rite of sacrificing Guru's kind to a hungry Rex-like dino-monster held in a cage. Being fed to the dinosaur evidently will be the *Idaho* crew's fate unless someone intervenes.

Craig is hard pressed to comprehend how such races of humanity could have lived so long ago without leaving a fossil record, yet he rationalizes:

What kind of creatures were the Ogrum? What secret lay behind their existence? They had left no mark on history as he knew it. So far as the human race knew, the Ogrum had never existed. And yet—the sudden thought was startling—there was a word in the English language that came close to describing these creatures—ogre! Ogre and Ogrum were very similar. Were these the original ogres, those mythological monsters who devoured human beings? Had the Ogrum, known, feared and named by the dawn men, come down through legends as ogres?[36]

Craig, Guru and company rescue the captured men, in the process triggering a dinosaurian stampede, trampling the Ogrum into bloody oblivion. By likening the brutality of modern war to ancient strife unrecorded by history yet involving dinosaurian might and power, Williams underscored the theme of prehistoric savagery in nature. The Ogrum wield chemical technology, a scientific field in which the Germans excelled during the World War II years. So the vicious, racially inferior Ogrum most likely represent Nazis—mockingly the antithesis of an Aryan race—literarily devolved into ancient ogres who also control prehistoric "props" as engines of brutality.

CONCLUSION

Since the 1850s, man's perception of nature and prehistory were shaped by two philosophies: (1) the myth of wild nature, where all species are considered to be at war with one another in an intense Darwinian struggle for existence, and (2) *prehistoric* nature, represented as a terrible, savage ordeal ruled by nature red in tooth and claw. As noted by Semonin, embracing such symbolism and metaphor justified white Europeans' usurpation of native Americans, or even other races in other places of the globe, because of a belief in genetic superiority. And because the nineteenth century "ladder of evolution" led inexorably (and, as some thought, atheistically) to the pinnacle, the creation of a white European race, then all that could have only been accomplished through countless millennia of prehistoric conflict.

In an evolutionary sense, not only had man ascended beyond the extinct dinosaurs, we had also conquered the other extinct races of man, such as Neanderthal. For example, in his 1920 short story "The Grisly Folk," H.G. Wells speculated how the Neanderthals were out-competed by the contemporary Cro-Magnon So, by the early twentieth century, it was socially acceptable to fantasize about dinosaurs and other prehistoric (or "primitive") societies and species as being somehow in conflict with modern civilized man, who would symbolically fire guns upon them, celebrating our superiority over prehistoria, broadcasting the silly message, "We beat them before and we still can today ... bang, bang—you're extinct and we're not." During the World War II period, certainly Nazis could be insultingly referred to as primitives or equated with ancient races of man and dinosaur species. And if the Nazis or wartime Japanese displayed "prehistoric" characteristics, then they could rightfully be rendered to extinction, in contemporary literature.

By the 1930s, movie-land dinosaurs were catching up to the prehistoria of fantastic literature, largely due to the successes of special effects animators. Using dino-creations made of clay, plasticine, rubber and fabric, film producers were learning how to suspend disbelief effectively, much as the masters of speculative fiction already had honed their craft with pen, paper and their fertile imaginations. And the world was in upheaval once again, as nations led the march to a second World War, climaxing with the detonation of two atomic bombs. Perhaps it just felt safer to read about or observe from a safe vantage point the real global war through an imagined war on dinosaurs, creatures which were emblematic of prehistoric savagery in nature, although now projected into modernity.

If Charles Darwin were alive today, perhaps he'd be astonished at the myriad, strange distortions of his theory. Dino-symbolism has evolved through 160 years to its present form. To the Japanese, however, derivation of dino-monsters and other prehistoria favored in the western world may seem less relevant than nuclear holocaust signified by Godzilla and alternative "kaiju," which we'll explore in the next chapter.

But today—neglecting their evolving symbolism and despite the associated destruction, blood and gore—doesn't the prospect of fantasy dinosaurs engaging our modern military still seem, well, somehow "cool"?

CHAPTER 4

Shadow of Gojira

BACKGROUND

On August 6, 1945, at 8:15 A.M., twentieth-century man—son of Frankenstein—unleashed the most terrible monster of all—*Pikadon*! Pikadon's fiery heat wave obliterated the Japanese city of Hiroshima, killing thousands in the first wave, and many more in weeks thereafter due to burns suffered and radiation poisoning.[1] Few victims understood what had hit them. Until then hardly anyone realized the might of atomic weaponry. Few had comprehended the awful consequences, adversities still affecting survivors today. But circumstances wouldn't end there, for shortly thereafter, Nagasaki was flashed into oblivion. Then Russia tested its first fission bomb. Scientists had created the first true weapons of mass destruction, triggering a means of warfare that was perhaps destined to happen. Although the Cold War ended politically, symbolically and in name in 1989, our nuclear bane, humanity's hellish plight, may prove everlasting.

In the aftermath of World War II and the dramatically successful Manhattan Project, atomic scientists refined their charges, building bigger bombs, including the hydrogen bomb, first exploded on November 1, 1952, at the Eniwetok Atoll. When, on March 1, 1954, a Japanese fishing vessel ironically named the *Lucky Dragon No. 5* strayed into waters subjected to hydrogen bomb testing near the Bikini Atoll, the monstrous proportions of modern warfare—Pikadons of unimaginable fury—were further realized. Spying a "sun rising in the west," the fishermen were soon coated with a "powdery white ash." The unfortunate crew had been exposed to massive doses of radiation, and tuna found to be contaminated with radiation was delivered to market. One crew member died; this person may be viewed, metaphorically perhaps, as "Godzilla's" first real victim. Japanese officials accused the United States of having unleashed yet another atomic attack.[2]

Thereafter and through the late 1960s especially, fears of atomic testing, nuclear war, and radioactive fallout gripped America. Unless you lived during those unsteady times, it isn't possible to comprehend the angst, that sense of fatalistic dread, like a sword of Damocles hanging precariously over our daily lives. When would the Soviet Union launch an atomic attack? Would the United States retaliate and would the war be escalated into a global holocaust? How lethal would exposures to radiation prove to be in populated areas? What were the latent health effects of atomic testing?[3] For those yet unborn, or for those who only dimly recall, there are those contemporary classic "B" movies—the ones involving radiation and mutation—serving as filmic artifacts characterizing assorted odd fears from Gojira's doomsday period.[4]

Godzilla, or *Gojira* as originally known to 1954 Japanese audiences, metaphorically represented a living form of radiation—war personified—a Pikadon incarnate towering over humanity, a virtually invulnerable creature that could only be destroyed by a weapon of even graver potential than atomic weapons: the "oxygen destroyer." *Gojira*'s creator stated, "The theme of the film, from the beginning, was the terror of the Bomb. Mankind had created the Bomb and now nature was going to take revenge on mankind."[5] *Gojira* (Toho, 1954) was in a thematic sense derived from preceding American film and literature, although due to its graphic nature and content was hauntingly, distinctly Japanese. No dino-monster film since has reflected the urgency and horror of nuclear holocaust, the coming of a Gojira. Steven Spielberg has stated that *Gojira* "was the most masterful of all the dinosaur movies because it made you believe it was really happening," a peculiar perspective because it's a stretch classifying Gojira, or Godzilla, as any kind of plausible "dinosaur."[6]

Given our emphasis on dinosaurs of fantastic literature, it would seem that Godzilla, or Gojira, was neglected by writers during the Cold War period, and yet we find that isn't entirely the case. Not only did science fiction and horror writers anticipate a "Godzilla," but published stories of the period also heralded grim and somber Cold War messages as projected through Toho's 1954 classic. When viewed in proper context it is evident how, like the rest of us then, writers of the period were standing in Gojira's fateful shadow.

FOG HORN REVERBERATIONS: THE PATH TO GOJIRA

Over half a century ago, the essence of an idea for one of the most enduring and influential paleo-themed stories ever written flashed in author Ray Bradbury's fertile mind. "Trusting his subconscious to give bread, as it were, to the birds," a lonely fog horn became symbolic in his 1951 short story "The Beast from 20,000 Fathoms," published in the *Saturday Evening Post* (June 23, 1951), and later re-titled "The Fog Horn" in anthologies. "I was in Venice, California at the time ... walking on the beach," Bradbury recalled for interviewer Will Murray, "... and came upon the strewn remains of the roller coaster; the Venice pier had just been torn down and I said to my wife, 'I wonder what this dinosaur is doing here on the beach.'

"Well, late that night, I woke up and heard something. The foghorn was blowing on the Santa Monica Bay. And I said, 'Yes, of course. The dinosaur thought he was going to encounter another dinosaur, came swimming in for the meeting, and found out it was only a foghorn in a lighthouse. So he tore it down and died of a broken heart on the beach.' I got up the next morning and wrote 'The Fog Horn' in three hours."[7] Bradbury didn't realize it then, but his brooding, atmospheric piece laid precedent for a swarm of "doomsday dinosaurs" featured both in pulp literature and in film during the Cold War period. Although Bradbury brooded poetically on the mysterious nature of the sea and its denizens, his vision wasn't as dark as the times. However, with his mystical dinosaur, Bradbury secured the beachhead, so to speak, opening avenues for subsequent saurian, atomic-age assault upon the civilized world.

James R. Bingham's painting of Ray Bradbury's "Foghorn" creature attacking a lighthouse. See text for further details. (Reprinted from *The Saturday Evening Post,* ©1951. Saturday Evening Post Society. Used with permission.)

In "The Beast from 20,000 Fathoms" (hereafter "The Fog Horn"), two lighthouse engineers, Johnny and McDunn, observe the majestic emergence of an ancient, ninety-foot-long monstrosity from the sea depths. The creature, whose desolate cry echoes down through the lonely abyss of time, is attracted by the sound of the lighthouse fog horn. It is a tale of profound sadness, an ironic "sadness of eternity" for life's brevity, one perhaps beyond the capacity for human understanding. "Fog Horn" is essentially a telling of the last dinosaur, trapped forever out of time, an "insanity of time" in solitude, caught in man's era.

Referring to the fog horn blowing steadily, McDunn remarks, "Sounds like an animal, don't it? ... A big lonely animal crying in the night. Sitting here on the edge of ten billion years calling out to the Deeps, I'm here, I'm here, I'm here. And the Deeps *do* answer, yes, they do." Then he relates occurrences that have transpired before, almost to the very date when "something comes to visit the lighthouse." Inevitably, the monster appears through the gloom, responding to the fog horn. "A cry came across a million years of water and mist. A cry so anguished and alone that it shuddered in my head and my body.... The sound of isolation, a viewless sea, a cold night, apartness. That was the sound." When the astonished Johnny declares how "impossible" is this apparition, McDunn answers, "No, Johnny, *we're* impossible. *It's* like it always was ten million years ago. *It* hasn't changed. It's *us* and the land that've changed, become impossible. *Us!*" Why has the dinosaur, a species more natural than humankind, survived? Eloquently, playfully, Bradbury penned, because it "hid away in the Deeps. Deep, deep down in the deepest Deeps. Isn't *that* a word now, Johnny, a real word, it says so much: the Deeps. There's all the coldness and darkness and deepness in the world in a word like that."

With great age comes despair and vast, ineffable solitude. The two empathize with the creature, McDunn explaining, "... that poor monster there lying ... a thousand miles at sea ... biding its time, perhaps it's a million years old, this one creature. Think of it, waiting a million years; could *you* wait that long? Maybe it's the last of its kind. I sort of think that's true." When they switch the fog horn off, the monster rushes the lighthouse tower, toppling it, moments after Johnny and McDunn scamper to safety in a secure basement underneath the crumbling wreckage. Now, with the tower down, they listen to the abject dinosaur bellowing into the night, a mournful sound surely to be mistaken by mariners rounding the Lonesome Bay horn for the extinguished lighthouse fog horn. Inadvertently, mankind summons a dinosaur from the depths, an ageless, superior being which conquers and effectively replaces mankind's technology.

The movie most closely tied to "Fog Horn" is *The Beast from 20,000 Fathoms* (Warner Brothers, 1953), directed by Eugene Lourie. However, there is but one scene described in Bradbury's story which appeared in the film, this being the sequence where the *Rhedosaurus* destroys the lighthouse. During the spring of 1952, several months following the publication of Bradbury's story, Lourie was asked to direct a picture with a script titled "Monster from Beneath the Sea." Decades later, it's a mystery deciding whether elements of "Monster from Beneath the Sea" or Bradbury's "Beast from 20,000 Fathoms" story came first, or the extent to which Bradbury's "Fog Horn" inspired the movie script used by producers Jack Dietz and Hal Chester.

Lourie recollects editorial work on the film was in progress already when the producers discovered Bradbury's *Saturday Evening Post* story.[8] Bradbury recalls being asked to read the script for a possible rewrite, only to determine how similar it was to his own. Author Bill Warren claims Bradbury didn't note the similarities until much later, *after* he'd screened the completed film. Animator Ray Harryhausen, however, thinks the script predates the *Saturday Evening Post* story. According to author Mark Berry, who carefully researched the murky associations between story and film for his *Dinosaur Filmography* (2002), "Harryhausen also reiterated that the illustration in the *Post*, of the creature attacking the lighthouse, made a big impression on Jack Dietz, and that's why Dietz wanted to buy the rights."[9] At any rate, the producers trumpeted the *Post* connection when promoting the film, and the coming attractions promised "The importance and impact of the *Saturday Evening Post* thriller that held millions spellbound!"[10] Artist James R. Bingham illustrated the "Fog Horn" creature for Bradbury's *Post* story.

As Bradbury recalled, he and Harryhausen, who shared deep admiration for *King Kong*, and who also were members (along with Henry Kuttner, of whom more shall be said in Chapter Six) of Los Angeles' Science Fiction League, "became fast friends ... forever dedicated to the proposition that dinosaurs were the greatest life-forms that ever strode the earth."[11] Bradbury and Harryhausen eventually became associated through *The Beast from 20,000 Fathoms*, the first dinosaur film animated by Harryhausen, with its famous lighthouse dino-demolition scene. In fact, Bradbury's 1962 short story "Tyrannosaurus Rex" was inspired by a demoralizing experience they'd had with a miserly Hollywood producer they declined to work for.[12] Also, that roller coaster which inspired Bradbury's "Fog Horn" creature became memorialized through Harryhausen's talents in *Beast*'s climactic scene, where the *Rhedosaurus*, rampaging in an amusement park, is killed using a radioactive projectile. And that metaphoric roller coaster appears again in *Gorgo* (MGM, 1961), also directed by Lourie.

Like the "Arctic Giant,"[13] Harryhausen's *Rhedosaurus* was freed from the ice, although the key plot element of the latter production involved nuclear weapons testing.

Since publication of Bradbury's "Fog Horn," fantasy dinosaurs of film and literature bearing somber messages have ascended from the ocean depths to threaten civilization— the *Rhedosaurus*, somber Gojira, *Paleosaurus*, Gorgo and even the laughable Reptilicus spring to mind. These were impossibly huge, invulnerable dino-monsters appearing at a pivotal episode in history. The United States had twice used atomic weapons in World War II, and the Soviet Union detonated its first nuclear weapon in 1949, ushering in the Cold War period. Hydrogen bombs were first tested in 1952, the Soviet Union following in suit with their first H-bomb test in 1953. Angst escalated over the health effects of exposure to radioactive fallout created during testing of nuclear warheads. The threat of atomic war, possibly ending civilization or even leading to our extinction, became instilled through these metaphoric, anachronistic creatures which represented annihilation and extinction. On the heels of studies proving the hazards of radioactive fallout came concerns over chemical pollution of the natural environment, culminating with publication of Rachel Carson's *Silent Spring* (1962).[14] Unlike Bradbury's "Fog Horn" creature, the *Rhedosaurus*, Gojira and the rest of these monsters (now sometimes referred to as *kaiju eiga*[15]) were often cast as demonic harbingers of Armageddon.

Like Bradbury's ambiguous "Fog Horn" creature, the previously named movie monsters hardly qualify as real dinosaurs. Dinosaurs were terrestrial animals, and couldn't hibernate or remain submerged for prolonged periods of time, let alone millions of years as did the Arctic Giant, the "Fog Horn" creature or even Gojira. *Gojira*'s premise sounds uncannily similar to "The Fog Horn," but with an added nuclear element. As recollected by *Gojira*'s creator, Tanaka Tomoyuki, the central theme was "What if a dinosaur sleeping in the Southern Hemisphere had been awakened and transformed into a giant by the Bomb? What if it attacked Tokyo?"[16] So in the original concept, Gojira was perceived as a dinosaur, an incipient, mutated species, sleeping in the deeps like Bradbury's "Fog Horn" creature until awakened by a technological device—a bomb instead of a fog horn.

James R. Bingham's illustration accompanying Bradbury's *Saturday Evening Post* story, although setting a standard for all later amphibious dino-monsters of the movies, doesn't resemble restorations of any dinosaur known to science.[17] So clearly, Bradbury established the growing tradition of fantasy dino-monsters which were amphibious rather than wholly reptilian based on their inferred natural history. Other primeval-looking, *amphibian* monsters of pop-culture include the Gillman of *The Creature from the Black Lagoon* (1954), Karel Capek's anthropoid "newts" described in his 1936 novel *War with the Newts*, and twentieth Century-Fox's *Gargantua* (1998).

Bradbury wrote four dinosaur stories, one of which, "The Fog Horn," spawned one of the most everlasting dino-monsters of the silver screen, the *Rhedosaurus*, followed by its derived "progeny" (e.g., Gojira, Gorgo, Reptilicus, etc.). "Fog Horn" was the first significant and widely known tale in literature to bring a huge, evidently carnivorous dino-monster to the brink of civilization. When destroyed, the coastal (phallic) lighthouse represented mankind's emasculation as well as our inevitable extinction.[18]

If the roller coaster became a metaphor for the dinosaur, then according to Bradbury, the fog horn "itself was a super metaphor of all the melancholy funerals and sad remembrances in history."[19] Of course, movie producers took things much further than Bradbury dared. At the time, Bradbury certainly wasn't intending to write a Cold War theme, but rather to explore "journeys to far metaphor." Bradbury stated, "We don't know why the worm changes into the larva, and from the larva becomes the butterfly. Science cannot give us the answer for this miracle, we can only observe its mystery and beauty. Mankind has always asked the question, why are we here, what is life all about? I would say that we are here to witness the universe. Without us there is no one to take the stage, no one to recognize the beauty, no one to probe the unknown. The universe would be an empty place without us."[20]

However, Bradbury's "Fog Horn" creature quickly became adapted to the growing threat from nuclear warheads, missiles and environmental degradation. Perhaps latter-day writers saw our plight foreshadowed in Bradbury's words: "No, Johnny, *we're* impossible. *It's* like it always was ten million years ago. *It* hasn't changed. It's *us* and the land that've changed, become impossible. *Us!*"

COLD-BLOODED COLD WAR

Surprise! Given that the novel *Gojira*, written by Shigeru Kayama from his screenplay,[21] has never been translated from Japanese into English, the contemporary novel capturing the essence of nuclear angst most effectively using dino-monsters symbolically is actually a largely forgotten pulp dismissed by most film historians for its "racy" nature.

How many of you realized there was a *Gorgo* paperback *novel*? Yes, in July 1960, or over half a year before MGM's February 10, 1961, release date of *Gorgo* (i.e., the movie), Carson Bingham's novel *Gorgo* was published by Monarch Books.[22] Writers note that *Gorgo* is the third in a string of dino-monster films directed by Eugene Lourie, following his successes with *The Beast from 20,000 Fathoms* (1953) and *The Giant Behemoth* (1959). However, the original idea for the story *Gorgo* was written by Lourie (with David Hyatt); of Lourie's three dino-monster films, *Gorgo* is the only example of "suitmation."[23]

One has an impression that of his *Beast*, *Behemoth*, and *Gorgo*, the last is Lourie's least favorite, despite the fact that it's the only story of the triad which he authored. But how does Carson Bingham's paperback novel, *Gorgo*, relate to the film? And to what extent is it related to Lourie's original story idea? In an informative article by Tom Weaver, Lourie explained, "The seeds of ... *Gorgo* were sown the day the director took his daughter to the *Beast from 20,000 Fathoms* matinee, with the tearful girl complaining that her daddy had killed 'the big, nice Beast': 'That is why, in *Gorgo*, I tried not to kill the Beast.... Gorgo escapes alive back to the sea. My daughter should have a writer's credit."[24]

While Lourie's original screenplay *Kuru Island* was never published, there is of course Carson Bingham's 1960 novel *Gorgo* to reflect upon. The title page of Bingham's novel adds these credits: "based on an original story by Eugene Lourie, screenplay by John Loring and David Hyatt." Bingham's novel is scarcely referred to today; probably most monster film buffs aren't even aware of it. It received poor ratings from sci-fi film expert Bill Warren, who labeled it a "preposterously sexy novelization."[25] Jeff Rovin, citing promotional advertising added to the book's back cover by an editor, referred to it as "an extremely racy novel."[26] Lourie doesn't mention Bingham's novel in his autobiography.[27] After reading the novel *Gorgo*, however, I must proclaim these are unfair assessments. In fact, I liked Bingham's rare and readily dismissed novel much better than the movie (meaning I enjoyed it more than my recent viewing of the video)! It is superior, despite its "risqué" nature.

The novel *Gorgo* explains why the movie characters are so despicable. The racy exploitation isn't unusual for its time and, by today's standards, is rather tame. Written nearly a year before release of the motion picture, Bingham's novel *Gorgo* captures the somber, atmospheric mood projected in prior 1950s films, *Beast* and *Gojira*.

The sixty-foot-tall Gorgo and his mother, the 200-foot-tall Ogra, are manifestations of evil which, when conjured by man, cannot be controlled. Leading up to the attack on London we have a tale of mounting apprehension and terror, stoked along by strong characters who guide the story along to its inevitable end.

Chapters within the book are divided into three sections titled "Cataclysm," "Gorgo," and "Armageddon." First, there is the emergence of a volcanic island in the North Atlantic, off the Irish coastal island of Nara; the eruption triggers tidal waves, metaphorically signaling the manifestation of sea monsters. The next morning, under calm skies, Captain Joe Ryan and his partner, protagonist Sam Slade, weigh anchor in the harbor and go ashore in search of supplies, including fresh water. As they row in toward the shore, they spy "startlingly grotesque abominations," dead, prehistoric fish with four rudimentary legs, which "exploded from the enormous pressure of great sub-oceanic depths." They encounter 12-year-old Sean McCartin and his archaeologist father, Kevin, who hires divers to haul up old Viking relics off the Nara coast. They also meet Sean's 20-year-old half-sister, Moira, "an ungodly beautiful girl," whose clothes occasionally slip off her body in the presence of men. With a promise of fresh water from alluring Moira, Slade's and Ryan's curiosity is piqued when a local diver surfaces, dying on their launch. His last whispered word is "Monster." Local folk have a legend of a monstrous sea serpent named "Ogra." Some say its horrible countenance is captured on the sculpted prow of Viking-age shipwrecks McCartin hauls up from beneath the waves.

Later, during a villagers' wake for the deceased diver, Moira pleads with Slade to take her to Ireland aboard the *Triton*, but her father spies the two and soon he and Slade are fighting on the sand. Then, as if fueled by their hatred, out of the deep strides a monster. "Men in the water began screaming for help.... The huge beast turned again, moving toward one of the swimming men.... It was like some prehistoric saurian, a giant marine lizard of some kind left over from the Mesozoic era. I'd certainly never seen its like in any textbook." Sean calls out excitedly, "It's Ogra," or what the promoters later decide to call "Gorgo." Hurling firebrands toward the monster's head averts the attack, and sixty-foot-tall Gorgo returns to the surf.

The elder McCartin strikes a deal with Ryan and Slade to capture the beast and haul it away from Nara Island, a bargain which Moira denounces, claiming of Ogra, "'Tis a manifestation of evil.... Don't you see? 'Tis the monster of the devil, making its appearance on earth to warn us all of the cataclysm.... Leave well enough alone. Heed the warning. Do not tempt the devil." If Slade and Ryan catch the monster, "It will be the death of us all." Afterward, when the monster is caught and hauled aboard the *Triton* in a steel shark net, following a famous scene involving a bathysphere reminiscent of a similar scene in *Beast*, Moira opines, "'Tis Ogra, the sea god. The beast is death. 'Tis like catching the devil by the tail. What do you do with it once you've got it?" Slade replies, "Frankly, it looks to me like some prehistoric link between the dinosaur age and ours." "Scientific nonsense," retorts Moira, sounding wise beyond her years.

Two Irish paleontologists, Professors Marius Flaherty and Desmond O'Brien, are interested in claiming the monster so they may study the creature. But Moira and Sean want it freed. Ryan, however, has another deal in mind, one that will make them rich. However, after Gorgo kills a shipmate with a talon, soul-searching Slade decides that probably Moira is right after all. Identifying with Gorgo, Slade reflects in a revealing passage,

> I could feel for it. I could feel the weight of that metal net on top of me. *I was the monster* [my italics], entrapped in a prison, not allowed my freedom.... I'd spent six months in a Red prison camp during the Korean war. I'd never been so close to madness in my life.... I'd never hoped to escape.... I glanced across at the beast. It glowered at me. Ogra, I thought, you've had it, old buddy. You'll never again see the bottom of the ocean. Small wonder the beast had killed. Small wonder it flailed and maimed. Manifestation of evil? Maybe. Or maybe a manifestation of man's evil to man. Maybe it was a warning, warning of destruction and disaster to come. Like with nuclear fission. Like with space exploration. *Like with the hydrogen bomb* [my italics]. Moira was right. I had to set the beast free. Too much was at stake if I didn't.[28]

Slade's change of heart proves ineffectual. A stream of water is fed onto Gorgo's tranquilized body to keep his skin moistened, the steady trickle running off into the sea with a phosphorescent glow.[29]

After docking in London, Professors LeRoy Flaherty and Hendricks of Dublin University arrive "to join ... in protest of this outrage. To deprive science of a creature unique in evolutionary biology! To turn it into a circus freak! It's too much, sir! Outrageous!" Then Hendricks cautions, "It may even carry disease-bearing parasites or unknown bacteria. And yet you take it into the heart of a great city before any observations can be made. Before any tests—without the slightest thought of what the results might be!"

Later it's revealed that Gorgo is a juvenile in its "early infancy," meaning that unless the volcanic eruption destroyed its parents, there could be a 200-foot-tall adult still swimming around. Now ever more despondent, Slade returns to visit Moria on Nara Island. Their romantic exertions on the sand seem to summon mother Ogra from the depths. "I turned. It was coming up out of the water, just as I imagined it might, rising like a giant formless thing, weaving back and forth in the darkness, scenting out the island, towering closer and closer, moving with its giant tail through the water, coming to Nara, coming to wreak vengeance on the world, coming to destroy us all." With its red eyes aglow, Ogra topples a lighthouse tower (as did the "Fog Horn" Beast) and proceeds to flatten Nara Island, killing everyone. Stuff of nightmares!

And so begins "Armageddon," the gripping conclusion of Bingham's novel.

For a time, London was the world's largest city, and Great Britain boasted the best navy in the world. But these factors mean nothing to Ogra, which has risen from below to claim her son! After the destruction of Nara, Ogra destroys a British aircraft carrier, the HMS *Royal Oak*, in dramatic fashion. Fortunately, however, the government decides not to use atomic weapons against Ogra, the military advising the populace to remain calm and stay indoors while tanks and cannon do the job. Now in London, Moira moans, "'Tis the end of the world!" And it must seem so.

Ogra rips through London's military defenses as if they are mere toys, crumpling city landmarks such as Tower Bridge, Big Ben, buildings at Piccadilly and the Houses of Parliament. Sirens scream. While their city burns, Londoners keep a stiff upper lip. Moria, Ryan and Slade escape falling debris (bodies and bricks) by fleeing into an underground subway, scrambling along the rails to safety. Missiles, fighter planes, and the last resort, four million volts of electricity ... nothing can stop Ogra!

Ogra reaches her Gorgo, rescuing him from his confines as Slade muses of his companions, "I saw something of satisfaction ... as if they all ... knew that this manifestation of man's greed and inhumanity would come to this end." As the two make their way slowly toward the Thames, Slade notes,

> I watched the flames from the city gas tanks mounting higher into the air. Darkness lay beyond. London had no electric power left. Everything was silence and stillness in the biggest city on earth.... Lifting her head to the heavens [Ogra] loosed a final rumbling roar, like distant thunder, a warning to us all, to mankind in general, and turned and vanished in the fog and mist.... I wondered if mankind would heed the warning. I doubted it.[30]

As I do!

It's the End of the World

A classic story bearing relevance to this Cold War era discussion has never before been included amongst tales of dino-monsters. But as paleontologists now see birds as modern, evolved dinosaur descendants, we must pause to consider Daphne du Maurier's (1907–1989) "The Birds" (1952).[31] This story, ostensibly about ecological disaster, forecasts the end of the world. Cold, a "black winter," is sweeping into the British Isles, "something to do with the Arctic Circle," and yet mysteriously, somehow, the Russians are to blame. Soon Nat Hocken's family is forced to hunker down in their home as they had during the air raids of World War II. Frustratingly, Nat senses how apathy led to their plight. His neighbors fail to recognize when they're in the clutches of impending doom. Furthermore, "There's been no time. Nobody's prepared" for the National Emergency that is declared. While no reason for the sensational havoc is ever defined, one character states anxiously, "They're saying in town the Russians have done it. The Russians have poisoned the birds."

War planes are sent out to destroy the flocking, shrieking, swarming birds, but to no avail; Nat and his family next hear sounds of aircraft crashing outside, their fuselages clogged with dead attacking fowl. Nat worries whether poison gas might be used to stop the birds, which would also contaminate the soil. In the midst of impending doom, Nat's wife can only mutter "Won't America do something? ... They've always been our allies.... Surely America will do something?" But Nat instead listens to the sounds of splintering wood as tiny beaks wear down their last layer of protection. He muses "how many million years of memory were stored in those little brains, behind the stabbing beaks, the piercing eyes, now giving them this instinct to destroy mankind with all the deft precision of machines." Then he smokes his last cigarette. But will America still even exist in the wake of such a staggering ecological onslaught? Or, worse, is the disaster ultimately our fault? A powerful allegorical story using winged "dinosaurs" (i.e., birds) as metaphor for the Bomb!

Next, we'll segue into Chapter Five, here focusing on time travel, with a dire warning of nuclear holocaust in Poul Anderson's (1926–2001) "Wildcat" (1958).[32]

A "wildcat" refers to someone who prospects for oil in an area of unknown productivity, such as during the Late Jurassic Period, which is what some 500 men have been doing for the Transtemporal Oil Company. Protagonist Herries, who's in charge of operations, directing the drillers and prospectors, is frustrated because they've only been provided with small caliber arms, inefficient for killing large predatory fauna which attack his men regularly. Meanwhile, back in the late twentieth century, while the Middle Eastern war rages, the United States is in an "atomic standoff," on the verge of global war, ready to launch deadly cobalt bombs. Herries is an intelligent, likable character; he's a thinker and a cynic. He views man as the "most sinister animal of all," and time travel as "fundamentally unhealthy ... an invention that only an ingrown mind would have made...." "The dinosaurs have more sense than we do," he declares to a priest.

Poul Anderson's time travel gimmick is the "inertial effect," which only permits travel to a minimum temporal "distance" of 101,300,000 years into the past; time travelers can make maximum leaps of one century into the future (i.e., *beyond* their original departure point in time). Also, if one spends one year in the past, then he can only return to their "present" one year beyond when he originally departed into the deep past. So, if one were to time hop a century into the future to learn the whether or not those cobalt bombs were ever launched, he'd have to travel 101-plus-million years into the past to deliver the information, "less the distance you went forward." Time travel consumes "fabulous amounts of energy," and the observations of future time-hopping beyond the twentieth century have been held by the American government as classified information. Not knowing their fate, or whether the passages of time are fixed and unalterable, proves frustrating to the time travelers, for "if our every action is foreordained, if we are doomed already, what's the use of trying?"

When Herries' boss Symonds informs him of a "special shipment" that is due to arrive shortly, Herries can only assume the worst, that a Jurassic military base will be built on their drilling operation. He speculates that the government will plant a few "husky" atomic cobalt bombs in geological formations underlying where future cities of the enemy will be built so they can be triggered a hundred million years later. Herries also ponders that, if the main time projector were ever destroyed by a bomb, then there'd be "five hundred womanless men in a world of reptiles. He'd take the future, cobalt bomb and all." Given time travel's propensity for total annihilation, it would have been far better to have first invented the means of infinite velocity necessary to travel to the stars instead. As Herries tells the priest,

> If we were sane, padre, we wouldn't have been so anxious for a little organic grease and the little military advantage involved that the first thing we did was go back into the dead past after it. No, we'd have invented that spaceship first, and gone to the stars where there's room to be free and to grow.[33]

Drunk and depressed after one of his men is killed by a Jurassic species of tyrannosaur, Herries pries into crates comprising the "special shipment" after it is transported from the twentieth century. Amazingly, the contents are not military hardware, but farming equipment instead. Turns out the time travelers who jumped into the future discovered that war erupted in the late twentieth century after all, beginning one year from their "base date," and sterilizing the planet for a hundred *million* years. And so, Herries is ordered to prepare for the next "special shipment," 500 precious women who will live with the men in the Jurassic Period. Ultimately, however, their descendants must "perfect the spaceships we know to be possible and take possession of the stars...."

The dreadful specter of the Cold War, doomsday and extinction were thought by many to be synonymous during the 1960s through the 1980s. Physicist Geoffrey A. Landis' brilliant "Dinosaurs" (1985) brought all of this together, linking our impending nuclear doomsday with the dinosaur extinctions.[34] Here, as part of a long-shot military project, individuals with strange powers or who are otherwise sensitive to the paranormal are trained to become "psychic assassins" for the U.S. government. One of these individuals is young Timmy, a paleontology buff who owns a nice fossil collection and has a passion for dinosaurs. His gift talent is time, being able to see into the future and the past as well.

When the Soviets launch their massive ICBM attack, after the efforts of his fellow psychics fail miserably, only Timmy is able to avert planetary incineration. Timmy is asked to concentrate on the incoming missiles. Suddenly, with only eighteen minutes remaining to impact, all the missiles just *disappear!* Several days later Timmy is spied flipping through a book he'd been reading, *The End of the Dinosaurs.* "Gee, Mr. Sanderson," Timmy asks ironically, "I wonder what really did happen to the dinosaurs." Mr. Sanderson solves the riddle, contemplating the iridium casings on the nuclear warheads.

> I could almost picture the warheads, six thousand of them, raining down on the forests of the Mesozoic. Poor dinosaurs, they never had a chance. And in sixty-five million years, even the last faint traces of radioactivity would have decayed to nothing.[35]

And so, it seems *we* finally did them in after all! But don't gloat. This is very bad because, remember, the dinosaurs are *us.*

Shades of Gojira.

CONCLUSION

In the prototypical Cold War era dino-monster tale, scientists—who brought us the Bomb—are not to be trusted. Formerly the strongest and most 'righteous' could be projected to prevail in (conventional) global conflict—a foreboding geopolitical extrapolation of Darwinism—now it seemed there might be no human successors in the aftermath of a nuclear holocaust.

Authors avail themselves of symbols and metaphors used as literary devices, such as diving bells and submersibles (i.e., penetrating the "underworld" lair of the beast), earthquakes and volcanoes (i.e., signaling an alarm to mankind through nature's fury), lighthouses or towers (i.e., phallic or cultural symbols which when destroyed or conquered represent mankind's emasculation), retaliatory nuclear or other weapons of mass destruction (i.e., symbolizing the degradation of our environment, our pending extinction and folly), the sea (i.e., a monster's emergence from the sea where life originated represents nature's retaliation), regeneration—as in Dean Owen's 1961 pulp novel *Reptilicus*[36] (i.e., the dino-monster, or *kaiju eiga,* cannot really be destroyed because it is within us and won't go away until our inevitable extinction), and prehistoric sense (i.e., an anachronistic revisiting of the prehistoric warns of extinction).

Yet not every "*kaiju* tale" relies on such devices. Mark Jacobson's *Gojiro* (1991), for example is a truly different and stylistic affair.[37] Here, Gojiro, a monitor lizard which was mutated in a hydrogen bomb test into Godzilla (although neither that name or "Gojira" are used for copyright reasons), is the main character of a highly unusual story. Gojiro has befriended "Komodo the coma boy," who survived the Hiroshima bombing. They have many adventures on their Radioactive Island and in Hollywood as well. It's "geek love on a truly epic scale and a bible for the world that was born out of the Manhattan Project."[38] And yet, because *Gojiro* is anything but like Marc Cerasini's formulaic Godzilla series novels, it surely was neglected by most Godzilla fans.[39] While college professors might rank Jacobson's peculiar entry as "literature" rather than pulp, I much prefer experiencing the somber, sincere contemporary messages cast in Carson Bingham's dino-monster novel.

The Cold War may have ended, yet the threat of "nuclear winter"—the full magnitude of which only became apparent after explorers of deep time contemplated the nature of sixty-five-million-year-old iridium deposits—remains omnipresent.[40]

So, as symbolized by doomsday dinosaurs of the Cold War period, nuking the planet may prove to be the quickest yet most horrific means for reverting to prehistoric times, perhaps even approaching the severity of an age before life, or a "neo–Precambrian" era. But a less facetious and far more technologically challenging and thought-provoking way into time's abyss would be through use of relativistic time travel devices ... which we'll now explore.

CHAPTER 5

Time-Relativistic Dinosaurs: Bradbury's Legacy

BACKGROUND

Jurassic Park aside, sooner or later, most dinosaur time travel adventures wind up in the *Cretaceous* Period. Why? Partly 'cuz that's where *Tyrannosaurus rex*, three-horned *Triceratops*, and even more demonic creatures known collectively as "raptors" dwell! But mainly because that's where Ray Bradbury staged the most influential dino-time travel tale ever written, "A Sound of Thunder."

Although H.G. Wells's influential *The Time Machine* (1895) is casually regarded as *the* landmark time travel tale, rather, Ray Bradbury's beloved "A Sound of Thunder" became the launching point for most time travel stories involving prehistoric life. Bradbury's three-fold legacy is apparent because, as in "Thunder," (1) the usual Mesozoic temporal destination is the Late Cretaceous (as opposed to, say, the Jurassic, Triassic or other geological periods), (2) *Tyrannosaurus*—or an equivalent dino-monster—is often encountered by the time travelers, and (3) there is often a "low-tech" time "safari" mission objective which backfires in extraordinary fashion. Developments in modern physics, recent paleontological discoveries and pervading socio-cultural factors may have altered the scope of dino-time travel fiction since "Thunder's" first publication in 1952; however, core elements of Bradbury's classic "A Sound of Thunder" are often cleverly retained.

In a sense, dinosaurs *embody* one of science fiction's most conventional themes—the time travel scenario. By luring men's fantasies to misty, primordial worlds, traditionally, dinosaurs have *represented* deep geological time.[1] In fact, from any dinophile's perspective, arguably, what good are time machines anyway, unless one can rely on them to travel backward in time to witness a primeval bestiary? Paleontology is inherently like time travel because in their reconstruction of prehistory, scientists and artists ("poets with brushes") must see through time, visualizing the deep past. Here, paleontology merges with pop culture as prehistoric monsters and other formidable prehistoria parade out of museum murals or stampede from the pages of pulp fiction and best-selling novels onto the silver screen. Until now, the nature of time travel stories involving prehistoric animals hasn't been carefully examined.[2]

In the 1867 edition of his epical *Journey*, Jules Verne relied on a *faux* time travel device, a combination of images and text suggesting paleontological movement through time's recesses, taking place deep within the earth. So instead, credit usually goes to H.G. Wells (1866–1946) for inventing the first time *machine*, although his accomplishment came fully a decade prior to the beginnings of an Einsteinian revolution in physics—the articulation of space-time Special Relativity. Curiously, time travel stories involving dinosaurs and other prehistoric animals weren't common for many decades. Partially this is because the prospect of finding dinosaurs alive in the present-day world, although in remote, primeval settings, seemed more romantic, if not downright plausible. Certainly it must have seemed easier (and somehow more factual) to escape into the past simply by chartering a voyage to some unexplored region of the world, akin to Kong's Skull Island, where dinosaurs and other prehistoric fauna may still be found, as opposed to finding the wherewithal of building a seemingly impossible device—a Wellsian time machine. After all, what could be more improbable than escaping into the past? For time travel is infinitely more difficult than storming the beachhead of any lost-world isle or continent.

Traditionally, writers rely on two means for bringing man and living dinosaurs together through use of time travel. For example, a time device may be devised for extracting a prehistoric organism from its native environment, moving it into our present for examination. This was the strategy employed by Isaac Asimov (1920–1992) in his acclaimed 1958 tale, "The Ugly Little Boy," in which a Neanderthal boy is snatched from the Pleistocene into a Stasis field where he can be observed in our present; author Malcolm Hulke employed a Timescoop to transfer dinosaurs from the Mesozoic into London in his 1976 novel *Dr. Who and the Dinosaur Invasion*. Alternatively, honest-to-goodness time machines are the favored means for traveling from our period into the deep past. This way, readers may explore a forbidden, primordial terrain inhabited by exotic creatures long extinct, yet alive in a younger world. (Although sometimes use of a time machine is merely implicit, as in Brian Aldiss' "Poor Little Warrior" (1958) or Michael Swanwick's 1999 story, "Riding the Giganotosaur.") Such time travel adventures are often coupled with the popular "time safari" lure, Ray Bradbury's legacy.[3]

H.G. Wells's *The Time Machine* wasn't by any means the first story written involving time travel.[4] Nor did it become the primary inspiration for later time travel stories involving prehistoric organisms. In this context, Ray Bradbury's classic 1952 story "A Sound of Thunder" was far more influential.[5] Primarily remembered for its 1960 projection onto the silver screen, Wells's story is perhaps the most famous time travel tale involving the remote future, while Bradbury's precocious tale is the most beloved story coupling the deep past with dinosaurs. Despite the literary perfection of Wells's classic 1895 tale, most dinosaur time travel tales owe their genesis to Bradbury's brilliance.

WELLS VERSUS BRADBURY

According to Bradbury, "A Sound of Thunder" was little more than a serendipitous *What if* experiment. "What if we could travel in time and run back to hunt the prehistoric beasts? This last was an experiment I tried in 1950. I simply sat down to my typewriter one morning with no idea where I would wind up, and hammered together a Time Machine, and shot my hunters back a few million years to see what would happen. Three hours later, after a butterfly had been stepped on, making it one of the first, and unconscious, ecology stories, the tale was done, the beast slain, and all political history changed forever."[6] Our eternal conflict with dinosaurs, evident in time safari tales, is a reflection of man's self-destructive tendencies and disregard for the environment.

In *The Time Machine*, after suspending disbelief through enlivened description of the nature of time's flow, as comprehended in Isaac Newton's day, and following discussion of temporal experiments conducted by the time traveler, Wells moves into his evolutionary theme forté. Wells, who studied under evolutionist "Darwin's bulldog" Thomas Henry Huxley (1825–1895), perceived *The Time Machine* as an "assault on human self-satisfaction." "In my student days we were much exercised by talk about a possible fourth dimension of space; the fairly obvious idea that events could be presented in a rigid four dimensional space time framework had occurred to me, and this is used as the magic trick for a glimpse of the future that ran counter to the placid assumption of that time that Evolution was a pro-human force making things better and better for mankind."[7] For as the time traveler discovers in the far-off future, 802,701 years hence, the course of evolution has split humanity into two species—the hideous subterranean Morlocks, and the gentle, childlike Eloi, who are subjugated by the Morlocks. And at an even more distant future, man ceases to be recognizable. Surely, for its time, this was thinly veiled social commentary on Victorian class structure.[8]

Wells, striving for a convincing level of technological realism, directed time travel toward man's future, whereas Bradbury, writing in a more enlightened period with respect to modern physics, pointed to the nostalgic abyss of time. By introducing the idea of the time safari, Bradbury—who never specialized in technological or scientifically (including evolutionary and paleontologically) founded fiction—illustrated mankind's technological folly.[9] Wells's vivid description of the mechanism and sensations of moving through time itself are not usually emulated in dinosaur time safari tales. In fact, most (terrestrially-based) time travel stories involving dinosaurs, the emphasis of this chapter, are inherently "low-tech," perhaps representing another aspect to Bradbury's legacy.

As opposed to dealing with hard science fiction, Bradbury confessed that, instead, many of his early writings probed the "psychological aura of loneliness."[10] Furthermore, by the early 1950s, Bradbury admitted, "I don't like what science is doing to the world.... I think science is a good thing to escape from."[11] As summarized by Isaac Asimov in 1980, "Bradbury ... created moods with few words. He wasn't ashamed to tug at the heartstrings and there was a semipoetic nostalgia to most of those tugs. He created his own version of Mars straight out of the nineteenth century, totally ignoring the findings of the twentieth century ... one gets the idea that Bradbury *lives* in the nineteenth century and in the small-town Midwest in which he grew up ... he can't drive a car. He still views science with intense suspicion, but supports the space program enthusiastically, largely because (I think) he finds it poetic."[12] While Bradbury may have seemed "antiscientific" to readers, Wells reveled in exploring the consequences of scientific advance upon impact human society.

Today, most would agree that time travel stories seem more convincing if they're founded in technical verisimilitude. Wells understood the importance of scientific explanation, stating, "It occurred to me that instead of the usual interview with the devil or a magician, an ingenious use of scientific patter might with advantage be substituted."[13] Wells's 1895 story preceded Albert Einstein's (1879–1955) Theory of Special Relativity, formulated in 1905. Wells may also have contemplated two limitations involving time travel into the past, the mind-boggling "grandfather paradox"—going back in time to kill one's grandfather, in which case the time traveler never would have existed in the first place—and the fact that sending a time machine hurtling into the past would immediately cause it to bump backward into itself, that is, in the fourth dimension. That collision would create something akin to a nuclear explosion! And if the explosion occurred even *before* the time traveler launched his time machine into the past, then one may ask how did the time traveler ever manage to trigger the explosion by pulling the lever of his time machine, because shouldn't he already have died? Paul Nahin suggests Wells avoided paradox in *The Time Machine* because he didn't know how to convincingly circumvent such absurdities.[14]

While Special Relativity presented means for time travel into the future, by 1916, Einstein offered a key for time travel into the *past* through his General Theory of Relativity. However, for decades, based on contemporary understanding of causality, physical laws and astrophysics, skepticism surrounded the *plausibility* of traveling into the past. So, perhaps understandably, the earliest, now rather obscure, stories in which modern humans confronted live prehistoric animals in their natural environments relied on unsophisticated means for experiencing geological history. Indeed, the earliest such tale, Pierre Boitard's (1789–1859) novel *Paris Before Man*, published in 1861, involved a demon, while in another, published in 1917, paleontologist Charles H. Sternberg (1850–1943) simply sleeps into prehistory! By 1931, John Taine envisioned television (or a "televisor") as a means for *seeing* into the Mesozoic, in his enjoyable novel *Before the Dawn*.[15] (See Appendix for more on this title.)

By the 1920s, readers of pulp magazines were expressing their reservations toward time travel into the past. One reader wrote in 1931, "There is only one kind of science fiction story that I dislike, and that is the so-called time-traveling. It doesn't seem logical to me. For example: supposing a man had a grudge against his grandfather, who is now dead. He could hop in his machine and go back to the year that his grandfather was a young man and murder him. And if he did this how could the revenger be born? I think the whole thing is 'bunk.'" This letter typifies how illogical, let alone paradoxical, the *What if* nature of traveling into the past must have seemed during the 1920s through the 1940s. And although, intellectually, the concept of time travel into the past may have seemed downright *fascinating* to them, physicists also derided the notion. Of course, by having his time traveler move into the future to meet Morlocks, Wells steered around such difficulties and criticism. By 1949, however, the shifting mindset offered further science fiction opportunities when mathematician Kurt Godel (1906–1978) published solutions to Einstein's field equations, reasoning that (for the special case of a rotating universe) it is "theoretically possible ... to travel into the past, or otherwise influence the past."[16]

Typically, the technological sophistication of time travel stories involving dinosaurs wasn't much to speak of until after the 1930s, and there's yet another, neglected reason behind this. British geologist Arthur Holmes (1890–1965) published the first relatively accurate, radiometric geological time scale in 1927. A decade later, researchers had pinned down the date to the Late Cretaceous, extending it to 68 million years, and the beginning of the Triassic Period at what must have seemed an extraordinary 193 million years! But although clearly there was time enough for all manner of fictional travels into the marvelous abyss of time, unlike Verne's adventurers in *Journey*, who toured the panorama of paleontological history, our intrepid time travelers continued to get hung up in the Cretaceous, often pondering *T. rex* and the great dinosaur extinction.

THE PATH TO BRADBURY

Beyond technological hurdles, stepping into prehistory is both foreboding and *forbidden*. Traveling through time into the deep past signals misery and death; metaphorically, the past is already dead and buried. It's like crossing the River Styx into Hades, or into the shadowy Underworld. Moreover, in the Mesozoic, coprolite happens! We see this illustrated in three stories which, collectively perhaps, paved the way to Bradbury's classic.

Frederick Pohl's 1949 story "Let the Ants Try" considered the aftermath of a limited atomic war.[17] A scientist who has built a time machine and is disgruntled by the human race decides to carry fertilized queen ants which have mutated into a new advanced species—evolving lungs as a result of exposure to twentieth century radiation fallout—forty million years into the past. The mutations, already superior to any other insect alive today, can now look forward to another forty million years of evolution. But the time traveler's "present" becomes infested by the horrific descendants of the ant colonies he established in prehistory. So when the time traveler attempts to alter the past a second time by going back to *prevent* his release of the queen ants, so that humans will instead later prevail, he is murdered by the insect race which has built their own time machine and traveled from the future to stop him. Without introducing a time safari element, Pohl's remarkable entry foreshadows elements of Bradbury's "A Sound of Thunder."[18]

As we noted in the previous chapter, dinosaur tales of the 1950s often bore dark, brooding messages concerning fears of atomic war and man's capacity (and rapacity) to degrade the planet. Such concerns are reflected in two science fiction tales published in 1950: Arthur C. Clarke's harrowing "Time's Arrow" and Asimov's foreboding "Day of the Hunters."

Clarke's "Time's Arrow" is a fusion of fears about subatomic experimentation and crimes against nature where, ultimately, a paleontologist confronts a fifty-million-year-old monster, known only to science through the gravity of its massive, stony footprints preserved in a desolate area.[19] The tracks are being unearthed under the blazing sun at an ancient watering hole, situated fortuitously near a new test facility operated by the Atomic Development Authority (ADA). When alive, the mass of this unknown monster, merely suggested by Clarke to be "dinosaurian" in nature, is speculated to be twenty or thirty tons, or much, much greater than any known theropod dinosaur. (*T. rex*'s mass is estimated at twelve tons.)

How intriguing to see where these tracks led—perhaps to a climactic end! What fateful tale can be told of the ancient footsteps? And to what extent is man merely a sterile, unmoving observer of nature? Fortunately in his classic tale, Clarke revels in such intrigue.[20]

Clarke's gimmick is "helium II," which has profound physical properties. Existing as a perceived form of liquid helium just above absolute zero, theoretically, helium II displays "negative entropy," which here is equivalent to negative time. (Positive entropy is also known as "time's arrow" because its tendency to increase sets a direction for time, always moving into the future.) An astonishing implication is that fiddling around with helium II can create movement against the normal course of entropy—into the past. Negative entropy—negative time.

As a much-anticipated experiment climaxes at the nearby Atomic Development Authority (ADA) facility, a hazy, rippling, half-mile-long wave of energy emanates across the horizon from the ADA towers. With their supervisor and his Jeep unaccounted for, the paleontologists notice a curious set of tracks imprinted in the sedimentary deposit—the zigzag pattern of *tire* tracks, which eerily weren't there *before*, and seem disturbingly orchestrated with the monster's movement: "... in one place the shallow tire marks had been completely obliterated by the monster's footprints ... as if the great reptile was about to make the final leap upon its desperately fleeing prey."[21]

In his "Day of the Hunters," after humorously brushing aside the troublesome grandfather paradox, Asimov introduces a college guy time machine inventor, converted into a raving alcoholic as a result of his traumatic experiences in prehistory. The professor observed Late Cretaceous dinosaurs to be sentient creatures, who, wielding weaponry, hunted for sport, not just for food. So, ultimately, when the dinosaurs' big game expired, they turned their weapons upon themselves, causing their own extinction. The dinosaurs' mistakes prove foreboding for mid–twentieth century humanity, standing at the crossroads of an atomic age, as "we're the second intelligence—and how the devil do you think *we're* going to end?"[22]

By degree, dinosaur *hunting* of one kind or another increasingly became an undercurrent theme of time travel to the deep past, although it was Bradbury who put it all together, inaugurating the idea of the time safari. Whereas Pohl's, Clarke's and Asimov's stories were printed in the traditional home for sci-fi tales, pulp magazines, Bradbury's "A Sound of Thunder" had wide exposure, first appearing in the slick *Collier's* (June 1952). Thereafter, "A Sound of Thunder" has been reprinted numerous times, including *Senior Scholastic Magazine* (November 1953), *Playboy* (June 1956), and as the dawn of the modern age of dinosaur fandom peaked, in several anthologies, including Bradbury's *Dinosaur Tales* (1983). Such a rich publishing history pattern is highly unusual for a science fiction short story.[23] Why has it aged so well? Asimov suggested, "People who didn't read science fiction, and who were taken aback by its unfamiliar conventions and its rather specialized vocabulary, found that they could read and understand Bradbury."[24] Perhaps also, its precautionary, culturally relevant message—to interfere with or destroy our heritage or harm nature often has dire consequences for our future—really dug home. After all, at heart, "A Sound of Thunder" *is* an ecological story.

DEBATING PARADOX: BRADBURY VERSUS SPRAGUE DE CAMP

"A Sound of Thunder" is perhaps the most influential and famous dinosaur time travel tale of all time.[25] Bradbury's magnificent story is possibly the earliest example of *dinosaur* science fiction and fantasy to employ an alternate universe gimmick. "Thunder's" protagonist, Eckels, pays the ultimate price for traveling back in time from the mid–twenty-first century with fellow thrill-seeking time travelers, courtesy of Time Safari, Inc., whose motto is "Safaris to any year in the past. You name the animal. We take you there. You shoot it."[26]

Once they arrive at their destination in time, sixty million years ago, Eckels and comrades are forewarned not to stride from the Path leading from the time machine's portal. The Path is a time and destiny stabilizing device made of antigravity metal that floats six inches above the ground. Metaphorically, it is also the "straight and narrow" path that mankind should never stray from. For an accidental killing of *any* organism encountered off the Path could set off untold disruptions and distortions in the future. Nor may they step on foliage, including grass (which didn't exist in the Mesozoic), because, "Crushing certain plants could add up infinitesimally. A little error here would multiply in sixty million years, all out of proportion."[27] As long as the time travelers remain entirely encapsulated within their self-contained, decontaminated suits, equipped with oxygen helmets so as not to release microorganisms into the Late Cretaceous ecosphere, and remain suspended on the Path, their future is secure.

So, if they can't even kill a single grass blade, how can Eckels be permitted to bag a trophy dinosaur? Time Safari, Inc. employees are skilled in their trade. Through prior trips to the Cretaceous, Time Safari guides had already established the time and spatial coordinates for when the particular rex Eckels has paid to shoot is supposed to die. So all they must do is return to that moment with hunters who have commissioned their services as guides. The time safari proceeds to the death setting several minutes before the time of the animal's natural death. The hunter then kills his dinosaur for sport with gunshot moments before it would have died through natural causes, thus placing infinitesimal constraints on the space-time continuum.

But the rex must be abandoned because, as the guide explains to Eckels, "the body has to stay right here where it would have died originally, so the insects, birds and bacteria can get at it as they were intended to. The body stays. But we can take a picture of you standing near it."[28] There is no trophy to carry home.

On this particular adventure, Eckels freaks out at his first sight of the monster—*T. rex*, or the "thunder lizard," as Bradbury refers to it for literary effect.[29] Terror-stricken Eckels retreats cowardly off the Path onto the jungle floor, his feet sinking into soft moss.

> It came on great oiled, resilient, striding legs. It towered thirty feet above half the trees, a great evil god, folding its delicate watchmaker's claws close to its oily reptilian chest. Each leg was a piston, a thousand pounds of white bone, sunk in thick ropes of muscle, sheathed over in a gleam of pebbled skin like the mail of a terrible warrior.... Its armored flesh glittered like a thousand green coins. The coins, crusted with slime, steamed. In the slime, tiny insects wriggled, so that the entire body seemed to twitch and undulate, even while the monster itself did not move.... The Monster ... lunged forward with a terrific scream.[30]

It is left to Eckel's fellow hunters to dispatch the nightmarish apparition with gunfire, only minutes before the trunk of a giant dead tree cracks and falls on the parasite-infested dinosaur's quivering cadaver—which would have been its natural fate had Time Safari Inc. not interfered. The "sound of thunder" *is* the *T. rex* itself, *and* the sound of the guns that kill it paradoxically millions of years prior to their invention, *and* it is also the last sound Eckels shall hear in the (altered) future they "return" to.

For Eckels had carelessly trod upon a butterfly, unnoticed until the crew returns in their machine to a future now haplessly distorted because of that second casualty. In the silent scream of Eckel's butterfly, an outcome far more harrowing than any *T. rex* roar awaits the travelers. For the future is (or has been?) altered. Or is it that their past never existed? In *Twilight Zone* fashion, their world and society are now oblivion, exchanged subtly and mysteriously for another that is unfamiliar. And so the Time Safari guide fires his gun, intending to kill Eckels, world destroyer, even as he pleads the unanswered question, "... can't we take it back, can't we make it live again? Can't we start over.... Can't we...."[31]

Well, could they?

Earlier, while Eckels journeyed backward through time into the Mesozoic, his guides

Jack Arata's vision of a key moment in Ray Bradbury's "A Sound of Thunder." See text for further details. (With permission.)

explained that time doesn't permit "a man meeting himself," invoking the odious grandfather paradox. Instead, "Time steps aside."[32] In other words, Bradbury's Path should be viewed as a Stasis field akin to Asimov's for snatching the Neanderthal boy in "The Ugly Little Boy," although extending into the past, or a means of circumventing the grandfather paradox. It would have been impossible for Eckels' guide to have first documented the exact time and place of the *T. rex*'s demise and then return *exactly* to those coordinates to shoot the same dinosaur without encountering himself, especially if they adhered to the Path—unless when time "stepped aside" they had entered an *alternate* Mesozoic universe. So perhaps Bradbury's Path also preserves (i.e., "collapses") the universe's quantum mechanical wave function. And perhaps we can forgive this minor inconsistency, a time paradox principle later magnificently exploited in Lyon Sprague De Camp's (1907–2000) similar and thought-provoking 1956 tale, "A Gun for Dinosaur."

    Author L. Sprague de Camp admitted how, in "1954, I read a story by a colleague, telling of a hunt for dinosaurs by time machine. I had been a dinosaur buff since the First World, or Kaiserian, War.... Fate denied me the lifetime role of paleontologist; but I still thought I saw egregious scientific errors in my colleague's story. These irked me to the point of writing my own story of dinosaur hunting by time machine, 'A Gun for Dinosaur,' trying to show how it should be done."[33] "Sprague," as Asimov lovingly referred to his friend, wrote a classic which led to further, brilliant time safari tales.

The time-honored formula employed by Sprague de Camp in his *Rivers of Time* collection is the recounting of memorable time travel safari tales by swaggering, rifle-toting Aussie Reginald Rivers for prospective, and rejected, clients. In "A Gun for Dinosaur," Rivers begins his story by claiming he can't take certain clients hunting late–Mesozoic dinosaur because of a tragic ending suffered on a prior safari. One must be large enough to handle the sort of rifle needed to bring down the great carnivores of the late Cretaceous, such as *T. rex*, and this particular gentleman, Mr. Seligman, isn't strapping enough to handle weaponry of the right caliber. And so on the way out of his office at the end of his business day, Rivers invites Seligman to a local bar where he tells him the tragic tale of one Courtney James.

Rivers and his partner, the "Raja," utilize Professor Prochaska's time machine at the "big University" for time safari journeys to nearly any period except anytime more recent than 100,000 years before the present, on up to about one billion years ago. Rivers explains the reason why one can't travel to less than 100,000 ago is that "if people could go back to a more recent time, their actions would affect our own history, which would be a paradox or contradiction of facts. Can't have that in a well run universe, you know. But before 100,000 B.C., more or less, the actions of the expeditions are lost in the stream of time before human history begins."[34] However, once a slice of time is visited by the safari guides, they must *never* revisit that exact sliver because it would be paradoxical to do so. The twenty-one-day-long safaris offered by Rivers and company are much desired by hunters because most of the large wildlife of the future has all but vanished. One must trespass into the past to hunt big game.

Courtney James and August Holtzinger were the *sahibs*, as referred to by safari guides Rivers and the Raja for this particular journey to eighty-five million years before the present. James is a playboy sort going plump; Holtzinger, an undistinguished Midwestern businessman, is rather slim yet desiring to prove himself worthy enough for his ordinary-looking fiancée. James becomes a royal pain in the neck, however, because he doesn't follow directions; James continually fires his gun at all manner of dinosaur, even when Rivers orders him to hold fire. Ultimately, James is intent on shooting a tyrant lizard, *Tyrannosaurus*, so he can mount its great head, while Holtzinger's sights are set on *Triceratops*. (There's that "Rex-Tops" pairing again!) According to Rivers, in the time period they've traveled to, it is the fictitious *Tyrannosaurus trionyches* (not *T. rex* itself), which is "bigger and more specialized."

As they move from camp to camp, with both barrels of James's gun blasting away at undesirable moments, Rivers smells a theropod nearby in the woods. They move stealthily until James's unexpected gunfire awakens *Tyrannosaurus trionyches*. Sudden sight of the monster incites panic, causing James—now without ammunition in his gun—to flee desperately. Holtzinger holds his ground, pumping smaller rounds into the advancing beast, which merely tickle its hide. Rivers and the Raja take aim, bringing down the brute, but only temporarily: "... the tyrannosaur got up again and blundered off without even dropping its victim. The last I saw of it was Holtzinger's legs dangling out one side of its jaws (he'd stopped screaming) and its big tail banging against the tree trunks as it swung from side to side."[35] It's all entirely James's fault, for he'd emptied his gun on a useless six-foot-tall pachycephalosaur and couldn't reload in time to shoot the tyrannosaur. James is incredulous, however, blaming Rivers for the sorry outcome.

To rectify matters on his own, James scrounges up a small fortune, lies to Prochaska about losing his wallet in the Cretaceous, and then travels in the time chamber to the very day of their lethal encounter with the tyrannosaur. A short time later there's a large explosion outside in the streets. As Rivers, who rushes out to find James's cadaver lying alongside his gun, relates: "... the instant James started to do anything that would make a visible change in the world of eighty-five million B.C., such as making a footprint in the earth, the space-time forces snapped him forward to Present to prevent a paradox. And the violence of the passage practically tore him to bits." So, as Rivers explains to Mr. Seligman in the bar, he's "... just not big enough to handle a gun for dinosaur."[36]

Not all writers fret over the grandfather paradox, or the far stranger *impossibility* of meeting oneself in the past. When it comes to time safaris, rules of time travel can be violated. For instance, time travelers in Clifford D. Simak's (1904–1988) 1978 novel *Mastodonia* seem oblivious to the possibility of creating paradoxical scenarios.[37] For his spirited, ecologically sensitive 1993 novel, *Tyrannosaur* (a "Gun for Dinosaur" clone), David Drake noted that the odds weighed statistically against one ever reencountering himself in the Cretaceous Period anyway, simply because time intrusion vehicles could not be calibrated to within less than an error of plus or minus 5,000 years![38] Over a decade *before* Bradbury's "A Sound of Thunder," in his 1941 story "By His Bootstraps," Robert Heinlein (1907–1988) wrote of a time traveler who repeatedly encountered himself.[39] Likewise, Michael Swanwick has no qualms about the grandfather paradox in his *Bones of the Earth* (2002), the beginning of which recalls John Taine's opening in *The Greatest Adventure*.[40] Here, a severed *Stegosaurus* head, remarkably with all soft tissues intact, is delivered to a paleontologist named Griffin, triggering a mind-bending series of paradoxes where time travelers can greet themselves in past, present or future. At one point, in homage to Ray Bradbury's "A Sound of Thunder," a *pair* of Dr. Griffins relate to an audience how "all your actions in the past—all your *future* actions, everything you *will* do—have already existed for millions of years, and are part of what led inevitably to this present moment. Don't obsess about the repercussions of simple actions. Step on as many butterflies as you wish—the present is safe."[41]

TIME MACHINE ALTERNATIVES

Besides reliance on time machines, within the past half century time travelers have visited the Paleozoic and Mesozoic eras using a remarkable alternate array of devices. Time slippage, time slips, chronotransference, dechronization, "minding," portals leading into the past, as well as the usual (or unusual) assortment of motor vehicles and airplanes, represent some of the bold and inventive ways conceived by writers of fantastic fiction for moving protagonists into prehistory without use of a conventional time machine, such as employed by Wells, Bradbury and Sprague de Camp.

Chronotransference, utilized by Robert J. Sawyer in his 1993 short story "Just Like Old Times," is the means of transferring a human consciousness back into an organism living in history, "superimposing his or her mind over that of someone who lived in the past."[42] In the year 2042 it's considered a proper means of euthanasia. The phrase "old times" in Sawyer's title isn't simply a trite nostalgic reference to good ol,' happy-go-lucky Mesozoic days, but, rather, a cruel pun. For in 2042, Dr. Robert Cohen is convicted of murdering thirty-seven people. During sentencing, Justice Amanda Hopkins claims that evil-minded Cohen is "the most cold-blooded and brutal killer to have stalked Canada's prairies since *Tyrannosaurus rex*...."[43] So, to pay for his serial killing, most judiciously, Hopkins condemns him to fate by chronotransference into the Mesozoic's most bloodthirsty killer of all—*Tyrannosaurus rex*. Cohen advises his attorney, "Kidding is not my forte.... *Killing* is. I want to know which was better at it, me or the rex."[44] Requiring an actual fossil specimen from which to "back-propagate," scientists complete the transfer. Soon Cohen's mind is at large within the skull of a *T. rex*, roaming through the Late Cretaceous landscape.

Unfortunately, the scientists erroneously placed reliance on one principle—that the transferred mind would have absolutely no impact on or control over the transferee. "Chronotransference worked precisely because the transferee could exert no influence, and therefore was simply observing things that had not already been observed. Since no new observations were being made, no quantum-mechanical distortions occurred. After all, said the physicists, if one could exert control, one could change the past. And that was impossible."[45] And yet Cohen's intellect proves so vastly overwhelming compared to the puny *T. rex's* brain that the "impossible" soon happens. (Also see the Appendix for more on Cohen's story.)

In paleontologist George Gaylord Simpson's 1996 novella, *The Dechronization of Sam Magruder*, slippage into prehistory occurs accidentally through "dechronization," founded on the philosophical prospect of *quantized* time. This happens randomly without use of a time machine. It is only possible to "slip" backward, not forward in time, because the future doesn't yet exist in any universe. Magruder's eighty-million-year-old, Late Cretaceous destination is an entirely random occurrence. The chances of anyone ever repeating the event are infinitesimal and it is impossible for protagonist Sam Magruder to return to his "present," the year 2162.[46]

Brian Aldiss crafted an unlikely means for time-traveling to the past in his remarkable 1967 novel *Cryptozoic*. Here, depressed artist and society dropout Ed Bush escapes from his awful "present" of 2090 into the abyss of time using a recreational drug—cryptozoic acid (CSD, akin to LSD). Time travel is accomplished as "mind-travel," meaning in their past destinations the travelers become wraith-like, only allowed limited interaction with materials or organisms in their visited past. In this well-crafted novel, Bush explains the principle of "minding." "If you think of the space-time universe, with the true present always at the point of highest energy and the furthest past at the lowest, then obviously as soon as our minds are free of passing time, they will fall backwards towards that lowest point...."[47] It is further explained that unlocking the secret of temporal mind travel required understanding the human "overmind," an organ evolved to falsely create a perceived state of passing time, or the flow of time from past to future.

In Clifford D. Simak's *Mastodonia*, where an ill-fated Late Cretaceous hunting party is exterminated by a pack of allosaurs, of a species previously unknown to science yet much larger than *T. rex*, prehistoric ages are accessed through portals one may simply walk through. In Rod Serling's story "The Odyssey of Flight 33" (1962), a jet airliner exceeding the sound barrier moves into the Jurassic Period. And in Lewis S. Brown's nicely illustrated children's book *Yes, Helen, There Were Dinosaurs* (1982), a Volkswagen "bug" doubles as a time machine to the Jurassic Period, 138 million years ago.[48]

TEMPORAL MECHANICS

Wells's Victorian time traveler moved deterministically through a rigid universe filling space and time, to which an omniscient observer would perceive concepts such as past, present and future as meaningless. This is quite the opposite of Bradbury's "Sound of Thunder" universe, in which small changes effected in the past significantly alter future realities. In Bradbury's tale, Eckels and fellow time travelers simply must remain in their suits, on the Path, or else all hell breaks loose. While Bradbury introduced the popular time safari concept, evidently his ideas about traveling into the past proved too restricting, prompting Sprague de Camp to loosen the reins somewhat in "A Gun for Dinosaur." Subsequently, most tales involving time travel into prehistory either ignore or soften the impact of alternate future histories caused by actions taken by time travelers in the past.

Reginald Rivers' safari teams, however, have far more mobility and freedom, provided they avoid interfering with prehistoric men in too recent an age (i.e., less than 100,000 years ago), or creating paradoxical situations such as time travelers encountering themselves in any time, or by otherwise causing anything to happen in the past—such as the dreaded grandfather paradox scenario—in which certain events logically shouldn't happen because they didn't *already* happen. In both Pohl's and Bradbury's stories, the future is vastly altered by actions taken by the time travelers. Throughout Sprague de Camp's eleven stories involving Reginald Rivers and company, however, despite one paradoxical calamity, the future is not even changed subtly by new actions taken in the past. The future is rigid, as in Well's story.

So Bradbury and Sprague de Camp represent extremes. What lies between?

Even though, following Bradbury's precedent, time travelers rarely describe the workings of their time machines in dinosaur science fiction, they do at least often contemplate the nature of time, expressing the author's theory of temporal mechanics. For instance, in David Gerrold's *Deathbeast* (1978), about a tragic safari hunt to the Late Cretaceous stalked by a vicious warm-blooded *Tyrannosaurus*, protagonist/guide Loevil muses about changing future history by their actions in the past—through the killing of prehistoric organisms. He decides, "History wouldn't be changed ... there'd been too many tests and simulations. Someone else would end up being someone's great umpteenth-great-great-grandfather—even the genetic loss was unimportant. A specific set of genes existed only for a single generation; it would be lost in just a few quick shuffles of the deck of chromosomes."[49]

In R. Garcia y Robertson's 1992 novella *The Virgin and the Dinosaur*, a scientific safari time-traveling team avail themselves of the latest in astrophysical theory—relying on the Hell Creek wormhole through space-time into the Late Cretaceous.[50] In physicist Geoffrey A. Landis' "Embracing the Alien" (1992), space voyagers return to the Earth's K-T boundary epoch, sixty-five million years ago, after plunging into a black hole. Upon their arrival, one of Landis' space-time travelers echoes the butterfly effect, cautioning, "*Don't* harm any of the animals you encounter! A change in history at this point could have severe consequences millions of years hence."[51] And in Robert J. Sawyer's superb 1994 novel *End of An Era*, we learn the Huang Effect, a principle facilitating travel to more remote ages in time because it takes exponentially more energy to travel backward to more recent ages. In fact, a postulated trip to within the last few decades would "require the harnessed energy of a small nova." Here, Sawyer pays homage to Bradbury's "A Sound of Thunder," in his tale about a pair of paleontologists who move backward in time 64.7 million years ago to the Late Cretaceous, K-T boundary event in their time machine named the *Sternberger*.

> As a boy, I'd read a short story by Ray Bradbury called "The Sound of Thunder" [sic]. It told
> of a time traveler who had stepped on a butterfly in the Mesozoic, and that one event—the
> loss of that butterfly—had cascaded down the eons to result in a different future. Well, we

Time safari guides lead an intrepid company into deadly combat in the Cretaceous Period with the "Deathbeast" in David Gerrold's gripping 1978 novel. For more on this title, see the Appendix. (Illustration after painting by Lariano by *Prehistoric Times* editor Mike Fredericks, reproduced with permission.)

knew now that small events like that do have a big consequence. Chaos theory tells us that the flapping of a butterfly's wing in China really does determine whether it later rains in New York.... But Ching-Mei said we didn't have to worry about any of that. The *Sternberger* was anchored to its launch point back in the sky over the Red Deer River. Her equations said that it would return there, regardless of what we did back here. She'd talked in terms I only half understood about the many-worlds interpretation of quantum physics, saying that our future would be safe.[52]

Ultimately their startling adventure results in "the future making the past what it must have been," thereby collapsing the universe's wave function to its proper state.[53]

And in Will Hubbell's pair of novels *Cretaceous Sea* (2002) and *Sea of Time* (2004), the "timestream" is viewed as a continuum. Future realities may be altered by travelers to past ages, provided their impact is sufficiently significant.[54]

All of history exists simultaneously. That is why time travel is possible. The past, present, and future are relative to your location.... Since there is only one [timestream], if it changes, we perceive the new version of history as having always been that way.... Entropy causes the timestream to have a current. The past flows toward the future.... It takes an extremely power-ful phenomenon to alter the course of time.... Stick your hand in a river, and you disturb it.... Water is displaced. Ripples form. Yet a few feet downward, nothing is different. Throw a boul-der in the current and the changes are greater, yet the river doesn't veer in a new direction. Time is the same way; it's not easy to alter.... History follows the optimal course.... It will always return to it whenever possible.[55]

Furthermore, excessive movement through time destabilizes the space-time continuum, and it's impossible to revisit the moment when a time traveler died in the past.

TIME SAFARI CULTURE: LIFE AND DEATH

While as noted previously, 1950s time travel expeditions into prehistory somberly cast shadows of the Cold War, two time travel safari themes have emerged in recent years: (1) the theme of artists experiencing prehistory, and (2) becoming an eyewitness to contingency, such as dinosaur extinctions. Such themes reflect 1980s popular emphasis on the well-publicized mass extinction theories and, secondarily, growing interest in paleoart—i.e., the restoration of prehistoric life. Here we have a merging of life and death, profoundly extend-ing Bradbury's artistically interwoven visions of ecology and multiplicity.

If certain dinosaurs can be regarded as monsters, then powerful forces engineering their extermination must be regarded as monstrous indeed!

The year 1978 saw publication of Bob Buckley's short story "The Runners," involving a more scientifically oriented safari to the Late Cretaceous period. By then, writers' inter-ests were being directed to another class of theropod—"raptors," which were more intelli-gent and cunning than *T. rex*, and carried such profound evolutionary potential, if only their world hadn't ended so abruptly. Buckley's tale features the relatively intelligent "dro-maeosaur" *Stenonychosaurus* (now *Troodon*), a raptor. After surveying the ancient Alberta land-scape, the protagonist stumbles upon a brooding *Troodon* female. When Rogers—the team astronomer—discovers that a star some two light years distant from our solar system has gone supernova, the team members realize the horrible implications. Within a year, as the earth's atmosphere is irradiated from space, "Only the smallest forms will survive....

Turtles, snakes, lizards, crepuscular mammals, fish. Creatures that tend to hide in the ground by day, or night, or are shielded by water. Anything larger than a dog that stays continually out in the open will find itself fighting cold and radiation sickness."[56] Blatantly against the rules, the expedition returns to their present bearing the nesting *Troodon*'s egg clutch. Like their intelligence, the future looks bright for *Troodon*.

Undoubtedly, the central science news story of the 1980s decade concerning (though not exclusively limited to) dinosaurs was the sensational mass extinctions theory advanced by Walter and Luis Alvarez, Helen Michel and Frank Asaro.[57] Their theory that a six-mile-diameter asteroid collided with our planet sixty-five million years ago in the Late Cretaceous, throwing up a sunlight-blocking dust cloud into the stratosphere which cooled temperatures globally for a geologically brief episode, leading to ecological devastation and extinctions of many marine and terrestrial organisms (plant, vertebrate and invertebrate), seemed "heretical" but was actually a sound theory offering workable scientific predictions. It was also the very essence of science fiction; it really got our juices churning! Naturally then, the return of Halley's comet in early 1986 and the growing threat of "nuclear winter" and globally extensive pollution caused by technological man carried more relevance to mankind. We began to see ourselves and threatened ecosystems cast in the dinosaur fate, no less fragile than the once mighty dinosaurs.

The overwhelming impact of this well-publicized controversy on scientific discourse, popular opinion, human philosophy and its daily influence on human imagination cannot be overstated. Future science historians may well have reason to view this episode as a revolution in earth science. Associating astronomical catastrophes with extinctions contributed substantially to the rising popularity of dinosaurian paleontology.[58] One of the earliest time travel adventure tales capturing the furor over mass extinctions and impact-caused ecological devastation was Peter Lerangis' interactive *Time Machine 22: Last of the Dinosaurs* (1988), where the book itself—replete with numerous illustrations by paleoartist Douglas Henderson—is the time machine.[59]

Fueled by such developments, writers crafted ingenious means for penetrating into the Cretaceous where time travelers ironically *cause* K-T boundary extinctions, unwittingly, as a consequence of their observations and actions. The last segment of David Drake's *Tyrannosaur*, for example, pleasingly offers an unusual twist on the theme. An asteroid didn't cause the dinosaurs' extermination sixty-five million years ago, after all, but (as paleontologist Robert Bakker suggested in 1986), disease instead. Except Bakker never speculated that the dinosaur-extinguishing illness—*ornithosis*, which sometimes afflicts modern birds—would be spread from the twentieth century, or that the disease would be borne by an afflicted tyrannosaur returned to the Cretaceous by the time safari team for sport. As did the Martian invaders in H.G. Wells's *The War of the Worlds* (1897), in Drake's tale, dinosaurs—which had built no resistance to our microbes—readily succumb to them. So it was the time safari itself which ended an era. And in Robert J. Sawyer's *End of an Era*, by fighting a Late Cretaceous dinosaur invasion threatening their future course of reality, two paleontologist time travelers who endeavor to observe what caused the extinctions ironically alter the past and hence their future in a parallel universe by *causing* the great dinosaur extinction.

L. Sprague de Camp's "The Big Splash" (1992) is the event Reginald Rivers considered his closest call.[60] Harvard and Yale scientists George Romero and Sterling Featherstone, respectively, enlist the Time Safaris team to take them back to the terminal Cretaceous in order to settle the debate over whether dinosaurs died out in the aftermath of the eruption of "super-volcanoes," or as a result of Enyo's (the name of the asteroid) impact. Also along for the ride are an artist, Jon O'Connor, and big game hunter Clarence Todd. CalTech Astronomer Einar Haupt joins the team to search the Cretaceous heavens for the asteroid. The plan is to travel back to the St. Louis, Missouri area, around sixty-six million years ago, and then move forward in ten-year jumps, making the appropriate measurements at each horizon, until they witness the event. Then, Haupt finds Enyo 800,000 miles distant, on an earth-intercepting course, due for impact in three or four days.

Meanwhile, O'Connor is busily painting Cretaceous landscapes—that is, until Enyo plunges into the sea near the Yucatan's east coast, south of their observing station, creating the most vivid, preternatural landscape imaginable. Painting a picture with words, de Camp narrates:

> The spot disappeared below the horizon, but almost at once a glow sprang up in the southeast. The glow of the coming sunrise in the east was already quite bright, but it was if two suns were rising at the same time, almost a right angle apart. The normal sunrise went on at its usual leisurely pace; but the other one brightened much faster. Then there was a perfect blaze of light from south-by-east. I shan't say it was brighter than a million suns; but for a few seconds it made the true rising sun in the east look like a mere candle.... The bright light faded, but then followed something the like of which I had never seen. A kind of illuminated dome thrust up over the horizon. This thing went up and up, becoming the top of a vast single column. It was of mixed colors, mostly red. Along the top it was a dark red, with a kind of ragged appearance, as if made of a million separate jets of steam or water or lava. Further down the column, the color brightened to a brilliant yellow at the base, and little blue flashes of lightning played all over the surface of the whole fantastic thing.[61]

And perhaps predictably, as the shock wave nears, a meat-eating raptor dinosaur *Stenonychosaurus* (i.e., *Troodon*), chased off from a cadaver by larger theropods, flees into the camp, leaping into the time chamber just as it launches toward Present.

Decades ago, archaeologist P. Schuyler Miller (1912–1974) wrote a story, revealing that artist Charles R. Knight's paintings of prehistoric life were so realistic because he availed himself of a time travel device whereby he could see the living animals.[62] This extraordinary idea was emulated for *T. rex: Back to the Cretaceous* (USA, Imax Corporation, 1998), in which Knight, played by actor Tuck Mulligan, is a character in the film who travels backward in time where he paints prehistoric wildlife. Here, young Allie, daughter of paleontologist Dr. Haden, undergoes a trip to the Late Cretaceous which turns out to be more than imaginary. Allie's school paper hypothesis that *Tyrannosaurus* laid clutches of eggs is doubted by her father. In a dreamlike state, Allie is transported to the past, where she has conversations with Knight, who is painting dinosaurs from life. He encourages Allie not to yield on her hypothesis until she's given it a fair shake. Ultimately, Allie proves her hypothesis when she notices an *Ornithomimus* (easily mistaken for a *Troodon*) stealing eggs from what turns out to be a *T. rex* nest. Then the K-T asteroid hits, *T. rex* dies, and the North American continent is covered in impact ash.

In Hubbell's *Cretaceous Sea*, dinosaur paleontologist Rick Clements is tempted into taking a time travel journey from his present year in 2050 to the Late Cretaceous. His dream of witnessing live dinosaurs soon becomes anyone's worst nightmare vacation. For the time machine is really an observation device for recording the K-T impact event, sixty-five million years ago. Rick deciphers the meaning of a strange set of fluctuating symbols found on a wall of their station; this device is really a *clock*, set to countdown the time remaining to impact, and doom. Rick and a woman named Constance are caught in an ordeal likened to eternal hell on earth. For example, Constance subsists for days underneath a ghastly, rotting *T. rex* corpse which becomes her source of food. With Rex extinguished, now the darkened, impoverished planet is ruled by predatory "nightstalkers," feathered, raptor dinosaurs which in more prosperous times formerly preyed on herds of three-horned dinosaurs, or rooted out small mammals from their burrows. Now Rick, Constance and follow traveler Joe find themselves hunted by the cunning, adaptable nightstalkers.

In Bradbury tradition, stemming from "A Sound of Thunder," time safaris usually target the Late Cretaceous where an obligatory encounter usually ensues with *Tyrannosaurus*. Whether they realize it or not, writers adhere to the "formula" in homage to Bradbury.[63]

Science fiction's "transition" from Rex to Raptor would appear complete with Hubbell's thought-provoking novel. While Rex ruled for nearly a century, now, besides Rex, the unsettling Raptors and their scaly brood chill us to the marrow.

IMPOSSIBILITY OF TIME SAFARIS: A MULTIPLICITY OF WORLDS

Clarke professed the impossibility of time travel in a 1960s essay, "Things that can never be done."[64] In another article Clarke speculated why time travelers from the future haven't reached our age, "by suggesting that Time is a spiral; though we may not be able to move along it, we can perhaps hop from coil to coil, visiting so many millions of years apart that there is no danger of embarrassing collisions between cultures. Big game hunters from the future may have wiped out the dinosaurs, but the age of *Homo sapiens* may lie in a blind region which they cannot reach."[65]

As Steven Utley illustrated in several of his Silurian Tales, time travel into the past, per se, may be utterly impossible, echoing Clarke's concerns, but not for reasons that perplexed Wells and annoyed sci-fi fans of the 1930s. In his 2002 tale "Walking in Circles," a scientist declares upon their materialization along a Silurian shore, four hundred and twenty million years ago,

> You cannot travel directly backward into our own Earth's own prehistoric past. You can only move diagonally, into some parallel Earth's Paleozoic. Therefore, nothing you do in this parallel Earth's Paleozoic can make any difference here in our proper matrix, our twenty-first century of the Christian era, *the present....* Time travel in the sense you people use the term violates the laws of physics ... a gross contradiction of logic.... There is a virtually infinite selection of these alternate worlds.[66]

The question, "Which is the 'real' universe?" is meaningless. Furthermore, when the scientists supposedly return from the Silurian Period to the present, they aren't returning to same world line they originally departed from.[67]

"Walking in Circles" and another of Utley's similarly themed imaginative tales, "Treading the Maze," are consistent with and fortify Bradbury's concept of past time travel, as there is no safe Path to guide, minimize or confine the actions of time travelers visiting the Silurian in Utley'stories. Utley's Siluria tales exemplify how the universe splits when humans interfere with the past, which is exactly what should happen according to quantum physics.

Incidentally, before Utley, Stephen Baxter provided another example of *mutiplicity*, in his attempt to update (although not improve stylistically upon) Wells' *The Time Machine* (1895). In Baxter's meaty "sequel" to Wells's seminal tale, a "quantum voyage" titled *The Time Ships* (1995), Wells's time traveler slides into many parallel universes, including a Paleocene epoch setting where he is menaced by the giant flightless bird *Diatryma*, the large croc *Pristichampus*, and a nuclear bomb.[68]

FINAL THOUGHTS

In this chapter the most noteworthy examples have been literary in nature. Curiously, despite the self-evident nature of dinosaurs associated with the time travel idea, few *movies* have exploited this connection. It seems the motion picture industry—relying on, emulating and milking the *Jurassic Park* "cash cowasaurus"—has found it challenging to keep up with the dizzying variety and pace of ideas in science fiction pulps and novels.[69]

As noted, beginning in the 1980s, an important consequence of impact theory was "contingency," where philosophers and scientists—Stephen Jay Gould prominently among them—speculated, "What if the impact event never happened, and the dinosaurs instead enjoyed another sixty-five million prosperous years of evolution?"[70] In other words, instead of a mere butterfly being extinguished, what would be the ecological consequences if somehow the Path leading into prehistory became altered in an extraordinary way? One speculative byproduct of this thought experimentation was paleontologist Dale Russell's "Dinosauroid," a hypothetical, technological dinosaur-man, sculpted in 1981 by Ron Seguin.[71] As we'll see in the next chapter, writers quickly thrust alien-looking dinosauroids into modern or futuristic parallel world settings where the K-T boundary asteroid was deflected from terrestrial impact and tool-using dinosaurs developed technological prowess, or even space-faring capabilities beyond our own.

CHAPTER 6

Dino-Trek

BACKGROUND

To our knowledge the only real dinosaur ever in orbit was the theropod genus *Coelophysis*, a fossilized skull of which was transferred from the space shuttle *Endeavor* to the Mir Space Station on January 22, 1998.[1] Yet that hasn't prevented writers of fantastic fiction from launching a Dino-Trek to the stars, populating vast and unknown corridors of the universe with many imaginative varieties of Earth's prehistoria. In order to access these most curious fauna, man must boldly go where dinosaurs have gone before!

Since the dawn of our Space Age, outer-space worlds have become traditional environments for Earth's prehistoric (extra-) terrestrial life forms. In some cases, alien prehistoria travel to Earth, where they cause hysteria, and in others human space travelers encounter indigenous organisms recognizable as "prehistoric" on other planets. Usually, conflict erupts between man and the extraterrestrial fauna that can only be resolved through ridding outer space (or the invaded Earth) of the reptilian (interplanetary) horde. Reflecting recent paleontological developments, intelligent dinosaurian forms often exemplify technological prowess or even cultural mores surpassing those of twentieth-century man.

When confronted by the prospect of cases of dinosaurs from outer space—or "exodinosaurs"—questions abound.[2] In the first place, how did the dinosaurs get to these other worlds? Or conversely, how did they reach Earth's Mesozoic Era from their home worlds?

What should an exodinosaur look like for it to be recognizable as a dinosaur? Should it truly resemble a terrestrial dinosaur, and if so, from which geological period? Or, given that exodinosaurs have no obvious organic ties to earth, wouldn't one expect them to have evolved different appearances and morphologies altogether?

In surveying this popular fictional form, three general patterns or schemes tried by creators of outer-space dinosaurian fauna become apparent. First, the dinosaurs and other prehistoric fauna indigenous to other worlds seem identical to or closely mimic Earth's Mesozoic life, due to presumed parallel evolutionary and paleoecological processes thought to have prevailed in the alien environments. Secondly, the dinosaurs are sometimes less recognizable as "dinosaurs" per se, even though science fiction writers and critics consider them to be loosely "dinosaurian"—or at least reptilian—in nature.

And, finally, dinosaurs can sometimes be entirely unknown to science, not simply because of unique evolutionary histories prevalent on their home planets, but either because they're not of *our* universe or since they escaped earth before their extinction here. In these latter cases, alien dinosaurs are often portrayed as intelligent evolutionary descendants of the latest dinosaurs which expired on Earth. It is with consideration of these interplanetary menaces where we must face the most unnerving evolutionary question of all: "Are the dinosaurs gradually gaining human attributes, or is mankind becoming more dinosaur-like?"

There have been numerous films and television programs about space travelers encountering prehistoric animals on other worlds. Typically, as in *Along the Moonbeam Trail* (1920), *On the Comet* (1970), and *Planet of Dinosaurs* (1978), indigenous prehistoric animals are noticeably terrestrial in appearance, that is, as known to contemporary science.[3] But as evident in the classic scaly monsters featured in *Twenty Million Miles to Earth* (1957), or *It! The Terror from Beyond Space* (1958), exodinosaurs of the movies can also take on quite unfamiliar forms. In *Planet of Storms* (*Planeta Burg*, 1962), Russian cosmonauts encounter *both* traditional-looking prehistoric reptiles and strange lizard-men approximating the human form (due to "suitmation") on Venus.[4] As we'll see in this chapter, avid readers are in store for a far more diverse array of prehistoria in classic literature.

So where does one draw the line as to what is and what isn't "exodinosaurian"? Surely there must be some grounds for exclusivity. An answer lies in the scientific theory supporting the existence of such fauna in each tale, the subject of this chapter. While a traditional purpose of science fiction literature involving or invoking prehistoric life is to provide a means of escapism from a "claustrophobic urban culture," ideas of evolution manifested in many such tales reflect mainstream pop culture. Classic stories such as these dazzle the mind with contemporary ideas about how life can or could evolve not only on earth but elsewhere in the cosmos.

Lost Worlds in Space

At first, prehistoric animals native to other planets could be regarded as inhabiting primitive lost worlds, although in outer-space settings. But doesn't the idea of dinosaurs in outer space seem more than a tad incongruous? Well, just consider—I mean, *alien dinosaurs*— what's cooler than that? Perhaps visual art reflecting contemporary science can further enlighten us.

For decades artists had pondered the possibilities of prehistoric animals being discovered on other planets. One vivid painting by Frank R. Paul (1884–1963), emblazoned on the back cover of the December 1945 *Fantastic Adventures* issue,[5] boggles our senses. We see human astronauts emerging from their spacecraft on a planet in the Aldebaran star system. The red-giant sun casts an ominous glow over the strange admixture of indigenous fauna— two gigantic allosaurs, giant Alley Oop–like humanoids and, in the distance, sauropod-like animals being ridden by the cavemen. A spaceman has already killed one allosaur with a laser rifle and is rescuing one of the cave men from the treacherous jaws of the other allosaur; blood issues from scaly corpses. Writer "Alexander Blade," a pseudonym for Edmund Hamilton (1904–1977), provides a generous caption for the scene.

> Artist Frank R. Paul, in painting his conception of what life might be like on a planet circling this giant red-sun ... does take into consideration the fact that the sun is capable of providing

light and warmth and life to a world that might conceivably be in the state Earth was 50,000 years ago (beg pardon, you geologists!) when the giant reptiles, the dinosauria, roamed the swamplands of a youthfully steaming earth. He has pictured a space ship from earth having landed on this primitive planet, and found, (here in subtle confirmation of an early legend of giant men on the earth at the time of the dinosaurs) eighteen foot humans contesting for supremacy with the towering reptiles whom they will eventually wipe out (if their history goes as Earth's did). These humans are regarding our heroes in much the same awe that our own giant prototypes might have regarded the visit of those "superhuman" beings from the "Ether" who came to Earth to set up our early religions.... In the background we see that the giant savages were not enemies to all the reptiles, but had actually tamed and subjugated certain types to use as beasts of burden and as steeds.... Mr. Paul has ably (more so than he realized) depicted here how the life of a world can be dominated by its environmental conditions. The red star, Aldebaran, can only produce such results as Mr. Paul has shown.[6]

Venus quickly became one of the earliest extraterrestrial habitats judged suitable for Mesozoic-like life. Few, for instance, may know that the earliest case of Venusian exodinosaurs was printed in Gustavus W. Pope's (1829–?) 1894 novel, *Romances of the Planets: N. 1, Journey to Mars*. In Pope's scientific romance, after being whisked out of the south polar sea to Mars, protagonist Tom Hallyard eventually is granted a tour of the Red Planet by the technologically advanced Martian race. In one scene the travelers see the twenty-foot-long "Gnakrip-Tihogos, or Alligator bat,"

> ... covered with black scales. Its neck was like a serpent's; its head and jaws like an alligator's, and armed with sharp teeth. Its wings were shaped like those of a bat with long hooks. Its hind legs were like those of a stork, with long curved talons. Its forked tail waved to and fro like a whip lash. As the hideous creature flapped its wings, its eyes blazing like coals of fire, it resembled one of the dragons of ancient fable.[7]

The creature clearly resembles contemporary views of terrestrial pterodactyls. It is explained that alligator bats were brought from *Venus* and transplanted to the Martian Zoological Gardens where they are used to "illustrate our studies in ancient natural history." While a fight spectacle soon erupts between some of the winged monsters, rationale for why pterodactyls would be found, in turn, on Venus is absent. The alligator bats are exodinosaurian paleoprops.

Until the early 1960s, scientists speculated that Venus had a watery, tropical climate due to its relative proximity to the sun and as we know—or at least as we think we know—where there's liquid water there could be life. Furthermore, even though by the twentieth century LaPlace's theory for planetary formation had been superseded by other astronomical theories, a corollary of the nebular hypothesis was that the oldest planets in the solar system were those furthest from the sun. Thus Mars was judged older than the Earth, and Venus was thought to be younger. How much younger? Possibly still in its geological infancy, perhaps still in its "Mesozoic phase"? During the 1930s, it wasn't difficult to imagine Venus as a veritable paradise for what were then perceived as cold-blooded, jungle-loving dinosaurs.

Our fascination with the possibility of Venusian dinosaurs perhaps culminated in the late 1950s with another dramatic portrayal.

During the pioneering stage of our space program, the March–May 1959 issue of *Space Journal: Dedicated to the Astro-sciences* featured on its covers Harry Lange's painting *Interstellar Space Ship Astra-Alpha Lands on Planet 'X.'* Here, dinosaurs from the Triassic and Jurassic vignettes of R. Zallinger's 1947 *Age of Reptiles* mural have been inserted into an extraterres-

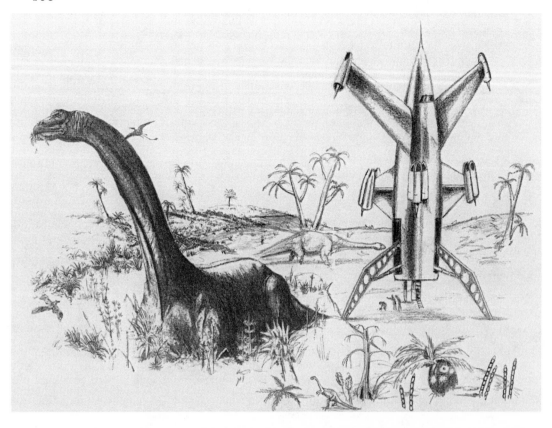

Even by the late 1950s, based on astronomical and geological theories, it was still popularly thought that astronauts *might* encounter dinosaurs on Venus. See text for further details. (Illustration prepared for this volume by *Prehistoric Times* editor and dinosaur artist Mike Fredericks; reproduced with permission.)

trial setting, replete with spacecraft and astronauts exploring the strange world. As the back cover caption informed, "the probability should earthman's first interstellar space travelers find a planet with near-earth environmental conditions, the planet would not be in the same evolutionary stage as Earth. This rendering shows the destination planet in its Cretaceous period of development. The monsters created by nature and man stand in stark contrast."[8]

Cretaceous period of development? A planet with near-earth environmental conditions? Well, it's apparent that Harry Lange's Planet X was inspired by contemporary views of Venus' "prehistoric swamps." An article in this issue, coauthored by Helmut Hoeppner and B. Spencer Isbell, addressing how means of interstellar might be achieved, concluded that, "In the event that planet 'X' is in a stage of evolution younger than Earth, then the scene illustrated [i.e., by Lange] may well be what the interstellar Space pioneers will first see when they arrive on planet 'X.'"[9] And geologist Philip N. Shockey's accompanying article "The ultimate necessity of space travel" suggested that on an Earthlike planet, "other things being similar, the colonists might encounter an environment like that on Earth around 100 million years B.C., when reptiles ruled the land. Dinosaurs, flying reptiles, and other terrestrial and marine animals and plants might confront the colonists who, through geologic deduction, would be prepared for such a spectacle."[10] Yes, even by the late 1950s real scientists still enjoyed speculating about such incredible things.

Certainly, then, Earth's sister planet Venus could be viewed as having a prehistoric ambiance, given that it may have formed from the solar disk gradually after Mars and Earth had already become planets. It wasn't too much of a stretch for imaginative sci-fi writers to envision the evolution of life on Venus (or on other similar planets) as proceeding in a life-through-time fashion along a "ladder of progress" parallel to Earth's own geological history.[11]

Other contrasting, although more accurate glimpses as to how contemporary scientists viewed Venus can be found in physicist Joseph Harold Rush's *The Dawn of Life* (1957). Rush rained on everybody's parade, however, noting, "Here, then, is an exciting picture: an earth-like planet, swathed in clouds over a steaming tropical land, suggesting the luxuriant vegetation of the fern forests of the Carboniferous Period, or the teeming life in our tropical rain forests today. Disappointingly, the picture stopped being exciting about 1932.... Venus ... appears to be devoid of the factor that we decided is most determinative for the development of life—water.... Instead of the sultry jungle scene that was formerly pictured, we have to think of an utter desert, a desiccated, sand-blasted rocky surface over which a sickly remnant of sunlight glows through a perpetual dust storm driven by winds of hurricane velocities."[12] While the accuracy of Rush's vision would be confirmed following Carl Sagan's theoretical treatment and Russia's successful *Venera* landings of the early 1960s, writers of the 1930s and 1940s couldn't help availing themselves of Venus's captivating organic possibilities.

In an anthology he edited, *Before the Golden Age*, Isaac Asimov refers to Stanley G. Weinbaum (1902–1935), a most influential sci-fi writer of the mid–1930s. Asimov claims, "After Weinbaum's coming, there was a period when it seemed that every writer was turning out stories of strange life-forms. Stories became extraterrestrial travelogues, though no one ever did it as well as Weinbaum. When I began writing sci-fi, I was not immune either."[13] Even though Weinbaum didn't write about exodinosaurs, anyone who's tuned in to *The Outer Limits*, *Twilight Zone*, or *Star Trek*, or who has enjoyed the *Star Wars* saga, can understand the appeal of "strange life-forms." Yet, prehistoric fauna continued to inhabit Venus long after Weinbaum inspired his colleagues. Let's proceed with four tales from this period involving Venusian "dinosaurs," beginning with one in which—upon careful reading, perhaps—Gojira's origins may be seen.

A VENUSIAN "BEAST"

For over two decades I'd been intrigued about a back-cover image on Donald F. Glut's *The Dinosaur Scrapbook: The Dinosaur in Amusement Parks, Comic Books, Fiction, History, Magazines, Movies, Museums, Television* (1980).[14] The illustration, borrowed from the front cover of an "extinct" science fiction magazine, the April 1940 issue of *Thrilling Wonder Stories*, shows an impossibly huge horned (ceratosaur-like) dinosaur crashing through the Capitol Building. A warplane fires upon the monster from above, while below, cannon and a heat ray emanating from a disk-shaped laser device blast the beast. The story mirrored a now-familiar movie monster theme, although over a decade would pass before Gojira's creation. So, is this archaic 1940 *Thrilling Wonder Stories* issue really where it all began, i.e., where for

A composite of two lesser known, yet significant Venusian dinosaurs. At left is Henry Kuttner's "Beast" from his 1940 short story "Beauty and the Beast," and at right we spy the "Whip" from Arthur K. Barnes' 1937 tale "The Hothouse Planet." See text for further details on these selections. (Illustration prepared for this volume by *Prehistoric Times* editor and dinosaur artist Mike Fredericks; reproduced with permission.)

the first time in print a science fiction author conceived a carnivorous dino-monster attacking a metropolitan setting?

The story in question, titled "Beauty and the Beast," was written by distinguished science fiction writer Henry Kuttner (1915–1958).[15] It was especially thrilling to read the word "Beast" in his title, for, to me, it represented continuity. About a decade earlier, plans to bring an incredible "beauty and the beast" tale (*King Kong*) to the silver screen were scarcely underway. Following publication of Kuttner's tale, another decade would pass before moviegoers cowered from sight of *the* quintessential "Beast" attacking New York City, a quadrupedal *Rhedosaurus* emerging all the way from 20,000 fathoms, Ray Bradbury's "deeps." Because we've all been accustomed to movie fare and extraordinary advertisement/poster art of the past half century featuring famed dinosaurian monsters stomping through our cities, today, Brown's front cover image, inspired by Kuttner's story, may seem stereotyped. However, under contemporary standards, both Brown's illustration and the story which inspired it were on the "Kutt"-ing edge.

Kuttner's "Beauty and the Beast," a welcome surprise, seems conceptually similar to one of Ray Harryhausen's stories. No, not *The Beast from 20,000 Fathoms* (1953), but instead more like *Twenty Million Miles to Earth* (1957), perhaps with a little of John Wyndham's *The Day of the Triffids* (1951) woven in for good measure.[16]

A rather unscrupulous farmer, one Jared Kirth, observes the crash landing of a rocket in a nearby New England forest. Turns out the rocket had been manned by astronaut Jay Arden, who had been presumed lost in space for several months. Arden had attempted the first interplanetary voyage to Venus. Kirth's inspection of the damaged hull reveals Arden's corpse, a small gem-shaped object, a notebook, some photographs detailing archaeological ruins from a lost Venusian civilization, and many seeds, all of which are brought to his farm.

Reading Arden's notes, Kirth learns that his "gem" is really an egg, which Kirth manages to hatch in an incubator. A small reptile shaped like a miniature "kangaroo" (an apt pre–1950s description for a theropod) emerges, which grows at an alarming rate (like the reptilian alien "Ymir" did in *Twenty Million Miles to Earth*). And as the creature grows, its "racial memory" stirs, "the first faint chords of memory vibrated ... memory of a previous life, half forgotten...." Meanwhile, from the Venusian seeds, Kirth successfully grows bright, beautiful flowers, which are a welcome source of income. Kirth intends to sell his carnivorous Beast when fully grown too ... if only its voluminous growth would ever cease!

The reptilian Beast is an intelligent animal, a remnant from Venus' ruined civilization, now learning to understand English, although without vocal cord capability. Initiating communication, it relies on the universal language—mathematics. The Beast wants to warn Kirth and Earth's inhabitants of a cosmic danger which wiped out Venus' reptilian race: "Death ... doom ... nothing could save them from the plague that had come from outer space." But nervous Kirth presumes the Beast's communication efforts are an attack and so he shoots it. Beast heads for the hills to hide. For the next few months,

> It grew unimaginably. Some effect of the Sun's actinic rays, not filtered as on cloud-veiled Venus, made the Beast grow far beyond the size it had been on Venus eons ago. It grew larger than the vastest dinosaur that ever stalked through the swamps of Earth's dawn, a titanic, nightmare juggernaut out of the Apocalypse. It looked like a walking mountain....

Soon it is attacked by planes, dropping bombs, yet only leaving superficial wounds.

Beast makes it way to Washington, its last-ditch effort to warn us of the looming danger. Bombed by planes, bombarded by cannon fire, Beast storms clumsily through Washington toward the Capitol.

> In the streets men and women fought and struggled and fled from the oncoming monster that towered against the sky, colossal and horrible.... A mighty forepaw reached out. The Beast had forgotten Earth's gravity ... the massive paw crashed through the Capitol's dome! Simultaneously the heat ray flashed out blindingly. It swept up and bathed the Beast in flaming brilliance. For a heartbeat the tableau held, the colossus towering above the nation's Capitol. Then the Beast fell....

Now in its death throes, readers learn of "Beauty," far more terrible than Beast. For Beauty is born of alien seed, the brilliant flowers which will release a deadly virus in about a month when the petals fall, "and then, all life on Earth will be destroyed, as it was on Venus, and nothing will exist on all the planet but bright flowers and the ruins of cities."

Notice how many elements of the modern rampaging dino-monster-on-the-loose sci-fi tale were all in place by the time of Kuttner's 1940 story: warplanes, a futuristic heat ray used to defend the city, buildings toppled by an enormous dino-monster as it relentlessly advances, a fleeing, screaming crowd, and a tragic demise for the ominous, yet misunderstood behemoth, which has been created (this time in an incubator) by humans meddling tragically once more with nature. As many of you realize, this wasn't the first time prehistoric monsters had been portrayed in such manner.[17]

Decades before Doyle, French astronomer Camille Flammarion (1842–1925), in his popular 1886 volume *Le Monde avant creation de l'homme, origines de la terre, origines de la vie de l'humanite*,[18] published an image of a gigantic *Iguanodon* as it would have appeared in a modern city setting, anticipating a "Godzillean" pose of a century later. And two decades before Flammarion's entry, George du Maurier (1834–1896) satirized the unsettling if not entirely nightmarish impact of prehistoric life on human psyche in a *Punch* cartoon (1868). Du Maurier illustrated a helpless little boy with snow-caked feet fleeing in terror up a typical English city street from a hideous Mammoth distortion. In 1992, Martin J.S. Rudwick stated this cartoon "is a striking early example of the ways in which fearsome dinosaurs have functioned ever since, serving psychological and perhaps cultural purposes of unfathomable depth."[19]

To date, I haven't encountered any story involving a theropod-like fantasy carnivorous dino-monster (like the *Rhedosaurus*, Ymir and Gojira) attacking cities, older than Kuttner's 1940 tale. So, is it possible that Kuttner's tale, or Howard V. Brown's striking illustration on the cover of the magazine, somehow influenced other writers and artists, leading however indirectly to further stories and imagery which have proved more lasting?

Today, dramatic imagery such as on the cover of the April 1940 *Thrilling Wonder Stories* issue would be regarded as visual cliché, even though for its time, Brown's artistry may have been prototypical.[20] During the nineteenth century, science fiction literature employing prehistoric animals usually relied on plesiosaurs, ichthyosaurs, pterosaurs and Cenozoic mammals, rather than the less-popular dinosaurs. Man's fictional encounters with such fauna typically took place in remote places, in prehistory itself, or even inside the earth. *Dinosaur* science fiction tales, however, are largely a product of the twentieth century, with the idea of ferocious dino-monsters menacing urban areas maturing during the World War II/Cold War era. Kuttner's neglected tale, involving a spectacular *Venusian* beast, presaging those to come in classic B films, recorded our first battle of Earth versus an exodinosaur.

EXODINOSAUR ZOOLOGY (I)

Sometimes it's difficult recognizing alien "dinosaurs." Usually, if they're reptilian or somehow saurian, that's sufficient to categorize them as exodinosaurs, but other times it's more obvious. A few examples will exemplify the problematic nature of identifying exodinosaurian biology.

Some nondescript cases are so sketchy that it's hard to judge. For instance, John Jacob Astor IV (1864–1912) wrote about reptile birds, saurians and "giant reptiles of prehistory" as inhabitants of Jupiter in his 1894 novel, *A Journey in Other Worlds: A Romance of the Future*.[21] In the prologue to Dan Simmons' outstanding novel *Hyperion* (1989), we read of "occasional vague, reptilian shapes [which] ... blunder into the interdiction field, cry out, and then crash away through indigo mists." These inhabit a "forest of giant gymnosperms." Robert Silverberg discusses the "Worsel" of E.E. Smith's (1890–1965) "Lensman" series, claiming, "Intelligent reptiles have long been a staple of science fiction, going back as far as E.E. Smith's

Lensman novels of sixty years ago, one of whose heroes is the fearless Worsel of Velantia, 'a nightmare's horror of leathern wings, of viciously fanged jaws, of frightfully taloned feet.' Smith ignores the question of Worsel's metabolism, but surely a four-chambered heart must have beaten in that saurian bosom."[22] However, a picture of winged Worsel appearing on a more recent add-on to the series written by David A. Kyle hardly appears pterosaurian, instead closely resembling the Grimalkin of Venus, discussed below.

Besides Kuttner's "Beast," contemporary writers Isaac Asimov, Arthur K. Barnes (1911–1969), and "G.H. Irwin" each conceived Venusian monstrosities meeting the loose zoological definition of exodinosaur. First, Barnes penned "The Hothouse Planet," featured in the October 1937 *Thrilling Wonder Stories*.[23] Barnes' tale showcased glamorous "interplanetary huntress" Gerry Carlyle (a female "Frank Buck" of the future), who is interested in capturing specimens for the Interplanetary Zoo. In one segment her team dispatches a Venusian version of a *T. rex* named a "Whip." "Fully fifty feet the monster towered into the mist, standing upright on two massive legs reminiscent of the extinct terrestrial *Tyrannosaurus rex*. A set of short forelegs were equipped with hideously short claws. The head was long and narrow resembling a wolf's snout, with large ears and slavering fangs." "Hothouse Planet" rated two illustrations by Howard V. Brown in the magazine—one on the front cover, both depicting the Whip attacking spacemen.[24]

Barnes stated on page 123 of the issue that "I have tried not to invent things that are too far removed from life as we know it on this Earth. The weird 'whip,' for instance, has its Earthly counterpart not only in the ant-eater, but in the sphinx-moth which sports a hoselike tongue a good deal longer than its own body." So evidently, there were no dinosaurian inspirations behind the Whip, although the depicted result certainly could lead one to believe otherwise. Regardless, imagine Gorgo (or Ogra), sporting their prominent ears, as also having a long, snake-like tongue added for good measure, described in the story as a "coiling sweep of flesh rope." That's the Whip.

Barnes' story is but one example of how the substantially warmer, presumably lush and swampy Venus could formerly be regarded as still being in the sultry Carboniferous or sometimes Mesozoic stage of development. Another is Isaac Asimov's "Half-Breeds on Venus." In fact, most would never have even regarded the "Centosaurs" described in Asimov's story as even approaching anything dinosaurian in nature—that is, until I saw the cover of the December 1940 *Astonishing* issue, in which the tale ran originally.[25] Despite their appearance, Asimov never suggests Centosaurs are dinosaurs in his story. Instead, they seem more like immense caterpillars, perhaps more akin to visions of H.G. Wells's *First Men in the Moon* "Moon calves" (1901), as they have twenty pairs of legs! But the two-hundred-foot-high beasts are also reptilian, so they may be exodinosaurian too. Interestingly, Barnes's, Asimov's and G. H. Irwin's (discussed below) tales are also exo-anthropological tales, involving the discovery and conservation of "lost" alien primate and amphibian-humanoid races known as "murri," telepathic "tweenies," and "Bunae," respectively.

Then there is the forty-foot-tall, winged "Grimalkin," described in G.H. Irwin's (pseudonym for Richard S. Shaver, 1907–1975) "Lair of the Grimalkin," published in the April 1948 *Fantastic Adventures*.[26] Appearing more or less like a winged dragon in three of Malcolm Smith's (1912–1966) spectacular illustrations, rather than truly pterosaur-like, the last living Grimalkin terrorizes colonists on Venus in the year 2020. Grimalkin is "a huge lizard with massive jaws and fangs, leathery wings, a long tail, and small forearms. The creature has three eyes as well as the power of "yarva" or telepathic "mind talk," which enables it to communicate telepathically with humans and the Bunae.[27] The legendary Grimalkin inhabits a noxious jungle swamp named "Despair," permeated by acid mists, and relies on a lost race of amphibious servants known as "Bunae," to do its awful bidding—finding sacrificial humanoids devoured by their great winged god.[28]

Venus has a distinctly reptilian fauna, one of which, the Grimalkin, is a legendary beast worshiped by the native green-skinned Venusians.[29] As on Earth, "Venusian mammals all show traces of reptilian origin." Colonists attempt to slay the beast by sliding a long spear over a cliff into its body. The wounded monster vengefully smashes through the roof of a plastic-domed city where it "gathered up a claw-ful of screaming, shrieking humans and mouthed them bloodily." Eventually the Grimalkin is bombed and dies.

EXODINOSAUR ZOOLOGY (II)

The distinctive dinosaurian nature of another traditional set of exodinosaurs is most obvious when they've evolved on Earth-like planets. Notable examples include novels by Anne McCaffrey (*Dinosaur Planet*, 1978), Donald F. Glut (*Spawn*, 1976), and short stories such as O'Neil De Noux's "Tyrannous and Strong" (2000) and Robert Silverberg's "Our Lady of the Sauropods" (1980, the significance of which shall be addressed in the next chapter).[30]

The premise behind Earth-like exodinosaurs is well stated in Sanz's *Starring T. rex!*

> To contemplate the possibility of the existence of dinosaurs on another planet (exodinosaurs) it is necessary to postulate that under similar conditions, the processes of organic evolution give rise to similar beings. This postulate means that on a planet that has a similar historical development and similar environments to that of Earth, the living organisms that arise over time will be similar.[31]

In O'Neil De Noux's gripping "Tyrannous and Strong" (*Isaac Asimov's Science Fiction*, Feb. 2000), following successful colonization of another world called Octavion, an aging recluse must protect his peaceful yet lonely existence from an invading *T. rex*. Noux's protagonist, MacIntyre, reflects, "While scientists like my father racked their brains, trying to discover why Octavion's dinosaurs are so similar to Earth's prehistoric beasts, we built a life. The scientists are no closer to solving this great riddle of the galaxy." At the climax, MacIntyre taunts a demonic Rex as it tumbles over a cliff, the majestic foe felled by its misunderstanding of a fundamental universal force—gravity.

In Anne McCaffrey's *Dinosaur Planet*, a xenobiology expedition abandoned on the planet Ireta encounters "real" dinosaurs mysteriously transplanted out of Earth's prehistory. However, the prehistoric animals' evolved five-fingered hands distinguishes them from terrestrial saurians. The team encounters a tyrannosaur, the "dawn horse" *Hyracotherium*, a flock of furry winged *Pteranodon*, hadrosaurs and a swamp-loving sauropod. After examining the animals' tissues, a chemist team member is hard-pressed to explain their existence on Ireta.

> It is patently obvious ... that someone has played a joke. Not necessarily on me, or us.... Those animals were planted here ... they didn't spring up in an independent evolution ... they *started* on Earth.... All you'd need is one common ancestor. Climate, food, terrain would bring about specialization over the millennia and the variety of types would evolve.... The possibilities are

infinite from one mutual ancestorx ... this is a splendid development. A planet that has remained in the Mesozoic condition for untold millions of years, and likely to remain so for unknown millennia longer.[32]

As in the case of "Tyrannous and Strong," circumstances surrounding Ireta's extraterrestrial dinosaur fauna aren't fully resolved in McCaffrey's novel, so we must probe further for comprehending the origins and nature of Earth-like exodinosaurs. Are Ireta's dinosaurs terrestrial-like because they evolved on Earth, yet remained thereafter in evolutionary stasis in Ireta's primitive ecosystem for another era of time? The mystery is resolved in McCaffrey's 1984 sequel, *Dinosaur Planet: Survivors*, where we learn that Ireta was established as a zoo, more or less like Glut intended in *Spawn*.[33]

Interestingly, as Glut is the only dinosaurologist as well as master dinosaur encyclopedist in this particular grouping of writers, here, for his potentially keener insights into exosauria, we'll focus on *Spawn*.

Departing Earth in the year 2149, space travelers have landed in the *J-17* rocket on the planet Dakka VII, an Earth-like world known to its sentient inhabitants as "Erigon." Erigon is in its Mesozoic stage of planetary evolution and the explorers commanded by Gene Bishop intend to obtain eggs of all the representative dinosaurian classes. These will be brought to Earth and incubated, and the growing animals will be placed in "Dino-World," a zoological park. Two paleontologists accompany the mission, David and Dian Grimsby. For them Erigon is a marvel because "we've been trying to piece together Earth's entire prehistory from incomplete fragments of bone, this moment is sheer ecstasy for us.... This is our first opportunity—the first any paleontologist has ever had, for that matter—to observe living dinosaurs.... And it doesn't matter that these saurians aren't quite the same as those that ruled our Mesozoic; they're close enough."[34]

How close is "close enough"?

Because by the twenty-second century man had overpopulated the planet and eradicated nearly all indigenous wildlife, for the sake of nostalgia and wonder, man has been ferrying alien fauna similar to Earth's extinct species (such as lions and elephants) back for public exhibition.

> Bishop had seen the faces of children and adults alike as they crowded and pushed through such famous wildlife parks as Africa-World and Asia-World to observe alien fauna that were similar to long-extinct Earth species. They could imagine what it had once been like on their own world, and it brought nostalgia and a conviction that if men had another chance, they'd do better the second time around. No one was too concerned with accuracy to complain that the "lions" of Africa-World had tiger stripes, or that the "elephants" of Asia-World had two sets of tusks.[35]

Yet, Erigon is the first world in the cosmos (besides Earth) where living examples of Earth's Mesozoic era have been identified.

Oddly enough, on Erigon, ruled by twin suns, there are representatives of all the suborders of Mesozoic saurians known to contemporary science, including plesiosaurs, ankylosaurs, flesh-eating carnosaurs, sauropods, horned dinosaurs, duck-billed dinosaurs, etc. However, there are notable differences. For example, carnosaurs have proportionally longer front limbs than did Earth's carnosaurs, ending with five digits, and a multi-horned styracosaur is found to also have thick ankylosaur-like armor plating covering its back. But while the dinosaurs rather resemble their extinct analogues on Earth, their behavior seems most peculiar. A congregation of Ireta's dinosaurs that should have been in fight-or-flight mode instead calmly observes the expedition when first encountered, until Dian notes that an "Allosaur" and a "Tyrannosaur," which are normally flesh-eaters, should be attacking the herbivores instead of communing with them. Then, almost as if conscious of her concerns, a carnosaur makes a feigned effort to bite one of the duckbills. Eventually it's discovered that these strange saurians are telepathic.

While exodinosaurs not resembling Earth's Mesozoic life so closely may have evolved according to adaptationist principles, those exodinosaurs which look most familiar to Earth's dinosaurian denizens must have inhabited planets most similar to Earth's prehistoric fauna. In *Spawn*, Glut proposes a parallel "evolutionary ladder" mimicking Earth's geological and organic history. But not only are extraterrestrial dinosaurs and other fauna from more recent ages found outside our solar system, but also *humanoid* forms. For, strictly in code with the anachronistic "lost worlds" theme prevalent throughout such tales, there's also a race of red-skinned cave-humans, who are psychologically enslaved by Erigon's telepathic saurians. Erigon's elepathic saurians recall Burroughs's race of Mahars in Pellucidar. After rescuing a female named "Leea" from a spined "Acrocanthosaur" endowed with hypnotic powers, Bishop is smitten with her beauty.[36]

Glut's story is one of the earliest involving more or less "real" dinosaurs which are artificially intelligent. And at the climax, the protagonist intriguingly becomes as one with the *T. rex*, through a mind-melding of sorts with "Oedipus rex."

"THAT'S ONE CLAWED STEP FOR DINOSAUR"

By the mid 1970s, writers were assigning heightened intelligence to dinosaurs of fantastic fiction, but what was the driving force behind the trend?

Certainly the film and novel *2001: A Space Odyssey* struck a chord with countless writers and science fiction enthusiasts.[37] Arthur C. Clarke's famous 1968 novel concerns discovery of a relic, a fifteen-foot-high alien monolith left on the moon's surface, only to be discovered millions of years hence, following the development of an intelligent, technological race evolving on Earth—*Homo sapiens*. In opening scenes of Clarke's novel, we read of "Moon-Watcher," an *Australopithecine*, whose hand-eye coordination and mentality are enhanced in a "Pavlovian dog" fashion, emanations from the monolith conditioning his senses.[38] Monoliths situated strategically throughout the *Australopithecine* habitat offer the species a means of survival. Soon Moon-Watcher's species develops enhanced abilities. The monoliths enable them to survive a pending extinction. And the *Australopithecines* eventually evolve into humanity, devising spacecraft and traveling to the moon, where Moon-Watcher's distant descendants uncover a monolith, fulfilling Clarke's prophecy. For "the destiny of the world" could be transformed with but a single success.

The "space race" of the late 1950s and 1960s, NASA's lunar landings and successful explorations of the solar system, combined with the influence of *2001*, triggered interest in possibilities for a mind-bending concept—the *paleontology* of outer space. In cases like *2001* and James P. Hogan's *Inherit the Stars* (1977),[39] the emphasis was inherently paleoanthropological, yet soon writers found themselves merging *dinosaurs* with space exploration too. And with good reason!

For there was mathematical basis suggesting the existence of life in the cosmos. By 1973, scientists had formulated an equation implying that there should only be one intelligent species presently broadcasting communications throughout the Milky Way galaxy, namely us. However, this equation also suggested that there should be 100 billion life-bearing worlds scattered about our galaxy too, one percent of which at some geological age would produce technical civilizations![40] Therefore, couldn't there be millions of planets existing out there now in pre-technical, "prehistoric" stages, just awaiting our discovery? And what if technological intelligence had evolved more than once on the same world? Had there been former races of intelligent saurians which had left Earth for the moon and stars? Would we ever learn of their existence or comprehend their intelligence? By the late 1970s, scientists like Carl Sagan had reason to believe that some dinosaurs were, indeed, relatively intelligent. A popular yet simple theme arising from such intrigue coupled dinosaurs with the moon.

Although dromaeosaurid dinosaur genera were first discovered over sixty years ago, it wasn't until the 1960s that vertebrate paleontologist Dale Russell enlivened interest in the cephalic characteristics of these animals. For example, the 6½-foot-long *Saurornithoides*, related to *Troodon* from the Late Cretaceous of Outer Mongolia, may have benefited from use of binocular vision and opposable fingers in catching small mammalian prey. The eyes of *Stenonychosaurus* (i.e., *Troodon*) have been compared to those of the modern ostrich, an animal which, except for the presence of bird-like wrists and hands bearing opposable fingers, it must have closely resembled.

By 1971, Russell stated that such "non-dinosaurian" features "were reminiscent of human attributes."[41] In 1977, astronomer Carl Sagan also became dramatically impressed by dramaeosaurid dinosaurs. He wrote, "If the dinosaurs had not all been mysteriously extinguished some 65 million years ago, would the *Saurornithoides* have continued to evolve into increasingly intelligent forms...? If it had not been for the extinction of the dinosaurs, would the dominant life forms on Earth today be descendants of *Saurornithoides*, writing and reading books, speculating on what would have happened had the mammals prevailed?"[42] Well, what if they had also devised means of space travel in past geological ages too, leaving mammals far behind in their astro-dust?

That's the premise of Frederick D. Gottfried's "Hermes to the Ages" (1980), when a well-preserved dinosaur fossil is discovered on the moon by Russian cosmonauts.[43] The specimen represents a tailless, intelligent species of dinosaur looking remarkably humanoid, and is aptly named "*Homosaurus*," personified with the nickname "Herman." Echoing Sagan, Gottfried's characters surmise that *Homosaurus* (or the "man-lizard") aspired to technological intelligence following evolution of an enlarged brain, upright walking stance freeing the forelimbs for non-locomotion grasping functions, a voice box used for complex verbal communications, and depth perception for handling tools. Besides man, only one class of animals bore evolutionary potential for attaining this advanced level—saurischian dinosaurs such as the carnivorous dromaeosaurs.

So where are all the dinosaurian tools then? Destroyed millions of years ago by forces of weathering and erosion on the Earth's crust. "Tools are barely distinguishable from the rocks in which they're found. It takes a trained eye to recognize them for what they are—something extremely unlikely if one has no reason to be looking for them." After deducing that Herman's kind wouldn't have abused nuclear power, the scientists conclude that instead,

Homosaurus had even invented biological weaponry, raising fears that the fossil may still be infested with prehistoric plague.

So American astronaut protagonist Lars self-righteously declares to the Russians as they prepare to board their space craft:

> You wouldn't listen to our theory. How the dinosaurs destroyed themselves. We believe that they type of war they waged was biological. If the individual you found was placed in suspended animation after that conflict, every part of him—every organ, every cell—must have been preserved intact. *And every living thing that might have been inside his body* [my italics]."[44]

To their astonishment and horror, the freeze-dried fossil rejuvenates itself from moist air aboard the spacecraft. Soon *Homosaurus* lives again and even communicates with its discoverers. "Herman" divulges that his race did indeed use biological warfare on their own kind, allowing a now-dead pathogen that preferentially attacked their sex cells to proliferate throughout their population so they couldn't reproduce. As one awed astronaut establishes, their racial suicide was deemed necessary because "their civilization became more like us." Herman's survival was a means for warning future terrestrial races. *Homosaurus*, messenger from the gods, would also *judge*, and if warranted, *destroy* humanity. Now it's up to us to prove our worthiness.[45]

Finding those as-yet-to-be-discovered dinosaurian tools, the theme of S.D. Howe's 1998 tale "Wrench and Claw," would be remarkable indeed.[46] Taking the probability of intelligent dinosaur races to a further degree than ever before, Howe's fictional paleontologist Dr. Heinrich Dietlief declares outrageously that if it takes 50,000 years for an intelligent race to become technological, then given the 165-million-year dinosaurs' Mesozoic reign, this means "there were *three hundred thousand opportunities* for a dinosaur civilization to rise up and disappear into oblivion." More pessimistically, if it requires on the average two million years for a technological race to evolve (the geological duration of "man-like creatures"), then as many as "eighty-two entirely different species could have arisen, become civilized, and died during the dinosaur reign." So, acknowledging the fossil record's incompleteness, where are the traces of all this supposed ancient technological activity?

On the moon, of course, although in Howe's tale paleontologists ironically miss making such discoveries. Instead "Wrench and Claw" uses the "wrench" as metaphor—handled by a hypothetical "saurian auto mechanic"—for what paleontologists should be looking for in their earthly digs instead of only fossilized organic remains. While wrenches would have rusted into unrecognizable condition after so many millions of years, surely chemical traces of their existence would remain, right? The answer is yes, although Howe's characters poohpooh Dietlief's silly allegations, ignoring the strange flecks of metal bits and zones of reddish-brown coloration—tool remnants—surrounding dinosaurs fossils they're uncovering in the field. At one of his popular lectures, Dietlief states:

> Paleontologists only take the tools to analyze what they expect to find. Thus, they only find what they expect—bones of simple animals.... If, around sixty-five million years in our future, a paleontologist ... happens to find a Neanderthal skull that we missed and none of our own, his conclusion will be we were slow, dull-witted bipeds who lived by searching for fruit and grubs. Not the intelligent, civilized, cultured population gathered here tonight.[47]

Had Howe's field paleontologists only selected proper field equipment (i.e., an X-ray fluorescence spectrometer used for detecting metals, rather than a ground-penetrating radar system), they'd have made an unholy discovery! But not this time. Howe wove two tales into

Front cover illustration for Dr. Thomas P. Hopp's 2002 novel *Dinosaur Wars: Counterattack*, reveals how the idea of the eternal conflict between prehistoria (in this case *Pteronychus* dinosaurs attacking from a lunar base) menacing modern man, is alive and well even today. (Reproduced with Thomas P. Hopp's permission.)

"Wrench and Claw." While in the present, paleontologist Dr. Dietlief spins his heretical notions about intelligent dinosaurs, it's also revealed what actually happened to dinosaur life on Earth sixty-five million years ago. Indeed, tools far more devastating and more advanced than any devised by man turned out to be their undoing.

Rather than *2001*, primary influences for genetic engineer and molecular biologist Dr. Thomas P. Hopp's *Dinosaur Wars* (2000) were *Jurassic Park* (1990, novel; 1993, film) and *Star Wars* (1977). Here, dinosaurs launch a massive attack from the moon in order to reclaim *their* planet. Whereas the likelihood of cloning dinosaurs from DNA preserved in real (terrestrial) fossils seems remote, Hopp's dinosaurs simply clone themselves and other vanished Cretaceous species prior to the attack. Or as Hopp clarified:

> What if the DNA sequences of every dinosaur on earth had been stored in a computer 65-million years ago? If that computer still existed, it would be possible to bring back the entire Cretaceous flora and fauna. That's what the invaders are up to in *Dinosaur Wars*. In *Dinosaur Wars*, the dinosaurs cloned themselves using fresh DNA, 65-million years ago. I dreamed up an intelligent, human-sized dinosaur species and had them do it. They put all the DNA information into a computer to outlast the asteroid impact that eliminated the other dinosaurs. Now, with the aid of some automatic clone-chambers—they're back! They've returned from space to reclaim their home world, and humans are the endangered species.... *Dinosaur Wars* was not that great a stretch of the imagination.[48]

Indeed, Hopp's premise is ingeniously simple; it's almost one of those "why-didn't-I-think-of-that-myself-first" story ideas. A sixty-five-million-year-old dinosaur cloning instrument on the moon is inadvertently activated when a lunar dinosaurian computer is repaired by meddling human astronauts. Next, dinosaur clones invade Earth firing death beams, laser rays and employing *Robocop*-like war machines controlled by a fictitious, intelligent regenerated dinosaur race, the feathered "*Pteronychus.*" Other more familiar Cretaceous dinosaur genera are reintroduced as part of the re-colonization strategy. The dinosaurs' vicious strike is swift and overwhelming, nearly annihilating Earth's military forces before the first counteroffensive. Led by hero Chase Armstrong, Earth's defenders, after defeating the first *Pteronychus* invasion, turn back another vicious offensive in Hopp's 2002 sequel, *Dinosaur Wars—Counterattack.*[49]

But in fantastic fiction, dinosaurs have traveled far beyond the moon and solar system. In fact, arguably the most memorable interstellar dinosaurs of all were introduced during the early 1990s in Robert J. Sawyer's *Far-Seer* trilogy.

QUINTAGLIO ODYSSEY

Indeed, Robert J. Sawyer's "Quintaglio" trilogy is a parallel universe setting, although founded on intelligent design in the cosmos rather than contingency. Collectively, Sawyer's *Far-Seer* (1992), *Fossil Hunter* (1993) and *Foreigner* (1994) the greatest trilogy of tales ever written about intelligent, space-faring dinosaurs.[50]

A "far-seer" is a device used to see far—in other words, a telescope! This is the instrument a young dino-astrologer "Quintaglio" named Afsan wields in Sawyer's engaging *Far-Seer* to view the heavens from his Earth-like satellite, "Land." Afsan determines that Land is one of many moons orbiting a gas giant, Jovian planet.

Theropod Afsan is the (combined) Columbus, Galileo *and* Copernicus of his times, who proves his satellite home world, Land, isn't flat but, in fact, round. Using astronomical observations, Afsan also demonstrates that the "Face of God," the deified Jovian giant in the skies above, isn't a god but instead a planet about which Land—where earthquakes have been increasing in intensity and frequency—orbits. Merging geological and astronomical data, Afsan foresees that Land is doomed. Land will inevitably self-destruct from gravitational and tidal forces due to its proximity to the gas giant.[51] Assuming the role of prophet, Afsan convinces governing officials that Land's time is limited. In order to survive, the Quintaglio race must develop means to travel to another, safer world in the heavens.

In *Fossil Hunter*, Afsan's son, Toroca, essentially the Charles Darwin of his race, discovers a large vessel filled with fossils buried in cliff-side strata. Here, it is further divulged that Land was deliberately seeded with terrestrial fauna, including the stock from which all warm-blooded Quintaglio evolved. Toroca's scientific team deduces the vessel is a spacecraft, providing impetus toward the goal of repopulating their place of origin in the stars. Finally, in *Foreigner*, the Quintaglio ultimately depart into space on a quest toward their planet of origin—Earth.

Sawyer's extraterrestrial dinosaurian fauna contrasts with Glut's and McCaffrey's in that inherently *intelligent* dinosaur species dominate Land. Yet these coexist with other traditional Mesozoic species—such as "hornfaces," "armor-back" ankylosaurs, long-necked "thunderbeast" sauropods, "shovel-mouth" hadrosaurs, and "blackdeath" tyrannosaurids. The odd admixture of evolved Quintaglio and conventional dinosaurs—which apparently haven't evolved (much) since Mesozoic times—remains puzzling until a revelation near *Fossil Hunter's* conclusion. Within the vessel—really a spaceship relic geologically corresponding to the "Bookmark layer" or the time before life existed (evidently emerging simultaneously) on Land—Toroca discovers mummified creatures, "very similar to the ones he knew." Yet these are also unfamiliar species, such as "a hornface with down-sized horns, like melted wax, unlike any hornface Toroca had ever heard of." So *all* the dinosaurians evolved on Land since the time of their curious Bookmark layer origin. Furry pterosaurs have evolved to even greater degree in arctic environments than have non–Quintaglio dinosaurs and pterosaurs on the more temperate Land: discovery of arctic pterosaurs facilitates Toroca's formulation of a theory of evolutionary speciation through natural selection. (On Land, birds became extinct long before the Quintaglio race evolved, while pterosaurs prospered.) *Nanotyrannosaur* stock evolved to much further degree than the rest of Land's fauna, eventually becoming civilized Quintaglio. But Quintaglio evolution has been guided by the *Jijaki*, who we find were very capable bioengineers as well.[52]

Throughout their recorded history, Quintaglio have suppressed their numbers through a breeding process presided over by a "bloodpriest," in which only one hatchling out of eight laid per egg clutch is permitted to survive. This form of artificial selection favors the strongest, fastest and most aggressive of the "egglings," producing a race of individuals so very aggressive they can barely stand to be in close proximity to one another. For proximity or physical contact can trigger an uncontrollable psychological state known as "dagamant," or the instinctive territorial bloodlust which can result in mass mortality. Toroca wisely decides that the Quintaglio's means of population control should be *randomized* instead of artificially directed. Within a few generations their passage through outer space under cramped, close quarters becomes possible without fear of triggering dagamant.

But the real mystery concerns how this peculiar fauna got to Land in the first place. The answer is that it was all engineered eons ago by a cosmic Watcher, an entity surviving from a previous universe on through our universe's Big Bang. But Watcher is lonely because while its former universe teemed with life, for billions of years ours remains sterile due to slightly differing universal laws and physical constants. Eventually, on the "Crucible" planet, on one out of all the worlds in the cosmos, simple life arose. And as certain forms developed, the Watcher transplanted them to several other ocean-bearing planets, so they wouldn't expire. One of the seeded worlds gave rise to the first intelligent species in the cosmos, known as the *Jijaki*, descended from the Crucible's *Opabinia*.[53] The *Jijaki* are summoned eventually by the Watcher to help resolve a dilemma which has developed on the Crucible planet.

It would still take a long time for real intelligence to develop on this planet—some 60 or 70 million Crucible years, I judged. But the mammals had already come up against a dead end. Intelligence, at least in the way these beings were trying to express it, required physical bulk—large, centralized, convoluted brains. The reptiles had long dominated every ecological niche for big animals; the rise of mammalian intelligence had ground to a halt. Not one, but two potential paths to sentience. Yet only one of them, it seemed, could make it on this world.[54]

Eventually, the *Jijaki* facilitate a vast transplantation effort, orchestrated by the Watcher (who is omniscient, yet not infinitely powerful with respect to physical forces and universal laws). First, the *Jijaki* terra-form an Earth-like satellite, chosen by the Watcher, with blue-green algae, and later import vast populations of dinosaurs, pterosaurs, mosasaurs, plesiosaurs and birds aboard ramscoop Arks. As you might have surmised by now, the Crucible is, of course, Earth, and the Earth-like satellite is Land. One of these Arks crash-landed only to be discovered on a seaside cliff by Toroca millions of years thereafter. As the Watcher mused, "I had hoped to leave no trace of my handiwork, but ... I had no way to remove (the) wreckage ... and every last *Jijaki* was now dead, so none could be summoned to clean up the mess." And so while the way has been paved for the success of Land's reptilian fauna, sixty-five million years ago, the Watcher causes the collision of a large comet with the Crucible planet so its mammalian fauna can triumph here. With niches available, intelligent life—humanity on Earth and Quintaglio on Land descended from terrestrial *Nanotyrannus*—arises on both worlds "nearly simultaneously."

The *Jijaki's* inventions foster the Quintaglio's success. Their development of "kiit"—a bluish-colored substance one hundred times stronger than diamond "which could be injection-molded like plastic"—permits the construction of interstellar ramjets, and a self-erecting tower which by the end of *Fossil Hunter* extends far into space. This vast tower is analogous to Arthur C. Clarke's monoliths; these symbols of intelligent design educate Quintaglio and *Australopithecines*, respectively, at pivotal moments in their species history—when they face extinction.

Nanotyrannus fossils are now scientifically regarded as juvenile *T. rexes*. So, in Sawyer's trilogy, we see not only how (instead of raptors) highly evolved tyrannosaurids conquered space, but also that they're on their way to Earth, perhaps to reclaim the planet for themselves. Earth versus the space-roving tyrannosaurs—what a spectacle that would be! Unless dinosaurs and man would conflict *culturally* instead.

If we established contact with intelligent, technological exodinosaurs, what sort of culture shock would we be in for? This was explored in James Patrick Kelly's gripping "Think Like a Dinosaur" (1995).[55] Here, humans must prove themselves worthy to a highly advanced race of interstellar dinosaurs before gaining privileges to their superluminary transfer wormhole technology. Following a rare transporter tragedy, instead of thinking *humanely* and in order to preserve "universal harmony," an earthman must learn to instead think *logically* "like a dinosaur," sacrificing the life of a human female space-time traveler for a greater good.[56] To be a dinosaur is to love the universe and nature, blood-red in tooth and claw.

DINOSAUROID DILEMMA

During the midst of unprecedented 1980s controversy surrounding the causes of mass extinctions in the fossil record, scientists and writers speculated how chance, rather than intelligent design, struck a blind course toward humanity. For it was a six-mile-diameter asteroid or comet[57] from space which wiped out the dinosaurs sixty-five million years ago, allowing the rise of increasingly intelligent mammalian forms. But some of the last dinosaur species alive were already quite intelligent. So let's reconsider the pivotal question once more. Had that cosmic bolide been deflected from its collision course with Earth, what would the dinosaurs have aspired to, say, granted another sixty-five million years of evolution? Perhaps as intelligent "dinosauroids"—evolutionary descendants of the brainiest Late Cretaceous species such as raptor dromaeosaurs, and troodontids—they might have developed space technology and, by now, populated the stars.

Unlike *Homosaurus*, *Pteronychus* and Quintaglio (or the Clan-Ru—discussed below, but also see note 62), *true* dinosauroids exist in universes alternate to our perception of reality. They represent a biological *probability*. In fantastic literature we find that dinosauroids are usually encountered during outer-space missions. (Sometimes the dinosauroids are themselves space-faring, in which case they're exo-dinosauroids.) The problem is that their very existence precludes mankind's. Just as matter is incompatible with anti-matter, dinosauroid and man should not coexist for they belong to separate universes, alternate realities. When conjured, dinosauroids may either represent mankind's ideals, or his worse nature.

Physicist's Geoffrey A. Landis's "Embracing the Alien" (1992) invokes a celestial entity, the Outsider, perhaps analogous to Sawyer's Watcher, which can travel via black holes throughout all of space-time.[58] On a visit to Earth sixty-five million years ago, Outsider inadvertently shifted the orbits of comets in our solar system's Oort cloud, causing a comet to collide with our planet. Now a scientist team comprising humans and two alien humanoids allied to mankind are whisked back from the Praesepe Cluster into our Mesozoic past through a gravitationally oscillating black hole. They've been sent there by the Outsider as a test, in order to select a future course of reality. Should the Outsider correct its mistake? Should the comet fall, or not? The decision ultimately rests on human shoulders as the Outsider cautions, "What does not exist cannot be destroyed. You are from the future. I will merely cause your species never to exist."[59]

The Outsider is a "lover of life" torn between alternatives. The Earth's primordial dinosaurian fauna is pleasing not only to the Outsider, but also to the human selected for this mission, First Mate Brown. As the Outsider reveals, there is great beauty in dinosaurian descendants who evolve into an interstellar, utopian society of dinosauroids. Brown votes *against* diverting the comet but, surprisingly, the Outsider recognizes humility in Brown's decision and so diverts the comet anyway. Dinosaurs will suffer extinction, mammals will proliferate, and the human race will evolve after all. Our future is intact, at expense of the dinosauroids,' but it was a very close call.[60]

Landis's tale reads more or less like a like a classic *Star Trek* episode script and is similar to a complexly woven novel, *Star Trek: First Frontier* (1995), a true "guilty pleasure" of mine co-written by Diane Carey and paleontologist Dr. James I. Kirkland, who in 1993 described the dinosaur genus *Utahraptor*.[61] Brown's dinosauroid dilemma is analogous to circumstances related in *First Frontier*, except *Enterprise* Captain James T. Kirk must make a universe-altering decision in the absence of a benevolent cosmic entity. Instead Kirk is guided by stoic Science Officer Mr. Spock, a mysterious device named "Guardian of Forever" which is "machine and being ... both and neither," as well as reliable "Bones" McCoy, who knows quite a bit of paleoanatomy.

Cast into prehistory by the Guardian to a time of critical convergence sixty-four million years ago, Kirk's crew makes an incredible discovery. A poorly understood race of reptilian humanoids known as the "Clan-Ru," who shun Star Fleet Federation and yearn to become unchallenged masters of the universe, have *also* entered the identical time-stream through the Guardian's time portal. The space-faring Clan-Ru are descendants of Earth's raptor dinosaurs, physically and temperamentally resembling Sawyer's description of the Quintaglio, although Clan-Ru possess two fingers on each hand with an opposable thumb. They're deviously attempting to alter their lowly fate in our "proper" universe by deflecting the asteroid that is about to hit the Earth so that dinosaurs can survive, evolving into dinosauroids. "Terrans" (earthmen) then will never evolve: buoyed by advanced technology, Clan-Ru can rule the universe.[62]

Except the Clan-Ru neglected an important matter! The alternate universe, void of mankind, as revealed by the Guardian, is one of nature blood-red in tooth, claw and phaser. Not only is the future scarred by perpetual war between Romulans and Klingons, but descendants of *Troodon* evolving into intelligent dinosauroids exterminate a Dietlief-like *succession* of their civilizations with nuclear warfare.[63] In fact, by the galactic epoch of space-roving Klingons, Romulans and Vulcans, intelligent dinosauroids have become long extinct on Earth, where humans never evolved. Once Oya, the Clan-Ru scientist captured during a skirmish, comprehends consequences of their plot (after Spock reveals the future history as altered by deflection of the asteroid, all recorded on a trusty Tricorder), she joins Kirk's team to overthrow her own warlike Clan-Ru race.

Granted a second chance after the Clan-Ru's asteroid deflector is destroyed, Kirk still must choose whether to destroy or not destroy the incoming asteroid with phaser hits. Unlike First Mate Brown in Landis's story, however, Kirk unwaveringly chooses humanity. Only after the asteroid collides with Earth does the Guardian of Forever mend the rift in space-time, simultaneously whisking Kirk and crew back to their normal universe. The asteroid strike is permitted, allowing evolution of Terrans who, adhering to the Prime Directive, will preserve a brighter tomorrow for all life. Also, from their low orbital vantage, the K-T impact event has been documented on Spock's Tricorder.[64]

As in Landis's startling 1992 story, *First Frontier's* dinosauroids have been precluded by fate. Or was it Kirk exercising free will who saved the universe?[65] Anyway, rather than a universe void of humanity, mankind may instead live long and prosper.

CONCLUSION

Over two decades ago, astronomer Carl Sagan related in his popular *Cosmos* (1980)[66] how conservative calculations suggested there are an estimated one hundred billion planets in the Milky Way Galaxy upon which life evolved. How many of these would be in a "dinosaur age"? Even if there *were* living exodinosaurs out there somewhere, first be advised of the obvious problem of bridging the vast gulfs of space. The chances are minuscule that we should happen to encounter any other Earth-like planet having undergone a terrestrial-like geological history that included timely intervals of cometary bombardment to stoke the fires of evolution in the wake of mass extinction, *and* having a sun optimally situated in a nurturing interstellar environment which itself is sufficiently similar in mass, stellar radiative output and age to our own. This would also be a water-bearing planet upon which life has evolved in Earth-like parallel fashion—such that creatures which we should recognize as terrestrial dinosaurs have developed. Also, we should necessarily and conveniently happen to stumble across these worlds during their dinosaurian age—a 160-million-year era of dominance on these respective planets. What are the odds? Likely or not, we love the chances of dinosaur discoveries being made out in the depths of space, as penned by writers of fantastic fiction.

"Hard" science fiction usually involves travel through space and time. In the previous chapter we considered how dinosaurs became an integral force to reckon with in *time*. But through recent years we find that dinosaurs have made even greater strides in outer space. As we've outlined here, with each passing decade, alien dinosaurs became ever more complex and varied, to the point where they had evolved distinctly human attributes, like dinosauroids and the Quintaglio. By comparison, the earliest nineteenth century exodinosaurs were simple—fantastic, yet implausible. Through the mid–twentieth century, exodinosaurs had become more cleverly founded in astronomical theory. These were more varied in type yet outwardly behaved, more or less, like the dimwitted brutes of our prehistoric past. Gradually, the lost-races theme pervading exodinosaur tales faded, to be replaced by more scientifically sophisticated themes and with worlds populated by more recognizable creatures—essentially *ourselves*, although in dinosaurian guise! For mysterious "lost races" of outer space worlds populated by dinosaurs inevitably evolved through annals of fantastic literature into even more human-like dinosauroid creatures, projecting a timeless intelligence-in-the-universe theme (with worlds seeded by an omniscient Watcher, an Outsider (or a *Thek* or Preserver—see notes 33 and 62). Increasingly since 1980, exodinosaurs, and in particular intelligent exo-dinosauroids, have become inherently woven into mainstream hard science fiction through scientific mysteries surrounding pivotal extinctions of the Late Cretaceous.

With dinosaurs becoming more intelligent and human-like through time, and as humans are increasingly cautioned to "think like dinosaurs," is there a happy point of convergence? And is there an easier, perhaps more likely way to suspend disbelief when it comes to crafting dinosaur "encounters of the first kind"?

Yes.

CHAPTER 7

Rise of the Raptor

BACKGROUND

So which came first—the raptor, or its DNA? And are today's most popularized notions concerning dinosaurs, alluded to by paleontologists, resultant of science or science fiction literature instead?

When it finally happened, the world was simply ready for a "Jurassic Park." Ostensibly, Michael Crichton's 1990 novel *Jurassic Park* became so influential, so prophetic. Rather surprisingly, however, taken at plot level, *Jurassic Park* isn't all that original. For the underlying science, imagery and fiction had been out there for well over a decade. True, Crichton added a few twists founded on chaos theory (popularized at the time through James Gleick's 1987 book *Chaos*), the prospect of contingency (i.e., chance opportunity) in the fossil record (prompted through paleontologist Stephen Jay Gould's writings and the 1980s mass extinctions controversy),[1] and hinted at a social problem—the idea of breakdown in the traditional nuclear family. But mainly Crichton memorialized a breed of ferocious, *unnatural* dinosaurs whose first representations were described from fossils in 1856—the raptors. As paleontologist Robert Bakker stated in 1994, "*Jurassic Park* needed an intelligent villain, one with formidable powers, one that could almost catch and kill and eat the human heroes.... It is the raptors that have come to symbolize all the revised scientific thinking about dinosaurs."[2]

Crichton's dino-fame and legacy rest in the cluster of 1990s science fiction stories borrowing from *Jurassic Park's* most prevalent, potent theory—cloning dino-monsters from fossil DNA, *especially* raptors. After all, today, the lab-sterilized, high-tech environment (i.e., melding computers with bio-technology) to restore living dinosaurs suspends disbelief far more effectively than the usual alternatives—outer space dinosaurs, building time machines to visit dinosaurs in the geological past, or finding cryptozoological dino-monsters in Earth's lost or forgotten places. Crichton's genetic force, likened to the impact of unleashing atomic power, an inherently Frankensteinian theme, is nearly two centuries old.[3]

According to paleontologists David E. Fastovsky and David B. Weishampel, "Made famous by Michael Crichton and Steven Spielberg, deinonychosaurs evoke more fear and nightmares than does *T. rex*. For these are the 'raptors' of *Jurassic Park* fame."[4] Yes, while *T. rex* played a prominent role in Crichton's pair of novels *Jurassic Park* (1990) and a sequel,

A fantasy vision of the 25-foot-long South American *Megaraptor*, illustrated by Jack Arata. The foot claw is now known to be a hand claw. (With permission.)

The Lost World (1995),[5] those nasty, sickle-clawed *Velociraptors* absolutely stole the show! The raptors took center stage in both novels and three *Jurassic Park* movies. But while no movie featured raptor dinosaurs before the *Jurassic Park* phenomenon, by then raptors had already stormed the beaches of science fiction literature.

What a curious Mesozoic ambassador is the raptor dinosaur breed! *Velociraptor* (1924) is merely one of several raptors known to science, that is besides *Troodon* (1856), *Dromaeosaurus* (1922), *Sauronithoides* (1924), *Deinonychus* (1969), *Sauronitholestes* (1978), *Utahraptor* (1993), *Megaraptor* (1998) and *Microraptor* (2000). (The dates refer to the first published scientific descriptions of these genera.) And yet while laymen may lack detailed circumstances corresponding to the natural history of each of these creatures, collectively, the raptors have become laden with unnatural pseudo-scientific and pop-cultural ideas. For besides fear and nightmares, now, simply the name *Velociraptor*—a dinosaur the name of which few knew thirty years ago—also evokes thoughts of DNA cloning, feathers and avian connections,[6] warm-bloodedness, and even the softer side of familial relations. Now raptors are veritable monsters not only due to their inherent savagery, but also for their crafty, menacing intellect. Indeed, the raptors are imbued with qualities far too human-like for our comfort. (One exception perhaps is "The Raptor," official mascot of the Toronto Raptors. It's no coincidence that the National Basketball Association welcomed an expansion franchise—the Toronto Raptors—in 1994 during the height of the *Jurassic Park* craze.)

Let's look at how these ideas surfaced in fantastic fiction in both the pre–Crichton era, and also how they proliferated in the years following *Jurassic Park*'s late 1990 publication. Besides just crafting a pair of decent *Jurassic Park* novels, what were Crichton's original contributions to the annals of dinosaur sci-fi and horror?

FIRST ITERATION: PRE-CRICHTON STIMULI

Perhaps the first unusual story involving laboratory recreation of an extinct animal was published in 1928, several years prior to release of the Universal film, *Frankenstein*. Author Max Begouen wrote a novel, *Quand le mammouth ressuscita*, concerning the Frankensteinian resurrection of a Siberian mammoth, using electricity.

> The galvanic currents were applied to the nerve centers, as biogenic rays bathed everything in an intense purple light.... Suddenly, the animal's legs quivered. The bent trunk seemed to lengthen. The tiny eye, once dull and lifeless, appeared to swell and come alive, gazing vaguely about. The body temperature rose, quickly ... then the chest appeared to rise. 'Oh, look,' said Nadia, pointing at the faint cloud of steam coming out of the trunk's twin openings in rhythmic puffs. Nadia seized Mougin's hands. '*It's alive*,' she cried. At that very moment, the mammoth's eyes blinked and a powerful blast of air roared from its rising trunk....[7]

John Taine's novel *The Greatest Adventure* (1929) is another early example. Here, a race of ancient bioengineers created a horde of gigantic pseudo-dinosaurians which evolved from spores over millions of years, ultimately leading to extinction of the ancient race. Three years later came Aldous Huxley's 1932 novel *Brave New World*, where a five class (i.e., clade) human society is cloned using Bokanovsky's Process. Although not involving prehistoric life, Huxley's classic modern tale may be regarded as a veritable *Jurassic Park* precursor.

Glimmerings of DNA-revived prehistoria remained on the science fiction frontier even following the revolutionary description of DNA's structure in 1953. DNA became educational introductory fare in most high school biology textbooks around the country by the mid–1960s. Writer Piers Anthony was stimulated by the spirit of the times to draft a 4,800-word story first rejected by the editor of *Data Processing Magazine* in 1966, a tale which finally became a published novel in 1990, the same year as Crichton's *Jurassic Park*. This was *Balook*, a tale concerning man's cruelty to animals.[8]

The original "Balook" story concerned a computer programmer married to a geneticist; the pair decide to link their knowledge in recreating a Miocene (thirteen- to twenty-million-year-old) rhinoceros, of the giant, twenty-six-foot-tall genus *Baluchitherium* (hence the story title, "Balook"). As Anthony related, "They crafted Balook, intending to promote the capacities of the computer. But Balook was a living creature, and they had not properly allowed for his nature in the modern world. A mean man saw him and took a potshot ... injuring him. Mean children laughed. That made them realize the enormity of the social problem. They had collaborated with a computer to play God, resurrecting an extinct animal. What price would Balook have to pay for their success?"[9] In a 2005 personal communication, Anthony further stated, "I can say from memory that the short story was different from the novel, and would be sadly dated by its references to computers at the time of their stone age. It was really more of a human story than a computer or paleontological story."

Anthony's story was also rejected by *Analog's* eminent editor, John W. Campbell, Jr. (1910–1971) who wrote, "Sorry—the story doesn't seem to me to accomplish anything....."[10] In fact, Anthony's story attracted no interest for two decades! Then, in 1987, inspired by Czech paleoartist Zdenek Burian's (1905–1981) painting of the related rhino genus *Indricotherium*, Anthony riskily decided to barrel on ahead, regardless—both with a miniature sculpture of "Balook" as well as, later, a completed novel written between 1986 and February 1987 without contract or promise of publication. *Balook* became, like *Jurassic Park*, a living, breathing melding of computers and chromosomes. Anthony described the biotech process in his novel, released in November 1990 by Underwood-Miller.

> Indeed, the process started with natural tissue, whose genetic blueprint was then modified by radiation and laser surgery and chemistry ... they chose a large animal. Not a dinosaur; the reptilian environment would have been too difficult to duplicate on that scale.... So it was *Baluchitherium*, the hornless rhinoceros of the Miocene epoch.... The experts had used a battery of computers to analyze the rhinoceros chromosomes, then had done the laser surgery on the living tissue: the fertilized rhino egg. A few small changes, meticulously scripted to make it conform to the pattern derived from painstakingly analyzed *Baluchitherium* bones and the sample was ready. It died. They made adjustments.... A hundred or more expensive cultures failed—but in the end five of them formed embryos.[11]

During the pre–Crichton period, a number of stories were published interrelating or involving prehistoric animals, DNA and bioengineering, or dinosaurs placed in a theme park. These included five novels—Donald F. Glut's *Spawn* (1976), Harry Adam Knight's *Carnosaur* (1984), and a trilogy of novels by Harry Harrison beginning with his *West of Eden* (1984)—and four shorter stories published in science fiction mags—Robert R. Olsen's "Paleontology: An Experimental Science" (1974), Frederick D. Gottfried's "Hermes to the Ages" (1980), Robert Silverberg's "Our Lady of the Sauropods" (1980), and Allen Steele's "Trembling Earth" (1990), the latter arriving in subscribers' mailboxes just a few weeks before copies of *Jurassic Park* hit book store shelves.

Of his *Spawn* with its alien exo-dinosaurians, Glut claims that it was basically a "ripoff of *Westworld* (1973) which was a Michael Crichton novel that I had in mind the whole time I was writing it. So, in no way am I going to claim that *Jurassic Park* was a ripoff of *Spawn*. I'm certain Crichton was totally unaware of *Spawn* at the time he wrote *Jurassic Park*. But the problem is one of similarity because both stories are about theme parks featuring dinosaurs where things go crazy. And so if you ever filmed *Spawn* it would look like a ripoff of *Jurassic Park*."[12]

It is more likely the case that Crichton knew about *Carnosaur*, Harry Adam Knight's page-turner dealing with dinosaurs (yes—and a plesiosaur too!) derived from DNA preserved in fossil bone. Following my first reading of *Jurassic Park* in early 1991, I confess I had a fonder recollection for *Carnosaur* years before.

Knight's novel is the first to feature a horrific DNA-derived raptor dinosaur, the eight-foot-long, 100-pound North American genus, *Deinonychus*. Perhaps it was fitting that *Deinonychus* became the first of this artificial (i.e., biotech) breed to be restored in the annals of fantastic fiction, because this was also *the* dinosaur which ushered in the first wave of the dinosaur renaissance during the late 1960s and early 1970s. Although *Deinonychus* had already made cameo appearances in David Gerrold's *Deathbeast*, in Knight's gruesome tale, *Deinony-chus* is the first dinosaur to score human prey. Knight's raptor is likened to a man, although in dinosaurian, genetic guise.

> Cartwright froze. He couldn't believe what he was seeing ... was absurdly reminded of some giant kind of giant plucked bird, like an ostrich, but this was definitely no ostrich. It had the head of a reptile.... They were cunning eyes too, almost intelligent, and this scared Cartwright more than anything. Even more than its claws.... Man and creature stood about 10 feet apart staring at each other.... Then the creature's tail ... suddenly stiffened and rose into the air behind it. This had the effect of pulling the upper body back until the creature was standing almost as straight as a man.[13]

Soon, human nature takes hold and the cloned dino-monsters escape from their cages within an English estate. Besides *Deinonychus*, a warm-blooded *Tarbosaurus* (an evolutionary cousin to *Tyrannosaurus*) that can sprint after cars at speeds up to thirty-five miles per hour, *Altispinax* (a spined theropod akin to *Spinosaurus*), a sexually frustrated male *Megalosaurus*, armored *Scolosaurus*, *Plesiosaurus*, *Brachiosaurus* and four others are terrorizing the pastoral British countryside of Warchester.

There are several uncanny similarities between the pair of novels. But while a compar-ison of *Jurassic Park* and *Carnosaur* would be enlightening, for sake of brevity here I'll point out several of the latter's most poignant passages.

Sir Penward, a dinosaur groupie of first-rate caliber, explains how he recreated his dinosaurs for his private zoo. Suspending disbelief with the real fact that sometimes excep-tionally well preserved dinosaur fossils do turn up—such as hadrosaur "mummies" found in Canada—Penward further suggests that genetic material could be extracted and decoded from the fossilized cells, using an electron microscope. This information is transferred into a computer and a dinosaur chromosomal map is developed. Using gene-splicing technol-ogy, DNA is recombined with embryo cells in chicken eggs. "Then, when the nucleus of the chicken cell is completely modified, a chicken ovum is enucleated and the doctored nucleus is implanted in its place."[14] So instead of chickens, dinosaur hatchlings emerge. In fact, Penward's technique sounds more viable than that employed by Hammond's Jurassic Park scientific team, as avians are evolutionarily closer to dinosaurs than are frogs.

Like Crichton (and Gould), Knight was influenced by *contingency* in the fossil record, although their writings took separate paths. To Crichton, contingency was connected to chaos theory through the degradation of complex systems and in the untestable principle that simple, perhaps unknowable factors—such as changes in dinosaurian behavior—may have caused their extinction. Knight's mad character Penward, however, is troubled by the fact that the dinosaurs were cut down in their prime by an asteroid collision sixty-five mil-lion years ago. To him, "the mammals inherited the earth—by *default*."[15] So, while Crich-ton's Hammond hopes to make a mint off his dinosaurs in a rapidly unraveling, unnatural setting, Knight's Penward, who predicts an atomic war on the horizon, strives to re-estab-lish dinosaurs on earth in order to "see who is the rightful victor in the struggle between mammals and dinosaurs."[16] For after man has been extinguished, either through his own means, perhaps aided by bloodthirsty dinosaurs like *Deinonychus* and *Tarbosaurus*, dinosaurs will rightfully re-inherit the earth!

In the very end, it is the unloved and sexually repressed who are punished. Lady Jane, Sir Penward's wife, unleashes the dinosaurian wave of terror to get even with her perverted husband who cannot satisfy her. A fate very much like that suffered by Dodgson at the climax of Crichton's *The Lost World*, published over a decade later, is reserved for Lady Jane, who is held in bondage while being steadily devoured by a pair of hungry tyrannosaur hatchlings armed with very sharp teeth. "Lady Jane's screams carried for a long way across the untended farmland, and continued for almost 12 hours, but no one heard them."[17]

Although only true raptors (i.e., winged birds of prey) appear in Harry Harrison's *West of Eden* (1984), discussed in previous chapters, the intelligent Mosasauroid-like "Murgu" or "Yilane" race menacing a primitive human civilization availed themselves of advanced bio-engineering methods unknown to mankind today. A Yilane motto reads "All life forms are mutable since DNA is endless in time."[18] (Also see the Appendix.)

While Steele's "Trembling Earth" brought those nasty raptors sharply into focus it was merely implied (left unstated) that the trio of deinonychi (named "Jason," "Freddy," and "Michael") were products of bioengineering. The sickle-clawed trio roam freely through the Okefenokee National Wildlife Refuge, as part of the Deinonychus Observation Project established by the Department of the Interior.[19] Gottfried's "Hermes to the Ages"[20] (discussed further in Chapter Six and the Appendix) is a launching point for three plot components often combined in post–1980s dinosaur fiction: (1) space-faring dinosaurs, (2) highly evolved (i.e., evolutionarily advanced or derived), technological dinosauroids, and, however simplistic, (3) references to biotech. In this case a human-like dinosaur mummy discovered on the moon, named *Homosaurus mercer*, thought to be an evolutionary descendant of *Deinonychus*, is biochemically restored from near-death suspended animation.

Olsen's earlier entry parodied the means of scientific discourse. Adopting a science journalistic writing style, Olsen explained through a series of mock "abstracts" how a 100-foot-long tyrannosaur species, *T. nevadensis*, came to be reconstituted from DNA preserved in fossilized bone and skin fragments. The dinosaur kills two researchers and escapes into southern California before its demise in a chilling November rainstorm.[21]

Silverberg's "Our Lady of the Sauropods" concerned dinosaur fauna of a Neptunian satellite named "Dino Island"—which, rather like Glut's *Spawn*, someday may be opened to tourists—that were restored (on Earth) through exploiting fossil DNA using the "Olsen-process," in homage to Robert Olsen's 1974 short story.

> We take what we can get. Olsen-process reconstructs require sufficient fossil DNA to permit the computer synthesis, and we've been able to find that in only some twenty species so far. The wonder is that we've accomplished even that much; to replicate the complete DNA molecule from battered and sketchy genetic information millions of years old, to carry out the intricate implants in reptilian host ova, to see the embryos through to self-sustaining levels. The only word that applies is *miraculous*.[22]

The dino-reconstructs, too dangerous for existence on Earth, were subsequently brought to Dino Island following a tragedy in San Diego involving a tyrannosaur, as described in Olsen's "Paleontology: An Experimental Science." In Silverberg's tale, Anne, who becomes stranded on Dino Island, becomes the holy priestess of the reconstructed dinosaurs. "I feel their strength, their power, their harmony. I am one with them, and they with me."[23] This passage exemplifies the distinctive *feminine* element reverberating through stories where living dinosaurs are recreated from non-life, a significant detail we'll return to shortly.

SECOND ITERATION: VISUAL STIMULI

One of the earliest visual representations of a dino-"raptor" published in a popular vein was the dinosaur *Troodon* issued in 1938 on a collectible Sinclair Dinosaur stamp. James E. Allen's restoration, hardly resembling modern raptor restorations and lacking characteristic sickle-shaped toes, is a relatively light-bodied sort curiously adorned with a pachycephalosaur-like dome. Paleontologist Barnum Brown's description in the collecting booklet no. 2 reads, "Length 6–10 feet, height 3–5 feet. Our list of strange creatures would be incomplete without this extraordinary dinosaur from the Cretaceous rocks of the United States and Canada. For seventy years it was known by a single tooth until an incomplete skeleton was described. The skull is 3–5 inches thick (an original bone-head); teeth small with long cusps on edges. Front legs much shorter than hind legs." Brown and Allen as well as Sinclair Gasoline's millions of patrons obviously had no idea what a sensation these light-weight dinosaurs would create half a century later, once it was possible to make more accurate reconstructions.

Discovery of *Deinonychus* from a butte hilltop in southern Montana on a hot afternoon in August 1964 went without much fanfare. John Ostrom and Grant Meyer of Yale University noticed several claw bones scattered on a hill slope, including one of the sickle-shaped variety. "In front of us, clearly recognizable, was a good portion of a large-clawed hand protruding from the surface."[24] After three summers of field work, four to five specimens belonging to an as yet unnamed new genus of dinosaur had been recovered. Following painstaking preparation in Yale's laboratory, mounting of bones and scientific illustration of each bone for Ostrom's technical report, Robert Bakker (who graduated from Yale in 1967) created the first life restoration of the evidently active dinosaur, named *Deinonychus* in July 1969. This was a superb illustration, and to boot, Bakker also prepared a skeletal reconstruction, both of which were published in Ostrom's monograph describing *Deinonychus antirrhopus*.[25]

Ostrom regarded the Early Cretaceous *Deinonychus* as ancestral to later genera—*Velociraptor, Dromaeosaurus, Stenonychosaurus,* and *Sauronithoides*. He claimed "the hind limbs of *Deinonychus* appear to have been powerful limbs for moderately, but not unusually, fast running ... there is a significant body of evidence that indicates it was a very active predator ... considered together, we have a rather convincing picture ... of *Deinoncyhus* as an active and very agile predator. It appears that this animal caught and held its prey in its fore hands and disemboweled it with the large pedal talons. This of course would require that *Deinonychus* stand, at least momentarily, on one foot while it ripped the victim's flesh with the claw of the opposite foot.... The modified tail of *Deinonychus* appears to have been the critical stabilizing mechanism as predator and prey struggled."[26]

While Ostrom's words and Bakker's images reached few at first, by 1972, the first popular images of an anatomically correct raptor stormed the beachhead of popular consciousness in a children's volume, *Life Before Man*, published by the editors of Time-Life Books.[27] In a chapter titled "The Bellicose Life Style of the Dinosaurs," artist Burt Silverman's illus-

Opposite: **Front cover design to** ***Asimov's Science Fiction Magazine,*** **showcasing Bob Walter's striking** ***Deinonychi*** **for Allen Steele's story, "Trembling Earth." (***Asimov's Science Fiction,*** **November 1990 cover, ©Dell Magazines. Used with permission.)**

tration showed how *Deinonychus* savagely dispatched prey—in this case an iguanodont known as *Tenontosaurus*. An accompanying restoration showed how *Velociraptor* was capable of ripping off spoils from larger predators. It should be said here that by this time, the Polish-Mongolian paleontological expedition had made a very significant discovery in Mongolia's Gobi Desert during the 1971 field season. A unique fossil of two "fighting dinosaurs" frozen together through fossilization had been unearthed. Ostrom's words of 1969 had been prophetic, as one of the combatants was *Velociraptor*.

Illustration by *Prehistoric Times* editor Mike Fredericks comparing the Late Cretaceous raptor *Troodon* with a hypothetical Dinosauroid as envisioned by Ron Seguin and Dale Russell. (Used with permission.)

Bakker's *Deinonychus* restorations would reappear in *Discovery* magazine (Fall 1969), in Adrian J. Desmond's *The Hot-Blooded Dinosaurs* (1975), where two chapters were inspired by the lively dinosaurs and the pair of recent discoveries, and in Donald F. Glut's popular *The New Dinosaur Dictionary* (1982), and the life restoration was published in John Noble Wilford's *The Riddle of the Dinosaur* (1985). Desmond wrote, "*Deinonychus* embodies all that is distinctly non-reptilian in dinosaurs."[28] By 1971, paleontologist Dale Russell went so far as to declare that non-dinosaurian features evident in the raptor breed "were reminiscent of human attributes."[29] Bakker did another study of *Deinonychus* for his book *The Dinosaur Heresies* (1986), although this time the fighting pair of dinosaurs were feathered.[30]

Thereafter, in those pre–*Jurassic Park* years, images of raptors—*Deinonychus* especially— would appear increasingly in popular books. During this period, perhaps the most influential illustrations were William Stout's stylish and speedy raptors published in *The Dinosaurs: A Fantastic New View of a Lost Era* (1981)[31], sickle claw-wielding monsters nobody would want to tangle with. Dino-aficionados spotted other raptors such as Peter Snowball's illustrations for paleontologist Alan Charig's *A New Look at the Dinosaurs* (1979), Margaret Colbert's illustration for Edwin H. Colbert's *Dinosaurs: An Illustrated History* (1983), John Sibbick's illustrations for David Norman's *The Illustrated Encyclopedia of Dinosaurs* (1985), and John Gurche's 1985 dramatic restoration showing a trio of vicious deinonychi leaping onto the left flank of a tenontosaur published in Volume 1 of *Dinosaurs Past and Present* (1986).[32] Near the end of his illustrious career, even inveterate paleoartist Zdenek Burian painted *Velociraptor* as a lithe and lively fast-moving creature in the years between 1974 and 1976 at a time when Bakker was still relatively unknown. This is something of a turning point as Burian was renown for his mid-twentieth century magnificent portrayals of sluggish, cold-blooded dinosaurs.[33]

Nature was turning blood red rapidly in tooth and sickle-claw! Certainly such images helped set the table for what was to come—the 1990s raptor invasion. However, besides a prior history of raptor imagetext—science fiction with visual representations—there was one additional, crucial ingredient needed to fuel *Jurassic Park's* fire: real laboratory experimentation conducted by scientists who were none too mad after all.

THIRD ITERATION: ANCIENT DNA'S FACT AND FICTION

DNA was first isolated as a chemical substance by chemists in 1869, although another eight decades would pass before its double-helical structure would be elucidated by Watson and Crick. Although today DNA is most often thought of perhaps in terms of the O.J. Simpson trial, Dolly the British sheep cloned a handful of years ago, and even Little Nikky, a Texas cat cloned from its progenitor, certainly DNA had been prominently in public consciousness at least since the early 1980s. For instance, many saw the 1986 film *The Fly*, starring Jeff Goldblum and Geena Davis, in which a computer inadvertently splices the DNA of Goldblum's character Dr. Brundle with a housefly, tragically, with monstrous results.[34]

Without success, as early as the late 1960s and '70s, Russian scientists had tackled the problem of extracting DNA preserved in frozen mammoth cadavers. Refinements in analytical chemistry allowed replication of the quagga's DNA to be extracted and recorded in the early 1980s. (The quagga is a zebra relative extinct since 1883.) Further refinements came about by the mid–1980s through development of the polymerase chain reaction (PCR) process, sort of a genetic Xerox machine allowing researchers to amplify an original DNA sample by a billionfold so minute amounts could be detected with lab instrumentation. Then by 1985, Svante Paabo extended the age range of DNA extraction and analysis to a 2,400-year-old Egyptian mummy. As Paabo indicated in his *Nature* article, "These analyses show that substantial pieces of mummy DNA (3.4 kilobases) can be cloned and that the DNA fragments seem to contain little or no modifications introduced postmortem."[35] In other words, analyzed samples didn't seem to be contaminated with recent DNA. The method worked, at least on historical specimens!

In his acknowledgments to *Jurassic Park*, Michael Crichton stated, "Certain ideas presented here about paleo–DNA, the genetic material of extinct animals, were first articulated by Charles Pellegrino, based on the research of George O. Poinar, Jr., and Roberta Hess, who formed the Extinct DNA Study Group at Berkeley." Actually, in January 1985, a *pair* of published articles hinted at the means through which one could clone a living dinosaur from fossil DNA. Charles R. Pellegrino's article "Dinosaur Capsule" appeared in *Omni*, and paleontologist Michael Benton's article "To clone a dinosaur" appeared in the January 17th issue of *New Scientist*. Pellegrino's article is rife with speculative ideas concerning the possibilities for fossil DNA, especially that preserved in insects sealed in amber. And it is here where Pellegrino noted in a popular magazine how Poinar and Hess "believed that the insect's DNA might still be capable of reproducing itself or at least of being 'read.'"[36]

Furthermore, Pellegrino speculated, "Three more decades of technological advance and we may be able to extract and read DNA from the flies' stomachs, where, if we are lucky, we will find the blood and skin of dinosaurs. Since flies flew among, and occasionally drew their nourishment from, dinosaurs, it's possible that we may one day publish the genetic codes of creatures known only from bones and footprints. If portions of the code are missing, we might conceivably figure out what belongs in the gaps and edit the lost 'paragraphs.' Perhaps we could borrow from currently living animals to provide a complete set of proteins necessary for the survival of the original dinosaur." He suggested dramatically, "Now think upon this: Some of the stones are filled with mosquitoes that bloated themselves, from time to time, on the blood of beings who then inhabited the earth. Oh, yes, it could be just like old times again!"[37]

In his *New Scientist* article, evidently unknown to Crichton during his preparation of the *Jurassic Park* manuscript, Benton didn't mention amber-preserved insects, although he suggested alternate means for reproducing ancient animals cloned from DNA extracted from fossilized bones. "Will we ever be able to clone a dinosaur...? The chances of success seem remote at present, so we may have a long way to go before biologists can produce a cloned dinosaur. For a start, they would have to get some dinosaur DNA, and no-one has found any of that yet; they have to clone it. And what on earth would you choose for a *surrogate mother* of a dinosaur?"[38] In other words, Benton's cloned dinosaur embryos would be placed inside a living female's womb serving as a surrogate mother.

But what were the perceived odds of being able to actually clone a dinosaur? Not very good, although it would have appeared quite the opposite to the general public as Crichton's novel made it to the silver screen in the summer of 1993. For reports of red blood cells discovered in *Tyrannosaurus* bone made headlines in early July 1993, nearly coinciding with the release of Universal's blockbuster *Jurassic Park*. A New York *Times* News Service head-

By the late 1990s, raptor dinosaurs—especially the six-foot-long *Velociraptor* (which by then were commonly thought to have been feathered creatures in life), ranked high among the dinosauria in popular consciousness due to the successes of *Jurassic Park* novels and films written or inspired by author Michael Crichton. (With permission of the artist, Jack Arata.)

line published in the July 1, 1993, *Chicago Tribune* stated boldly "Tyrannosaurus DNA may be Extracted"!

Few realized that a year prior to publication of Crichton's novel, efforts to clone ancient DNA had been mounting since April 1990, when researchers cloned a chloroplast DNA sequence from an exceptionally well preserved 17-to-20-million-year-old magnolia leaf.[39] Fueled by this remarkable news, and perhaps even by *Jurassic Park*, experimenters claimed that DNA had been successfully extracted in 1992 from a 25-to-30-million-year-old termite species, another successful DNA extraction in 1992, this time from a thirty-million-year-old bee preserved in amber, and then, in 1993, from a Jurassic-aged weevil.[40] Authors of the weevil paper saw their paper published one day prior to the release of *Jurassic Park*, although they claimed it was a coincidence. Lead investigator Raul Cano stated, "The possibility of cloning dinosaurs is ... probably impossible. But we have now at least shown that DNA from the age of dinosaurs actually has survived."[41] Next, in 1994, it was claimed that DNA had been sequenced from eighty-million-year-old dinosaur bone fragments.[42]

By 1997, however, the amber bubble burst, as "serious doubts" had been cast on all such alleged laboratory successes conducted to date.[43] Problems with lab contamination and DNA preservation difficulties were cited. So, if one couldn't extract geologically old DNA, then how could any dinosaurs ever be cloned? In the realm of fantastic fiction did it really matter?

FOURTH ITERATION: JURASSIC PARK'S UNNATURAL HISTORY

I've triple-checked, and that key phrase "Clever girl," uttered by Muldoon in the film *Jurassic Park* just prior to his demise, doesn't appear in Crichton's novel. And yet, to me, this line delivers the essence of what the *Jurassic Park* "genre" is all about—female perspective and "good mother lizards." In fact this illustrious theme has a longstanding history. *Jurassic Park* is more than dinosaurs being restored through an ingenious melding of high-tech with bio-tech.

As in many monster movies, traditionally there's the scene early in the film where a survivor mortally wounded by the beast is nursed by rescuers, only to utter in a dying breath the monster's name. In Crichton's 1990 novel this monster turns out to be the "Raptor," a dino-monster term effectively representing all of the bioengineered breed on Isla Nublar and Isla Sorna, and even those escaping to the mainland. Crichton provides a Costa Rican translation for this term, which also means the *hupia*, or "night ghosts, faceless vampires who kidnapped small children."[44] While this particular victim suffers from the poison of a *Procompsognathus* bite, the name "raptor" quickly became synonymous with those insidious *Velociraptors*. These are so frightening not only because of their manlike size and upright posture, but also due to their wicked intelligence and ability to kill, cruelly ... like humans are so capable.

> They killed for the pleasure of killing.... Raptors were at least as intelligent as chimpanzees. And, like chimpanzees, they had agile hands that enabled them to open doors and manipulate objects. They could escape with ease. And when, as Muldoon had feared, one of them finally escaped, it killed two construction workers and maimed a third before being recaptured.[45]

And in Crichton's *The Lost World*, we read how in once scene, "The raptors were all snarling and licking the blood off their snouts, wiping their faces with their clawed forearms, a gesture oddly intelligent, almost human."[46]

Crichton's Jurassic Park environment blends elements of the traditional dino-monster story, as 292 dinosaurs inhabit (infest) a pair of long neglected ("lost") islands, where due to the unnatural grouping of creatures representing different geological ages, "time stands still." Also, at least one species of dinosaur—*Procompsognathus*—has already escaped to Costa Rica. And then we have the usual assortment of greedy souls, villains, mad scientists, eggheads and, of course, heroes. However, following Crichton's description of the process for cloning dinosaurs (and with considerable attention to detail, unlike predecessor writers who more or less waved a wand over the crypto-technology), we learn that the fragments of cloned dinosaur DNA had to be doped into DNA of extant animals. This is the crucial error permitting the populations of dinosaur species—all initially *female*—to breed. From there things steadily unravel, chaotically. For Hammond, Nedry, Malcolm, Wu, Drs. Grant and Sattler, Muldoon, and the rest, it's going to become a really bad day at the lost world!

The first baby dinosaur witnessed by Dr. Grant in Hammond's laboratory, newborn into the modern world, is a *Velociraptor mongoliensis*, the very sort of dinosaur he'd just excavated from a deposit in Montana. This prompts a remark from Wu to the effect that "All the animals in Jurassic Park are female." Disbelieving, mathematician and chaos theory expert Malcolm challenges, "... is that checked? Does anyone go out and, ah, lift up the dinosaurs' skirts to have a look?"[47] Later, Malcolm proclaims prophetically, "You're going to engineer a bunch of prehistoric animals and set them free on an island? Fine. A lovely dream. Charming. But it won't go as planned. It is inherently unpredictable, just as the weather is.... Because the history of evolution is that life escapes all barriers. Life breaks free. Life expands to new territories. Painfully, perhaps even dangerously. But life finds a way."[48]

Only after geneticist Dr. Wu reveals that besides that besides avian DNA, dino-DNA strands had to be spliced with gender-bending amphibian (e.g., frog) DNA, is it understood that the dinosaurs must be breeding, and that the raptors must be roaming at large throughout the park, even sneaking onto the boat headed for the mainland. In Jurassic Park, life is finding a way because clever *girls* have found a way to breed—no, have been *granted* means of reproduction due to human folly. Like his predecessor, Dr. Frankenstein, Hammond—whose empty glass is always half full—is the real monster. Hammond recollects, "My colleagues and I determined ... that it was possible to clone the DNA of an extinct animal, and to grow it. That seemed to us a wonderful idea, it was a kind of time travel—the only time travel in the world. Bring them back alive, so to speak. And it was so exciting, and since it was possible to do it, we decided to go forward."[49] Malcolm's perspective on mankind's arrogance is the antithesis of Hammond's. "[S]cientific power is like inherited wealth: attained without discipline. There is no discipline lasting many decades. There is no mastery.... There is no humility before nature. There is only a get-rich quick, make-a-name-for-yourself-fast philosophy. Cheat, lie, falsify—it doesn't matter."[50]

Much of the main body of the novel is about Dr. Grant—who in the 1993 film doesn't like kids—and Hammond's two grandchildren, Lex and Tim (children from a broken home), fleeing from dinosaurs throughout the park and visitors' compound. Meanwhile, back at the compound, Sattler, who likes the idea of having children someday, nurses the wounded Malcolm. In the end, Grant and Sattler observe a family of raptors on the volcanic southern end of Isla Nublar, intent on migrating to the mainland. "There was a female with a distinctive stripe along her head.... that same female had stayed in the center of the nesting area ... like certain monkey troops, the raptors were organized around a matriarchal pecking order, and that this striped animal was the alpha female of the colony."[51]

This represents a curious, disjointed family affair both for dinosaurs and mankind, as in the 1993 movie, Sattler and Grant, who are unattached, become the children's surrogate parents—while man becomes the surreal parent of dinosaurs. According to sociologist John

O'Neill, "Without a family, Lexis and Tim ... risk losing their chance of reentering the family by so confirming Alan's [i.e., Dr. Grant's] distaste for children that even Ellie's combination of feminist independence and maternal desire is helpless to win him over. Of course, both Alan and Ellie have to be seduced away from their dead love of paleo-pets for the kids to be removed from the endangered species list."[52]

But is *Jurassic Park* merely, as O'Neill proclaimed, "the new Easter of the dino-egg fertilized by the marriage of science and consumerism ... an infantile fantasy of bypassing the primal scene of reproduction through a combination of lab, computer, and art skills that the superkid can master, renewing human history as a game run by and for children"?[53]

Harnessing DNA power is no child's affair. As the anonymous television announcer once cautioned, "Don't try this at home, kids!"

FIFTH ITERATION FRANKENSTEIN VS. *JURASSIC PARK*

It was a woman who, in effect, created the modern dino-monster! Dinosaur genetic force, misused by man and mightier than atomic power, is inherently female.

The roots of today's modernized, high-tech dino-monsters can indeed be traced to Mary Shelley's *Frankenstein*—perhaps the first true sci-fi novel reflecting fears and futuristic hazards of bio-tech, written over a century before publication of Aldous Huxley's (1894–1963) *Brave New World*, 1932.

Two monstrous pinnacles of fantasy literature, seemingly unassociated, are in fact from the same ideological mold—Mary Shelley's *Frankenstein: or the Modern Prometheus* (1818 and 1831 eds.)[54] and Michael Crichton's *Jurassic Park* (1990). *Jurassic Park* can be viewed as a modernized version of *Frankenstein*, perhaps the tale Mary Shelley (1797–1851) would have written had she been born 150 years later. Fittingly, *Frankenstein* was written during an important period of discovery, when the first fossilized bones of extinct saurians, later to be classified as dinosaurs, came to light. While Shelley discourages use of the contemporary, emerging science of electricity and chemistry to reveal God's benevolent design, Crichton exposes our fears and uncertainties over the misguided use, or abuse, of biotech. (For, if bloodthirsty and cunning dinosaurs could be cloned, why not the most contemptuous *humans*—modern "Frankensteins"—as well?)

Given steady bombardment of our senses by classic horror tale screen adaptations and monster fan literature, it is all too easy to accept "traditional" views on the nature of "real" monsters. In Shelley's story, Frankenstein's monster was horrific to behold, a murderer. It was an unholy, rejected "offspring" of its creator, instilled with unrealized potential. (In the 1931 film starring Boris Karloff as the monster, however, Dr. Frankenstein's creation proved psychologically unstable due to deterministic causes, basic human error—the inadvertent substitution of a criminal brain for that of a superior specimen of mankind.)

A modern renaissance in the science and art of dinosaurs budded during the heyday of 1960s monster fandom. Because they were once real animals, like the lions and tigers and bears of today, dinosaurs are rarely given their due as true monsters. Yet from human perspective, the largest and most ferocious of *Jurassic Park*'s carnivores (i.e., *T. rex* and the vicious *Velociraptors*, a.k.a. raptors) would have seemed scarier if encountered in-the-flesh than would have Shelley's original conception of Frankenstein's monster. (Frankenstein's monster even spoke *French!*) If you could politely avert your eyes from his ghastly countenance, it would have been possible to sit down to dinner with Frankenstein's monster, engaged in artful conversation, although *Jurassic Park*'s raptors rudely disembowel their dinner guests.

Jurassic Park's dinosaurs are encoded from insensate DNA biomolecules, analogous to how Frankenstein's monster was resurrected from lifeless matter. As depicted on-screen and in his novel, Crichton's creatures certainly seem monstrous and terrifying. However, his raptors and *T. rexes* may also be viewed as malicious, modernized, genetic reincarnations of Mary Shelley's Frankenstein. Billed as idealized restorations of our planet's former "lords of creation," much as Frankenstein's monster—stitched together from corpses—was intended to be a model human being, *Jurassic Park*'s dinosaurs—formed by stitching together strands of DNA—quickly go berserk. The moral is clear. Ultimately, with their vile (and soon disowned) creations on the loose creating unspeakable terror, men of science and greed are transmogrified into the real monsters! After all, havoc, mayhem and even chaos are anticipated consequences whenever scientists, stricken with hubris, corrupt natural order.

We've become so accustomed to Universal's classic "universe" of Frankensteinian horror, that many of us may have forgotten the inherent fear-behind-the-science of Mary Shelley's novel. In weaving *Frankenstein* from a recalled nightmarish dreamscape, Shelley was influenced by the experiments of Erasmus Darwin (1731–1802)—Charles Darwin's grandfather. Erasmus was a pioneer in the philosophical understanding of evolutionary principles. He also invented new types of pumps, carriages and other mechanical devices, proposed (if not actually tested) a means of rocket propulsion using hydrogen and oxygen, and reflected on a "Big Bang" theory explaining the origin of stars from chaos. But Shelley recalled in 1831 one particular experiment where "(Erasmus) Darwin ... preserved a piece of vermicelli in a glass case till by some extraordinary means it began to move with involuntary motion. Not thus, after all, would life be given. Perhaps a corpse would be re-animated; galvanism had given token of such things. Perhaps the component parts of a creature might be manufactured, brought together, and endued with vital warmth."[55]

Shelley's protagonist, the ingenious Victor Frankenstein, studies medieval alchemical texts of Paracelsus (1493–1541) and Albertus Magnus (circa 1200–1280) prior to gaining the modern scientific knowledge necessary for stimulating life from cadavers. Interestingly (according to Historian of Science Allen G. Debus), "Paracelsus wrote about generating the 'homunculus' (i.e., a miniaturized 'essence' of a human being) in a chemical flask, and Albertus Magnus was thought to have fashioned a head of brass that talked."[56] Today, we can't speculate to what degree Dr. Victor Frankenstein, through Mary Shelley, was shaped by knowledge of their unusual, alleged preoccupations.

Apart from his unfortunate predilection, Dr. Frankenstein's ultimate failure stems from psychological character flaws. Victor is a loner, on the level of a Jeffrey Dahmer type, a real weirdo anyone with a teenage daughter should be wary of! He is delusional, eventually branding himself a madman. At first, he has prototypical visions of grandeur, desiring of his creation that, "A new species would bless me as its creator and source." He rejoices in the fruit of his two-year labors, an eight-foot-tall abomination. (Given that the materials for his giant were furnished both from the "dissecting room and the slaughterhouse, one wonders whether he used any animal parts too, perhaps foreshadowing H.G. Wells' *The Island of Dr. Moreau* in 1896.) Later, after infusing his creation with "a spark of being," Victor, stricken with "breathless horror and disgust," condemns the nightmarish apparition. "A mummy again endured with animation could not be so hideous as that wretch."

Taking its first convulsive breath, the creature joins the living, although without benefit of the electrical gadgetry and laboratory special effects seen in the 1931 film, and without the creator's dramatic exultation, "*It's alive!*" Quite conversely, in the novel, by omitting details on how to reanimate the dead, Shelley opted to suspend disbelief in Victor's ability to do the unthinkable. Then, haunted by his ghastly creature, Victor requires medical asylum. After a prolonged convalescence, Victor—himself a "modern Prometheus" like Benjamin Franklin (1706–1790) who experimented with lightning—finally spies his murderous creation framed in preternatural lightning glare on a dark and stormy night. Mired in despair, Victor laments his strange progeny, a "living monument of presumption and rash ignorance which I had let loose upon the world," much like John Hammond would seventeen decades later in *Jurassic Park*'s fictional setting. Ultimately, his maniacal mission to destroy the monster becomes all-consuming, ending tragically in Victor's death.

Whereas in *Frankenstein*, Victor suffers for boldly going where no man should, in *Jurassic Park* many people are eaten and trampled by dinosaurian monsters set in motion by a chaotic turn of events. Victor pays mightily for his sin of playing God, while in *Jurassic Park*, chaos, unpredictability and catastrophe become natural manifestations of the universe's controlling force. *Jurassic Park*'s somber message is that no ordered system is failsafe, no matter how many safeguards are employed, especially when creatures that should no longer be alive—i.e., bloodthirsty dinosaurs and other prehistoric animals—enter the picture, destabilizing natural order through becoming integral components of that system. Chaos personified will even pass judgment on those who have disturbed natural order. In Crichton's novel and the 1993 movie, this message comes across as, "Don't mess with Mother Nature, or you'll be devoured."

SIXTH ITERATION: IN THE BELLY OF THE BEAST

Frankenstein and *Jurassic Park* share two other themes, those of consumption and replication.

Jurassic Park's dinosaurs go on a rampage, eating everything in sight, including humans. After all, eating is a dinosaurian preoccupation. And from the outset of our fascination with such prehistoria, humans *have* been consumed within the "belly of the beast"—by dinosaurs and other prehistoric horrors. In fact, in 1853, British Victorian scientists celebrated New Year's Eve wining and dining themselves into the wee hours of the morning within the life-sized mold of a dinosaur sculpted and cast by Benjamin Waterhouse Hawkins for the world's first such exhibition of prehistoric animal statues. To be consumed with (or by) dinosaurs is not far removed, metaphorically, from how fully Dr. Frankenstein becomes self-absorbed in his maniacal quest to create a person from non-living body parts. In *Frankenstein*, self-absorption leads to enslavement by the creature, and ultimately ... death. In a sense, tormented Victor has been psychologically *consumed* by his monster, not unlike the way Crichton's victims have been savagely devoured by rampaging rexes and raptors.

The first true American monster, every bit as imaginary as Frankenstein's monster, predates Shelley's invention. This, as claimed by Paul Semonin in his fascinating account

American Monster (2000),[57] was an early perception of a prehistoric beast—our American *Mastodon*, originally regarded as a fearsome carnivore. Intriguingly, on Christmas 1801, participants celebrated at a dinner staged *within* the first reconstructed skeleton of an American *Mastodon*, foreshadowing the dinner-inside-the-*Iguanodon* half a century later! Thus, metaphorically, we sense a continuum, from the first real "American monster" through Mary Shelley's *Frankenstein*, leading to *Jurassic Park*'s raptors, and beyond.

Perhaps the gravest, ultimate crisis facing mankind today is overpopulation, yet it is the least acknowledged environmental crisis. But when the monsters begin spawning at an out-of-control rate, then we have reason to fear. So, in relative safety we face down our fears of overpopulation through favored sci-fi books and movies. For instance, how can we readily forget the horrific alien replication featured in Ridley Scott's *Alien* (1979) and its sequels? From self-replicating robots of the sci-fi pulps, Karel Capek's madly spawning Newts, frightening vampires of Stephen King's *Salem's Lot* which multiply at a geometric rate, vast clutches of baby-Godzilla hatchlings invading New York City in TriStar's *Godzilla* (1998), to armies of human clones in a recent *Star Wars* prequel or even those cuddly *Star Trek* Tribbles (created by *Deathbeasts* author David Gerrold) ... we've seen 'em all.

The association between bioengineering, prehistoric biotech-wielding monsters and the softer gender (i.e., Mary Shelley's) is keenly felt through Harry Harrison's trilogy of *West of Eden* novels concerning the Yilane, a race of intelligent Mosasauroids which might have evolved from marine Mosasaurs by recent Ice Age times had the K-T boundary asteroid never collided with the Earth sixty-five million years ago. For Yilane society—including its commanders, warriors and workers—is dominated by females. Male Yilane have but one function—they are necessary for reproduction *and* even give birth! (Talk about role reversal!)

Jurassic Park's were bioengineered to be all females, to *prevent* their replication. But because missing strands of dinosaur DNA were selected from modern amphibian DNA, male dinosaurs also hatched—allowing the dinosaurs, the vicious raptors poisonous "compys" especially, to reproduce and spread at an alarming rate. In *Frankenstein*, published thirteen decades before the discovery of DNA, Mary Shelley's Dr. Frankenstein creates a female companion for his creation. But in revulsion he destroys the "bride" before the experiment reaches the point of no return. If he hadn't, conceivably, an unholy union of reanimated supermen and women would replicate the world over. In one passage of Shelley's novel, Victor Frankenstein reflects on the demon seed to be spread "if they were to leave Europe and inhabit the deserts of the new world ... one of the first results of those sympathies for which the demon thirsted would be children, and a race of devils would be propagated upon the earth who might make the very existence of the species of man a condition precarious and full of terror. Had I [the] right ... to inflict this curse upon everlasting generations?"[58]

Had Shelley written a sequel to *Frankenstein*, wouldn't that have been the natural plot— a tale of futuristic Frankensteinian generations challenging our species for supremacy? Or, in a sense, is *Jurassic Park* indeed Shelley's "sequel"? (Incidentally, filmed sequels to *Jurassic Park*—*The Lost World: Jurassic Park* (1997) and Spielberg's *Jurassic Park III* (2001), as well as all the Universal movie spin-offs following the 1931 film, are in themselves forms of literary and filmic replication.) In monster stories, replacement of the human race by races of superbeings (genetically reconstructed dinosaurs, self-replicating robots, or supermen) remains a conceivable outcome of replication.[59]

The connections between Mary Shelley's *Frankenstein* and Crichton's *Jurassic Park* are inescapable. Dinosaurs and Frankenstein's monster(s) (i.e., including its "bride") are forever linked thematically, historically and metaphorically. We must acknowledge the dawning association between monsters of literature and the first known fossil reptile later claiming status as a dinosaur. For Gideon Mantell (1790–1852), a co-discoverer of the bones of *Iguanodon*, claimed of its probable life appearance as he attempted an early 1830s reconstruction how he was appalled at the gigantic ". .being which rose from his meditations ... like Frankenstein."[60] *Iguanodon*, perhaps the "Frankenstein" of dinosaurs, became the creature immortalized through the famous New Year's Eve celebration of 1853, with humans—those consumed engaged in *consumption, reconstruction* from inanimate (fossilized) remains, and even *replication* (i.e. from cast/sculpted dinosaurs)—dining within its restored abdomen. Thus, from early perceptions of America's *Mastodon*, through Shelley's *Frankenstein*, through an inaccurately restored *Iguanodon* of Victorian times, into the *Jurassic Park* era of CGI-replicated dinosaurs, the spirit of Frankenstein's monster lives on.

SEVENTH ITERATION: CRICHTON'S LEGACY?

Following on the heels of *Jurassic Park*'s bookstore and box office successes, scores of other sci-fi tales involving raptors or fossil DNA appeared, including, for example, Victor Appleton's *Tom Swift—The DNA Disaster* (1991), and Ian McDowell's "Bernie" (*Asimov's Science Fiction*, August 1994), the latter a horrifying spoof of "Barney," the alarming, TV-land purple dinosaur. Frank M. Robinson's 1993 short story "The Greatest Dying"—where a disease-infested, amber-preserved raptor claw threatens extinction of the human race—was a treat, while Penelope Banka Kreps' rather obscure pulp novel *Carnivores* (1993) tried to capitalize on *Jurassic Park*'s fame.[61] In Thomas Hopp's *Dinosaur Wars* (2000) and a competent sequel *Dinosaur Wars—Counterattack* (2002), we see a merging of the *Star Wars* theme with *Jurassic Park*.[62] Hopp speculated about a technologically advanced race of space-faring dinosaurs who attack Earth from the moon after being reconstituted from sixty-five-million-year-old dino-DNA preserved in a lunar base. Hopp's insidious race of "Pteronychus" therefore represents a rather ingenious example of the outer space dinosauroid theme as well.

Stories by Bill Johnson, and Lori Selke, respectively—"The Vaults of Permian Love" (*Analog*, May 1999) and "The Dodo Factory" (*Asimov's Science Fiction*, March 2005)—exemplify how influential *Jurassic Park* has been through such intricately conceived speculative means for reproducing extinct fauna genetically.[63] Now, thanks to Crichton, one nearly needs a college class or two to be able to fully understand speculative fiction involving fossil DNA.

In the midst of all this dino-DNA, tabloid-ridden hype, it was easy to gain an impression that evildoers of the world were about to unleash regenerated dinosaurs upon civilization, more or less like Harry Adam Knight's Sir Penward intended to do. So, for those desiring peace of mind, Rob DeSalle and David Lindley clarified in their informative book *The Science of Jurassic Park and the Lost World* (1997) that it's pretty darn near impossible to regenerate a dinosaur the way Crichton speculated it could be done.[64] Meanwhile, scientists scored successes in extracting DNA from Neanderthal Man bones and the 23,000-year-old Jarkov Mammoth from Siberia.[65]

Paleontologist Robert Bakker twice wove speculative tales of realistic dinosaurs, first in his 1994 essay for *Earth* magazine, "Cretaceous Park," concerning a fictitious *Utahraptor* attack. Next, the artistic Bakker refined his ideas for his 1995 novel, *Raptor Red*, in which he traced the life of one *Utahraptor* individual in the Early Cretaceous. "I'm a method pale-ontologist," Bakker once said. "I want to be Jurassic. I want to smell what the megalosaur smells. I want to see what he sees."[66] Bakker is an expert "environmental vertebrate paleon-tologist," taking particular care to understand the paleoenvironments dinosaurs lived in. And his knowledge of the Cretaceous ecological system deeply enhances *Raptor Red*.

In spinning his tale of Early Cretaceous North American dinosaurian fauna, Bakker has scored another strike for originality! Readers may delight in an elaborate illustration of how dinosaurs lived their lives, conveying far more than would ever be possible in any paint-ing or sculpture (which would merely focus on an *instant* in time). Bakker has woven many ideas concerning the evolution and behavior of dinosaurs, albeit extrapolated from what is known of living species, into his story.

Since the mid–1990s, while raptors haven't become our *favorite* dinosaurs, they've cer-tainly become the most intriguing dinosaur breed, a trend set in motion perhaps since publi-cation of Sagan's *The Dragons of Eden* (1977). We've become accustomed to seeing realistic raptors, such as Wayne Barlowe's 1992 restoration of a *Velociraptor* gazing into the twilight, or those appearing in recent speculative documentaries, such as *Walking with Dinosaurs* (2000) (i.e., *Utahraptor*), *Dinosaur Planet* (2003) (i.e., a Mongolian CGI *Velociraptor* pack featuring the tale of "White Tip" and "Blue Brow"), and even Disney's animated *Dinosaur!* movie released in 2000 with its nasty *Velociraptors*.[67] These days it's easy to associate DNA with things prehistoric as genetics have surfaced in a variety of popular, post–*Jurassic Park* films such as *Relic* (1996), *Godzilla vs. Biollante* (1989), *Sabertooth* (2002) and *Anonymous Rex* (2005).[68] And while Douglas Lebeck's raptors described in his *Memories of a Dinosaur Hunter* (2002) are wholly vicious, raptors inhab-iting artist James Gurney's imaginary *Dinotopia* (1992) are sensible, energetic and hard-working scribes that contribute to society. Following the 1996 discovery of feathers associated with cer-tain Chinese dinosaurs, now raptors are thought to be fine-feathered fellows as well. We've come a long way since the quagga, not only in science but also in the pop-cultural realm!

Conclusion: Hubris and Bio-tech, "Been There, Done That"

And just when you thought it was safe to visit an uncharted Pacific isle, such as Kong's Skull Island (i.e., *Kong: King of Skull Island*, 2004), where, as envisioned by Joe DeVito, vicious raptors dwell, came news that scientists were dabbling in dino-DNA once more. While reports of early–1990s efforts to extract ancient biomolecules from dinosaur bone and other fossils had been contested, finally came positive findings that seemed beyond question. For in 1997, first, molecules indicative of the presence of insect chitin—preserved in twenty-five-million-year-old specimens—were identified, followed by the dramatic discov-ery of ancient heme structures in a *Tyrannosaurus* bone sample possibly representing origi-nal components of dinosaur blood.[69] Eight years later, researchers claimed they'd found soft tissue micro-structures such as flexible, hollow blood vessels and "cellular features" in another *T. rex* bone sample.[70] The discovery had researchers thinking about fossil bones in a whole new light! For if one kept his or her eyes open they might find the key to a brave new world of examining the past.

One of Harry Harrison's intelligent, militaristic Yilane, equipped with a bioengineered dart gun known as a *hesotsan*. See chapter text and Appendix for details. Illustration by Lisa R. Debus. (Reproduced with permission.)

Where could such experimentation lead? When, if ever, will we learn that human folly knows no bounds? Rather than finding Gilligan and his shipmates, someday shipwrecked castaways may find themselves rowing frantically away from Raptor Island instead.

But hadn't we been there in the "B.C." era, that is, Before Crichton? For Aldous Huxley had already brought us the delights of "paradise engineering" with its sexless forms of (cloned) human reproduction and an apparent end to the era of Darwinian evolution. Huxley's "brave new world" was inspired by technology, with his novel beginning in the year 632 A.F. (i.e. "after Henry Ford"). Forming humans in a lab "hatchery" will control population growth and generate a socially compatible caste structure. Writing fifteen years after *Brave New World's* publication, Huxley sardonically opined:

> It is only by means of the sciences of life that the quality of life can be radically changed. The sciences of matter can be applied in such a way that they will destroy life or make the living of it impossibly complex and uncomfortable.... All things considered it looks as though Utopia were far closer to us than anyone ... could have imagined.... I projected it six hundred years into the future. Today it seems quite possible that the horror may be upon us within a single century. That is, if we refrain from blowing ourselves to smithereens in the interval.[71]

Six years before *Jurassic Park's* publication, Harry Harrison's Yilane race of Mosasauroids descended upon Ice Age humans in a parallel world setting in which the K-T boundary asteroid never exterminated the dinosaurs, ammonites and marine saurians. According to a surviving Yilane manuscript, "Only when we stop evolution can we begin to understand it."[72] Incredibly, the cold-blooded Yilane have mastered bio-technology to the point where they've held their evolution and that of other saurians in stasis for over thirty million years by controlling the reproduction process! Yilane society is very much the saurian "brave new world" equivalent.

Tinkering with dino-DNA strands was intended to prevent any dinosaur reproduction whatsoever, other than that controlled by scientists—never a good or wise thing. Crichton, through Ian Malcolm, echoed Huxley's Luddite, anti-technological sentiments, stating, "Discovery is always a rape of the natural world. Always."[73] As in his *Jurassic Park* introduction, Crichton expressed that "The commercialization of molecular biology is the most stunning ethical event in the history of science, and it has happened with astonishing speed."[74] When the dinosaurs escape, it becomes the fulfillment of chaos theory—the biotech "threat" fully realized.

So, how original was Crichton, given that DNA- engineered dinosaurs and mosasauroids had been storming the pages of science fiction for years, the concept of hubris—daring to master nature and delve in things which should be left to God—was expressed by generations of writers gong back to Mary Shelley, and that even the rising science of molecular paleontology was in place prior to *Jurassic Park*? Think of it this way, the way science fiction maven Bill Warren explained it to me using a Latin term, *post hoc, ergo propter hoc*, meaning "if it came after, it must have been based on what came before." This, of course, is a fallacy.[75]

To a certain degree, Crichton stood on the shoulders of giants to view the future, then he wrote about it. To an even greater extent, Crichton is a darn creative person who can spin a great yarn, from *Westworld* to *Jurassic Park*.

So does this mean the DNA came first, or is it the other way around?

CHAPTER 8

Infiltration: Living with Dinosaurs

BACKGROUND

Beginning with the 1980s, a period marked by a heightened pop-cultural love-fest for dinosaurology,[1] the American public increasingly saw itself cast *as* dinosaurs, a morphing reflected perhaps in some of the most fantastic dinosaur fiction of all. In a peculiar resonance, dinosaurs rapidly gained human attributes while humans increasingly acquired dinosaurian characteristics. It was as if a new race of dinosaur-men walked the earth. This blurring of distinctions between intelligent, talking saurians and man mirrored a number of socially relevant matters, including enhanced scientific understanding about dinosaurs and their world—so analogous to the human condition or plight—and the fact that dinosaurs were seen just about *everywhere!* The extraordinary dino-happy pop-cultural situation was sarcastically presaged in Jack Dann's and Gardner Gozois' 1981 story "A Change in the Weather," where nuisance dinosaurs metaphorically rain down from the skies, getting in everybody's way.[2]

After sixty-five million years of dormancy, dinosaurs had become an iconic, socio-culturally relevant breed of animals. The fact that dinosaurs were victimized by environmental devastation caused by an asteroid (or comet) impact at the peak of their evolutionary development cast them as the most tragic characters of all time. After all, *T. rex, Velociraptor* and *Triceratops* had been unjustly, cruelly cut down in their prime—sort of like Sandy Koufax or James Dean. Yet humans would never have evolved had the dinosaur reign continued unabated. Moreover, scientists had shown how dinosaurs were in certain ways *superior* to mammals and man! So if *they*—the mighty Mesozoic gods—were exterminated, what chances of survival had we?[3] Beyond (and running countercurrent to) Michael Crichton's mainstream *Jurassic Park* phenomenon, dinosaur fiction of recent times also reflected a new breed of dinosaur—often cast as non-belligerent, intelligent reptiloids. While during the 1910s through 1920s, fears of ape-human miscegenation were projected in dinosaur fiction, during the 1990s, similar affairs between man and dinosaur were not only tolerated but embraced. Why? Because by this time and for a variety of reasons people *identified* with dinosaurs.[4]

The fantastic trend toward what could be labeled loosely as intelligent dinosaur-men had begun decades earlier, of course—as far back as Wells's "In the Abyss" and Curtis's "The Monster of Lake LaMetrie." In the early 1930s, H.P. Lovecraft's *The Shadow Over Innsmouth* concerned a "Palaeogean" species of scaly, bipedal anthropoids with fishy faces inhabiting the northeast Atlantic coast.[5] These mate with human victims and through biological degeneration threaten extinction of the human race. Quite racy stuff for the 1930s, indeed! Tarzan faced a race of "Horibs," scaly man-like reptiles populating Pellucidar in Edgar Rice Burroughs' novel *Tarzan at the Earth's Core* (1930). Then came Capek's warlike "Newts" reflecting the contemporary human condition, followed by Universal's prehistoric Gillman from *The Creature from the Black Lagoon* (Universal, 1954), which *Dr. Moreau*-like scientists attempted to further humanize through vivisection in a filmed sequel. Before the "decade of the dinosaur" (i.e., the 1980s) was in full swing, we also encountered pseudo-dino-humanoids in a 1967 *Star Trek* episode (i.e., the "Gorn" race) and *Dr. Who* (e.g., the "Silurians").[6] However, dinosaur- men, such as Gottfried's *Homosaurus*, never really caught on until after scientific evidence supported a popular case for warm-blooded, brainy and nurturing dinosaur species, that is, after the late 1970s.[7]

Beyond children's books, perhaps the first story which explored the infiltration theme involving a creature named as a dinosaur was Italo Calvino's (1923–1985) *Cosmicomics* (1968). Calvino's chapter, titled "The Dinosaurs," is told from point of view of the last surviving, fifty-million-year-old dinosaur named "Qfwfp." But while the legend of dinosaurs persists among the predominant mammalian "pantothere" race, known as the "New Ones," many doubt whether dinosaurs ever really existed. By now, dinosaurs are a shadowy myth and the New Ones don't recognize Qfwfp for what he is—a real dinosaur. After a genuine dinosaur skeleton comes to light, the New Ones are unable to associate its form with Qfwfp's; the New Ones still don't believe him even after Qfwfp comes right out and confesses that he *is* a bona fide dinosaur! If the New Ones are regarded allegorically as humans, then dinosaur Qfwfp has achieved perfect assimilation into our society.[8]

The Russell/Seguin dinosauroid model discussed in Chapter Six revolutionized our concept of intelligent, essentially humanoid dinosaurs. Humanoid anatomy—outlines of which are evident in dinosauroids—was seen by some as a hypothetical example of evolutionary convergence, evident in intelligent, technological species. Unlike Gojira, *Carnosaur*'s crafty *Deinonychus*, or Bradbury's *T. rex* "thunder lizard," Russell and Seguin's dinosauroid wasn't scary or hellbent on destruction. Russell speculated that "the dinosauroid-human form may have a non-negligible probability of appearing as a consequence of natural selection within the biospheres of earthlike planets."[9] Yet, as mankind can testify, intelligent species—such as ourselves mirrored in dinosauroids or scaly dinosaur-men—can exploit or otherwise become a blight on the natural environment through war, pollution and, especially, overpopulation.

In the first wave of dinosaur fiction, humans sought living examples of dinosaurs and other prehistoric animals for scientific reasons, first in the earth's remote or forgotten places, and later in the vastness of space-time. When colossal prehistoria mounted our shores we repelled them, often with dire consequences. But as science humanized dinosaurs during the 1980s, we accepted their ubiquitous presence. For these dinosaurs not only reflected mass pop-culture; they also had important stories to tell about the tragic human condition. Conjured from a misty past, personified dinosaurs were just trying to come home to live in a community alongside human brethren, if we'd only give them another chance. And so, building on its mythic foundation of lost worlds and other speculative encounters with man, dinosaur fiction of the late 1980s and 1990s turned in a new direction—the infiltration of dinosaurs into human society.

By the late 1980s, in context of the dinosaur story, it was as if cave-people of former dino-fiction had transformed into strange reptile-men, occupying and fulfilling their niche. It is perhaps through this most recent iteration, therefore, that dinosaur fiction merges closest with anthropological fiction.

ENVIRONMENTAL PROTECTION

If humans are so darn smart, then why can't we protect our precious living environment the way any intelligent species ought to? As America entered the 1960s, gloomy Cold War despondency clouded our lives; the times were well captured in Steven Utley's "Getting Away" (1976), published a few years after Godzilla battled Toho's famous "Smog Monster" on-screen.[10] In Utley's depressing tale, Bruce Holt is afflicted with "temporal dislodgement." He's possessed by chronopathic flashbacks sending his mind back to the Late Cretaceous for brief moments. He becomes a pterosaur, a gorgosaur and a plateosaur on different occasions. At the age of 38, Holt—disgusted by the smog and pollution of his world—has lost hope for the future. His affliction is "triggered by despair" for the worsening environment and a loss of faith in our future. He's obsessed with extinction and with times before "the smell of extinction was in the air." For the dinosaurs were "nobler monsters than men." Evidently, man can read his own fate in the dinosaurs'.

> When the dinosaurs died, they left a clean world. They walked out of their world and it was still full of living things. The dinosaurs died out gracefully. When we die out, we'll take the whole world with us, one way or another.[11]

A few years following publication of Utley's story, it became evident that the dinosaurs died out anything but "gracefully," not with a whimper but with a huge bang!

During the 1960s, fears of pending global nuclear warfare and radiation poisoning gradually spilled over into concerns about chemical pollution of the environment and our own swelling masses of humanity. Marine biologist Rachel Carson (1907–1964) set a wave in motion with her classic bestseller *Silent Spring* (1962), illuminating how chemical companies and application of carcinogenic pesticides were polluting our surface waters and other environmental media. Sensitive freshwater ecosystems were on the brink of disaster as a result of chemical agent overloading. Birds were becoming sterile, laying infertile eggs. While the environmental movement gained momentum, by 1970 culminating in the creation of an Environmental Protection Agency in America, President Richard M. Nixon claimed, "The 1970s absolutely must be the years when America pays its debt to the past by reclaiming the purity of its air, its waters, and our living environment. It is literally now or never."[12]

Shortly thereafter, in 1975, paleontologist Adrian Desmond likened the dinosaurs' end–Cretaceous extinction to an environmental plight suffered by man and birds exposed to pesticides in the mid-twentieth century. Desmond claimed that "in the last few years of its dominion the dinosaur was subjected to unbearable pressure ... with their hormonal systems hopelessly out of tune, the dinosaurs reacted by laying weak-shelled eggs, and in so doing sealed the fate of their own offspring."[13]

Strangely enough, there are relatively few contemporary dinosaur tales mirroring man's fears over environmental pollution. Two titles hardly merit mention here, Leigh Clark's *Carnivore* (1997) and K. Robert Andreassi's *Gargantua* (1998), neither of which were published during the height of the 1970s environmental movement.[14] But by the early 1970s, a (literally) ever-growing threat caught the attention of skilled writer Clifford D. Simak. At a time when credence in one slogan ("Zero Population Growth") had replaced another "("Chemistry for Better Living"), people feared how the world's billions could ever cope with steadily diminishing resources.[15] For then the world's population was estimated to be doubling every thirty-five years! A "population bomb" indeed. Also, more people meant increased pollution, an insurmountable problem we're still wrestling with today. Simak got down to the heart of the overpopulation theme with a pair of novels, *Mastodonia* (1978) and *Our Children's Children* (1974), viewing the past as a great (even nostalgic!) place to escape from present and futuristic dangers—a place of salvation, if we only had the means.[16]

As the 1980s dawned, with dinosaurs enjoying more popularity and media coverage than ever before, man recognized his probable future in the dinosaurs' fate—global environmental deterioration. As an organic group, dinosaurs had survived for an incredible 160 million years, while *Homo sapiens* has only been around for a mere 50,000 years The forces which ultimately devastated their paleo-environment were entirely beyond their control, while the scourge that is man willingly pollutes and overpopulates. What could we learn from dinosaurs in order to protect ourselves? What could those eminently successful dinosaurs teach us about racial longevity and planetary conservation? Maybe if some of them had survived, gaining intelligence, they could show us the folly of our ways.

Maybe, hopefully—if disbelief can be ingeniously suspended once more—they're still around. Could they help us to help ourselves? Could dinosaurs become mankind's salvation? Maybe together man and dinosaur could valiantly find a way to thwart the inevitable—pending extinction caused by self-imposed environmental threats. Formerly viewed as unsuccessful brutes worthy only of extinction, dinosaurs—the new superheroes—offered valuable lessons for man and possibly a means of survival!

DINOTOPIAN SOCIETY

By the 1980s, authentic dinosaurian lost worlds were coming closer to home! We didn't always have too far to turn to lost worlds—essentially our own back yards—like the American west, where dinosaurs still roam with the buffalo out there yonder in Indian territory. For instance, in S.N. Dyer's (pseudonym for Sharon Farber) "The Last Great Thunder Horse West of the Mississippi" (1988), real paleontologists Othniel C. Marsh (1831–1899) and E.D. Cope (1840–1897) vie for possession of and scientific rights to a valuable specimen, a living sauropod discovered by unscrupulous prospectors in the late nineteenth century American west.[17] The two scientific combatants' greed and arrogance ultimately lead to destruction of the innocent creature. In Harry Turtledove's "The Green Buffalo" (1992), field assistants working for Professor Marsh hunt a live *Triceratops* stampeding with the buffalo. Later, they feast on its flesh (which tastes like chicken). Ironically, a paleontologist who dines with them doesn't even notice the bones he's chewing on are the same as those of the fossilized skeleton his crew has been hammering out of the rocky hillside.[18] Rather than a coordinated infiltration of dinosaurs within our ranks, Dyer's and Turtledove's cryptozoological dinosaurs were merely endangered species, a sign of the times—*our* times.

However, within the friendly confines of a fabled lost world—a southern island continent isolated from the rest of the world, known as "Dinotopia"—dinosaurs have withstood the test of time, managing not only to survive alongside humans but to convey their wisdom and philosophy to those of us who'll listen. Dinotopia is sometimes regarded as fare for younger readers; however, the two books, written and illustrated by James Gurney—*Dinotopia: A Land Apart from Time* (1992) and *Dinotopia: The World Beneath* (1995)—are read and enjoyed by adults as well, hence their inclusion here.[19] Gurney wove a number of classical ideas into the Dinotopia history and lore, influences of his archaeological training. Intriguingly, the origins of Egyptian monuments and civilization, the biblical story of Noah's Ark, and the myth of Atlantis are all associated historically with the land of Dinotopia, where man is the interloper.

But strangest of all are the indigenous fauna, intelligent dinosaurs who communicate with humans stranded on Dinotopia's shores. Set in the mid–nineteenth century, the two books comprise journal writings and sketches of Arthur Denison and his young son Will, shipwrecked off the Dinotopian coast while en voyage to Hong Kong. Soon they're confronted by a bevy of friendly dinosaurs—including many genera which, according to the known fossil record, never coexisted (or had not been discovered by 1862—the year of their shipwreck).

The premise for Gurney's "time stands still" admixture of prehistoric animals is that

James Gurney's popular *Dinotopia* volumes of the early 1990s really caught the eye and imaginations of those who longed to live alongside real dinosaurs in a lost-world setting inhabited by friendly, intelligent dinosaurs who had welcomed humans into their ancient society. (With permission of the artist)

... everything living in Dinotopia is extinct elsewhere, and everything living elsewhere is extinct on Dinotopia. So you won't find dogs and horses on Dinotopia.... Early on, I explored the idea of applying the principles of evolution that actually happen to a population that is isolated on an island: dwarfism, etc. But it's far simpler to work with creatures just as they appear in the fossil record. The minute you begin speculating about extrapolated evolution, you're dealing in fantasy, and I'd rather deal with the real dinosaurs.[20]

Arthur and Will learn how to communicate with the dinosaurs and their exceedingly content people. They soon find Dinotopia's "Code" engraved on a tablet lodged into a pyramid atop Waterfall City which, translated, reads:

Code of Dinotopia

Survival of all or none.
One raindrop raises the sea.
Weapons are enemies even to their owners.
Give more, take less.
Others first, self last.
Observe, listen, and learn.
Do one thing at a time.

Sing every day.
Exercise imagination.
Eat to live, don't live to eat.
Don't pee in the bath.[21]

All good words to live by. In short, Dinotopia is more politically and environmentally correct than any other country or civilization. And yet this isn't satire. Gurney's perspective is that:

The idea of wise, intelligent dinosaurs piques our interest because we all grew up thinking dinosaurs were dim-witted sluggards. The turning point for the evolution of the idea was to suggest that perhaps the dinosaurs domesticated the humans, rather than the other way around. The core appeal of Dinotopia is that we can share a world with other humans and with the natural world and do so peacefully. I tried to avoid a lot of laws or rules because if you're not careful utopias can turn into dystopias.[22]

The Denisons travel throughout Dinotopia, escorted by dinosaur guides, but near the end of *Dinotopia: A Land Apart from Time*, Arthur Denison decides to travel through a waterfall "portal" into the fabled "world beneath," a dark place where dinosaurs rode out ecological havoc caused by the K-T asteroid impact event. Here they hid "long, long ago, before humans started coming, [when] ... the sky went black with dust and it got cold"[23] So, naturally in *Dinotopia: The World Beneath*, Arthur explores the vast underground network of caverns and the ancient cities preserved below. Alan Dean Foster's "spin-off" 1996 novel *Dinotopia Lost* blends the nature of *Treasure Island* with the essence of *King Kong*, introducing a nineteenth-century band of brigands to Dinotopian shores in search of treasure.[24] During a 1997 *Dinosaur World* interview, Gurney slyly suggested that Dinotopia's existence may be protected from satellite surveillance in the modern day by a "cloaking device" invented by dino-engineers.[25]

Essentially, this is Charles Dickens's vision of Holburn Hill with that misty megalosaur striding along except with many more dinosaurs besides moving constructively in tow, and—incredibly—all part of an accepted dinosaur-human society! Gurney's imaginative artwork

A.C. Farley's illustration showing "Stennie," the human boy whose genes have been "twanked" so he resembles a raptor-like dinosaur. See text for further details. (With permission.)

is mesmerizing, differing stylistically as well as in content from Riou's 1867 portrayals of *Journey*'s prehistoria encountered deep inside the earth. Dinotopia is sort of a dino-lovers' Oz, although far more "prehistorical" than Terrybubble's airborne island. In his own distinctive way, Gurney has transformed (combined) elements of the lost race/lost world novel, blended images with text (into absorbing imagetext), and reconfigured the time-stands-still theme into an utterly new dinosaur infiltration mythos highly appreciated both by adults and younger readers.

If we could learn to "think like a dinosaur," ours would be a Dinotopian society.

From humans ensconced in a dino-utopia, we move on to dinosaurs fully infiltrating human society.

DINO-PEOPLE AND PURITY CONTROL

One of the oddest tales ever conceived involving a "dinosaur" wholly assimilated into human society, James Patrick Kelly's "Mr. Boy" (1990), involves a futuristic, late twenty-first century human society in which people can radically alter their morphology into any chosen organic form through genetic "twanking."[26] One human character in the story, figured on the cover of the magazine issue in which Kelly's story first appeared, has become a *Stenonychosaurus* (i.e., *Troodon*) known to his pals as "Stennie." Stennie isn't a real dinosaur; he's a genetically-altered human. However, A.C. Farley's cover art shows us Stennie looking exactly like any raptor dinosaur should, just hanging out with his human pal Mr. Boy. Twanking represents a means for the rich to escape society's mores through self expression, such as later in the story when Stennie asks for sex with his friend's twanked mother (but here we digress).

Another odd case of a (pseudo-) dinosaur having infiltrated human society is Mark Jacobson's 1991 novel *Gojiro*, wherein a certain, famous B-movie actor, a personified Godzilla-like character, who can change his height at will from a 500-foot-tall "cancerous size" to human-sized, befriends a human, "Komodo" the Coma Boy.[27] Jacobson's novel offers stylized social commentary on the atomic age and our nuclear plight, often from the perspective of the virtuous Gojiro, who lives alongside humans. Unlike Carson Bingham's *Gorgo* and lacking scenes overflowing with toppled buildings and crushed military hardware, *Gojiro* is about integrity and (inter-species) relationships.

"Mr. Boy" and *Gojiro* aren't exactly revered by today's (male-dominated) dino-enthusiasts who perhaps prefer action-packed dino-fiction laden with toppled buildings, ray-gun fire and a world in peril. So instead, the dinosaur infiltration literary theme would reach a fitting culmination a decade later with a mainstream pair of humorous detective novels that, interestingly, few hardcore dino-philes even know of.

Dinosaurs in Eric Garcia's two amusing novels, *Anonymous Rex* (2000) and *Casual Rex* (2001), can be read essentially as people in dinosaur guise, although that's opposite Garcia's premise.[28] Instead, dinosaurs have survived the K-T extinction (referred to as the Great Shower), first opting for human camouflage during the Pleistocene so they would blend in with people. And today, although you wouldn't realize it, there's a complete dinosaur society out there, seamlessly merged within the fabric of human culture. In fact, approximately five percent of the world's "human" population is made up of dinosaurs. Included among the hallowed ranks of famous dino-people are James Earl Jones, Elvis, and J. Edgar Hoover. Furthermore, the Mormon movement was "not religious in nature; rather it was reptilian." And although we humans haven't caught on, disguised dinosaurs functioning as museum technicians have even faked their extinction sixty-five million years ago.

Both of Garcia's novels are told from the perspective of an intelligent *Velociraptor* protagonist named Vincent Rubio, a private detective, who believes, "Deception is fun; human deception is a spectator sport." Dinosaurs aren't at all fond of people. As Vincent explains,

> Two-legged mammals are bad enough by themselves—rude, ego-centric, generally sporting bad hygiene—but an entire pack of the filthy apes gives me the willies. It's a visceral reaction, a subconscious tug at my gut that I'm sure is somehow representative of my shared genetic dislike and discomfort. My forefathers watched these creatures evolve from nothing more than hairy toads, and it must have pained them to no end to realize that at some time in the future, they would be forced to recognize the existence of this separate but sentient species. Sure, my ancestors could have killed them off, stomped the little Neanderthals into pâté with a few good whacks of a tail, but by that point they'd already decided to try and live in peace with the humans, even to mimic them if the need arose. Bad move.[29]

Dinosaurs conceal their identity through an intricate system of clamps, foamed skin, false teeth, elaborate masks and fake hair. For all practical purposes, every member of the sixteen surviving dinosaur species looks and sounds human; only dinosaurs can identify one another through their distinctive smells using an enhanced olfactory sense. Occasionally dinosaur individuals suffer from "Dressler's Syndrome," a psychological condition where they find themselves believing that they're human. There are also cases of effeminate dinosaur "cross-dressers," and Progressives who yearn for restoration of a (pre-human) dinosaurian condition where they no longer must wear their uncomfortable human costumes. While one marvels how a sixty-foot-long *Diplodocus* can ever squeeze into human-sized tuxedo, or how a bony, horny *Triceratops* head frill could be stuffed into a baseball cap, Garcia merely hints that dinosaur descendants of all species surviving the Great Shower somehow "evolved into our kind sometime during the last sixty-five million years."[30] ("Don't ask, don't ask!") This interchanging of guises and shape-shifting of forms can become rather confusing. At one point a dinosaur exclaims, "So let me get this straight ... this one here is a human pretending to be a dino pretending to be a human?"[31] But then these *are* detective stories.

Once a particular human costume is registered with the Dinosaur Council for a dinosaur individual, said dinosaur isn't permitted to alter his or her appearance, unless subtly to reflect the aging process. Yet we find that dinosaurs consistently violate their customs and taboos, just like humans do. Especially when it comes to sex, as suggested by Garcia's play-on-words, come-on "rexy" titles.

Ostensibly a detective story, *Anonymous Rex* is a spoof of *Jurassic Park*. Not only are dinosaurs committing the sacrilege of inter-dinosaurian species sexual intercourse, but far worse—having sex with humans! Eventually, Rubio uncovers the grand scheme of a dinosaurian scientist named Dr. Vallardo attempting to tamper with nature in order to satisfy the awful desires of a human female. Vallardo has combined her human genes with a male consort's *Carnotaurus* DNA in order to create a mixed, or cross-mated infant dinosaur-human, the love child of the dino-human couple hatched from an egg.

In Garcia's novels an underlying theme is "coming out of the closet," much like homosexuals did in American society during the 1990s. For as it's explained at the climax, a mixed dino/human child would represent a "settlement between the humans and the dinos, to introduce his kind to our kind in as peaceful a way as possible ... to bring the dinosaur community out into the open. To bring us 'out of the closet,' as he put it...."[32] However, in Garcia's sequel, the path leading out of the closet is militaristic.

Casual Rex is a prequel to *Anonymous Rex*. Here, a dinosaur faction intent on taking the planet back from unwitting humans feigns alliance with a strange cult in which dinosaurs try to get back to their natural state, by casting off human customs and increasing their hormonic purity through field exercises such as sleeping in nests, deadly red-in-tooth-and-claw combat, swimming with real crocodiles and eating raw flesh. These uncivilized activities are practiced in wild, secluded "nudist camps." Cultist Progressives blame the first dinosaur to don an "ape-suit" a million years ago as the "catalyst" leading to their eventual downfall. (In fact, the first "lady" to burn her bra was a *Brontosaurus* in human guise, "who had dealt with one strap too many"!) Progressives earn money for their cause through their chief industry, making faked fossil bones—up to 87 percent of West Coast fossil discoveries—and dinosaur skeletons which can be "authentically" planted in the ground only to be dug out later and then sold to unsuspecting humans for a mint. A regular cash-cowasaurus!

So, while Rubio and his partner set out on a case to reclaim a fellow dinosaur's stolen prosthetic penis ("Don't ask, don't ask!"), instead they're whisked into the Progressives' camp where they uncover a plot to take over the world. Following a climactic battle astride a colossal fake dinosaur skeleton named "Frank," the dino-terrorists are defeated and the world is safe once more for man and dinosaur, perfectly assimilated into human society, cross-dressers and all.

Awful Homecoming

Maybe it's fundamentally impossible to think like dinosaurs after all: therefore, maybe it'll never be possible to live with them.

In Barry B. Longyear's 1989 novel *The Homecoming*, a space fleet piloted by a race of five-fingered intelligent dinosaurs returns to Earth after seventy million years. The "Nitolans," intent on reclaiming *their* world, abhor humans' swelling populations, political strife, pollution and warlike tendencies. After a Nitolan mind-melds with an Earth representative, a negotiator named Baxter, the dinosaurs conclude how fundamentally *alien* is *our* thinking. Our humorous adage, "We're only human," is to the Nitolans a major copout. Although born of Earth, isn't Mankind aberrant?

> As lifeforms, you are freaks—self-destructive, murdering freaks! And what is your answer? 'We are only hue-man.' You use this phrase to excuse it all. But Baxter, this defines you as a lifeform. It defines you as flawed, unworthy. And this is how you define yourselves. You take pride in it. You wallow in your imperfections.[33]

So after *rejecting* an option of living alongside us on Earth, the Nitolans also decide to spare us from their powerful laser weapon—known as "the Power." Instead, they elect to return to space for another few centuries. Their expectation is that we'll have eliminated ourselves by then and Earth (or Nitola) will be naturally, rightfully theirs without need for interspecies conflict.

And maybe we should be content with that outcome *because* we're already as "dinosaur" as can be, even without the "real" variety lurking around. The dinosaurs walk among us—because they *are* us, we have become them! Through adaptive literary convergence, Man has become as one with Dinosaur, sharing a mutual fate—the riddle of the dinosaur. Let us seal our own fate, for that ability defines our uniqueness.

So, *why* the dinosaur story?

Like never before, the dinosaur has become culturally relevant, much like Bradbury's *The Martian Chronicles*. In Bradbury's conclusion, Earth's last survivors—a family consisting of three young boys and their parents—gaze into a reflecting pool.

> The Martians were there ... in the canal—reflected in the water. Timothy and Michael and Robert and Mom and Dad. The *Martians* stared back up at them for a long, long time silent time from the rippling water.[34]

How wholly analogous to John Noble Wilford's succinct conclusion to his *The Riddle of the Dinosaur*.

> In our exploration of time, we have driven down a highway and searched the junipers for some dinosaur bones and come face to face with *ourselves*.[35]

After all this, is the answer to the sphinx-like riddle of the dinosaur so simple: in a word—*man*?

CONCLUSION

In Verne's heyday adventurers were cast through a sequence of geological time periods. Increasingly, however, the Late Cretaceous—when the path of organic evolution was shaped through a cosmic accident for humans—became a focal point of intrigue.

Dinosaur *stories* (not necessarily the supporting cast of outlandish dinosaurs and other paleo-prop prehistoria themselves) consistently reflect the human condition. Mirroring humanity through dino-fiction has evolved historically in tandem with contemporary ideals and a pop-cultural pulse. Accordingly, dinosaurs have increasingly assumed more pivotal roles in dino-fiction, from simply symbolizing extinct times and prehistoric savagery—to be tempered or overthrown by civilized human interlopers—to becoming final arbiters for mankind.

Through a peculiar retrograde "de-volution," principal characters and protagonists reflecting the human condition in dino-fiction have moved steadily downward in evolutionary scale, from (in the earliest tales) Victorian intellectuals penetrating prehistory's lair, to Cro-Magnon or Neanderthals anachronously living alongside dinosaurs, through super-ape Kong darkly instilled with human attributes, to scaly dinosauroids superior to man, and ultimately through Eric Garcia's novels, intelligent dinosaurs interspersed throughout human society.

How fitting that through dinosaur stories intended to be about us, we have gradually transformed into dinosaurs! What better way to comprehend ourselves through dinosaur fiction than by literally *becoming* dinosaur?

Appendix: Dinosaur Stories and Other Noteworthy Paleo-fiction

Given space limitations, until this point it wasn't possible to mention or sufficiently describe certain dino-fiction which ought to be represented in this book. Therefore, this appendix complements previous individual chapters and associated notes. Readers may be able to glean how the following entries relate to the evolving history of fantastic literature involving dinosaurs and other prehistoric animals as conveyed through prior chapters. While much of this presentation is in plot summary form, I've striven to note unusual or otherwise interesting aspects for each entry. If summaries, below, appear uneven as to length for respective entries, this merely reflects that certain works "grabbed" me in some fashion more than others: a subjective and capricious guiding principle. There's insufficient space to summarize all published dino-fiction here. However, if certain significant or otherwise noteworthy stories received short shrift elsewhere in this volume, then I've further elaborated or summarized those titles below in this appendix. Above all, I've captured the imaginative *variety* of published stories.

It should be apparent by now that *Dinosaurs in Fantastic Fiction* isn't limited to just science fiction. In this endeavor I've encountered and considered a wide variety of fantastic fiction, although the two primary kinds might be loosely classified as science fiction and horror. (However, horror elements sometimes may simply reflect dread for the workings of science or for what may be lurking in a paleontologically founded prehistory—in which case horror would still be considered science fiction.)

But don't stop here. The following anthologies and collections are highly recommended, offering a delightful variety of more recent stories (several of which are outlined in the appendix). Also, consult with your local reference librarians and search the Internet for additional information about dino-fiction and consult the Bibliography for additional sources.

A. Bradbury, Ray. *Dinosaur Tales.* New York: Bantam Books, 1983.
B. Dann, Jack, and Gardner Dozois, eds. *Dinosaurs!* New York: Ace Books, 1990.
C. Dann, Jack, and Gardner Dozois, eds. *Dinosaurs II.* New York: Ace Books, 1995.

D. De Camp, L. Sprague. *Rivers of Time*. Riverdale, NY: Baen Books, 1993.

E. Greenberg, Martin H., ed. *Dinosaurs*. New York: Donald I. Fine Books, 1996.

F. Resnick, Michael, and Martin H. Greenberg, eds. *Dinosaur Fantastic*. New York: Daw Books, Inc., 1993.

G. Resnick, Michael, and Martin H. Greenberg, eds. *Return of the Dinosaurs*. New York: Daw Books, Inc., 1997.

H. Silverberg, Robert, Charles G. Waugh, and Martin H. Greenberg, eds. *The Science Fictional Dinosaur*. New York: Avon Books, 1982.

I. Silverberg, Robert, ed. *The Ultimate Dinosaur*. New York: iBooks, 2000.

The best way to get started on your grand tour of the not-so-irrecoverable dinosaurian past as seen through fantastic literature is to simply start reading (or maybe writing your own stories as well). And consider too the legends, natural history traditions, theoretical notions and myths of Native Americans and the ancients founded upon real fossil bones and skeletons. Classical folklorist Adrienne Mayor has thoughtfully discussed what could in a sense be regarded as very early examples of dino-fiction in her two books, *Fossil Legends of the First Americans* (Princeton: Princeton University Press, 2005), and *The First Fossil Hunters* (Princeton: Princeton University Press, 2000).

For those interested in reading the tales listed below, I've included literature references. Following certain summaries, letter designations—e.g., (A.), (B.), (C.), etc.—refer to anthologies as cited above. If no such designation appears, please consult the Bibliography for the citation. For additional titles, see pp. 698 to 700 in *The Complete Dinosaur* (1997), edited by James Farlow, Michael Brett-Surman and Robert Walters. Below, titles of novels are *italicized*.

Aldiss, Brian. "Poor Little Warrior" (1958). In British writer Brian W. Aldiss' most famous piece of dinosaur fiction, a humorous short story, dinosaur hunter Claude Ford suffers a most unfortunate outcome with an unlikely and most disgusting prehistoric monster. "Poor Little Warrior" offers an ironic twist on the time safari theme. Ford is poised, ready to shoot a "sitting duck," a defenseless yet smelly and otherwise repugnant *Brontosaurus* wallowing in a swamp. Bush muses, "...here horror had reached its limits, come full circle and finally disappeared up its own sphincter." While observing the great dull-witted beast, Ford notes the lobster-sized parasites swarming over its epidermis.

Why, then, did Bush place himself in such a dreadful situation? Aldiss narrates, "You just wish you could forget yourself ... that was, after all, the reason you had to come the long way here. *Get Away from It All*, said the time travel brochure, which meant for you getting away from Claude Ford, a husbandman as futile as his name with a terrible wife called Maude. Maude and Claude Ford. Who could not adjust themselves to each other, or to the world they were born in. It was the best reason in the as-it-is-present-constituted world for coming back here to shoot giant saurians...." Ford pulls the trigger, and slowly, relentlessly, the brontosaur expires before him. "Nothing is left to you now but to slink back to your time-mobile with a belly full of anticlimax." However, Ford neglected to anticipate a result of death—that the parasites would leave the great carcass to find other hosts, such as *himself*! Soon, Ford is screaming in agony as "something lands socko on your back, pitching your face forward into tasty mud. You struggle and scream as lobster claws tear at your neck and throat.... You wrench at its shell, but it giggles and pecks your fingers off.... Already they are picking your carcass loving clean. You're going to like it up here on top of the Rockies; you won't feel a thing." (B.)

Aldiss, Brian W. "Heresies of the Huge God" (1966). Although not quite a real dinosaur by any stretch of the imagination, even pseudo-dinosaur Godzilla would be puny when scaled against the proportions of Aldiss's "Huge God." Suddenly, out of the depths of outer space, a gigantic creature alights upon the Earth. This animal is continent-sized: its head stretches into the stratosphere! Although it's difficult surmising the Huge God's nature and origin, "if living," it may qualify as an exodinosaur because in one brief passage Aldiss remarks, "...it somewhat resembles an eight-footed lizard...." Mankind can do nothing but humbly pray to the Huge God, even as its mass upsets the Earth's orbital rotation and, alarmingly, increases the radial distance to the Sun. (See Aldiss's *Man In His Time*.)

Anderson, Poul. "Unnatural Enemy" (1992). A forty-foot-long *Elasmosaurus* named "Harpoon" is the protagonist of this late Cretaceous tale. After losing a flipper to an eighty-foot *Carcharodon* shark, Harpoon eventually regains strength to fend it off from its territory in a titanic marine struggle. (I.)

Asimov, Isaac. "A Statue for Father" (1958). A physicist invents a "Chrono-funnel," increasing temporal "permeability" such that specimens can slide from the Mesozoic Era into modernity. Dinosaur eggs which pass through the funnel hatch, and after one-half grown juvenile accidentally destroys the Chrono-funnel device, the scientists sample its tasty charred flesh. The dinosaurs breed like crazy, and soon people everywhere are snacking on "dinachicken." A statue is erected to the great scientist who, inadvertently, solved the world's hunger problem. (H.)

Bakker, Robert T. *Raptor Red* (1995). Sometimes the means of scientific discourse (leaden, technical terms interspersed through technical journals and trade publications) must seem as lumbering and stodgy as cold-blooded dinosaurs. Perhaps unsatisfied with the conventional rites of scientific expression, throughout his career as a vertebrate paleontologist, Bakker offers alternative, tantalizing glimpses into his visions of the dinosaurian world. A female *Utahraptor*, identified as "Raptor Red," and several close kin seem a bit too human in nature. This apparent problem is a minor difficulty, however. For Bakker has only encountered one of the major paradoxes science fiction writers routinely encounter. This is how to convincingly write about an "alien" race without revealing the fact that the writer is, after all, a human who is incapable of thinking like an alien (or in this case, a dinosaur)!

So, when Raptor Red expresses loving emotions, the reader must wonder whether a dinosaur can really love anything. *Utahraptors* were probably among the most intelligent dinosaur species known, yet who is to say whether they could love their offspring, or not? Well, to dinosaur aficionados, if it isn't strange reflecting on the fact that humans love dinosaurs, the idea of intelligent dinosaurs somehow "loving" their kin may not seem so bizarre. Actually, the characters were extrapolated from Bakker's ideas of how hawks would perceive their world had they been clothed in dinosaur flesh instead.

In providing a series of vignettes concerning how Raptor Red interacts with her environment through the course of a single year, Bakker leads us through the realm of Early Cretaceous North America. He effectively couples his original thoughts on dinosaur behavior to established ideas about genetic transmission and sensory adaptation in species. Realistic, believable dinosaur encounters are the end result.

Raptor Red relies on her wits and senses to hunt prey and compete socially against other females in her quest for a mate. Prior to mating, the male must present himself in a way that proves instinctively appealing to Raptor Red, but also, as Bakker explains, so as to demonstrate lack of genetic defects, disease, and parasites. The raptorial mating rituals may seem strikingly avian, yet today few would condemn the analogy's appropriateness. However, analogies are also made to African predators whenever the *Utahraptor* pack skillfully brings down prey in an orchestrated, "feline" fashion.

Most interesting were Raptor Red's numerous encounters with non-dinosaurs, an assorted cast of turtles, crocodiles, fuzzy mammals, ammonoids, plesiosaurs, and pterosaurs, all known on the basis of fossil evidence to have coexisted with the star characters. Bakker's insights into just what a *Utahraptor* such as Raptor Red might have thought about other species in its environment are amusingly and enjoyably portrayed, and no stranger than similar speculations often made on televised wildlife shows.

Bakker illustrates just how harrowing and difficult it was for *Utahraptor* to survive in its hostile world. Floods, diseases and injuries sustained while hunting (or in curious play) plague the species. Being powerful, quick and bloodthirsty doesn't guarantee success in any ecosphere. Mere survival is hard-won and risky. Yet there are occasions for raptors to playfully explore and even savor their surroundings too.

If we detect a bit of Bakker himself woven into the story, it may be in the guise of a wise old pterodactyl character, who carries on a sort of symbiotic, peaceful existence with Raptor Red, soaring in the skies and spying on the dinosaurs below.

Rather than killing off his tightly woven characters in an asteroid collision, volcanic eruption cliché, or battle to the death, Bakker provides a "happy" ending. Both the "dactyl" and Raptor Red have found new mates to continue their (genetic) struggle for existence.

In a scene staged on the shore of the epicontinental sea dividing western North America in the Early Cretaceous, Raptor Red encounters a marine *Kronosaurus*, which hurls itself through the surf in search of unsuspecting prey. Bakker has given us new insights as to how these whale-sized monsters may have hunted. The thought of a kronosaur lunging out at you on the beach seems truly frightening, and Bakker creates a dramatic scene, eventually pitting the wits of Raptor Red versus the bulk of the mighty *Acrocanthosaurus*, which falls victim to the amphibious hunter.

As in the case of many of his other popular publications, *Raptor Red* is illustrated with many of Bakker's fine drawings. Bakker's thought-provoking artistic style lets us see his dinosaurs with feeling, enhancing the narration.

Baxter, Stephen. *Evolution* (2000). Baxter's moving *tour de force* illustration of the entire history of primate evolution is artistically woven. Baxter chronicles primate evolution through the geological ages from the Late Jurassic Period on into "a far distant futurity," half a billion years from today. Yet while the novel's title is *Evolution*, it might have also been entitled "Extinction." For Baxter offers ominous warnings about how mankind's behavior threatens our fragile ecosystem, placing our futurity in jeopardy.

Sandwiched between *Extinction*'s beginning and end are two quotations from Charles Darwin's *The Origin of Species*. Darwin's prefatory statement reads, "Judging from the past, we may safely infer that not one living species will transmit its unaltered likeness to a distant futurity. And of the species now living very few will transmit progeny of any kind to a far distant future." Baxter introduces an elaborate, delightfully written vignette about "Purga," our remote squirrel-like primate ancestor, an omnivore (*Purgatorius*) which walked in the shadow of the last of the dinosaurian giants. This embellished "pen-picture" personifies Purga, fossil teeth of which are found by early twenty-fist century (fictional) paleontologist Joan Useb. When Useb fantasizes about little *Purgatorius*'s life, the primitive primate comes to life in a dramatic tale of death and survival, one so pivotal for the as-yet unborn human race.

Although *Purgatorius*, known from Late Cretaceous sediments in Montana, is thought to have resembled a squirrel, Purga is humanity itself personified. Baxter succeeds by allowing her struggle for survival become *our* struggle too. We must pull for Purga because if she—of all the individual members of her species—dies without passing her genes along to the next generation through surviving young, then the human race will never evolve. As Baxter says, "Life always had been chancy." And so our great- great, etc., ancestor not only must survive saurian threats, such as one hungry yet "insane" raptor and vicious pterodactyls, but Purga's life span also coincides with the most terrible catastrophe of the past 100 million years on planet Earth. For the K-T comet is already visible in the heavens above, although none of Earth's creatures can comprehend what is about to happen, or how within a single hour an era will end.

To Purga's mind, "[D]inosaurs were a force of nature, as beyond her control as the weather. In this huge dangerous world, the burrow was home. The thick earth protected the primates from the heat of the day, and sheltered the still-naked pups from a night's chill. The earth itself was Purga's shelter against dinosaur weather." And yet after a 160-million-year reign, all this was about to dramatically change. From Purga's protective burrow and ovaries would spring the human race. Purga loses one brood to predators, and then eventually another set of pups to a male competitor of her kind. It seems as if she won't propagate after all.

Then Baxter swiftly turns back the clock eighty million years earlier to the Late Jurassic Period, providing another pen-picture concerning dinosaurs unknown to science, which may have been conjured out of Asimov's short story "Big Game." Here human-sized "orniths" resembling "large, sparsely feathered bird(s)" who have learned how to communicate and make simple weapons stalk and hunt a herd of *Diplodocus*. The orniths are personified as well, as one swears vengeance after one of his fellow hunters is slashed mortally by a "Diplo's" whip-like tail. Eventually, however, the orniths disappear without leaving a trace. "They didn't build fires, which might have left hearths. Their stay had been too brief; the thin strata would not preserve their inflated skulls. When they were gone the orniths would leave no trace for human archaeologists to ponder, none but the puzzle of the great sauropods' abrupt extinction."

Baxter returns to Purga's tale, and the human plight, in a dramatic chapter titled "The devil's tale," which is a vivid, graphic description of the fateful end of an era founded on up-to-date scientific information concerning logistics of the K-T boundary impact event. As the comet bores down toward the Earth, "In one place a crowd of ankylosaurs, their dusty armor glistening, like a Roman legion in formation" stare into the skies. Yes, metaphorically speaking, the mammalian horde is about to sack Rome following a most incendiary event. Fire storms, tidal waves, hurricane winds and quakes of unimaginable intensity, incendiary fallout from the stratosphere, and an eternal chill still the alien landscape. Yet while the mighty dinosaurs all meet horrible fates in a swift series of comet-driven ecological insults, Purga, hunkered down in her hole, is spared. As is one solitary pup who is born into the new era.

As Baxter states, "At least with death there was the consolation that your descendants would go on after you, that something of your kind would linger on. Extinction took away even that comfort. Extinction was the end of your life—and of your children, and all your potential grandchildren, or any of your kind, on to the end of time; life would go on, but it would not be *your* kind of life." That is why we can empathize with Purga, because she's our very ancestor and represents *our* kind of life.

The grand story continues with more vignettes from primate history painted through the subsequent Tertiary Period through modern times and on into the far distant future. While Baxter hopes *our* kind of life won't succumb to extinction, he ends with Darwin's words which now ring ominously, "There is grandeur in this view of life ... that ... from so simple a beginning endless forms most beautiful and most wonderful have been, and are being evolved." And that life need not be mammalian.

In a latter segment, Baxter describes late-surviving miocene dinosaurian Antarctic fauna. These ten-million-year-old relics from the Mesozoic Era have outlived the dinosaurs known to science, living in isolation on a steadily cooling continent. Ultimately, as Baxter relates, "there would be no trace left to say [the] ... world of tundra, and the unique life that had inhabited it had ever existed" (p.196).

Bear, Greg. *Dinosaur Summer* (1998). In this lighthearted "sequel" to *The Lost World* set in 1947, Willis O'Brien, Merian C. Cooper and Ray Harryhausen escort young Peter Belzoni on a mission to return circus dinosaurs to Venezuela's El Grande plateau. Interestingly, Bear breaks tradition with the time-stands-still theme by introducing dinosaurs evolved from Mesozoic ancestors, such as *Neostruthiomimus* and *Communisaurus*. Before escaping from the uncharted territory, the explorers witness a climactic, titanic struggle between *Stratoraptor* and a theropod *Venator*.

Beecham, John Charles. "Out of the Miocene" (1914). Geologist Bruce Dayton encounters a sickly, elderly scientist, Eugene Scott, in the southwest American desert. Scott's aim is to "make some contribution to our knowledge of Evolution, the great science, the science of beginnings." For, "Only by knowing the story of life can we ever solve the mystery of life." So, quite mystically and hypnotically, Scott casts the protagonist's spirit into "some period of the world's infancy, when from the womb of Mother Nature there sprang those forms that are now the amaze of scientists," so he may actually witness them alive like he has. Feeling feverish, Dayton faints, only to "awaken" as a hairy primitive hominid. In atavistic form, Dayton feels urges toward a female of the local tribe, and their wanderings soon take them past non-crocodilian, "huge lizard-like creatures" and "huge lizards of the dinosaur type." Eventually, on the ancient Kansas Sea, they witness a bloody sea battle waged between a *Zeuglodon* from the Tertiary Period and a *Mosasaurus* of the Cretaceous. Dayton also must cope with cavemen species more advanced than he, as well as with the savage beast within himself, that raw, uncivilized part of his hominid body into which his spirit has been transplanted. Meanwhile, they savor geological wonders of the past, as Dayton marvels,

"Everywhere was intense, brooding heat and excessive moisture, limitless production, cataclysm of storm, violence and destruction. Building up and tearing down, the process was ceaseless; all making for nature's crowning creation, man." The twelve-foot-long turtle *Archelon*, a blind cave bear and ancestral horse *Hyracotherium* are thrown in anachronistically for good measure in this timeless tale. Dayton comes to, only to discover that he's been comatose for sixty days and that Scott has passed away.

Benford, Gregory. "Shakers of the Earth" (1992). Over the course of sixty years scientists establish a small herd of *Seismosaurus* penned in a "Kansas Sauropod Park," regenerated from DNA extracted from well-preserved fossilized bone (not amber). (I.)

Bierce, Ambrose. "For the Ahkoond" (1909). Here is the account of an explorer reporting on the condition of the western United States in the year 4591 following a meteorological cataclysm involving "terrific cyclones" and a "glacial period." In the aftermath of the landscape-transforming geological events, saurians reappear (i.e., "flocks of pterodactyls," ichthyosauri, and an *Ignanodon*, the latter of which drags "his obscene bulk in indolent immunity"). Thus, decades before the Alvarez asteroid theory for K-T extinctions, Mesozoic saurians already represented geological upheaval too. Or as Brian Aldiss stated in his *Trillion Year Spree* (1986), "The theme of nature reasserting its dominance can be clearly related to evolutionary thought. If humanity does not prove fit to rule the world and itself, then it will be overwhelmed. Earth will be green once more. The wilderness will come again."

Bishop, Michael. "Herding with the Hadrosaurs" (1992). Two boys who pass through the Time-Slip discontinuity are orphaned after their parents, attempting to establish a homestead in the Late Cretaceous, are eaten by a tyrannosaur. They survive after becoming adopted by a migrating hadrosaur herd, dodging pirates who exploit the indigenous fauna. (C.)

Burroughs, Edgar Rice. *Pellucidar* (1915). After reaching the surface in *At the Earth's Core*, David Innes decides to return to the inner surface world known as Pellucidar, driving the same mechanical drilling device as before. Innes unifies the human tribes of Pellucidar, creating an army which engages the horrible Mahars with their enslaved servants, the Sagoths. Innes also learns about the last male Mahar and obtains the "Great Secret," without which "this maleless race must eventually become extinct. For ages they had fertilized their eggs by an artificial process, the secret of which lay hidden.... So long as the powerful reptilian race of Pellucidar continued to propagate, just so long would the position of man within the inner world be jeopardized. There could not be two dominant races." Commanding a neolithic navy, Innes defeats the Mahars and becomes ruler of the Empire of Pellucidar, with Dian the Beautiful at his side.

Burroughs, Edgar Rice. *Tarzan the Terrible* (1921). Tarzan, who has been captured by Germans, encounters dinosaur fauna, known as *gryfs*, and a lost race of primitive pithecanthropine humanoids in the paradisiacal land of Pal-ul-don, a lost African setting. The *gryfs* have evolved since the Mesozoic age. For instance, *Triceratops* has become a carnivore. Tarzan discovers the "missing link" between apes and man.

Burroughs, Edgar Rice. *Tarzan at the Earth's Core* (1929). Burroughs' most popular hero, Tarzan, is enlisted to rescue David Innes from Pellucidar. Jason Gridley, Tarzan

and fellow compatriots descend in a 997-foot-long Zeppelin named the "0–220" into Pellucidar through a north polar passage leading inward to the Earth's interior. After arriving at their primeval destination, the party is soon separated following confrontations with fierce mammal species long extinct on Earth's outer surface, such as sabertooths, *Mastodon* and mammoths. Tarzan befriends an ape-like Sagoth. They battle a giant flightless bird, *Phororhacos*. Tarzan also confronts a giant winged pterodactyl known to the inhabitants of Pellucidar as a thipdar, and a brutish cave bear. Eventually, Tarzan encounters the monstrous "Horibs" who, riding their "Gorobors" (which are descendants of Permian pareiasaurs), slay *Triceratops*, which as Tarzan notes bears a striking resemblance to the *gryf* of Pal-ul-don. Tarzan is transfixed by the spectacle. "As Tarzan gazed in fascination upon the Horibs, whose 'blood ran cold and who had no heart,' he realized that he might be gazing upon one of the vagaries of evolution, or possibly upon a replica of some form that had once existed upon the outer crust and that had blazed the trail that some, to us, unknown creature must have blazed from the age of reptiles to the age of man. Nor did it seem to him, after reflection, any more remarkable that a man-like reptile might evolve from reptiles than that birds should have done so, or as scientific discoveries are now demonstrating, mammals must have." Meanwhile, Gridley kills a *Stegosaurus* (here known as a "dyrodor") which angles its plates horizontally to catch the wind and glide down to the ground from a cliff. Emperor Innes is finally discovered by members of the 0–220 expedition, yet they are forced to ascend to the outer crust without one of their party, Lieutenant William von Horst.

Burroughs, Edgar Rice. *Back to the Stone Age* (1936, 1937). This very readable sequel to *Tarzan At the Earth's Core* traces the remarkable adventures of von Horst through Pellucidar. From the get-go, the novel is exciting as "Von" is captured by a winged marsupial reptile known as a "Trodon" which paralyzes him with venom and drops him into a nest inside a volcanic cone. Hatchlings emerge with regularity feeding on paralyzed mammalian prey (not unlike the concluding scene in Harry Adam Knight's 1984 novel *Carnosaur*). Certainly Von has more than his share of prehistoric perils to overcome, but *Stone Age* is primarily about loyalty, friendship and the tendency for civilized man to revert to primitive ways in a prehistoric environment. What keeps Von above the rest of Pellucidar's "Gilaks," however, is his evolved sense of trust, kindness to fellow man as well as beast, and loyalty, concepts which are poorly understood in Pellucidar. For as one Pellucidarian explains, "If everyone felt that way here there would be too many gilaks in Pellucidar and all the game would soon be killed off." So, according to Burroughs, in order for the Pellucidarian ecosystem to survive, altruism and cooperation must be suppressed. Eventually, Von falls in love with a beautiful cave woman, La-ja. Although "rescued" by David Innes, it's very clear that Von prefers to remain in the enchanting Pellucidar instead of returning to the outer crust.

Cerasini, Marc. *Godzilla 2000* (1997). Godzilla and the mutated *Pteranodon* Rodan fend off a plague of monsters unleashed by a swarm of asteroids.

Chester, William L. *Kioga of the Unknown Land* (1938). On a landmass in the Arctic known to Shoni natives as "Nato-wa," a Tarzan-like, Caucasian individual named Kioga,

Opposite: **A recreation of assorted stylized prehistorians as envisioned for science fiction pulp magazine covers of the 1920s, typically by artist J. Allen St. John. (Illustration by Jack Arata—used with permission.)**

the "Snow Hawk," leads a party of American explorers through tunnels and burial chambers inside a lofty mountain, descending toward a mysterious city where living woolly mammoths are beasts of burden. Kioga seeks to preserve the ecology from "those who would despoil mankind's last wilderness wonderland."

Costello, Matthew. *King Kong: The Island of the Skull* (2005). Costello's story is the "official" prequel to the story of King Kong previously novelized by Delos W. Lovelace, and rewritten by others in 2005 including DeVito and Strickland, and, separately, Christopher Golden (based on a screenplay by Fran Walsh, Philippa Boyens and Peter Jackson). In *Island of the Skull*, Kong makes a symbolic appearance only through a roar heard by island interlopers during a lightning storm near the end of the novel. Pearl divers and seamen are forced to land at Skull Island following an attack by a enormous marine reptile. Afterward they're assaulted by a "V. Rex," or a "King of the dinosaurs ... vast mountain of lizard." This novel explains how Carl Denham came into possession of the mysterious map charting the Skull Island's position in the Indian Ocean. Skull Island is also explained as a place "...where time had stopped sixty million years ago."

Crichton, Michael. *The Lost World* (1995). In Crichton's sequel to *Jurassic Park*, Malcolm, who is presumed dead at *Jurassic Park*'s conclusion, turns out to have survived after all. Now, rather reluctantly, he's ready to confront living dinosaurs once again. The premise is that Hammond's "dirty little secret—Site B," a Pacific island named Isla Sorna, near Isla Nublar, served as a proving ground for bioengineered dinosaurs. It is here that Hammond's biotech group learned how to circumvent a prion-viral agent, akin to mad cow disease, which afflicted some of his earlier experiments. These dinosaurs escaped their cages long ago, have grown to adult sizes and have been roaming free for years, in the absence of man. The unscrupulous Louis Dodgson wants to exploit the dinosaurs by seizing fertilized eggs from every dinosaur species on the island, while Malcolm's associate, Berkeley paleontologist Richard Levine, simply wants to explore the island to observe the dinosaurs.

Levine treks off to Isla Sorna. Soon, however, his alarming cell phone message eventually prompts Doc Thorne, Malcolm and two genius kid stowaways to Levine's rescue. This trio are later joined on Isla Sorna by Sarah Harding, who survives Dodgson's assassination attempt. The kids crack the island's computer system and manage to glean the purpose of Site B, which was where the dinosaurs were originally reconstructed from bits of DNA found in fossil insect tissue preserved in amber.

Dodgson's rival party reaches the island, and the dinosaur attack is in full swing, as under Crichton's talents, a nesting tyrannosaur pair, a pair of hungry carnotauri, and, of course, those savage raptors soon descend upon Malcolm and company. Malcolm's objective of deciphering the "greatest mystery in the history of our planet: extinction" through observation of the complexity of interacting dinosaur groups goes unfulfilled after Levine interferes with and alters the dinosaurs' (un)natural behavior. Dodgon's deserved demise—being eaten alive by a brood of *T. rex* hatchlings—recalls a horrifying climactic scene in Knight's *Carnosaur*.

Curtis, Wardon Allan. "The Monster of Lake LaMetrie" (1899). In Curtis' short story, first published in the September 1899 issue of *Pearson's Magazine*, an *Elasmosaurus* plays a prominent role, in homage to Mary Shelley's *Frankenstein*. Explorers James McLennegan and Edward Framingham journey to Wyoming's Lake LaMetrie which seems to extend into the very bowels of the planet (with references made to John Symmes and the "hollow earth" theory, as in Obruchev's *Plutonia*). Framingham, who has a serious malady, spends most of his time fishing in the lake where traces of living flora and fauna no longer alive elsewhere are expelled. Following a great lake disturbance, a living elasmosaur is found floating on the lake, and McLennegan beheads it. After he removes the conveniently human-sized brain, and replaces the head back onto the sinuous neck, the elasmosaur's body continues to live! Then Framinghan dies and McLennegan transplants his brain into the elasmosaur body. The saurian begins singing and understands his human companion, but the human brain lodged in the elasmosaur steadily regresses and the elasmosaur murders McLennegan. Tragically, the elasmosaur is killed by U.S. infantrymen who are shocked at the sight of the insanely laughing monster.

Debus, Allen A., and Diane E. Debus, "Mesozoic Miasma" (2002). In this pseudo-scientific farce inspired by a George Carlin concert, Mother Nature becomes the protagonist in a sinister, Late Cretaceous plot to rid the world of pesky dinosaurs who from their rears foul the atmosphere with methane, a greenhouse gas. (This was published in an essay collection, *Dinosaur Memories*.)

De Camp, L. Sprague. *The Day of the Dinosaur* (1968). Besides "A Gun for Dinosaur," De Camp published nine additional twists on the time travel scenario, eight of which involved Rivers and his noble friend, the Raja. The story not involving the likeable pair of intrepid safari guides appeared in Chapter One of *The Day of the Dinosaur*, coauthored with his wife, Catherine Crook de Camp. This time machine flight of fancy takes readers to the dawning Cretaceous world, where various genera of dinosaurs are observed. At the climax of their story, two carnosaurs battle over a hadrosaur carcass.

De Camp, L. Sprague. "Crocamander Quest" (1992). In this lark, Reginald Rivers and the Raja guide a paleontologist and a couple, the Alvarados, to the Late Triassic Period, where the latter's stormy affair serves to help date the breakup of Pangaea. Inez Alvaredo ends up teasing members of the party, prompting Rivers never again to take women on a time safari, even if he's charged with being a male chauvinist. As Rivers concludes, "It's not the dinosaurs and other animals that cause the main problems; it's the human beings." (D., I.)

Delaplace, Barbara. "Fellow Passengers" (1993). A *Blatant Enquirer* female reporter tracks the story of a *Deinonychus* which escaped from the Zoological Gardens in the American west. "The Claw"—as it's known—infuriates ranchers whose cattle are being slaughtered. The wolfish brute is subdued with a tranquilizer gun and returned to its cage. When animal rights activists free the dinosaur once more so it can live naturally, the reporter reflects how the last passenger pigeon died forlornly in a zoo, surely an unbecoming fate for the last proud dinosaur. (F.)

DeVito, Joe, and Brad Strickland, *Merian C. Cooper's King Kong* (2005). Essentially an updated, vivid and "seamless" retelling of Cooper's Kong story, quite similar overall to Lovelace's 1932 novel.

DiChario, Nicholas A., and Jack Nimershein. "The Land That God Forgot" (1997). In the year 2212, Pope John Paul IV elects to have his consciousness permanently downloaded into computer "SimSpace." This is because God had come to him and said, "Go to SimSpace, go to the dinosaurs. Give them freewill and the intelligence of Man, and we will start anew." The Pope aspires to convert dinosaurs to Catholicism before the asteroid impact event. Following the fiery inferno, both he and a tyrannosaur named Rexanne wrestle with why God would wreak such havoc upon their world. So what had Pope John Paul IV accomplished if all were destroyed by His wrath? He finds comfort when his dim K-T boundary campfire light attracts furry ape-like creatures who appear to listen to his readings from the Bible. Then he knows that someday "God's message would echo throughout all of SimSpace." (G.)

Garcia y Robertson, R. "The Virgin and the Dinosaur" (1992). In R. Garcia y Robertson's 1992 novella, Jake Bento, FTL (faster than light) time-guide employee, uses a hyperlight "navmatrix" to penetrate back sixty-five million years through the Hell Creek wormhole anomaly with *memsahib* Peg, a female dinosaur expert, Ph.D. They're the very first time-travelers ever to visit the Mesozoic era. Upon their arrival, Peg sheds all her clothes, filling Jake with lust. After all, Jake muses, in this virgin territory, it's "Just like Adam and Eve...." Here in this forbidding, time-relativistic "Garden of Eden," Peg is Jake's temptress. Throughout their journey across the Late Cretaceous landscape in a fusion-powered balloon—named *Challenger* after Conan Doyle's Professor Challenger—Jake finds it difficult to concentrate on his work as bare, fetching Peg parades before him, naively and nakedly. Although Peg hired Jake's services through FTL to make observations of living sauropods, at first they're mesmerized by a herd of *Triceratops*, tracked by a pack of tyrannosaurs.

With Jake distracted by the condition of his loins, Peg continually places herself in dangerous situations, like nearly being trampled by half a dozen *T. rex* on their way to a *Triceratops* stampede, or lovingly patting a dozing *T. rex* on the noggin. She rationalizes her rash actions, "That creature has no natural enemies, nothing to fear or defend against. If you are not afraid, or appetizing, you have nothing to fear from it." For her brazen recklessness, Jake considers her a "brainless waif," while Peg criticizes his state of "testosterone frenzy." Following a tumultuous storm in the proto–South Atlantic, they spy mountains on the horizon. With thunderheads towering in the distance, and a curious *Quetzalcoatlus* soaring near their craft, to pass the time, Jake plays the Doors' "Riders on the Storm" on the *Challenger's* microamps before their inevitable crash.

The climax of Robertson's tale occurs after they survive smashing into a sequoia on a hillside. Only after Jake and the virgin consummate their relationship does Peg spot her first sauropod, *Alamosaurus*, foraging high up from tree limbs on which their shattered craft is suspended above the ground. With her passion for dinosaurs having borne fruit in the form of *Alamosaurus*—with its long, snaky, sinuous neck, metaphorically likened, perhaps, to Eden's snake—the rite of passion is stimulated. Following man's successful "penetration" into the (fertile) Mesozoic, the time-travelers navigate through the Hell Creek wormhole anomaly back to a historic period. (C.)

Gerrold, David. *Deathbeast* (1978). David Gerrold's highly-charged novel reads like a *Star Trek* tale set in the Early Cretaceous period of North America; the safari arrives at their temporal destination—one hundred million years ago—in a "Nexus" time-craft. Two Time-Hunt Ltd. guides, Megan and Loevil, escort six clients on a three-day dinosaur hunt. The alpha male of the group, Ethab, is intent on slaying a *Tyrannosaurus*, even though Time-Hunt's policy officially advises customers against such derring-do. For the crimson-eyed, nine-ton Tyrant King is far too dangerous, and as Megan cautions, no one has brought one down before. Best to set sights on smaller quarry instead. Even though the team is fully equipped with portable scanners, high-tech crossbows and blazer rifles, supposedly the right sort of "gun for dinosaur," such weaponry proves ineffective against *T. rex*, "the Deathbeast, god of prehistoric fear." For science fiction's first example of a warm-blooded rex relentlessly pursues the hunters across the prehistoric landscape, picking off safari members in one gruesome scene after another.

Like Melville's Captain Ahab, loner Ethab, likened to an unfeeling android, becomes obsessed with destruction of the Deathbeast, and for his hubris, believing himself perfect enough to challenge the "god-beast, god of lizards, dinosaurs, and demons ... master of terror," must pay the ultimate sacrifice. In a disturbing scene, Loevil views "the deathbeast ... poised ... Ethab bloody in his mouth—and Ethab still alive!... 'Kill him, dammit—' [Loevil] breathed. The awful part of the whole thing was that even as he struggled, Ethab *smiled.*" Loevil and two other survivors lure Deathbeast into a tar pit, igniting the flammable substance. Then with time running out, the trio must run like hell to the Nexus before its programmed return to their twenty-first century present.

After beguiling himself into believing they've killed the monstrosity, now Loevil feels transformed into a "deathbeast" himself, assuming Ethab's former role in the group! He knows what killed the dinosaurs—fear of Man, the hunter! "It was humanity who taught this world how to *fear* ... human beings strode among them and the world *trembled, changed....* The beasts looked up, and for a moment *wondered*—and in that wonderment, *they died ...* somehow, gradually across a million years, the lesson would sink in—the dinosaurs were dying...."

But in best horror tradition, Deathbeast, likened to "something from the shadows of the soul ... something ... monstrous moving through the nightscape of your dreams, always behind you...," strides forth from the tar pit, menacing the time travelers even as the Nexus warning sirens signal its scheduled departure. Deathbeast, blinded and mortally wounded by fire and blazer blasts, heaves itself onto the Nexus disc ... only to die, a magnificent trophy.

In a short preface to Gerrold's exciting entry it's explained that *Deathbeast*'s descriptions of dinosaurs were founded on the latest theories concerning dinosaurian physiology: warm-bloodedness. In fact, this also marks the first fictional appearance of a famous raptor dinosaur, *Deinonychus*, which savagely attacks the safari team shortly after they materialize in the Cretaceous. Although in *Deathbeast* two deinonychi are dispatched rather easily with blazer rifle fire, raptors wouldn't succumb so readily in science fiction and horror that were to come.

Gerrold, David. "Rex" (1993). This curious tale opens with the line "Daddy! The tyrannosaur is loose again. He jumped the fence." This tale is a dark dino-equivalent of that old 1950s song "How much is that doggie in the window?" Poor Rex, the miniature tyrannosaur, is getting too big for his basement confines and after escaping eats other miniature dinosaur household pets which live in Johnathan Fillmore's beloved dinosaur diorama. His eight-year-old daughter Jill and his wife Joyce have been feeding Rex—who should only be eating Purina Dinosaur Chow—fresh beef, accelerating his growth to the point where Rex, at two feet high, has become downright dangerous, even to humans. Now Johnathan is contemplating getting rid of Rex somehow, as he's rapidly attaining the legal limit of thirty-six inches tall. However, the market for trendy dwarf dinosaurs has diminished considerably. "At one time it had been fashionable to own your own miniature *T. Rex*; but the fad had passed, the tyrant-lizards had literally outgrown their welcome, the price of meat had risen again ... and a lot of people—wearying of the smells and the bother—had finally dropped their pets off at the zoo or turned them over to the animal shelters. Because they were protected under the Artificial Species Act, the cost of putting a mini-dino down was almost prohibitive." Rex's upkeep is also causing terrific fights between Johnathan and his wife, whom he no longer loves and has grown tired of. Johnathan feels totally handcuffed by his domestic dilemma. Then, after Rex nearly rips a burglar to shreds, Johnathan witnesses what a ferocious guard animal Rex is. Malevolently, Johnathan decides they can keep Rex after all—even though, while he's conveniently away on a two-month business tip, their pet may soon fulfill his dark desire of tearing the flesh from Joyce's raw bones, the thought of which provided "an odd thrill of pleasure." (F.)

Glut, Donald F. *Frankenstein in the Lost World* (1976, revised and reprinted 2002). Glut unites his two literary passions—prehistoric animals and the Frankenstein monster. Electrochemist and biologist Dr. Burt Winslow and his beautiful fiancée Lynn have captured and subdued Frankenstein's monster. They intend to transport the monster to Winslow's laboratory in Ingolstadt, Germany, where it will be dissected and destroyed. But a terrorist stowaway causes the Lear Jet to veer off course into an inexplicable cyclonic force field, which may instead be a "chronal" eddy, possibly some kind of time warp. Following an aerial encounter with a *Pteranodon*, the craft plummets into a lake where it remains afloat just long enough for Lynn, Burt, the terrorist and eventually the Monster to escape. There are prehistoric animals aplenty on this misty, uncharted volcanic haven. A strange admixture of prehistoric wildlife representing the Permian, Jurassic, Cretaceous and Tertiary Periods and the Pleistocene epoch inhabit the lost-world landscape, beset by "weird temporal properties" in which the "rules of time and geography have all gone haywire." Giant ground sloths, glyptodonts, tyrannosaurs, allosaurs, *Triceratops*, sabertooth cats, giant winged pterosaurs and cave bears are soon encountered. Most imposing, however, are the Neanderthal tribe, and a gigantic, Kong-sized ape named "Tor." After saving a Neanderthal woman from reptilian peril, Winslow finds his way to the Neanderthals' cave. There, he finds captive, bare-breasted Lynn, who has caught the roving eye of the chieftain named Kaz. There is yet another captive, a long-forgotten professor of paleontology, a "Maple White"-type character named Dr. Marvin Sara, whose plane was also lost in the vortex surrounding this land during World War II. Sara's vintage biplane, equipped with machine guns, offers a means of escape! Frankenstein's monster fights and kills a fin-backed *Dimetrodon*, while Tor seizes Lynn and kills a *T. rex* before the predictable, climactic volcanic eruption. Glut's enjoyable *Frankenstein in the Lost World* was obviously inspired by classics such as *King Kong*, Conan Doyle's *The Lost World*, and Burroughs' Caspak trilogy.

Glut, Donald F. *Dinosaur Valley Girls* (2006). Uncannily, upon recognizing ancient relics stored in the Raymond M. Alf Museum, dashing, handsome actor Tony Markham—disenchanted with his coterie of Hollywood groupies—is magically whisked into a mystical parallel-universe-type valley, where dinosaurs and cavepeople coexist. In this primitive society cavegirls have separated from their crude, foul mates. The cavefolk are reunited and Tony is smitten by spear-wielding temptress Hea-Thor. After demonstrating the art of love to many of the buxom, scantily clad cave-beauties, Tony defends the cave clan from a rampaging *Allosaurus*. Tony returns to his proper universe, only to willfully transport himself back to voluptuous Hea-thor in dinosaur valley once more. The book is a novelization of Glut's script for his tongue-in-cheek, independent 1996 film *Dinosaur Valley Girls*, which he directed.

Golden, Christopher. *King Kong* (2005). Golden's engaging novelization of the screenplay by Fran Walsh, Philippa Boyens and Peter Jackson further promoted Peter Jackson's Universal blockbuster *King Kong* during the fall of 2005. The novel effectively explains the special relationship between Ann Darrow and Kong, as well as Denham's obsessive, ulterior motives for exploiting the burly, heroic beast. While in general outline Golden's is similar to DeVito's and Lovelace's novelizations, the former offers a few surprises. For instance, there are bloodthirsty raptor dinosaurs present. And the former, foreboding presence of a mighty civilization on the (steadily sinking) volcanic Skull Island is keenly felt. The "tyrannosaurs" are renamed "*V. Rex*" for the species' apparent voraciousness, and wordsmith Jack Driscoll (here a playwright) names dinosaurs and other species new to science as they're encountered. The trek through the jungle in pursuit of Kong is likened to a military World War I venture, with Tommy guns ablaze.

Gottfried, Frederick D. "Hermes to the Ages" (1980). In this tale published in the dawning dinosaur renaissance, a mummy preserved in the vacuum of space is discovered on the moon by Soviet cosmonauts. Word of the discovery spreads to the Americans, and soon paleontologist Lars Hansen and his female assistant Eleanor Mercer meet them aboard the Russian space station *Gargaringrad*. Hansen theorizes that the specimen is a derived form of intelligent dinosaur, possibly representing an evolutionary descendant of the brainiest Mesozoic forms such as *Deinonychus*, *Dromaeosaurus*, or *Stenonychosaurus* (now *Troodon*). Gottfried suspends disbelief by suggesting that the species found by the cosmonauts "may not have existed long enough to leave a permanent geological record" (i.e., on Earth) ... the enlarged cranium above [promised] a brain the equal to man's—if not greater." The creature is named *Homosaurus* for its "extremely manlike" attributes. Following concerns over the possibility of encountering harmful microorganisms, the Russians manage to revive the freeze-dried creature and, aided by the Americans, communicate with it. The humans learn from *Homosaurus* how after their society became much like that of humans today, the intelligent dinosaurs modified their environment leading to their decision to commit "deliberate racial suicide," although through means and for reasons left unexplained. Now fearing that *Homosaurus* commands knowledge capable of exterminating mankind, the humans soberly realize they must convince him that the human race is "worthy." (H.)

Harrison, Harry. *West of Eden* (1984). Spear-wielding humans are pitted against ancient bio-engineers and "intelligent preservers" of ancient life known as the Yilane—evolutionary descendants of Cretaceous marine mosasaurs—in this imaginative novel staged in a parallel universe setting where the K-T asteroid never struck. Here, young Kerrick, born into a Cro-Magnon (human) "sammad," is captured by the cold-blooded Yilane, where upon he learns about their female-dominated, millions-of-years-old culture. Kerrick even has sexual intercourse with the Yilane female commander, Vainte. Conflict begins when an ice age

This obscure illustration from the 1899 story "Silas P. Cornu's Divining Rod," written by Henry Hering, shows how dinosaurs could sometimes be cast as mere "paleo-props" in early examples of dino-fiction. (From *Cassell's Magazine*, 1899.)

threatens the Yilane's home world of Africa. Fleeing to what would be our Florida, the Yilane confront humans—known as ustuzou—for the first time as they *grow* their city, likened to an ant hive, using bioengineering techniques. As in the case of Karel Capek's "Newts," soon the Yilane are at war with the humans, as Kerrick escapes and finds a way to destroy Vainte's armies with the first true weapon of mass destruction—*fire*, a technology which the Yilane never mastered. Bio-engineered dinosaurs are beasts of burden for the Yilane, and many of their tools, naval vessels and weaponry are actually highly derived organisms adapted for their specific uses by Yilane scientists. While humans are highly adaptable, the Yilane's fatal flaw becomes their ultra-conservatism. For the Yilane, "the future would be as the past, immutable and unchangeable. New species were added to the world by careful gene manipulation; none was ever taken away." Unlike the ustuzou, Yilane cannot ever use their language to lie. In Harrison's sequels, *Winter in Eden* (1986) and *Return to Eden* (1988), obsessed Vainte vengefully pursues Kerrick, leading to her inevitable defeat and humiliation. The Yilane are unable to cope with deadly planetary forces exerted upon them by evolution of mammalia taking place in foreign lands such as North America, and through climatic change.

In his 1992 short story "Dawn of the Endless Night," Harrison offered yet another alternate view, where the Yilane confront an asteroid collision sixty million years ago, dooming the Yilane while permitting eventual ascendancy of the despised ustuzou. (I.)

Heilmann, Gerhard. *The Origin of Birds* **(1926).** Ornithologist and paleontologist Gerhard Heilmann (1859–1946) wrote a highly descriptive account, or a "pen-picture" as he referred to it, in a chapter of his landmark *The Origin of Birds* titled "Some Fossil Birds— *Archaeornis* and *Archaeopteryx*." Using his considerable talents, Heilmann described a Jurassic setting and assemblage of crocs, dinosaurs, pterosaurs and fossil birds known on the basis of actual fossil evidence from Bavaria's Solnhofen deposits. Heilmann prefaced his fictional description, "In the following pen-picture, the only forms mentioned are those well known in Paleontology, the whole organization of which were thus able to reconstruct; hence it is no fairy-tale with which I wish to entertain my readers. The description of their coloration is of course only guesswork, but nevertheless based on that of creatures now living under nearly similar conditions. Let us imagine ourselves standing on one of the large islands in the Jurassic sea...." Six pages later, Heilmann concluded, understating his intentions to provide an accurate glimpse of the evolutionary state of Jurassic period organisms, "the reader may possibly form some conception as to the stage of evolution at which the animal world at this period had arrived." In a subsequent chapter the artistic Heilmann also painted another "pen-picture" with words, this time involving two other fossil birds of the Cretaceous Period, *Ichthyornis* and *Hesperornis*, interacting with their contemporaries.

Hering, Henry A. "Silas P. Cornu's Divining Rod" (1899). An articulated "dinysorus" skeleton, named *Dinysorus Tontinus Gigantissimus*, is used as a metaphoric paleo-prop in this tongue-in-cheek yarn about gold mining in mid-nineteenth century Dakota country published in *Cassell's Magazine*.

Holmes, John Eric. *Mahars of Pellucidar* **(1976).** In the grand finale to Edgar Rice Burroughs' seven acclaimed Pellucidar stories, psychologist Chris West beams down by wire transmission to the inner, primeval world, facing winged Mahars and Thipdars in a bloody struggle for survival. We learn that male Mahars have survived after all, and that Mahars' telepathic sense is a form of "radio sense." We also tour the Mahars' egg-incubator rooms and once more witness Mahar sadism in their temple of despair. West is himself subjected to psychological experimentation conducted by Mahar scientists before escaping to the forest beyond the city walls. West and his party confront many prehistoric dangers along the way, at one time finding themselves in the midst of a climatic battle waged between an enraged three-horned *Triceratops* and a monstrously sized *Tyrannosaurus*.

Hulke, Malcolm. *Doctor Who and the Cave-Monsters* **(1974).** The BBC series hero Doctor Who is summoned to resolve a mystery at an underground atomic research station located in Wenley Moor, England, where losses of power continually occur and a man has gone insane, reverting to a prehistoric psychological state. Soon, men are confronted by strange, subterranean, intelligent "reptile-men" possessing a powerfully hypnotic third eye and humanoid posture. It's revealed that one hundred million years ago these reptile-men (known as "Silurians" in 1970s televised programming) ruled Earth. When a planetoid hurtled their way through outer space the reptile-men, fearing the Earth's atmosphere would be gravitationally sucked away, hibernated in shelters under the ground. This planetoid, or our moon, became locked in Earth orbit and a sufficient proportion of atmosphere was retained following the catastrophe so that the little furry mammals could survive. Now the revived reptile-men, referred to as *Homo reptilia*, are stealing atomic power to resuscitate their kind from deep hibernation so that they may reclaim *their* world. A *Tyrannosaurus* fighting lizard is employed to attack British soldiers, and the reptile-men scientists unleash a viral plague to wipe out mankind. They also plan to destroy Earth's Van Allen belt so that the environment will become unsuitable for inferior mammalian life. Doctor Who invents a serum to stop the spreading affliction and tricks the reptile-men to withdraw into their caves, which are then sealed by the British military.

Lackey, Mercedes, and Larry Dixon. "Last Rights" (1993). Dinosaur rights activists, who abhor GenTech Engineering's practices of restoring dinosaurs from ancestral DNA within the genome of modern chickens and other birds, free various genetic revenant dinosaurs from their pastures and confines. They're opposed to seeing dinosaurs as "P.O.Z.'s" (prisoners of zoos). After freeing several dinosaurs to the wild, one activist suffers a fatal "incident" with a *Deinonychus* mistakenly thought to be herbivorous. (F.)

Laumer, Keith. *Dinosaur Beach* (1978). Four hundred million years after life has disappeared from Earth, Timesweep cyborg Agent Ravel's mission is to preserve the temporal stream and repair entropic strands in time's continuum, the results of tampering caused by incidents of time travel. One Nexx Central time station is situated in the Late Mesozoic Era, where dinosaurs are used as elegant paleo-props.

Lebeck, Douglas. *Memories of a Dinosaur Hunter* (2002). Vertebrate paleontologist David Williams is a lonely and highly depressed individual, sent on a strictly one-way venture into the Late Cretaceous Period in a time machine built by astrophysicist Dr. Dermot. Lebeck provides a detailed description of the workings of Dermot's time machine with discussion of the experience of space-time travel through a wormhole. But life in prehistory turns out to be oppressive; it's no Garden of Eden by any means. Williams' doleful character seems somewhat modeled after Simpson's Sam Magruder, even though Williams traveled into prehistory willingly. "I came to this time for a reason. I came here to see for myself what the real truth was about life seventy million years before the common era. And even though I had seen a lot, there was still so much more to learn, so much more to experience.... I was looking for a reason to keep on living." Williams makes dangerous first-hand observations of a variety of dinosaurs, including duckbilled dinosaurs, *Velociraptor*, *Triceratops* and the elusive *T. rex*. But, overall, despite trying to keep his spirits up, he's miserable. His time machine is equipped with a computer so he can record his observations and data for posterity when it's dug up by paleontologists in his (former) present, after he's long dead and perhaps fossilized. In the end, after he cheated certain death numerous times, a volcanic eruption forces him to forever abandon his time machine and he watches a bloody battle between *Triceratops* and *Tyrannosaurus*. But salvation arrives in the form of his girlfriend lover, a fellow paleontologist named Susan, who had slipped into a coma over a decade before, just prior to when Williams ventured into the deep past. Now they're ecstatic because they'll never be separated again.

Majewski, Erazm. *Professor Antediluvius* (1898). This little-known foreign title (unread by this writer), written by Polish archaeologist Majewski (1858–1922), concerned a trio of intrepid explorers who penetrate a crevice leading into the earth in Bosnia, and subsequently travel through landscapes representing the earth's geological ages.

Matthew, W.D. "Scourge of the Santa Monica Mountains" (1916). In this vivid "pen-picture," real paleontologist William Diller Matthew (1871–1930) highlighted discoveries being made at Los Angeles's Ranco La Brea Tar Pits during the early 20th century. In this tale of the Ice Age, a saber-tooth cat stalks a giant ground-sloth. Both predator and prey become entrapped in the sticky asphalt. In the end, they're "...hopelessly doomed... to an awful and lingering death in the black and sticky depths of the asphalt pool, from which rose now, faster and faster, bubbles of oil and malodorous gas as the struggling animals sank lower and lower beneath the suface." Matthew's story, published in *The American Museum Journal* (vol. 16, no. 7, pp. 469–72) generated interest in an American Museum display, the first of its kind, showcasing animals featured in the story.

McHugh, Maureen F. "Down on the Farm" (1997). Grace Sabiston, a female *Oviraptor* rancher, faces being put out of business by the Federal Drug Administration. At the last minute, fretting over how she'll survive without being able to breed her dinosaurs for profit, her attorney apprises her of an agreement arrived at between AgriGene (which holds the patent on her *Oviraptors*) and the FDA, hinging on an important technicality. Sabiston's dinosaurs are classified as "genetically *enhanced* animals," rather than "genetically engineered," meaning she can keep her farm after all. (G.)

Merritt, A. *The Face in the Abyss* (1931). Abraham Merritt's (1882–1943) fantasy tale of right versus evil in the Andean wilderness, or the "Hidden Lands," thrilled readers with its odd assortment of lost races and anthropo-reptilian fauna. A million years ago, a mythic society of humans and lizard men, presided over by the Snake Mother, emigrated from their cooling native continent of Antarctica into prehistoric Mexico. Their ancient civilization is discovered by treasure seekers, one of whom—Graydon—witnesses the Xinli, predatory dinosaurs relied on for sport, and as fear-instilling steeds driven into battle. It is suggested that the Yu-Atlanchi, "a people so old that their ancient cities were covered by the Antarctic ice!," and who inhabit the Hidden Lands, may have learned the secret of "devolution," or how to reverse the evolutionary process. Xinli are "ravening devils" relied upon by an evil emissary, "Lantlu." Over 200 were counted among the hunting packs and a couple dozen are used as a makeshift "cavalry." Xinli sporting races are held in a great amphitheater, where combats are also staged between the dinosaurs and captured "lizard-men." As Graydon discovers, scaly Xinli are vulnerable to lancing under the jaw area. In one passage, Graydon also discovers an ancient mural depicting the history of this odd, prehistorical society.

Nye, Nicholas. *Return to the Lost World* (1991). Challenger, Malone, Summerlee and Roxton venture back to Maple White Land where they discover traces of a former advanced civilization, debate evolutionary theory and encounter more pterodactyls and dinosaurs. Challenger considers the ape-men as a relic population of Neanderthal; back home in England, as a joke, he perpetrates the Piltdown forgery.

Obruchev, Vladimir A. *Plutonia* (1924). A contemporary life-through-time novel (the Russian "lost world" story) was written by an esteemed Russian geologist Obruchev (1863–1956), borrowing elements from Conan Doyle as well as Verne's *Journey* and Burroughs' *At the Earth's Core* series.

Plutonia is the world inside the earth, formed on the inner surface of our hollow planet. At the center of the hollow earth resides a small sun which is named Pluto. Much of the astrophysical science of Plutonia is founded on eighteenth and nineteenth century pseudo-science and speculations which have long been overthrown. (Geologist Obruchev, of course, didn't believe any of these offbeat theories; he was simply writing an entertaining tale.) In Plutonia, a team of Russian scientists sets out for the Arctic region in 1914 aboard the *North Star*, although at first their purpose is mysteriously ill-defined. As they progress across the tundra, anomalous meteorological readings imply they are penetrating into the earth when they seem to have moved over flat ground. Under foggy skies, they spy a herd of mammoth, shooting one specimen. The climate grows steadily warmer with each passing day, until they spy a sun positioned in the sky nowhere near where it should be located in the heavens. Has there been a celestial catastrophe involving the sun? Meanwhile, Ice Age mammals keep turning up, and eventually they realize they've entered the earth's interior through an enormous hole in the Arctic, which has shifted their overland course so gradually that they didn't even notice the change in their direction.. The Russians keep shooting prehistoric life, gaining specimens to take back with them upon their return.

From their observations of Pluto, one scientist theorizes that "This central luminary, or actual core of the earth, is in its last stage of burning. It's a dying red star. A little more time and it will be snuffed out! The inner surface [i.e., of the planet] will be plunged into darkness and cold, and this flourishing wild life will gradually become extinct." Later they hypothesize that a meteorite impact most likely tore a hole through the earth and became the radiant "star," Pluto. Fauna would have eventually inhabited the inner surface, and judging from the ancient fauna they find in Plutonia (none older than Jurassic age), they surmise that this catastrophe occurred no later than the Jurassic, and most likely during the Triassic period.

Obruchev's is another life-through-time adventure, given that the farther they travel in a southerly direction (i.e., on the earth's inner surface) the older becomes the fauna, geologically. There is a central river which they decide to sail after constructing a raft for passage along the coast and to the sea, and so this water body becomes a "river of time" in the story. They encounter saurians including an enormous crocodile, plesiosaurs, pterodactyls, prehistoric birds, and, of course, dinosaurs. A giant kangaroo-like dinosaur, *Iguanodon*, is encountered first, and soon they witness an attack by a ceratosaur, before shooting the carnivore with cameras and then rifles. They also spy a *Triceratops*, prompting this exclamation from one of the scientists, "That means we're in the Cretaceous period now!... And the farther downstream we go, the more of these monsters we'll probably meet." Later they find a stegosaur which they urge on its way by firing guns in the air and yelling. "The frightened monster made off at top speed, joggling along with the large plates on its back slapping against each other and clacking loudly."

After several scenes involving giant ants and volcanic eruptions, the expedition encounters a Neanderthal race, which captures two of the Russian party. They escape, returning to the *North Star*, only to find the outer world engaged in a deadly world war. Their specimens are confiscated and lost, and the only remaining record of their findings is their manuscript notes, titled "Plutonia."

Pelkie, J. W. "King of the Dinosaurs" (1945). "Everybody loves ball games; but who wants to play the part of the ball—especially if the players are dinosaurs." That's the premise of this unusual story about a band of cave men who strangely coexist in the past with intelligent dinosaurs ("Big Snakes"). Cave men become unwilling "balls" of the dinosaurs, who play prehistoric, "Flintstones-like" baseball.

Petticolas, Arthur. "Dinosaur Destroyer" (1949). University athlete and scholar Lewis Varjeon relates his story of reincarnated past lives—especially his existence as "Daarmajd The Strong"—to an astonished colleague. In the first chapter of Petticolas' novella, Daarmajd slays a "dragon," really a *Tyrannosaurus.* "Imagine a gamecock thrice the size of an elephant; a gamecock covered with iridescent scales instead of feathers; a gamecock with a great lashing tail, one blow of which would have smashed an average modern dwelling into kindling wood; with legs like the legs of a gamecock but bigger than an elephant's and covered with scales; and three-toed feet big enough to have broken every bone in the body of a horse they stepped upon ... in the dragon's jaws, pierced through by its long, sharp teeth, was the body of the warrior who had fled into the forest—my warrior, crushed and mangled, his blood dripping in a crimson stream from the creature's slobbering jowls." Daarmajd hurls a great stone at the tyrannosaur's scaly head, killing it.

Preston, Douglas. *Tyrannosaur Canyon* (2005). When a near-perfect specimen of a *Tyrannosaurus* is discovered—with soft tissues and integument preserved—in a New Mexico desert, a wave of intrigue is triggered far surpassing that which enveloped the famous *T. rex* skeleton known as "Sue." For this specimen is contaminated with an alien viral strain that the U.S. government seeks to eradicate before it spreads. This virus was carried to Earth aboard the asteroid which struck the Earth sixty-five million years ago. However, in Preston's novel, dinosaur extinctions are attributed to the spreading of disease through particulate dispersed into the atmosphere in the aftermath of deep impact. It is further suggested that the virus instead may be a "nanomachine," devised "to ensure the extinction of dinosaurs. Perhaps it is a machine built to manipulate or direct evolution, which was seeded on an asteroid headed toward Earth—perhaps even on an asteroid *pushed* toward Earth.... To make way for the evolution of human beings."

Preuss, Paul. "Rheas's Time" (1992). Preuss' tale updates the idea of the "waking dream," as a comatose patient experiences all of geological history and its past life in the course of a single year. (I.)

Rivkin, J.F. *Age of Dinosaurs #1: Tyrannosaurus rex* (1992). Christine Fawcett organizes an expedition to find traces of her relatives who disappeared in the 1920s while exploring the Brazilian rain forest. She discovers a fresh fragment of *Tyrannosaurus* bone in an old crate which was shipped by her ancestors years ago. Members of the Yanomani tribe (actually discovered in the 1920s) take Christine and party to an ancient Mayan pyramid with a pentagonally shaped room inside, adorned with crystalline skulls; it's really a magical time transport device keyed to the Late Cretaceous. As they inadvertently discover, clapping one's hands causes instant transport to the dinosaur age, where Christine finds her uncle alive although much worse for wear. A *T. rex* egg is stolen, and on the river voyage back to civilization, a five-foot-long baby hatches. This story pays homage to Conan Doyle's *Lost World* and his real life South American plateau explorer associate, Col. Percy H. Fawcett (b. 1867; missing in the Amazon jungle as of 1925), incorporating a time travel gimmick in order to encounter dinosaurs in the past.

Roberts, Charles G.D. *In the Morning of Time* (1912). In this well-done novel, first serialized in *The London Magazine*, Roberts paints a remarkable picture of prehistory. Although this is principally a "nature red-in-tooth-and-claw" cave romance, in his first chapter Roberts considers "The World Without Man," offering a glimpse of contemporary understanding about life in the Mesozoic era. Here we witness a battle between the "colossus" *Diplodocus*, and a horned theropod, *Ceratosaurus*. Shaking off its attacker, the wounded colossus swims to a distant shore, only to become mired in quicksand, where it is gobbled by hungry pterodactyls and crocodiles under the watchful eyes of bloodthirsty marine lizards. In the next chapter, Roberts provides a most anachronistic description of the combat between the "king of the triple horn" (i.e., *Triceratops*) and *Dinoceras*, a uintathere which lived some twenty-five to thirty million years *after* the great dinosaur extinction. As Roberts narrates, "Nature, pleased with her experiments in the more promising mammalian type, had turned her back upon them [i.e., the reptilian dinosaurs] ... and was coldly letting them die out. Her failures, however splendid, have always found small mercy at her hands." The bulk of the novel, however, is about how a Cro-Magnon family, Grom and his bride A-Ya, survive in prehistory, outflanking attacks from a host of vicious prehistoria, learning the control and use of fire (the "shining one") for defensive purposes as well as cooking, inventing the bow and arrow and primitive sailing vessels, and thwarting the more primitive ape-like races in battle. *In the Morning of Time* was published in four segments beginning in May, overlapping the time when Conan Doyle's *The Lost World* was running in *The Strand Magazine*.

Robeson, Kenneth. *The Land of Terror* (1933). No doubt influenced by Lovelace's novel *King Kong*, Robeson cast his superhero Doc Savage to the dawn of time on uncharted volcanic Thunder Island in the Pacific, inhabited by dinosaurs and other prehistoric animals. In a chapter titled "Where Time Stopped," Doc theorizes that the prehistoric life forms have been "forced to remain here through the ages" after an earthquake sealed passages leading to and from the now ocean-filled crater. Evolution and extinction haven't operated here because the warm environmental conditions haven't changed in eons. Following action that mimics scenes from Burroughs' *Out of Time's Abyss* (aerial combat between plane and pterodactyl) and Conan Doyle's *Lost World* (carnosaurs which incongruously leap in kangaroo fashion), the terrible reptiles are extinguished in lava from a volcanic eruption triggered by the adventurers. "Robeson" was a pseudonym for Lester Dent (1904–1959).

Rovin, Jeff. *Fatalis* (2000). Sabertooth cats slink and slash through modern southwest California in Rovin's thriller. Combining state-of-the-art scientific technology such as DNA sequencing with knowledge of ancient native customs and traditions, paleoanthropologist Jim Grand and newspaper reporter Hannah Hughes decipher how and why a pack of bloodthirsty *Smilodon fatalis*, supposedly extinct for 11,000 years, has suddenly emerged from a labyrinthine cave network in hills near Santa Barbara and Los Angeles. The huge cats—not mutations but genuine Pleistocene relics—were evidently preserved in the cave system through a peculiar freeze-drying process involving volcanic action, then restored to life after excessive La Nina-caused rainwater percolated into their underground lairs. Grand and Hannah, who want to rescue the cats from vengeful police and military called in to exterminate the rampaging carnivores, understand the cats must be attracted to the smell of asphalt (tar), formerly a source of food (i.e., trapped prey). "If a cat is slain how many lives does its spirit demand in exchange?" Grand wonders, as he struggles mightily to save the last adult cat outside Los Angeles' George C. Page Museum, as the alpha male *Smilodon* becomes trapped in the La Brea Tar Pits alongside life-sized sculptural restorations of *Mastodon*. The savage adult can't be rescued, but preservationists Grand and Hannah discover a litter of mewing kits in a hillside cave which are spared and returned to the wild.

Sagara, Michelle M. "Shadow of a Change" (1993). When a lonely, neglected outcast, April Stephens, begins feeling unusual urges, at first she believes she's coming down with an illness. She's absent from work, eats raw meat and notices that the texture of her skin is changing—becoming scaly. Her teeth are becoming more prominent and sharper too. But her doctor finds nothing out of the ordinary with her. She eats her pet cat and then despondently decides to simply hide out in her basement. When a visitor stops by to check on her, April—now a full-fledged carnosaur—devours the good Samaritan. Although she had "never been in control of her life or the things that changed it and shaped it," now she "had never felt so free as this.... She strode out, primitive, great, old—a thing of memory, a dream of children, a walking death." (F.)

Sawyer, Robert J. "Just Like Old Times" (1992). Isn't man-as-terrible lizard, perhaps, the ultimate dino-monster fantasy? The phrase "old times" in Sawyer's title isn't simply a trite nostalgic reference to good ol,' happy-go-lucky Mesozoic days, but, rather, a cruel pun. In 2042, Dr. Robert Cohen, convicted of murdering thirty-seven people, is sentenced to a "chronotransference" fate. Chronotransference is the means of transferring a human consciousness back into a organism living in history, "superimposing his or her mind over that of someone who lived in the past." It's considered a proper means of euthanasia. Cohen takes Hopkins' cue and suggests an appropriate, yet most unusual target organism—*Tyrannosaurus rex*. Confronting his attorney, John Axworthy, Cohen notes, "That damned judge said I was the most cold-blooded killer to stalk the Alberta landscape since *Tyrannosaurus rex*.... The idiot. Doesn't she know dinosaurs were warm-blooded? Anyway, that's what I want. I want to be transferred into a *T. rex*." Axworthy replies, "You're kidding." Cohen sets him straight. "Kidding is not my forte, John. *Killing* is. I want to know which was better at it, me or the rex." Requiring an actual fossil specimen from which to "back-propagate," scientists complete the transfer. Soon Cohen's mind is free at large within the skull of a *T. rex*, roaming through the Late Cretaceous landscape.

Cohen directs his new *T. rex* body into a tumultuous battle versus a large three-horned *Triceratops*, mainly for the thrill of the hunt and to experience "Pain. Exquisite, beautiful pain." Delighted that blood still appears red to his reptilian retinas, Cohen dispatches the three-horn, and vengefully, yet paradoxically, moves onto a far more devious undertaking..

Spying tiny mammalian *Purgatorius*, "not just any mammal ... the very first primate," Cohen tortures the little creature:

> The rex leaned in close, and Cohen saw the furball's face, the nearest thing there would be to a human face for another sixty million years. The animal's eyes went wide with terror.
> Naked raw fear.
> *Mammalian fear.*
> Cohen saw the creature scream.
> *Heard* it scream.
> It was beautiful.
> The rex moved its gaping jaws toward the little mammal, drawing in breath with such force that it sucked the creature into its maw. Normally the rex would swallow its meals whole, but Cohen prevented the beast from doing that. Instead, he simply had it stand still, with the lit-

tle primate running around, terrified inside the great cavern of the dinosaur's mouth, banging into the giant teeth and great fleshy walls, and skittering over the massive dry tongue.

Cohen savored the terrified squealing....

It was just like old times.

Just like hunting humans.

With his superior mind lodged inside the *T. rex* braincase, Cohen steers his rex body away from the calamity which in a parallel-world setting would have normally ended the rex's life. Thus, the rex avoids an otherwise fatal fall into a fissure, causing Cohen to select a new career—the systematic extermination of *Purgatorius*—because "if he killed enough of these little screaming balls of fur, they wouldn't have any descendants. There wouldn't ever be any *Homo sapiens* ... he *was* hunting humans—every single human being who would ever exist." As previously noted in Chapter Five, the idea of exterminating humanity's existence from the future fabric of space-time was anticipated by Pohl in his "Let the Ants Try." (E., F.)

Sawyer, Robert J. *End of an Era* **(1994).** Dinosaur paleontologist Brandon Thackeray, beset by a mid-life crisis, and his rival, the cool, calm and collected "Klicks," present a most satisfying fictionalized solution to that time-honored question, "How did the dinosaurs become extinct?" Protagonist Thackeray, favoring a volcanic "smoking gun" alternative, counters geologist Klicks, the self-professed "impactor," who incidentally has stolen Thackeray's wife.

In order to ensure a safe "throwback" to 64.7 million years ago, Sawyer's flying saucer-shaped timeship, named the *Sternberger*, must be dropped with Thackeray and Klicks aboard from a height of over 3,000 feet above the Alberta Badlands. During its descent they're transported from A.D. 2013 way, way back to the Cretaceous, where they soon encounter living dinosaurs, including *Troodon* who seem suspiciously more intelligent than anyone would have anticipated. Curiously, Earth's gravitational field is substantially less than in the present.

Turns out the Late Cretaceous is really dominated not by dinosaurs but instead by a hive of space-faring protoplasmic Martians. Sawyer's Martians are viral yet sentient, and can assimilate themselves into living tissue. In fact, due to their large cranial capacities, the malicious *Troodon* turn out to be the preferred medium through which the hive mind of the Martians communicates with Thackeray and Klicks. Using gravity-suppressing satellites, the Martians have reduced Earth's gravity to equal Martian gravity. They have bio-engineered the evolution of Cretaceous dinosaur species adapted to the diminished gravitational field, explaining why some dinosaur genera became so huge. Automatons such as *T. rex* serve as engines of destruction in the Martians' war waged against other aliens living on a planet existing in the orbit now occupied by the asteroid belt. The Martians, who have not invented time machines of their own, learn from Thackeray and Klicks that global extinctions will take place shortly in a geological instant, a peril that can only be avoided if they hitch a ride back to 2013 with the time travelers.

The Martians launch a massive dinosaur offensive in their bid to control time and Earth's future. But their attack is thwarted only after Thackeray and Klicks manage to destroy the gravity suppressors using radio signals, a victory that ironically *causes* the K-T boundary extinction! Following an intensified, unrelenting global earthquake, "It was a different world. Klicks and I were the only large creatures still able to walk around. Dinosaurs were everywhere, flopped on their bellies. Some still clung to life. The hearts of others had already given out under the hours of doubled gravity. Those that did survive would eventually starve, unable to move around to forage."

While Sam Magruder never returns to his present in Simpson's novella, for Thackeray there is salvation. Afterward, back in 2013, Thackeray finds solace in a mended, alternative reality in which time travel was never invented and his marriage survived.

Schwartz, Susan. "Drawing Out Leviathan" (1997). In biblical times, Leviathan's mate Behemoth has been killed. Then God tells Noah to build an Ark because a Great Flood will drown sinners of the world. One male and female of every living species should board the Ark, but Leviathan (a nondescript dinosaurian) cannot enter the Ark since she's the last of her kind. Lacking a prospective mate, her race must succumb to extinction. (G.)

Sheffield, Charles. "The Feynman Saltation" (1992.). A patient afflicted with a positronic brain experiences the deep geological past in reverse chronological order. (I.)

Silverberg, Robert. "Hunters in the Forest" (1992). Evidently inspired by Brian Aldiss' classic tale "Poor Little Warrior," a time traveler named Mallory encounters a lovely lady who attempts to seduce him to remain there with her in the Late Cretaceous, stranded for all time. Turns out, though, that she's just been enjoying a little dangerous fantasy of her own, and Mallory doesn't regret his return voyage to the present after all. (I.)

Simak, Clifford D. *Mastodonia* (1978). Overpopulation is the theme of Clifford D. Simak's (1904–1988) delightful "closet classic" *Mastodonia*, documenting the most catastrophic time safari ever in the annals of science fiction. Asa Steele and his female companion, Rila, encounter a reclusive, godlike alien named Catface whose spaceship crash-landed on Earth fifty thousand years ago. Catface is capable of opening "time roads" which are soon exploited by entrepreneurs intent on visiting the past. Sensing a cash cow opportunity in the making, Asa and a small party journey to the Cretaceous Period to secure evidence of their time travel capabilities. They soon spy a number of dinosaurs including an *Ankylosaurus*, a *Triceratops* herd and, in homage to L. Sprague de Camp, a *Tyrannosaur*, "maybe a trionychid. Maybe another kind of tyrannosaur we've never found a fossil of...." Furthermore, the party acknowledges the dinosaurs may be warm-blooded, so the party must remain on guard during the night.

Then, "Coming down the slope ... was a monstrosity that made me catch my breath: no other than the old rex himself. There was no mistaking him. He didn't look exactly as our twentieth-century artists had depicted him, but he was close enough that there was no mistaking him.... Below the lower jaw hung an elaborate dewlap that no artist could have been aware of—a dewlap that displayed an awful, iridescent beauty. It shone in the sunlight with colors that seemed to ripple across its surface—purple, yellow, blue, red and green— ever-changing colors that reminded me momentarily of the stained glass windows I had seen at one time in an ancient church...." Two tyrannosaurs charging in for the kill are shot dead in their tracks. Rila captures their terrifying attack on film, but it's a darn good thing Asa and party carried guns suitable for dinosaur.

Having seen the incredible footage, Safari, Inc. contracts with Asa's newly formed Time Associates for access rights to the Late Cretaceous Period where hunters can kill the greatest carnivores ever to walk the planet. Because modern big game teeters on the verge of extinction, hunters are willing to pay a fortune to travel back in time to experience the thrill of the hunt, no matter what the risk. A movie company, interested in filming the evolution of the Earth through time, desires a contract to visit all of the geological periods. With money soon about to roll in hand-over-fist, tragedy and turmoil soon upset the pastoral Minnesota setting, encouraging Asa and Rila to set up a base operation in an Edenic setting tagged "Mastodonia," situated in the Sangamon interglacial stage of the Pleistocene. But Hiram— the only person capable of communicating with Catface—is bitten by a rattlesnake. Then Safari, Inc. sends four hunting expeditions to the Cretaceous, each spaced 10,000 years apart in time. When only three safari teams return, a rescue party is sent in after the fourth, and a grisly scene is discovered. A pack of allosaurs previously unknown to science, carnivores considerably larger than any tyrannosaur, have slaughtered every member of the fourth expedition. Other legal and political snafus seem to leap out at Asa and Rila, like snakes in the grass.

Consequently, the government places restrictions on Time Associates' operations, but following the intervention of Senator Freemore, a deal is struck. Time Associates may remain in the time safari business after all, provided time roads are opened allowing the poor and impoverished masses of world society to pioneer homesteads in the Miocene epoch, twenty-five million years ago. While Asa sarcastically claims this ploy is merely aimed to get these individuals "out of our hair," the senator counters that he's seeking to avoid mass starvation and lifelong privation. The Miocene would be ideal because grasses had evolved by then, permitting agriculture. Furthermore the Miocene is sufficiently far back in time such that there would be no possibility of the pioneers clashing with modern humans. Eventually, an evolved Catface is recalled to his celestial abode.

Sparhawk, Bud. "Fierce Embrace" (1997). Two paleontologists, Hans Koenig and Regina Quinn, who have sparred professionally, debating whether *T. rex* was an active hunter versus a scavenger, find themselves falling for one another at a dig site. Their passion is consummated following their discovery of a pair of tyrannosaurs which—as they determine— died during coupling, their fossilized limbs interlocked eternally in a "fierce embrace." (G.)

Sternberg, Charles H. *Hunting Dinosaurs: In the Bad Lands of the Red Deer River, Alberta Canada* (1917). After publication of Conan Doyle's *The Lost World*, paleontologist Sternberg (1850–1943) privately published this volume. Curiously, in the midst of personal recollections about his career as a collector of fossil vertebrates, Sternberg incorporated several "pen-pictures" and a quaint science fiction tale, a "waking dream" three chapters in length. After entering a coal miner's tunnel, Sternberg travels backward in time successively from the Late Cretaceous, next to an earlier stage of the Cretaceous in western Kansas, and then ultimately to the Permian Period. According to David A. E. Spalding, "Sternberg's inclusion of the story suggests that it satisfied some deep personal needs. It was not, perhaps, written as entertainment but started as an extension of his descriptions of animals in life. Sternberg the fossil collector must often have longed to see the animals he was collecting as they were when they lived, and the appearance of Sternberg as a character in his own story allows this to happen in fictional terms."

The means of time travel? Like Rip Van Winkle, Sternberg simply falls asleep in the field. Waking, he writes, "I was overcome with surprise, I could not tell whether I had awakened in eternity, or Time had turned back his dial, and carried me back to the old Cretaceous Ocean." After surveying this younger world he concludes that he's has been transported "three million years" to the Age of Reptiles. Sternberg, wondering whether he'll survive this incredible experience, offers himself up to the Almighty who will guide him according to His will. Next, he spies a passive, herbivorous *Trachodon*, inspiring Romantic poetic verse. While *Trachodon* finishes its breakfast, Sternberg makes scientific observations, which in a self-serving way confirm his own scientific speculations about the animal's life appearance and natural history.

Suddenly Sternberg's *Trachodon* is attacked by the "Tiger of the Everglades," *Tyrannosaurus*, quite likely the first time this species appeared in any science fiction tale. "The noble lizard, seeing that he could not escape his foe, bravely faced him, and as if to hurry the end, he exposed the most vulnerable part of his body, by rising on his hind limbs. The enemy hurled himself at full length upon the defenseless victim, and with great claws of hardened horn, fully ten inches long, he ripped his body down and red blood flooded the mossy way. As he fell to earth and death, this tyrant of those early days tore open his body and fed upon the quivering flesh and running blood in the very shelter of the redwood forest.... After gormandizing to his heart's content he drifted off into the forest, and I saw him no more." After further observing the Rex "conquerer," Sternberg paddles his boat to the shore where he slumbers, only to reawaken the next day along another, more ancient ocean shoreline.

For Sternberg, prehistory is nostalgic. In the Early Cretaceous, Sternberg is joined by his own dear daughter, Maud, who had tragically died several years before the book's publication. Reunited in fantasy, the pair set up camp in a cave overlooking Mosasaurian Bay and observe aquatic saurians such as the mosasaurs *Tylosaurus* and *Clidastes*, as well as giant fish native to this Kansas chalk environment. Dozing off once more, Sternberg awakens in the Permian Period, "twelve million years ago," where he encounters a ten-foot-long salamander, *Eryops*, as well as other forms of ancient life and risks becoming his own fossil. Sternberg's tale of reverie is remarkable as it appears in what otherwise what would be considered as a scientific manuscript. In his introduction to the 1985 edition, Spalding further suggests, "From the modern perspective ... Sternberg can undoubtedly be seen as a pioneer science fiction writer, yet in the artistic sense he is a 'primitive.' He gives no direct evidence of being influenced by other writers of science fiction, or indeed of regarding the material as fiction at all." The devout Sternberg's vivid description of a living *Tyrannosaurus* foreshadowed man's forthcoming preoccupation and identification with the lordly beast.

Strickland, Brad, with John Michlig. *Kong: King of Skull Island* **(2004).** This imaginative novel, both a prequel and a sequel, created and illustrated by Joe DeVito, elucidates what happened both prior to King Kong's capture by Carl Denham, who returned Kong's body to Skull Island, and during the late 1950s aftermath following a return visit to Skull Island by Jack Driscoll and Denham's son, Vincent, who is a paleontologist. We learn that Kong was the last survivor of a primate "kong" species otherwise unknown to science which lived alongside highly evolved intelligent raptor dinosaurs, including the fearsome "queen" of the raptors, named "Gaw" by the islanders. After the raptor pack slays his parents, lonely Kong eventually triumphs in battle over Gaw. Upon his return to New York, Vincent wisely decides to withhold knowledge of the island's rich past, revealed to him through a storyteller. Also, Skull Island's location will never be divulged. Driscoll states, "You know, all these years I thought those islanders were the most primitive of savages, but ... they may be the greatest ancient civilization the world has ever known."

Swanwick, Michael. "Riding the Giganotosaur" (1999) George Weskowski, a business executive diagnosed with terminal cancer who is also seeking freedom from a stifling, futuristic working world, much like that of today, signs on with a science team who transfer his mind into the forty-foot-long titular theropod. Having traveled backward in time to the Patagonian Cretaceous Period, George is granted a new lease on life, if only he'd come to his senses. With a transmitter chip installed into the Giganotosaur's speech center to facilitate communication between George's mind and paleontologists studying the natural history of this genus, George turns renegade, abandoning the scientists. Then "George" makes his first kill, rejoicing, "No more bosses! No more networking, no more memos, no more meetings! He'd never see the inside of an office again, sweat out another cold sell, face another IRS audit…. Since this morning he had experienced pride, anger, gluttony, and—now—sloth. Four of the seven deadly sins in the course of a few hours. By God, that was the way to spend a day!" And then, ironically, George muses, "This was the life for a man."

When confronted by the scientist team after failing to make his first report from the field, George is found devouring the remains of fresh kill, an *Australotopsian*. George's "muzzle was wet with blood. His eyes surely glittered with the savage joy of the kill. He knew that he must look the perfect image of Satanic fury. He grinned." The team's "transition psychologist," becoming deeply concerned with George's transformation as well as his failure to keep his end of the bargain, pleads, "…you can't simply break all ties with humankind. Strong as you are, big as you are, you can't exist on your own." Arrogantly, George dismisses the scientists with, "You forgot it make it *enforceable*. You forgot to come up with a way to make Mr. *Giganotosaurus* give a damn."

Next, George is joined by three lovely females of "his" species, giganotosauruses which he names Eve, Slut, and Scarface. George is smitten with a newfound carnal pleasure—"dino sex," another deadly sin. Although he initially expresses revulsion for bestiality, in fact, dinosaur sex turns out to be the best sex he's ever had. Now George's "queens filled his days with sex and companionship," and even bring him food prior to copulating. George's reaction to this marvelous attention is simply "Take a number, ladies."

Life is good—that is, until the queens turn on him. Having planted seed in his harem, he is of no further use to the females, and a deadly chase ensues. "So this is what terror feels like, he thought crazily." Panic-stricken, George stumbles into a mound of broken tree trunks where he ends up hopelessly entangled with a broken leg, awaiting a cruel fate. But the queens' snapping jaws can't reach him through the logjam, and so they depart. Also entrapped with the pile is a little protorat, whose progeny, symbolically, would opportunistically inherit the post-dinosaurian world. Here was "quite possibly the direct ancestor of Man." Although in a previous encounter, George had urinated on the squeaking protorat, now he muses, "Come to get your revenge, have you?… Going to defend the honor of your kind by gnawing on my bones?"

George weighs how he could reach out and pop the little protorat into his maw, a final cold-blooded act of cruelty. Trapped in the log pile, much as he had been trapped in his human life with a bad marriage and caught up in a joyless job, George laments on how little he has left in the world. "He'd made a pot of money over a long lifetime running with the wolves in the financial markets, and spent it all on a much shorter lifetime running with the giganotosaurs in the wild. And in the end, everybody—humans and dinosaurs alike—he'd trusted had turned on him…. It only confirmed what he'd learned long ago. There was no loyalty in this world. Every man lived alone, and he died alone as well." Unlike Sawyer's evil-minded Cohen-as-rex, however, Sawyer's giganototaur character George becomes further transformed.

"All right, you sonofabitch … live!" Summoning his waning strength, George heaves two logs aside just sufficiently for the terrified protorat to escape; then he prepares to die, alone. As his consciousness fades, he hears a whirring—the sound of helicopter blades. Tested by nature, realizing his life's mistake, George is granted another chance, a reprieve, rescued by the scientists. Although melded within a dinosaur body, rehabilitated George becomes more human than ever before.

Swanwick, Michael. "A Great Day for Brontosaurs" (2002). Creatures disguised as humans—but presumably dinosaurian in nature as they are "feathered"—are delighted with one "Mr. Adams's" enthusiasm for the genetic cloning of dinosaur species. They are prepared in a "Phase Two" to establish a world with a "permanent breeding population," provided their interview with "Eve" goes as well.

Taine, John (pseud. for Eric Temple Bell). *Before the Dawn* (1934). Scientists discover a means for glimpsing prehistory through a peculiar "televisor," relying on the properties of incidental light as it once reflected on fossil objects. The televisor was inspired by early experimentation with television in America. The investigators use the technique to follow the life history of a huge theropod which they name Belshazzar, a creature invested with humanlike courage and loyalty. The novel—Taine's favorite, although certainly not his best—has been regarded as a celebration of Victorian attitudes toward might and power. Taine's dinosaurs are never identified by species. Ultimately and symbolically, Belshazzar confronts his dino-nemesis, "Satan."

Turtledove, Harry. "The Green Buffalo" (1992). Othniel Marsh's real bone collector, John Bell Hatcher, a specialist in *Triceratops*, amusingly doesn't realize he's munching on cooked "Tops" meat, which tastes like chicken, after a buffalo hunt. Turtledove suggests the lone *Triceratops* may have passed inexplicably into 1890s Wyoming through a time slip. (I.)

Twain, Mark (pseud. for Samuel Clemens). "Was the World Made for Man?" (1904). Twain, who met Charles Darwin in 1879, wrote satires about evolution. In this satire, Twain opined that after the *oyster* had gradually, painstakingly evolved, they might "jump to the conclusion that the nineteen million years was a preparation for *him*; but that would be just like an oyster, the most conceited animal there is, except man." Continuing, Twain went on to satirize the course of geological history and the pageant of life. Taking on the Mesozoic Era, Twain facetiously described how, "The Paleozoic time limit having now been reached, it was necessary to begin the next stage in the preparation of the world for man, by opening up the Mesozoic Age and instituting some reptiles. For man would need reptiles. Not to eat, but to develop himself from. This being the most important detail of the scheme, a spacious liberality of time was set apart for it—thirty million years." In another essay published in the *Daily Record-Union*, Twain opined that fossil tracks discovered near Carson City had been instead imprinted by a drunken Legislature following their adjournment one evening. "It had rained all the evening outside, and it had rained whiskey all the evening inside.... It was then that they made the tracks.... I was there and saw them march. The primeval man was absent; the Irish Elk did not arrive; the Cave Bear responded not to the summons.... The menagerie was entirely local." Several of Twain's evolutionary satires were collected in the book *Letters From the Earth* (1938).

Verne, Jules, with Michel-Jules Verne. "Humbug: The American Way of Life" (1910). This tongue in cheek examination of American culture, possibly inspired by the Cardiff Giant hoax of 1869, was drafted by Jules Verne (probably) in 1870, yet modified by his son Michel prior to publication. This is the tale of an enormous alleged fossilized skeleton found in a field outside Albany. While early speculation hints that the colossal skeleton might be that of a *Mastodon*, a woolly mammoth or even a plesiosaur, instead, when unveiled, the specimen is purported to be a 120-foot-tall human! "If the fact was true (and everybody accepted it as such), the geological theories with the most solid foundations, must necessarily be changed, since fossils had now been found well below the alluvial deposits—meaning that they had been deposited before the Flood." Newspaper accounts claim the human race sprang from American soil. The "humbug" is identified by the protagonist as a heap of recent bloodstained buffalo bones, but not before its promoter has made a mint.

Williams, Robert Moore. *Jongor of Lost Land* **(1940).** In his interesting lost-world tale, Williams introduces a Tarzan-like hero named Jongor, whose parents perished on a trip across Australia's desert wastelands through lofty mountains into a hidden valley. The grown Jongor rescues Ann Hunter from her two unscrupulous male associates, Hofer and Varsey, as well as a colony of monkey-like survivors from the lost continent of Mu (which in legend sank into the Pacific Ocean centuries ago) who inhabit the mysterious Lost Land. After enormous pterodactyls killed John Gordon's parents years ago, young "Jon-Gor" was forced to fend for himself in this forbidden land against winged teros, the apelike "Muros" and dinosaurs. In Lost Land, where the "time clock was keeping lost and forgotten centuries ... the mad savagery of a primeval world," dinosaurs and teros are controlled telepathically, aided by Muros' advanced technology. Ann Hunter is intent on finding her brother who was recently lost during an expedition to Lost Land, but unbeknownst to her, her comrades plan to ransack the Muros' gold and diamond treasure, and steal their weapon of mass destruction which is capable of delivering tremendous tornado wind blasts to populated centers. Hofer and Varsey plan to hold the world for ransom, threatening global powers with this device. Following capture by the Muros, Ann will be sacrificed to the sun. But riding a theropod dinosaur into combat, Jongor saves Ann from the evil Muros' clutches (including "Alcan," who covets her lecherously), outmaneuvering traitorous Hofer and the cowardly Varsey in a deadly struggle. At one point in the story, when Hofer spies a dinosaur wallowing in a swamp, he declares, "...it is logical enough. Where we find pterodactyls, dinosaurs we will also find. But who would have thought that such things anywhere on earth had remained alive in the Twentieth Century." In a later passage it is revealed that one reason why Jongor decided not to kill Hofer and Varsey outright after first spying them—even though Varsey wounded him slightly with a rifle shot—was because, like him, they're of his own Caucasian race.

Wolverton, Dave. "Siren Song at Midnight" (1992). A scientist who restores a Triassic bipedal animal (a dinosaurian ancestor), *Euparkeria*, from fossil DNA contemplates ecological devastation in a futuristic society populated by DNA-enhanced humans, the marine Sirens. (I.)

Yep, Lawrence. *Monster Makers, Inc.* **(1986).** Before Crichton's monsters were cloned, Yep conceived a scientist creating miniaturized versions of dinosaurs (e.g., *Hadrosaurus*) and even a fire-breathing, three-foot tall Godzilla for sale as pets and to assist in the colonization of other planets. These animals are a product of biogenetic engineering experiments.

Notes

Preface

1. Adrian Desmond, *Huxley: From Devil's Disciple to Evolution's High Priest* (Reading, Mass.: Perseus Books, 1997), p. 427.

2. Philippe Taquet, *Dinosaur Impressions: Postcards from a Paleontologist*, trans. Kevin Padian (Cambridge: Cambridge University Press, 1998), p. 146. According to French paleontologist Philippe Taquet, Efremov's "Shadow of the Past" concerns an unusual discovery in the Gobi Desert. Taquet relates, "Efremov imagines that the rock face of a cave in the mountain, coated with resin, has served as a photographic film on which the features of an enormous carnivorous dinosaur have been permanently fixed, because the cave has become a natural darkroom." The paleontologists "watch in fascination as the rays of the setting sun bring out the apparition of this monstrous dinosaur ... first to bone, and then in the flesh! The dream of every dinosaur paleontologist." In Efremov's *Star Ships*, extraterrestrial humanoid prospectors, seeking radioactive elements in the Earth's crust to power their magnificent spacecraft, visit our planet in the Late Cretaceous. As noted by paleontologist Jose Luis Sanz in his *Starring T. rex* (Bloomington: Indiana University Press, 2002), "The arrival of the aliens results in a serious conflict with the dinosaurs, and the aliens decimated them. The proofs of this conflict are evident: enormous cemeteries discovered by Soviet paleontologists in eastern Russia and central Asia, and bones perforated by wounds caused by projectiles. Finally the scientists find the cranium of a humanoid and some advanced tools next to the skeletons of the dinosaurs" (80).

Introduction

1. Leon E. Stover and Harry Harrison, eds., *Apeman, Spaceman: Anthropological Science Fiction* (New York: Doubleday & Co., Inc., 1968), p. 14.

2. Allen A. Debus, "The Lost Worlds of Science Fiction," *Cosmic Landscapes* 1, no. 6 (October 1983): pp. 20–21, 24.

3. That is, between 1990 and 1993, with four articles printed in the *Earth Science Newsbulletin*, with titles such as "Searching For Fantasy Dinosaurs (Parts 1–2)," "Fantasy Dinosaurs—Revisited," and "More Fantasy Dinosaurs." Then, sometime in the early 2000's, I learned through a package of assorted documents from paleontologist and historian of science William A.S. Sarjeant (1907–2000) that Sarjeant was indeed working on a manuscript concerning the history of dinosaurs and geology in science fiction. There's no telling how that intriguing study would have turned out or what relation it would have borne to this volume.

4. Science fiction writer Robert Silverberg has recently stated that all fiction can be boiled down to his "universal theory" of the story, which is, "A sympathetic and engaging character, faced with some immensely difficult problem that it is necessary for him to solve, makes a series of attempts to overcome that problem, frequently encountering challenging sub-problems and undergoing considerable hardship and anguish, and eventually, at the darkest moment of all, calls on some insight that was not accessible to him at the beginning of the story and either succeeds in his efforts or fails in a dramatically interesting and revelatory way, therefore arriving at new knowledge of a significant kind." See Silverberg's articles titled "Toward a Theory of Story," Parts 1 to 3, *Asimov's Science Fiction* (April/May 2004), (June 2004), (July 2004), pp. 4–9 in each issue.

5. Allen A. Debus, "Sorting Fossil Vertebrate Iconography in Paleoart," *Bulletin of the South Texas Geological Society* 44, no. 1 (September 2003): pp. 11–24; Allen A. Debus, "Images Out of Deep Time," *Prehistoric Times* 12, no. 67 (2004): pp. 52–54. I've thrice lectured on this topic, such as in my presentation to an audience at the Burpee Museum of Natural History's annual "Paleofest" in February 2003, titled "Paleoart—a History."

Chapter 1

1. The first edition of Verne's *Journey* was published in 1864. For more on the 1959 film, see Mark F. Berry, *The Dinosaur Filmography* (Jefferson, NC: McFarland & Company, Inc., Publishers, 2002), pp. 147–151. For more on use the "gagged-up" lizards of dino-monster filmdom, see my article, "Get Real! Dinosaur Masquerade," *G-Fan* no. 65, (Nov./Dec. 2003): pp. 28–34. To eliminate confusion, it should be mentioned that character names differ in Verne's original novel from those in the film. For instance, "Alec" (played by Pat Boone) is "Axel" in the 1864 novel, and Professor "Lindenbrook" (played by James Mason) is instead "Lidenbrook." There is no female companion participant in Verne's novel, and character names in 1860s French editions were changed to young "Harry" and "Pro-

fessor Von Hardwigg," respectively, in 1870s English editions.

2. W.J.T. Mitchell, *The Last Dinosaur Book: The Life and Times of a Cultural Icon* (Chicago: The University of Chicago Press, 1998), pp. 51–52.

3. Martin J.S. Rudwick, *Scenes From Deep Time: Early Pictorial Representations of the Prehistoric World* (Chicago: The University of Chicago Press, 1992), pp. 35–36.

4. Allen A. Debus, "Sorting Fossil Vertebrate Iconography in Paleoart," *Bulletin of the South Texas Geological Society* 44, no. 1 (Sept. 2003): pp. 5, 10–24; Allen A. Debus and Diane E. Debus, *Paleoimagery: The Evolution of Dinosaurs in Art* (Jefferson, NC: McFarland & Company, Inc., Publishers, 2002), p. 8. As noted by Debus and Debus, paleoartists (a term coined by Mark Hallett in 1986) have been viewed as "(modern) artists who create original skeletal reconstructions and/or restorations of prehistoric animals, or restore fossil flora or invertebrates, using acceptable and recognized procedures. Paleoartists could themselves be scientists or individuals who are well informed about the relevant science concerning the organisms they seek to reconstruct and restore." In 2001, the Society of Vertebrate Paleontology (*www.paleovert.org*) further defined "paleoart" on their Web site as "the scientific or naturalistic rendering of paleontological subject matter pertaining to vertebrate fossils." Perhaps reflecting that over 90 percent of normal human sensory perception is optical, such definitions and an associated term, "paleoimagery," emphasize the visual nature of prehistoric animal imagetext, while giving short shrift to its verbal component. So the definition of paleoartist should be amended to incorporate artists who *write* speculatively about fossil vertebrates, inclusive of the more detailed (yet inherently speculative) scientific end, along a continuum to a more elaborately fictionalized terminus. Thus, especially since words form pictures in our mind's eye, in its broadest sense "paleoart" can refer to literary works of fiction as well as visual depictions.

5. Martin J.S. Rudwick, "The Emergence of a Visual Language For Geological Science 1760–1840," *History of Science* 14 (1976) p. 150.

6. Marianne Sommer, "The Romantic Cave? The Scientific and Poetic Quests for Subterranean Spaces in Britain," *Earth Sciences History* 22, no. 2 (2003): pp. 172–208; quote from p. 175.

7. Scientific investigation also freed caves of imaginary subterranean creatures such as fairies, dragons and chimeras of birds, which according to myth and folklore lurked in mysterious caves. Instead, geologists noted fossilized bones of *real* former "monsters" deposited in caves, such as hyenas and cave bears. Their remains became synonymous with geologists' early visions of prehistory, as is the case today.

8. Sommer, *op. cit.*, p. 193.

9. Rudwick, 1992, *op. cit.*, p. 20–21.

10. Full text of Conybeare's poem and the image itself are reprinted in Rudwick, 1992, pp. 41–43.

11. This depiction was reproduced on page 195 of Sommer, *op. cit.*

12. Rudwick, 1992, *op. cit.*, p. 47; also see note 55.

13. The entire poem is reprinted in Jordan D. Marche II, "Edward Hitchcock's Poem: The Sandstone Bird (1836)," *Earth Sciences History* 10, no. 1 (1991): pp. 5–8. The poetic (speculative) life-through-time tradition was continued through the early twentieth century, the premier example of which must be Henry Robert Knipe's (1855–1918) *Nebula to Man* (New York: J.M. Dent & Company, 1905).

14. Hitchcock cited in Marche, p. 7, lines 104–105.

15. Two early works not traceable by this writer include

J. Mill, *The Fossil Spirit: A Boy's Dream of Geology* (London: Darton Books, 1854), referenced on p. 699 of *The Complete Dinosaur* (Bloomington: Indiana University Press, 1997), eds. James O. Farlow, M.K. Brett-Surman and Robert Walters, as well as Alexandre Dumas' (1802–1870) *Isaac Laquedem* (1853), discussed on p. xviii of Butcher's Introduction to the Oxford World's Classic edition (1998) of Verne's *Journey*, as well as by Arthur B. Evans, "Literary Intertexts in Jules Verne's *Voyages Extraordinaires*," *Science Fiction Studies* 23, no. 2 (July 1996): pp. 172–173.

16. For more on the "hollow earth" leanings of Poe and Symmes, see William Goetzmann, *New Lands, New Men* (New York: Viking Penguin, Inc., 1986), pp. 258–264; Arthur B. Evans, *op. cit.* July 1996, pp. 172–173; John Cleaves Symmes (Captain Adam Seaborn, pseud.), *Symzonia; Voyage of Discovery* (1820; reprint, New York: Arno Press, 1975).

17. William Butcher, Introduction to *Journey to the Center of the Earth*, by Jules Verne, trans. William Butcher (Oxford: Oxford University Press, 1998), pp. x, xxvi.

18. John Breyer and William Butcher. "Nothing New under the Earth: The Geology of Jules Verne's *Journey to the Center of the Earth*," *Earth Sciences History* 22, no. 1 (2003): pp. 36–54, quote from p. 53.

19. Breyer and Butcher, *op. cit.*, p. 37.

20. My finding, that *Journey*'s principal, recurrent theme is life-through-time, wasn't previously recognized by Peter Costello in his *Jules Verne: Inventor of Science Fiction* (New York: Charles Scribner's Sons, 1978), was omitted by Breyer and Butcher, *op. cit.*, who stressed *Journey*'s geological elements while neglecting cave metaphor, wasn't fully acknowledged by Butcher, *op. cit.* (1998), and was neglected by Rudwick, *op. cit.* (1992). The overall significance of imagery in Verne's *Les Voyages Extraordinaires* was recently documented in Arthur B. Evans, "The Illustrators of Jules Verne's *Voyages Extraordinaires*," *Science Fiction Studies* (July 1998): pp. 241–270.

21. Breyer and Butcher, *op. cit.*, p. 53.

22. As I.O. Evans stated in his 1964 introduction to the Ace Books Fitzroy edition of Verne's *The Village in the Treetops* (1901; reprint, New York: Ace Books, 1964), "Fascinated as he was by every branch of science, Jules Verne could not but be interested in the controversy over the Darwinian controversy."

23. Costello, *op. cit.*, p. 83.

24. Jules Verne, *Backwards to Britain* (New York: Chambers, 1992). Verne stated, "As the train passed over the housetops, Jacques glanced for the last time at the Thames and at St. Paul's Cathedral. He caught sight of the magical Crystal Palace of Sydenham, although it was only a fleeting glimpse" (p. 208). So it appears as if Verne may not have actually visited the island of prehistoric monsters.

25. Quite opposite from Verne's unifying theme in *Journey* is George Sand's *Laura: A Journey Into the Crystal* (London: Pushkin Press, 2004). Sand's short novel delves more fully into mineralogical themes and symbolism than *Journey*, while relegating paleontology to minor significance. Boitard's *Paris Before Man* is discussed in Rudwick, 1992, *op. cit.*, pp. 166–172.

26. Rudwick, 1992, *op. cit.*, chapters 4 and 5.

27. Miller quoted in Arthur B. Evans 1998, *op. cit.*, p. 250. To date, Edouard Riou's illustrations published in Figuier have not been compared to those published in *Journey*.

28. See Michael Dirda's afterword to *A Journey to the Center of the Earth* (New York: Signet Classic, 1986), p. 299.

29. Rachel Laudan, *From Mineralogy to Geology: The Foundations of a Science 1650–1830* (Chicago: The Univer-

sity of Chicago Press, 1987). Laudan describes Davy's experimental erupting model volcano on page 186. See also Davy Humphry, "On the phenomena of volcanoes," *Philosophical Transactions of the Royal Society* 118 (1828) pp. 241–50. For a closer look at Davy's geological and paleontological ideas in light of Verne's *Journey*, see my article "Humphry Davy's *Consolations*," Parts 1–2, *Journal of Avocational Paleontology* 12 (2006), no. 5 (May 2006): 14–17 and no. 6 (June 2006): 14–17, and my (in press) 2006 *Science Fiction Studies* article.

30. All quotations from Verne's novel are as found in Jules Verne, *Journey to the Center of the Earth*, trans. William Butcher (Oxford: Oxford University Press, 1998). (This particular quote is found on p. 98 of Figuier's).

31. Verne, *Journey*, p. 100.

32. Verne, *Journey*, p. 120.

33. Verne, *Journey*, p. 142.

34. Verne, *Journey*, p. 147.

35. Verne, *Journey*, p. 150.

36. Verne, *Journey*, pp. 99–100.

37. Louis Figuier, *The World Before the Deluge* (retranslated as *Earth Before the Deluge*), trans. Henry W. Bristow (London: Cassell & Company, Ltd., 1867), Plate VII, p. 104.

38. Verne, *Journey*, p. 151.

39. Figuier, *op. cit.*, p. 125.

40. Verne, *Journey*, pp. 152–153. This is the text of the "waking dream." "I take the telescope and examine the sea. It is deserted. Doubtless we are still too near the coast. I look up. Why should not some of the birds reconstructed by the immortal Cuvier be flapping their wings in the heavy strata of the atmosphere? The fish would provide quite sufficient food. I search the space above, but the airs are as uninhabited as the shores.

Nevertheless, my imagination carries me away into the fantastic hypotheses of paleontology. I am in a waking dream. I fancy I can see on the surface of the water those enormous Chersites, those tortoises from before the flood, as big as floating islands. Along those darkened shores are passing the great mammals of the first days, the Leptotherium found in the caves of Brazil, the Mericotherium, all the way from the glacial regions of Siberia. Further up, the pachydermatous Lophiodon, that gigantic tapir, is concealing itself behind the rocks, ready to do battle for its prey with the Anoplothere, a singular animal taking after the rhinoceros, the horse, the hippopotamus, and the camel, as if the Creator, in too much of a hurry in the first hours of the world, had put together several animals in one. The giant mastodon, twisting and turning his trunk, uses his tusks to break up the rocks on the shore, whereas the Megatherium, buttressed on its enormous legs, is excavating the earth for food, all the while awaking the sonorous echoes of the granite with his roaring. Higher up, the Protopithecus, the first monkey to appear on the face of the globe, is clambering up the steep slopes. Still higher, the pterodactyl, with its winged claws, glides like a huge bat on the compressed air. Above them all, in the topmost layers, are immense birds, more powerful than the cassowary, greater than the ostrich, spreading their vast wings, about to hit their heads against the roof of the granite vault.

This whole fossil world relives in my imagination. I am going back to the biblical ages of the Creation, long before man was born, when the incomplete Earth was not yet ready for him. My dream then goes ahead of the appearance of the animate beings. The mammals disappear, then the birds, then the reptiles of the Secondary Period, and finally the fish, the crustaceans, the molluscs, and the articulata. The zoophytes of the Transition Period themselves return to nothingness. The whole of the world's life

is summed up in myself, and mine is the only heart that beats in this depopulated world! There are no longer seasons; no longer climates; the internal heat of the globe is increasing unceasingly, and canceling out the effect of the radiant orb. The vegetation is multiplying exaggeratedly. I pass like a shadow amongst arborescent ferns, treading uncertainly on the iridescent marls and rainbow-coloured sandstones underfoot; I lean against the trunks of giant conifers; I lie down in the shade of Sphenophyllas, Astrerophyllites, and Lycopoda a hundred feet high.

The centuries are flowing past like days! I am working my way up the series of earthly transformations. The plants disappear; the granitic rocks lose their purity; the liquid state is about to replace the solid under the action of a greater heat; the waters are flowing over the surface of the globe; they boil; they evaporate; the vapour is covering up the entire Earth, which stage by stage becomes nothing but a gaseous mass, heated up to red- and white-hot, as big as the sun and shining as bright!

In the centre of this nebula, 1.4 million times as big as the globe it will one day form, I am being carried off into planetary space! My body is being subtilized, subliming in turn and commingling like an imponderable atom with these immense clouds, which inscribe their fiery orbit on infinite space!

What a dream! Where is it taking me? My feverish hand jots down the strange details. I have forgotten everything; the professor, the guide, the raft. A hallucination has taken hold of my head."

41. Unmentioned by De Paolo (see note 58, reference to "cave romances") is Jack London's interesting *Before Adam* (New York: The Macmillan Co., 1907), where on p. 139 the protagonist, a twentieth-century human although in atavistic form, experiences an "epiphany" much like Axel's waking dream. Unlike Verne, however, London was rather pro–Darwin.

42. The other scene showing us the Lidenbrock Sea shoreline was a frontispiece shaped as an oval. Although highly similar to the larger rectangular image, here Riou added the Mushroom Forest to the distant left of the frame, thus jostling any apparent life-through-time organization.

43. Verne, *Journey*, pp. 159–160.

44. No one before Verne had written such a dramatic, fictionalized account involving prehistoric "monsters." Bearing in mind that modern viewers have become desensitized to visual imagery of dinosaurs through myriad book illustrations, televised programs, movies, CGI sequences, and dramatically posed skeletal casts displayed in museums, Riou's illustrations showing the explorers' harrowing experience would have seemed highly original, effective and even terrifying in 1867. Combined with Verne's language, the imagetext may be regarded as a precursor to Peter Benchley's *Jaws*, or to Poul Anderson's 1992 short story "Unnatural Enemy." Thus, through the most dramatic imagetext crafted by that time, Verne (with Riou) allowed readers to "sample" specimens from Earth's Secondary Period, monsters which must have seemed alive and frightening.

45. Rudwick, 1992, *op. cit.*, p. 186.

46. Verne, *Journey*, p. 178.

47. Verne, *Journey*, p. 178.

48. Verne, *Journey*, p. 180.

49. Verne, *Journey*, p. 183.

50. Verne, *Journey*, p. 184.

51. Verne, *Journey*, p. 187.

52. Verne, *Journey*, p. 186.

53. Rudwick, 1992, *op. cit.*, pp. 202–214.

54. Costello, *op. cit.*, p. 85. In America, Albert Koch (d. 1867) was the first to prove the contemporaneity of pre-

historic man and beast. See Koch's *Description of the Missourium, or Missouri Leviathan; Together With its Supposed Habits and Indian Traditions Concerning the Location From Whence it was Exhumed: Also, Comparisons of the Whale, Crocodile and Missourium, With the Leviathan, as Described in 41st Chapter of Job*, 2nd ed. (Louisville: Prentice and Weissinger, Printers, 1841), "Evidences of Human Existence Contemporary with Fossil Animals," pp. 19–20. For more on Koch see my article, "Albert Koch's 'Missourium Leviathan' of 1841," *Fossil News: Journal of Avocational Paleontology* 11, no. 4 (April 2005): pp. 7–11, 14–15. For more on Boucher de Perthes, see Erik Trinkhaus and Pat Shipman, *The Neanderthals: Changing the Image of Mankind* (New York: Alfred A. Knopf, 1993), chapter 3. In Figuier's 1867 edition, Riou's idealized portrait of the "Appearance of Man" differs considerably from his 1863 effort, showing a more realistic vision of Ice Age times. However, in the latter edition, human figures are essentially modern in physiognomy, differing considerably in appearance from how Pierre Boitard characterized them—as monkey-like brutes. Verne's views on paleoanthropology and organic "progressionism" are beyond the scope of this article. However, besides addressing the possibility of fossil man and questioning whether prehistoric humans coexisted with other extinct, fossilized "antediluvia," Verne wove evolutionary ideas pertaining to the "degeneration" of fauna through time as well. For more on this see Breyer and Butcher, pp. 48–52. In *Journey*, Riou's portrait of the huge, upright anthropoid is shadowy, perhaps intentionally, to reflect contemporary controversies over prehistoric man. Furthermore, fossils and flora found in the field of bones as well as the Tertiary forest, respectively, seem oddly "mixed up. " What is the implication of such imagetext? Here and in other passages, Verne may have been reflecting the jumbled, sketchy, or uncertain nature of Boucher de Perthes' artifacts and fossils, as found *in situ*.

55. Martin J.S. Rudwick, "Caricature as a Source for the History of Science: De la Beche's Anti-Lyellian Sketches of 1831," *Isis* 66 (1975): pp. 534–560, quote from pp. 557–559.

56. Brian W. Aldiss with David Wingrove, *Trillion Year Spree* (New York: Avon Books, 1986), p. 31. Aldiss regards "cave romances" as a distinct science fiction subgenre. Here I treat "dinosaur fiction" as yet another subcategory of prehistoric-land fiction.

57. Sommer, *op. cit.*, p. 173.

58. Mary Shelley, *The Last Man* (1826; reprint, Oxford: Oxford University Press, 1994), pp. 3–4.

59. Besides the iconic cave, another metaphor for time is the "river of time." A classic example of its use in association with prehistoric animals would be in Karel Zeman's 1955 Czech film *Cesta do Praveku*, or *Journey to the Beginning of Time* (USA release, 1966). Here, however, the juvenile time explorers who move backward in time on a raft begin their journey navigating through a *cave*.

60. A thesis of this book is that prehistoric animal science and horror fiction may perhaps be historically categorized into four post–Verne "periods" (while recognizing there is considerable overlap between each of the periods). The corresponding "heyday" for each of these periods may be labeled "Lost World Dinosaurs" (circa 1912 to 1933), "Wartime Dinosaurs" (circa 1934 to mid–1950s), "Space-time Dinosaurs" (circa 1940 to early 1990s), and "Recombinant Dinosaurs" (circa 1980 to present). Of course, modern man's encounters with prehistoric animals are often associated with themes in evolutionary biology, as well a recurrent theme. Here, I am excluding from discussion a bevy of "cave romances," defined as stories about Stone Age people cast in contemporary settings. For more on this category of stories, see Charles De Paolo,

Human Prehistory in Fiction (Jefferson, NC: McFarland & Company, Inc., Publishers, 2003). Verne incorporated both cavemen and exotic reptilians into *Journey*. To me, however, Verne's cave metaphor didn't directly lead to or inspire the "cave romances" in prehistoric-land fiction of the early twentieth century. For a listing of strictly dinosaur fiction tales, see James O. Farlow, Michael Brett-Surman, and Robert Walters, eds., *The Complete Dinosaur* (Bloomington: Indiana University Press, 1997).

61. Arthur Conan Doyle, *The Lost World* (1912; reprint, New York: A.L. Burt Company, Publishers, 1925), pp. 112–113.

62. An intriguing title I've encountered without being able to locate is E.D. Fawcett's *Swallowed by an Earthquake* (1894), mentioned on p. 699 of *The Complete Dinosaur* (1997), which involved dinosaurs. Taine's *Greatest Adventure* not only incorporated a decisive cryptogram deciphered inside a great Antarctic cavern, but also employed the Frankenstein theme as the pseudo-dinosaurs encountered by explorers were machinations of a prior technological race which got out of control.

63. Vladimir Obruchev, *Plutonia* (1924; reprint, Moscow: Raduga Publishers, 1988). Majewski's work, evidently based on Verne's *Journey*, has eluded this author. According to Polish paleontologist Zofia Kielan-Jaworowska, *Professor Antediluvius* was originally published in Polish, and later in Czech and Russian. "The hero of the story is Leszek Przedpotopowicz, Polish professor of paleontology at Oxford University, who is accompanied by his British friend Lord Puckins and a young Stanislaw when he enters a crevice formed after a great earthquake in Bosnia. The first part of the book describes their journey down the crevice as they examine successively older formations and fossils. When they reach Cambrian beds after several days, an earthquake cuts off their return route, but a rescue expedition finds them unconscious days later. In the second part of the book the three heroes visit the lost world in Prof. Przedpotopwicz's dream, traveling back through fossilized landscapes of ancient life from Cambrian to the present...." This quotation is excerpted from an unpublished review of John Lavas' *The Lost World of Arthur Conan Doyle* (Panmure, New Zealand, 2002).

64. Delos W. Lovelace, *King Kong* (New York: Grosset & Dunlap, 1932). Lovelace's (1894–1967) novelization of *King Kong*, differing in particulars from the movie script, preceded the RKO film.

65. In the context of *Journey's* 1867 edition, Verne and Riou interacted as "paleoartists." One might argue that elements in *Journey's* life-through-time movement were a natural consequence of Verne's style of describing settings (e.g., flora before fauna) and his tendency to enliven Figuier's 1863 text. But no matter, because however unwittingly they arrived at their accomplishment, the life-through-time theme resonates throughout. According to Butcher, certainly Dumas' (author of the unfinished *Isaac Laquedem*) acquaintance with Verne may also have been an important influence behind the life-through-time theme.

Chapter 2

1. W.J.T. Mitchell, *The Last Dinosaur Book: The Life and Times of a Cultural Icon* (Chicago: The University of Chicago Press, 1998), p. 32.

2. This was a lively period in the development of modern biology and study of the "biosphere," a relatively new term coined in 1875. Scientists and laymen alike pondered the chief mysteries of evolution—the origin of species, the origin of life, the mechanisms which caused evolution to

happen and the means for extinction. However, the relevance of fossils to these deep questions was often misunderstood. While the nature of ape fossils (e.g., Eugene Dubois' Java Man, Raymond Dart's Taung baby, and the peculiar Piltdown Man) sparked evolutionary debate, from a popular view, other species like dinosaurs and brontotheres seemed inherently symbolic of deep time and extinction.

Evolution had stirred a revolution in biological understanding, but by the 1910s, "Darwinism" (i.e., natural selection) was fighting a defensive battle against views of early geneticists Hugo de Vries, Carl Correns, and Erik von Tschermak, who had by 1900 discovered Gregor Mendel's (1822–1884) work. Experimental geneticists were elevating the study of the "germ plasm" as a controlling influence of heredity, or, more precisely, that random mutations formed the basis for evolution, instead of natural selection which Alfred Russell Wallace (1823–1913) fought for vociferously. Furthermore, physicists had discovered radioactivity; by 1912 cosmic rays had been detected. By 1917, biologists such as T.H. Morgan realized that exposure to radiation caused genetic mutations carrying the potential to disrupt or modify evolutionary processes through alteration of chromosomes. And by 1920, population geneticists conceived the concept of evolutionary "adaptive landscapes."

Paleontologists like E. Ray Lankester (1846–1929) and Henry F. Osborn (1857–1935), however, realized that genetics alone wouldn't satisfactorily explain the evolutionary process. So Lankester labored to meld genetics with Darwin's concept of natural selection, a framework known as "neo-Darwinism." Meanwhile, Osborn, who regarded Darwin's survival-of-the-fittest principle as a cause of evolution, although not an "energy of evolution," invented a host of nonexistent, nonmaterial processes and "energies" allegedly operating independently of environmental conditions.

While Louis Dollo (1857–1931) refined his premise that evolution wasn't reversible, based on his examination of a bevy of *Iguanodon* specimens from Bernissart, Robert Broom (1886–1951) was teasing out evolutionary relationships between mammals and reptiles through his studies of South African "mammal-like" reptiles. Meanwhile, Richard Swann Lull (1867–1957) interpreted the extinction of dinosaurs as a consequence of orthogenesis, or "racial senility." In other words, dinosaurs were inexorably driven to a foreordained fate of extinction, independent of environmental factors. However, Lull still believed that dinosaurs weren't "useless experiments" of evolution, but instead species "dynasties" which waxed and waned as did great nations and civilizations of history.

But this also was a time when many felt encumbered by evolution's culture shock. Dinosaurs (such as the magnificent North American *Diplodocus*) carried social messages about "survival of the fittest," which, as espoused by, for example, Andrew Carnegie (1835–1919), really meant survival of the rich and powerful. On a lighter note, author Mark Twain (1835–1910) satirized the "evolutionist" state of affairs through a series of splendid essays. However, social Darwinism took a dangerous, dark turn through the writings of German paleontologist Ernst Haeckel (1834–1919), who encouraged his countrymen to think of themselves as the "master race." The famous trial of Tennessee high school biology teacher John T. Scopes (1900–1970) began on July 10, 1925, pitting "religion versus evolution" in a visible public forum. While there is no single reference covering all these matters and it would be beyond the intended scope to do so here, the following references may be of further interest: Garland Allen, *Life Science in the Twentieth Century* (Cambridge: Cambridge University Press, 1978); Richard Milner, *The Encyclopedia of Evolution* (New York: Facts On File, 1990); Cynthia Eagle Russett, *Darwin In America: The Intellectual Response* (San Francisco: W.H. Freeman and Company, 1976); Ronald Rainger, *An Agenda for Antiquity: Henry Fairfield Osborn and Vertebrate Paleontology at the American Museum of Natural History, 1890-1935* (Tuscaloosa: The University of Alabama Press, 1991).

3. Marc Angenot and Nadia Khouri. "An International Bibliography of Prehistoric Fiction," *Science Fiction Studies* 8, no.1 (1981): pp. 38–53. According to Marc Angenot and Nadia Khouri, "the simian origin of man had already been narrated in the guise of satirical conjecture as far back as the eighteenth century." Furthermore, "the odd fact concerning these narratives about ambiguous humanoids is that they appeared much earlier than the Darwinian dispute and the polemics on the simian genesis of man. Fiction here had indeed preceded scientific statements.... No matter what power religious authority may have exerted in curbing some of the most audacious assertions about the origins of man, fiction still remained the field where almost anything could be safely asserted, without being attacked for systematizing scientific beliefs."

4. J.P. Vernier, "The SF of J. H. Rosny the Elder," *Science Fiction Studies* 6 (July 1975): pp. 156–163. In another tale, "The Treasure in the Snow" (1922), Alglave discovers a race of primitive people surviving in the north polar region alongside mammoths. Alglave rescues the hardy population from extinction and transfers them to North Africa, where they miscegenate with modern natives.

5. Brian W. Aldiss with David Wingrove, *Trillion Year Spree: The History of Science Fiction* (New York: Avon Books, 1986), p. 136; Professor Thomas D. Clareson, introduction to *Kioga of the Unknown Land*, by William L. Chester (New York: Daw Books, Inc., 1978), pp. 5–8. Clareson, of the College of Wooster, declared that the "'lost race, lost land' novel ... developed as a response to widespread public interest in archaeology, geology, anthropology, and the last wave of exploration during the late years of the nineteenth century.... One ... may see the frontier ... in terms of fantasies of escape from the restrictions imposed upon the individual by society. Another may see them in terms of a rejection of the modern urban-industrial civilization which had already taken its fundamental shape" by the late nineteenth century.

6. C.J. Cutcliffe Hyne, "The Lizard" (1898), in *The Birth of Science in Fiction*, ed. Isaac Asimov, Martin H. Greenberg, and Charles G. Waugh (New York: Knightsbridge Publishing Company, 1981), pp. 295–303.

7. *Ibid.*

8. C.J. Cutcliffe Hyne, *The Lost Continent* (1899; reprint, New York: Ballantine Books, 1972), pp. 202–203.

9. Ignatius Donnelly, *Atlantis: The Antediluvian World* (New York: Harper & Brothers, 1882; reprint, ed. Egerton Sykes, New York: Gramercy Publishing Company, 1949). Donnelly attempted to link together many lost and ancient civilizations across the globe through Atlantean "relics."

10. Wells, H.G. "In the Abyss" (1896), in *The Birth of Science in Fiction*, pp. 257–274.

11. Frank Mackenzie Savile, *Beyond the Great South Wall* (New York: Arno Press, 1978; originally published by Grosset & Dunlap in 1901).

12. Jack London (1876–1916) not only wrote a cave romance (i.e., *Before Adam*), but an anachronistic tale with cryptozoological flavor as well, "A Relic of the Pliocene" (1901). Here, an old ruffian trailblazing through the Yukon recounts how he killed a woolly mammoth. However, London's readable tale wasn't half the sensation that "Harry

Tukeman's" 1899 story "The Killing of the Mammoth" proved to be, in which a modern man kills the last mammoth alive, thus rendering extinct the "great monarch of the recent Ice Age." "A feeling of pity and shame crept over me as I watched the failing strength of this mighty prehistoric monarch.... It was as though I were robbing nature, and old Mother Earth herself of a child born to her younger days, in the Dawn of Time." Murray C. Morgan noted that Tukeman (pseudonym for American story writer H.T. Hahn) saw his story published in the October 1899 issue of *McClure's* magazine sandwiched between credible articles by Theodore Roosevelt and Admiral Dewey, in turn lending a sense of credence to the mammoth yarn. In 1938, William L. Chester's (1907–1960) lostworld tale of the Arctic, *Kioga of the Unknown Land*, incorporated living Ice Age mammoths witnessed by American scientists.

13. Rainger, *op. cit.*

14. This account was republished in Roy P. Mackal's *A Living Dinosaur?* (Leiden, The Netherlands: E.J. Brill, 1987), pp. 216–221.

15. Dr. Dwight Smith and Gary S. Mangiacopra, "Carl Hagenbeck and the Rhodesian Dinosaurs," *Strange Magazine* no. 5 (1990): p. 51.

16. Roy Pilot and Alvin Rodin, *The Annotated Lost World: The Classic Adventure Novel by Sir Arthur Conan Doyle, The Creator of Sherlock Holmes* (Indianapolis: Wessex Press, 1996), pp. xi–xii. For more on crypto-prehistoric life see Allen A. Debus and Diane Debus, "The Truth is Out There: On the Trail of Living Dinosaurs," Chapter Fifteen, in *Dinosaur Memories: Dino-Trekking for Beasts of Thunder, Fantastic Saurians...* (Lincoln, NE: Authors choice Books, 2002), pp. 280–292.

17. Milner, *op. cit.*, pp. 252–254; Cooper wrote, "When you told me that the two Komodo Dragons you brought back to the Bronx Zoo, where they drew great crowds, were eventually killed by civilization, I immediately thought of doing the same thing with my Giant Gorilla. I had already established him in my mind on a prehistoric island with prehistoric monsters, and I now thought of having him destroyed by the most sophisticated thing I could think of in civilization, and in the most fantastic way ... to place him on the top of the Empire State Building and have him killed by airplanes" (Cooper, quoted in Milner, p. 252); as John R. Lavas recounted in his *The Lost World of Arthur Conan Doyle: Collector's Anniversary Edition* (New Zealand, 2002), pp. xliii–xliv, this period was an age of discovery. Real lost worlds such as the Inca city Maachu Pichu had been discovered in South America by Hiram Bingham in 1911, and formerly unknown species such as the longhaired mountain gorilla, the Siberian brown bear, the okapi and others were all discovered in the years 1900 to 1904.

18. Dougal Dixon, *The New Dinosaurs: An Alternative Evolution* (Topsfield, Mass.: Salem House Publishers, 1988), pp. 109–110.

19. Dixon, *op. cit.*; see David M. Raup, and Steven M. Stanley, *Principles of Paleontology*, 2d ed. (San Francisco: W.H. Freeman and Company, 1978), Chapter Eleven, for information on factors effecting the longevity of species.

20. Dixon, *op. cit.*

21. The best reference available today on dinosaur films is Mark F. Berry's *The Dinosaur Filmography* (Jefferson, NC: McFarland & Company, Inc., Publishers, 2002).

22. Jose Luis Sanz, *Starring T. Rex!: Dinosaur Mythology and Popular Culture* (Bloomington: Indiana University Press, 2002), p. 57.

23. Sanz, *op. cit.*

24. Arthur Conan Doyle, "The Terror of Blue John Gap," *The Strand Magazine* 40 (September 1910): pp. 131–141; Dana Martin Batory, and William A.S. Sarjeant, "'The Terror of Blue John Gap'—A Geological and Literary Study," *ACD—The Journal of the Arthur Conan Doyle Society* 5 (1994): pp. 108–125. For those interested in the early popular magazines in which early science fiction such as Doyle's for *The Strand Magazine* was published, before the advent of the "pulps" during the 1920s, see Sam Moskowitz, "A History of Science Fiction in the Popular Magazines, 1891–1911," in *Science Fiction by Gaslight* (Cleveland and New York: The World Publishing Company, 1968), pp. 15–50.

25. Peter J. Bowler, "Holding your head up high: Degeneration and orthogenesis in theories of human evolution," in *History, Humanity and Evolution: Essays for John C. Greene*, ed. James R. Moore (Cambridge: Cambridge University Press, 1989), p. 338.

26. H.G. Wells, *The Time Machine*, in *The Science Fiction Hall of Fame*, vol. 2A, ed. Ben Bova (New York: Avon Books, 1973), pp. 452–526. Evolutionary ideas run prevalently through H.G. Wells contemporary writings, notably *The Time Machine* (1895), *The Island of Dr. Moreau* (1896), and *War of the Worlds* (1897). Like many of his contemporaries, Wells also wrote "prehistoric romances" such as "A Story of the Stone Age" (1897), although he and Verne refrained from writing about live dinosaurs, per se. In particular, *The Time Machine* explored mankind's future evolution, "the theme of human degeneration in a society stripped of competition," according to Adrian J. Desmond, *Huxley: From Devil's Disciple to Evolution's High Priest* (Reading, Mass: Perseus Books, 1994) p. 642. Here *Homo sapiens* has evolved into a new species known as the Morlocks which preys on a weaker variety, the Eloi, over 800,000 years hence. Perhaps it is no puzzle that evolutionary ideas were woven into Wells's fiction, for he studied evolution under the influential Thomas Henry Huxley during the 1880s. Much later in life, Wells coauthored a popular book on evolutionary biology with Huxley's grandson Julian Huxley (1887–1975), titled *The Science of Life* (1925). The far-distant future of man's evolution was also forecasted by Olaf Stapledon (1886–1950) in his two novels *Last and First Men* (1931) and *Star Maker* (1937); *Last and First Men and Star Maker: 2 Science Fiction Novels by Olaf Stapledon* (New York: Dover Publications, Inc., 1968). Besides his "In the Abyss," Wells also wrote "Aepyornis Island" (1905), about an island castaway who, at first, befriends the largest prehistoric bird ever; and in a chapter titled "The Dreary Megatheria," in his 1929 novel *Mr. Blettsworthy on Rampole Island*, Wells described a colony of living *Megatherium*. The sloths' survival into modernity is compared to the cultural survival of antiquated social customs and societal institutions.

27. Bowler, *op. cit.*, p. 329.

28. Mitchell, *op. cit.*, p. 169.

29. Doyle, *The Lost World*, p. 257. One ferocious, treeclimbing ape-man is described by Malone as having "a human face—or at least it was far more human than any monkey's that I have ever seen. It was long, whitish, and blotched with pimples, the nose flattened, and the lower jaw projecting, with a bristle of coarse whiskers round the chin. The eyes, which were under thick and heavy brows, were bestial and ferocious, and as it opened its mouth to snarl what sounded like a curse at me I observed that it had curved sharp canine teeth." These creatures are arguably more orangutan-like than the Piltdown men envisioned by British scientists. In my opinion, Doyle's "missing link" ape-men seem derivative of another fictional tribe of apehumans described by Jack London in his imaginative novel, *Before Adam*, published in 1907 by the Macmillan Company. Also, Doyle's Indians-versus-"links" tribal war seems reminiscent of climax scenes in London's 1907 novel.

30. Pilot and Rodin, *op. cit.*, p. 40.

31. This implies that evolution doesn't operate here only because climatic conditions haven't changed. See Pilot and Rodin, *op. cit.*, p. 127.

32. Doyle, *op. cit.*, p. 241.

33. *Ibid.*, p. 211.

34. Pilot and Rodin, *op. cit.*, p. 187.

35. E. Ray Lankester, *Extinct Animals* (London: Archibald Constable, 1905). For more on Lankester, see "Sir Ray Lankester, K.C.B.," *The Strand Magazine* 42, no. 249 (September 1911): pp. 312–317.

36. Pilot and Rodin, *op. cit.*, p. 13.

37. J.H. Winslow and A. Meyer, "The Perpetrator of Piltdown," *Science* 83 (September 1983): pp. 32–43. For my views on the affair, see Allen A. Debus, "Skullduggery: a Piltdown 'Elementary,'" *Fossil News: Journal of Avocational Paleontology* 10, no. 3 (March 2004), pp. 14–18; no. 4 (April 2004), pp. 14–17; and no. 5 (May 2004), pp. 15–18. Although certainly politically incorrect by today's standards, it was common then for readers to find articles such as the following anonymously written item printed in popular magazines: "Which is the Finest Race?" *The Strand Magazine* 43, no. 254 (February 1912), pp. 148–155.

38. Irwin Porges quoted in "Back to Barsoom," by John Carter Tibbetts, in *Filmfax* no. 104 (October/December 2004), p. 80.

39. Edgar Rice Burroughs, *At the Earth's Core* (1914; reprint, New York: Ace Books, 1978). How did the strange fauna get inside the earth? During the earth's formation, because the inner crust cooled more slowly than the outer crust, the evolutionary state of the inner world is "primitive" relative to the outside of the planet. Therefore, Pellucidar became inhabitable at a much later geological period relative to events of the earth's outer crust. As stated previously, Burroughs was a master at suspending disbelief. For further discussion of the Mahars in Burroughs' *Earth's Core* series, please see Allen A. Debus, "Terrorsaurs," *Prehistoric Times* no. 65 (April/May 2004): pp. 12–14.

40. Burroughs, *op. cit.*, 1914, p. 38.

41. Edgar Rice Burroughs, *The Land That Time Forgot* (1918; reprint, New York: Ace Books, 1963). Originally published in *Blue Book Magazine*; in 1924, this Caspak trilogy, as it became known, was published in book form. Famed artist J. Allen St. John provided illustrations for the 1924 volume. *The Land That Time Forgot* is the first "dinosaur novel" I ever read, after having been attracted to a 1963 paperback Ace edition cover painted by Roy G. Krenkel, Jr. Appearing on the cover were a soaring pterodactyl and a ceratosaur clawing at an iguanodont, while in the foreground an immense sabertooth straddled its mammoth prey. A diminutive human observed the saurian combat. *The Land That Time Forgot* is an adventure tale beginning with a manuscript found in a bottle penned by Bowen J. Tyler, Jr., who was fatefully "marooned in a lost land of Dawn Age monsters."

42. John Taliaferro, *Tarzan Forever: The Life of Edgar Rice Burroughs, Creator of Tarzan* (New York: Scribner, 1999), p. 136.

43. Two plot elements evidently borrowed from Doyle's *Lost World* in Burroughs' *At The Earth's Core* involve a Mahar escaping to the surface world (akin to Challenger's *Rhamphorhynchus* escaping into the London fog), and a curious statement on p. 51 of *Earth's Core*, where Burroughs character Innes remarks, "I had forgotten what little geology I had studied at school—about all that remained was an impression of horror that the illustrations of restored prehistoric monsters had made upon me, and a well-defined belief that any man with a pig's shank and a vivid imagination could 'restore' most any sort of paleolithic

monster he saw fit, and take rank as a first class paleontologist." This recalls Tarp Henry's statement in *Lost World* where it is opined that "If you are clever and know your business you can fake a bone as easily as you can a photograph," a statement which has been said to bear implications for the Piltdown Man forgery.

44. Burroughs, *op. cit.*, 1918, p. 72.

45. *Ibid.*, p. 86.

46. Edgar Rice Burroughs, *The People That Time Forgot* (1918; reprint, New York: Ace Books, 1979).

47. Burroughs, *ibid.*, p. 91.

48. Burroughs further reveals that, rarely, sometimes people in Caspak are born from man and woman, as opposed to the "cor sva jo," who "come from an egg and thus on up *from the beginning*." Furthermore, there is an even higher race of man, a winged variety known as the Weiroo. The evolutionary process leading to the development of Weiroo from Galus no longer operates in Caspak. In order to sustain their race at all, Weiroo must mate with Galus women. Also, not every organism is destined to progress beyond certain levels of evolutionary progress. Some remain as Alus, or Bo-lu, etc., never progressing to the Galus stage, or even, presumably, dinosaurs. Finally, in a further sequel, *Out of Time's Abyss* (1918; reprint, New York: Ace Books, 1979), as his heroes dodge another set of reptilian and paleolithic foes, Burroughs fortifies the course of Caspakian evolution. As Burroughs explains in one significant passage, "all but those who were cos-ata-lu came up corsva-jo, or from the beginning. The egg from which they first developed into tadpole form was deposited, with millions of others, in one of the warm pools and with it a poisonous serum that the carnivora instinctively shunned. Down the warm stream from the pool floated the countless billions of eggs and tadpoles, developing as they drifted slowly toward the sea. Some became tadpoles in the pool, some in the sluggish stream and some not until they reached the great inland sea. In the next stage they became fishes, or reptiles.... Always there were those whose development stopped at the fish stage, others whose development ceased when they became reptiles, while by far the greater proportion formed the food supply of the ravenous creatures of the deep.... In each stage countless millions of other eggs were deposited in the warm pools of the various races and floated down to the great sea to go through a similar process of evolution outside the womb as develops our own young within; but in Caspak the scheme is much more inclusive, for it combines not only individual development but the evolution of species and genera. If an egg survives it goes through all the stages of development that man has passed through during the unthinkable eons since life first moved upon the earth's face" (pp. 72–74).

49. Charles Darwin, *The Origin of Species: By Means of Natural Selection Or the Preservation of Favoured Races in the Struggle for Life*, 6th ed., with a foreword by George Gaylord Simpson (1872; reprint, New York: Collier Books, 1905).

50. *Ibid.*, p. 483.

51. Charles Darwin, *The Descent of Man and Selection in Relation to Sex* (London: Murray, 1871).

52. H.G. Wells, "The Man of the Year Million" (1893), in *Apeman, Spaceman*, pp. 121–126. (Quote excerpted from p. 125.)

53. Constance Reid, *The Search for E.T. Bell: Also Known as John Taine* (Washington, D.C.: The Mathematical Association of America, 1993), pp. 80, 267–269.

54. John Taine, *The Greatest Adventure* (1929), in *The Antarktos Cycle: At the Mountains of Madness and Other Chilling Tales*, ed. Robert M. Price (Hayward, Calif: Chaosium, Inc., 1999), pp. 165–304; John Taine, *The Iron Star* (1930;

reprint, Westport, Connecticut: Hyperion Press, Inc., 1976). Also see the Appendix.

55. Taine's *Iron Star* is the ideological opposite of Edmond Hamilton's "The Man Who Evolved" (1931), reprinted in *Before the Golden Age*, ed. Isaac Asimov (New York: Doubleday, 1974), pp. 23–39), in which X-rays are experimentally used to convert a scientist into (predictable) futuristic renditions of humanity, millions of years hence. In Hamilton's short story, borrowing from H.G. Wells' 1893 essay, "Man of the Year Million," we learn that in the penultimate stage, man will evolve into a great brain that just sits there cogitating. However, as the experimenters divulge, after 250 million years, "The last mutation results in a mass of simple protoplasm. This was the end of man's evolutionary road, the highest form to which time would bring him, the last mutation of all! The road of man's evolution was a circular one, returning to its beginning!" (perhaps reflecting British geologist Charles Lyell's early nineteenth-century theories of organic evolution as illustrated through De la Beche's cartoon "Awful Changes"). In these stories, while man is viewed as evolution's pinnacle, degeneration into past or future forms takes place along a predictable orthogenetic "ladder" or pathway. Another example is Hamilton's 1936 story, "Devolution" (reprinted in *Before the Golden Age*, pp. 796–809), in which alien forms have "degenerated" into mankind due to exposure to radioactive minerals present on the primordial Earth. The protagonist makes this dramatic discovery after the protoplasmic beings trace the entire course of terrestrial organic evolution within his mind in order to chart the devolution process. Incidentally, as we'll see in Chapter Four, use of radiation-induced mutations to produce evolutionary relatives through "saltation" was an early twentieth-century biological theme later commonly used in dinosaur film and fiction of the Cold War period. (Also see Note 2.)

56. Taine, 1929, p. 212.

57. Most likely Taine's *Greatest Adventure* influenced American horror writer H.P. Lovecraft's later crafting of *At the Mountains of Madness*, written in 1931, among the eeriest of all lost-world tales, concerning aliens which interacted with earth's prehistoric indigenous fauna. The "Old Ones," "makers and enslavers of life," populated Earth billions of years ago and ruled "a haunted, accursed realm where life and death, space and time, have made black and blasphemous alliances in the unknown epochs once matter first writhed and swam on the planet's scarce-cooled crust." Soon, members of an expedition led from Miskatonic University to Antarctica determine that the ancient aliens harnessed intelligent creatures "in the age of dinosaurs [which] were not dinosaurs, but far worse." And we read how "In the building of land cities the huge stone blocks of the high towers were generally lifted by bat-winged pterodactyls of a species heretofore unknown to paleontology." They even altered the evolutionary course of dinosaurs to suit their insidious purposes (*The Antarktos Cycle*, Chapter 7)! Dinosaurs, pterodactyls and Mesozoic marine saurians are also mentioned in Lovecraft's creepy tale "The Shadow Out of Time" (1934–5).

58. Linda Nochlin, "The Darwin Effect," *Nineteenth-Century Art Worldwide: a journal of nineteenth-century visual culture* (Spring 2003, posted on the Internet). F. Gardner's frontispiece for Charles G.D. Roberts' *In the Morning of Time* (1919 ed.)—see Appendix to this volume—showing a primitive ape-like human named "Mawg" carrying off the fetching cave girl "A-ya," further illustrates this theme. Such artistry, perhaps, revealed contemporary fears of miscegenation; certainly white women had been captured and raped by Native Americans during America's westward expansion, and especially during the early twentieth century,

interracial sex was viewed with disdain by society. Such fears were amplified by its objectionable form—copulation of civilized white women with lesser-evolved humans out of prehistory, and apemen.

59. Jules Verne, *A Journey to the Center of the Earth* (New York: Signet Classic, 1986), Chapter 40.

60. Quote excerpted from Milner's entry on "Gorillas" in Milner, p. 196.

61. *Ibid.*, p. 253; A real gigantic, ten-foot-tall fossil ape, the Asian genus *Gigantopithecus blacki*, was described by paleontologists in 1935. *Gigantopithecus* became extinct a million years ago in the Middle Pleistocene. Some believe this animal may still survive, providing basis for the Yeti of legend. *King Kong* is often cited as "conceived by" both Cooper and British novelist Edgar Wallace (1875–1932), although Wallace died shortly after completing only a draft of Cooper's story. According to James V. D'Arc, Curator of the Merian C. Cooper archive at Brigham Young University, "Cooper nevertheless kept Wallace's name on the film and in publicity connected to *King Kong*, both because of his promise to Wallace and for its publicity value." See Joe DeVito and Brad Strickland, *Merian C. Cooper's King Kong* (New York: St. Martin's, 2005), pp. xii–xiii. In addition to Grosset and Dunlap's novelization of the story, Walter F. Ripperger's "King Kong" was serialized in *Mystery Magazine* (Feb.–March 1933). Lovelace, a journalist by trade, also wrote a historical novel, titled *Journey to Bethlehem* (1953).

62. And the earliest plausible subterranean world environments were created by early seventeenth-century scientists such as Athanasius Kircher and Thomas Burnet, or nineteenth-century pseudo-scientist John Cleves Symmes. Beyond ancient writers such as Virgil, who wrote about the Underworld in his *Aeneid*, recently Peter Fitting edited a fascinating book, *Subterranean Worlds* (Middleton, CT: Wesleyan University Press, 2004), focusing on writers who considered the earth's interior in a fictional vein. Ten selections are highlighted, originally published between the years 1721 and 1838. Intriguingly, several of these authors populated their subterranean realms with lost races—or sometimes with several races. Some, such as the pseudonymous "Captain Seaborn" in his *Symzonia* (1820), even speculated on the nature of a pre–Darwinian "evolution," pondering whether life on the outer crust was somehow derived from creatures that initially developed in the earth's interior. In Edward George Bulwer-Lytton's (1803–1873) novel *The Coming Race* (1871), in which Darwinian influences are apparent, a "monstrous reptile resembling that of the crocodile or alligator, but infinitely larger than the largest creature of that kind," devours one unfortunate soul upon his descent. There is also a race known as the Vril-ya, evolved from prehistoric frogs of the outer crust, who threaten inhabitants of the surface world with our ultimate destruction. Interestingly, the Vril-ya or the "coming race," are evidently "descended from the same ancestors as the Great Aryan family, from which in varied streams has flowed the dominant civilization of the world...." (p. 182). Paul K. Alkon, in *Origins of Futuristic Fiction* (Athens: The University of Georgia Press, 1987), views Thomas Burnet's late seventeenth-century *Sacred Theory of the Earth* as speculative proto-fiction, rather than a contemporary scientific account. Also see my summary of A. Merritt's *The Face In the Abyss* (1931; reprint, New York: Collier Books, 1992) in the Appendix to this volume.

63. Taliaferro, *op. cit.*, pp. 168–171, 173, 175, 181, 211.

64. *Ibid.*, p. 14.

65. *Ibid.*, p. 211. As Tarzan's author, Burroughs felt somewhat obligated to submit an article on this theme to the *New York American*; it ran in the July 6, 1925, issue during the height of the Scopes trial.

66. Russett, *op. cit.*, p. 176.

67. Erling B. Holtzmark, *Edgar Rice Burroughs* (Boston: Twayne Publishers, 1986), p. 48.

68. It should be stated here how evolution is regarded today. Prominent biologist Dr. Richard Dawkins has stated, "It is a theory of gradual, incremental change over millions of years, which starts with something very simple and works up along slow, gradual gradients to greater complexity. Not only is it a brilliant solution to the riddle of complexity; it is the only solution that has ever been proposed." Quoted by Claudia Wallis, "The Evolution Wars," *Time* (August 15, 2005), p. 32.

Chapter 3

1. For a brief discussion of this term, see the entry for "social Darwinism" in Richard Milner's *The Encyclopedia of Evolution* (New York: Facts On File, 1990). Also see entry for "Aryan Race, Myth of." For the impact of contemporary biological sciences on the social Darwinian mindset, see pp. 107–109 in Garland Allen, *Biology In the Twentieth Century* (Cambridge: Cambridge University Press, 1981). Herein, Allen addresses the influences of Darwin's "survival of the fittest" tenet applied to American capitalism and industrialism. Allen observes, "Science is not divorced from the cultural period in which it develops" (p. 107).

2. During America's Civil War, in 1862, American writer and science critic Henry Brooks Adams (1838–1918), who was fascinated by the ideas of evolution, opined, "I tell you these are great times. Man has mounted science, and is now run away with. I firmly believe that before many centuries more, science will be the master of man. The engines he will have invented will be beyond his strength to control. Some day science may have the existence of mankind in its power, and the human race commit suicide by blowing up the world." See Cynthia Eagle Russett, *Darwin in America* (W.H. Freeman and Co., 1976), p. 138. Adams also predicted that "explosives would reach cosmic violence." This sense of angst and impending doom, perhaps even to be realized someday as a self-fulfilling prophecy, became reflected in science fiction tales of future war.

3. Brian Aldiss with David Wingrove, *Trillion Year Spree*, pp. 126–127.

4. *Ibid.*, pp. 120–121. Metaphorically, Ray Bradbury's *The Martian Chronicles* (1950) related the demise of the remnant Martian race to our taking-over of Native American lands in nineteenth-century North America.

5. Dan Dinello, "4th World War," in *Chicago Tribune*, June 19, 2005, section 7, pp. 1, 9.

6. Milner, *op. cit.*, p. 207; also see Paul Weindling, "Ernst Haeckel, Darwinismus and the secularization of nature," in *History, Humanity and Evolution: Essays for John C. Greene*, ed. Martin J.S. Rudwick (Cambridge: Cambridge University Press, 1989), pp. 311–327.

7. James Gurney, *Dinotopia: A Land Apart From Time* (Atlanta: Turner Publishing, Inc., 1992).

8. Dahlgren's "Hypsirophus" painting is discussed in *Paleoimagery: The Evolution of Dinosaurs in Art*, by Allen A. and Diane E. Debus (Jefferson, NC: McFarland & Co. Publishers, Inc., 2002), pp. 73–74. (As an aside, in 2004, this writer discovered a much older, curious *Stegosaurus* restoration originally published in the April 1882 *Scientific American* issue. For more on this, see Allen Debus, "Stego-Record Breaker! The Oldest Known Stegosaur Restoration," *Prehistoric Times* no. 68 (October/November 2004): p. 52.) Charles G.D. Roberts (1860–1943) wrote one of, if not the earliest of fictional passages concerning a *Stego-*

saurus battling furiously for its life, published in Chapter One, "The World Without Man," of his *In the Morning of Time* (London: Hutchinson & Co., 1919; first published in *The London Magazine*, Parts 1–4, May to August 1912). See the Appendix for more concerning this title. Knight's mammoth restoration was reproduced in Sylvia Massey Czerkas and Donald F. Glut's *Dinosaurs, Mammoths and Cavemen: The Art of Charles R. Knight* (New York: E.P. Dutton, Inc., 1982), p. 7.

9. Allen A. Debus, "…Versus: Ancient Nemeses as perceived in the 'Prehistoric World,'" Parts 1 and 2, *Prehistoric Times* nos. 56–57 (October/November 2002 to December/January 2003): pp. 17–18, and pp. 18–19. In literature, Jules Verne and Charles G.D. Roberts were among the earliest to write about titanic saurian struggles in the Mesozoic age. Many may not realize that favored restorations, scientifically yet speculatively prepared by paleoartists to represent savage events in prehistory (usually involving bloodthirsty dinosaurs), are allied to exploitative efforts of the motion picture industry, through an evolving medley of "versus." Hence in our favored sci-fi film features, dinosaurian contestants created via the magic of stop-motion animation or "suitmation," fanciful dinosaurs and prehistoric creatures afflicted by sequel-itis, battle outrageously toward an unbounded, bitter and bloody end. While at first man observed prehistoric animals fighting for their survival, in time man would be drawn into the fray, himself competing with dinosaurs and other prehistoria for survival.

10. *Ibid.* Knight's "Rex vs. Tops" paintings are reproduced both on the front cover of the author's *Paleoimagery*, and on pp. 50, 159.

11. Later in the nineteenth century, after the docile, herbivorous nature of America's *Mastodon* was more properly understood, focus shifted to Mesozoic prehistorians, beginning with the aquatic marine reptiles *Plesiosaurus*, *Ichthyosaurus*, and *Mosasaurus*, and creepy bat-winged pterodactyls. In particular, paleoartist John Martin (1789–1854) captured the violence of prehistory as perceived during the early nineteenth century through his restorations of ferocious, battling marine reptiles. (Note: Peruse early chapters of Martin J.S. Rudwick's *Scenes From Deep Time* [Chicago: The University of Chicago Press, 1992] and Chapter Four of *Paleoimagery: The Evolution of Dinosaurs in Art* [2002], by Debus & Debus, for more on Martin's prehistoric visions.) The striking image of battling sea-saurians, a theme also favored much later by grandmaster paleoartists Edouard Riou and Zdenek Burian, has persisted into the "dinosaur renaissance." Four years after Alfred, Lord Tennyson (1809–1892) penned the phrase "nature, red in tooth and claw," (published in his 1850 poem "In Memoriam"), a magnificent exhibition featuring full-sized sculptural restorations of "antediluvian" animals opened at the Crystal Palace grounds at Sydenham, outside London. This prehistoric landscape was the handiwork of British paleoartist Benjamin Waterhouse Hawkins (1809–1889), who was supervised by British anatomist Richard Owen (1804–1890). By this date, before publication of Charles Darwin's *Origin of Species* (1859), the "savagenature" theme in art had become well established in an emerging paleoart genre. For John Martin had depicted a lurid vision, titled "The Country of the Iguanodon," for the frontispiece of Gideon Mantell's popular book *Wonders of Geology* (first ed. 1838), showing (anatomically incorrect) hulking dinosauria battling to the death. In 1860, following publication of Darwin's monumental book, Hawkins published a wall chart incorporating a series of illustrations emphasizing the "Struggles of Life among the British Animals in Primaeval Times." The wall chart featured imagery of extinct, sparring mammalian megafauna—

woolly rhinos, sabertooth cats, mammoths, Irish deer and cave bears. However, during the 1860s, it was French artist Riou who captured the nineteenth century's most popular (European) conceptions of prehistoric violence—aquatic combat between *Ichthyosaurus* vs. *Plesiosaurus*, and dinosaurs, *Megalosaurus* vs. *Iguanodon*—in illustrations prepared for editions of L. Figuier's *Earth Before the Deluge* (and also, in the case of marine reptiles, for the 1867 edition of Jules Verne's *A Journey to the Center of the Earth*). During the late 1860s and 1870s, Hawkins brought his vision of combative saurians to America, as exemplified in surviving design drawings prepared for the ill-fated "Palaeozoic Museum," and in a painting depicting Cretaceous life of New Jersey, completed for Princeton University. These restorations dramatically paired ancient American nemeses, *Laelaps* vs. *Hadrosaurus*, with blood-thirsty elasmosaurs lurking in the shallows. Evidently, America's elasmosaurs and *Laelaps* were perceived as even more deadly than its by-then demystified "incognitum" (i.e., the *Mastodon*). By the 1870s, certain dinosaurs were restored in upright bipedal stance, as shown in a restoration published in C. Flammarion's (1842–1925) book *Le Monde avant la creation de l'homme...* (1886). From this period forward, the theme of savagery in nature was best exemplified through traditional dinosaurian nemeses—e.g., *Laelaps* vs. *Hadrosaurus*, or *Megalosaurus* vs. *Iguanodon*, depending on which side of the Atlantic you dug fossils on. However, in visualizing the prehistoric world, whereas Knight refrained from illustrating graphic violence in prehistory, compatriots such as Hawkins, Riou and F. Long ignored censorship, focusing on the feral, bloody and combative nature of restored dinosaurs and Tertiary mammals. Also see my article, "From *Incognitum* to Odo: Prehistoric Roar," in *G-Fan* no.76, Summer 2006 (pp. 38–41) for elucidation of Thomas Jefferson's (1743–1826) previously unsuspected role in promoting imaginative, figurative battles of the primeval.

12. Paul Semonin, *American Monster: How the Nation's First Prehistoric Creature Became a Symbol of National Identity* (New York: New York University Press, 2000), pp. 259–262. Also see Semonin's afterword, "The Myth of Wild Nature," pp. 392–411, *op. cit.* For a closer look at the savagery-in-nature theme as applied to restorations of prehistoric men in the late nineteenth and early twentieth centuries, see Chapter Five, "The Scientific Vision of Prehistory," in Stephanie Moser's *Ancestral Images: The Iconography of Human Origins* (Ithaca, NY: Cornell University Press, 1998).

13. Paleontologist Christopher McGowan claims, "Today, thanks mainly to television, we know that animals in their natural habitat are not locked in eternal battles to the death. We know ... that combat between meat eaters, or between any other groups of animals, rarely becomes an overt conflict of tooth and claw. Rather it is a subtle competition for resources and for living space. People in Regency England rarely had the opportunity to witness interactions between animals in the wild. Some individuals had seen lions and tigers in menageries, and could see how fierce they were. It was therefore natural for them to suppose that such animals spent most of their time in open conflict in the wild. It is not surprising, then, that the early fossilists were so obsessed with depicting combat among the denizens of the prehistoric world." *The Dragon Seekers: How an Extraordinary Circle of Fossilists Discovered the Dinosaurs and Paved the Way for Darwin* (Cambridge, MA: Perseus Publishing, 2001), p. 74.

14. As explained in the previous chapter, atavism—a tendency to revert to ancestral (often perceived as "lower" or more primitive) genetic traits—mirrored fears of the civilized man toward "low culture." Jack London wrote in

racial undertones, believing that the fittest (i.e., the Anglo-Saxon race) would survive through Darwinian processes, while his contemporary, writer Frank Norris, speculated that atavistic tendencies might take a lupine rather than apish turn, through lycanthropy. For in Norris' 1914 novel *Vandover and the Brute*, a young gentleman of upper class breeding psychologically degenerates, through "habits of drunkenness and sexual immorality," into an imagined werewolf. Similar themes were explored in Jack Williamson's 1940 novel *Darker Than You Think*, published in *Unknown* (December 1940), wherein a modern man subjected to witchcraft has the power to metamorphose into prehistoric ancestors such as a pterodactyl and a sabertooth tiger. Ultimately the shape-shifter is killed by radioactivity.

15. Debus and Debus, *Paleoimagery*, Chapters 21 and 25.

16. Charles Hazelius Sternberg, *Hunting Dinosaurs: In the Bad Lands of the Red Deer River, Alberta, Canada*, with an introduction by David A.E. Spalding (1917; reprint, Edmonton: NeWest Press, 1985), pp. 130–176.

17. Harley S. Aldinger, "The Way of A Dinosaur," *Amazing Stories* 3, no. 1 (April 1928): pp. 35–37; Alexander M. Phillips, "The Death of the Moon," in *Flight Into Space: Great Science-Fiction Stories of Interplanetary Travel*, ed. Donald A. Wollheim (New York: Frederick Fell, Inc., 1950), pp. 95–107 (originally published in *Amazing Stories*, February 1929).

18. Decades after Aldinger's story, writers such as Bill Fawcett still yearn to write of titanic battles between Rex and Tops, such as his "After the Comet" (1993), published in *Dinosaur Fantastic*, ed. Mike Resnick and Martin H. Greenberg (New York: Daw Books, 1993), pp. 95–112.

19. L. Taylor Hansen's "Lords of the Underworld," *Amazing Stories* 15 (April 1941): pp. 8–47, offered a climactic battle between *Tyrannosaurus* and the great sabertooth cat *Smilodon*. Here the prehistoric animals are mere props in this odd tale about an archaeologist who uses a "time chair" to go back 20,000 years, where he witnesses lost races of South America, which expire in a flood. During the mid–1990s Newt Gingrich ordered a *T. rex* cast skull for his Washington D.C. office, underscoring the national symbolism of America's favorite cult dinosaur.

20. Allen A. Debus, "The Great and Terrybubble," *The Baum Bugle* 48, no. 2 (Autumn 2004): pp. 20–23.

21. Ruth Plumly Thompson, *Speedy in Oz* (Chicago: The Reilly & Lee Co., 1934); illustrated by John R. Neill.

22. The best painted restoration of *Andrias scheuchzeri* was done by Czech paleoartist Zdenek Burian in 1963, as Plate XXIII for Josef Augusta's beautifully illustrated volume *The Age of Monsters* (London: Paul Hamlyn Ltd., 1966). In Burian's restoration, we see the great, three-foot-long salamander waddling down to a river bank, where it seems poised to catch fish. In the background there is a little waterfall, which, at first glance, artist Jack Arata mistook for a "deluge." Well, perhaps this "mini-deluge" is what Burian symbolically intended to portray, especially given the genus' curious history.

23. This is despite the fact that Scheuchzer held advanced notions concerning the nature of fossils—perceived as the remains of true, living organisms. Scheuchzer was a convert from the *vis plastica* doctrine, which held that fossils were produced inorganically within the earth, a theory which he abandoned as he accumulated knowledge through his great fossil collection. Furthermore, he became an adherent of the Flood theory through the writings of British physician and proto-geologist John Woodward (1665–1728), particularly his *Essay Toward a Natural History of the Earth* (1695), essentially a ("Newt"-onian) account of how and why the universal Deluge happened. Scheuchzer was so taken by Woodward's treatise that he

even zealously translated its contents into scholarly Latin, published in 1704. Before his death on June 23, 1733, Scheuchzer wrote prolifically, authoring several noteworthy publications on fossils, four of which merit mention here. The first item of note is his *Piscium querelae et vindiciae* (1708), or "Complaints and Justifications of the Fishes," in which Scheuchzer revealingly created a fishy narrator—a personified pike fish emerging from Lake Constance, who instructs, in Latin no less, that fossils aren't the "mineral offspring of stone and marl," but instead relics of formerly living organisms. Another volume, Scheuchzer's *Herbarium diluvianum* (1709), or "Herbarium of the Deluge," remained a valuable reference on paleobotany on into the nineteenth century, and earned him the reputation of founder of paleobotany.

Perhaps his largest and greatest work, which is expounded upon by Martin J.S. Rudwick in Chapter One of *Scenes From Deep Time* (1992), was *Physica sacra* (1731–1733), or "Bible of Nature." Rudwick noted how a "deep past" extending beyond recorded Scripture would have been inconceivable to Scheuchzer. His sequences of "scenes" from recorded biblical history in *Physica sacra* therefore underscored how all fossils were actual Flood "witnesses" bearing testimony to this catastrophic historical event. Finally, his *Helveticae stoicheiographia* (1716–1718) is revered today for its consideration of the geophysics of the Alps, to which he made annual excursions.

24. Herbert Wendt, *Before the Deluge* (New York: Doubleday & Company, Inc., 1968).

25. John Woodward's contributions to diluvial geology must be examined in order to enhance our understanding for why his self-appointed protege, Johann Jakob Scheuchzer, so unquestionably allied himself with the Flood theory for the origin of all fossils. Woodward evidently borrowed another naturalist's precept—Nicolaus Steno's (1638–1686)—explaining how fossils could become buried and embedded within sediment deposited in horizontal superposition. Fossils, real remnants of antediluvian creatures, settled out of the aqueous suspension in order of specific gravity, with the densest kind sinking fastest into the mud deposit. It mattered little to Woodward that fossils often didn't resemble extant fauna or flora species because it seemed reasonable that organisms found in fossilized condition may simply not have been discovered yet in the ocean depths, and "that there is not any one species of Shell-fish, formerly in being, now perish'd and lost" (i.e., extinct). A lingering question remains: did Scheuchzer read something in Woodward's *Essay Toward a Natural History of the Earth* which triggered a thought that human fossils would also be found in diluvial deposits, prophetically leading to Scheuchzer's later "discovery" of the *Homo diluvii testis*? Indeed, Woodward does discuss disposition of drowned "terrestrial bodyes" which would have presumably included humans. Being dense, "bodyes" such as those of animals and birds wouldn't have "precipitated" from the flood slurry until the last and so would have been deposited at the top of the mud pile. Yet, throughout Woodward's *Essay*, there is conspicuous absence of discussion about fossil men, which would doubtlessly have been by far the most exciting discovery. In his 1977 book, *Dr. Woodward's Shield: History, Science, and Satire in Augustan England* (University of California Press), pp. 276–277, historian of science Joseph M. Levine stated: "Despite all the plenty and variety of fossil remains so far come to light, no one had yet discovered any sign of antediluvial man ... what happened to the many men who must also been destroyed in that event? ... Woodward proposed an explanation ... but he had raised no objection to discovering a human fossil, and there was obviously every incentive for doing so." So I wonder whether

Scheuchzer's interpretation of the *Homo diluvii testis* fossil was the misguided result of an early naturalist's effort to identify a paleontological "Holy Grail," a most extraordinary find—the first antediluvian human fossil known to science. Is it possible that Scheuchzer was driven by visions of grandeur toward his erroneous conclusion? Besides the published description of Scheuchzer's pamphlet about *Homo diluvii testis*, 1726 was also the year in which another naturalist, Johann Beringer (1667–1740), published his book, *Lithographiae Wirceburgensis*. Therein appeared Beringer's elaborated interpretations of strange fossils he had discovered near Wurzburg. These fossils actually turned out to be stone carvings planted by detractors. Beringer had been had; he was the victim of an awful hoax. Cardboard history paints Beringer as an advocate of the *vis plastica* theory for origin of fossils, when it really wasn't that simple. However, Beringer's embarrassment over the deception may have furthered the demise of the plastic force theory of fossil origins. As Herbert Wendt characterized the chain of events, "The Beringer case ... dealt the final blow to the doctrine of vis plastica and ushered in the victory of the Diluvian school.... The Diluvians of the Scheuchzer school restored a good name to the science." And yet, Scheuchzer's good name has become sullied too.

26. William J.T. Mitchell, *The Last Dinosaur Book: The Life and Times of A Cultural Icon* (Chicago: The University of Chicago Press, 1998), pp. 34, 36–39.

27. Aldiss, *op. cit.*, pp. 179–180. My copy of Capek's 1936 novel *War With the Newts* is a 1985 translation by Ewald Osers, published by George Allen & Unwin (Publishers) Ltd. All quotes from Capek's novel have been excerpted from this edition.

28. Louis Figuier, *Earth Before the Deluge: Newly Edited and Revised* (London: Cassell and Company, 1867), pp. 367–369.

29. Expert French anatomist Baron Georges Cuvier (1769–1832) offered a correct interpretation in the early nineteenth century. In 1809, Cuvier obtained an illustration of the fossil, allowing a reinterpretation. He concluded the *Homo diluvii testis* was no more than a fossil of large salamander dating from the Tertiary period (Miocene). Subsequently, during an 1811 trip to the Netherlands, he viewed the fossil at the Haarlem Museum, excavating it further. On this occasion he scraped away matrix, dramatically revealing bones he predicted would be found based on his salamander hypothesis. That same year he renamed *Homo diluvii testis* as *Andrias scheuchzeri*, noting the extinct variety is closely related to the Japanese Giant Salamander (*Cryptobranchus japonicus*). Cuvier wrote, "Nothing less than total blindness on the scientific level can explain how a man of Scheuchzer's rank, a man who was a physician and must have seen human skeletons, could embrace such a gross self-deception." His identification of the fossil was published in the fifth volume of *Reserches sur Ossemens fossiles*. As Levine, *op. cit.*, reflected in 1977, "What had gone wrong? Obviously Scheuchzer in his eagerness to demonstrate his theory had leaped from a superficial resemblance to a dogmatic conclusion."

30. Isaac Asimov, "Big Game," in *Before the Golden Age: A Science Fiction Anthology of the 1930s*, ed. Isaac Asimov (Garden City, NY: Doubleday & Co., Inc., 1974), pp. 810–812.

31. Isaac Asimov, *The Early Asimov* (Garden City, NY: Doubleday & Co., Inc., 1972), pp. 386–387.

32. John York Cabot, "Blitzkrieg In the Past," *Amazing Stories* 16, no. 7 (July 1942): pp. 8–47; Robert Moore Williams, "The Lost Warship," *Amazing Stories* 17, no. 1 (January 1943): pp. 8–56.

33. Cabot, *op. cit.*, p. 36.

34. *Ibid.*, p. 40.

35. Admittedly, time travel devices discussed in this chapter are rather unsophisticated in nature. As the theme of time travel in dinosaur fiction didn't mature until the early 1950s, dino-time-travel stories will be more fully addressed in Chapter Five.

36. Williams, *op. cit.*, p. 43.

Chapter 4

1. *Pikadon*, literally a "flashboom," is defined in Dr. Michihiko Hachya's *Hiroshima Diary* (New York: Avon Books, 1955; copyright the University of North Carolina Press) as a "glitter, sparkle, or bright light, like a flash of lightning" with a "boom! or loud sound." This Japanese word "came to mean the atom bomb" (p. 223). One witness stated that "She thought it was the coming of the Lord, because the sun rose in the west that day": Felicia Fonseca, "Thousands mark 60th A-bomb anniversary," *Chicago Tribune*, July 17, 2005. An estimated 100,000 individuals perished in the Hiroshima blast, which would have been equivalent in energy to 10,000 Oklahoma City bombs.

2. William Tsutsui, *Godzilla On My Mind: Fifty Years of the King of Monsters* (New York: Palgrave Macmillan, 2004), pp. 18–19. For an in-depth look at the 1954 film *Gojira*, see Peter H. Brothers' article "The Truth is the Truth," *G-Fan* no. 70 (Winter 2005): pp. 20–36.

3. Spencer Weart, "From the Nuclear Frying Pan Into the Global Fire," *The Bulletin of the Atomic Scientists* (June 1992): pp. 19–27. Also, in his *In Joy Still Felt: The Autobiography of Isaac Asimov—1954–1978* (New York: Doubleday, 1980), pp. 9–10, Isaac Asimov recounted a little-known tale leading to the nuclear weapons test ban in which, independently, he and Linus Pauling wrote papers discussing the danger of radioactive carbon 14 in the human body. Pauling's more important and widely recognized paper was published in the November 14, 1958 issue of *Science*.

4. Allen A. Debus, "The Doomsday Dinosaurs: Cold-Blooded Relics," *G-Fan* no. 61 (March/April 2003): pp. 12–17. Also see Richard Schwartz's *Cold War Culture: Media and the Arts, 1945–1990* (New York: Facts On File, 1998).

5. Tsutsui, *op. cit.*, p. 18.

6. *Ibid.*, p. 24.

7. Bradbury quoted by Will Murray, "Ray Bradbury's Dinosaur Chronicles," in *Dinosaur: Dinosaur Movies—The Complete History* (New York: Starlog Telecommunications, Inc., 1993), pp. 56–57.

8. Ray Bradbury, "The Beast From 20,000 Fathoms," *Saturday Evening Post* (June 23, 1951): pp. 28–29, 117–118.

9. Mark, F. Berry, *The Dinosaur Filmography* (Jefferson, NC: McFarland & Company, Inc. 2002), pp. 30–34.

10. *Ibid.*, pp. 31–32.

11. Murray, *op. cit.*

12. Ray Bradbury, "Tyrannosaurus Rex," reprinted in *Dinosaur Tales* (New York: Bantam Books, 1983), pp. 121–142.

13. In *The Arctic Giant* (1942), a Superman cartoon directed by Dave Fleischer, an enormous *T. rex* found frozen in Siberia goes on the rampage. The icy slab is delivered to Metropolis' Museum of Natural Science. Lois Lane is dispatched to cover the story of the possibility that, if thawed, the monster may recover and live once more. "Boy, what a story," Lois muses. When an oil can falls into the machinery of the "special refrigeration unit," the temperature rises to the fated "danger level," melting the ice. Fleischer's *T. rex* is huge, about Gojira-sized, although it seems to grow throughout the story, from an initial 100 feet in height to a towering 250 feet high! It has enormous fins along its spine and its face even resembles Gojira's. The *T. rex* smashes its way though buildings, destroying an elevated train line, a dam and a bridge before Superman trips it using cable on its approach toward a sports coliseum. Lois Lane's headline, "Superman Subdues Arctic Monster," graces the cover of the next *Daily Planet*. Also, in 1953, Frederick Pohl published a short story, "The Ghost-Maker" (*Beyond*, Galaxy Publishing), about a magic amulet used to summon the spirit of a long-dead *Tyrannosaurus* skeletal display in a downtown museum. Pohl's *T. rex* doesn't escape its confines, however. Momentum built steadily from that time forward, as Gojira and Ray Harryhausen's "exodinosaur," the "Ymir," are only a few (conceptual) strides removed from Kuttner's "Beast"—to be discussed in Chapter Six.

14. Rachel Carson, *Silent Spring* (New York: Fawcett Crest Book, 1962). In his *Bulletin of the Atomic Scientists* article (see note 3 above), Weart discusses how fears of radioactive poisoning transformed into America's environmental movement of the 1960s.

15. Allen A. Debus, "Alternative Kaiju (Part 1 of 3)," *G-Fan* no. 69 (Fall 2004): pp. 22–27. A literal translation of "kaiju eiga" would be "giant mysterious beast." J.D. Lees, however, ponders whether "Maybe the essential quality lies in the 'mysterious' part of the term. Perhaps there has to be something inexplicable in the nature of the creature." I feel that the term may also apply to non–Japanese mysterious monsters.

16. Tsutsui, *op. cit.*, p. 15.

17. Bingham's fabulous illustration of the "Fog Horn" creature appears on pp. 28–29 of this magazine.

18. One reader, whose letter was printed in *Filmfax* no. 107, objected to my comment on this matter. See my article, "Reverberations of the Fog Horn," *Filmfax* no. 106 (April/June 2005): pp. 62–66. I stand by my original remark, but you can judge for yourselves.

19. Jerry Weist, *Bradbury: An Illustrated Life—A Journey to Far Metaphor* (New York: William Morrow, 2002), Bradbury quoted from his introduction, p. xxi.

20. Weist, *op. cit.*, pp. 179–180.

21. J.D. Lees and Marc Cerasini, *The Official Godzilla Compendium* (New York: Random House, 1998), p. 12. Here, the authors note that Kayama was a "renowned Japanese science-fiction author."

22. Carson Bingham, *Gorgo* (Derby, CT: Monarch Books, Inc.,1960). For this section, all quotes from the novel, whether indicated by page number or not, are from *Gorgo*, unless otherwise cited. In the author's profile "Carson Bingham" is identified as "the pseudonym of Bruce Cassiday, who has published several novels under his own name.... He ... is presently fiction editor of a large national men's magazine." Of note, Cassiday was a U.C.L.A. graduate who served during World War II. The man could write a page-turner too.

23. *Beast* and *Behemoth* were filmed using stop-motion animation puppets. For its time, dinosaur film experts such as Donald F. Glut recognized *Gorgo* as being one of the better "maninsuitasaurus" examples. *Gorgo*, the British film, seems to have borrowed plot and theme elements generously from *Beast*, *Godzilla: King of the Monsters* (1956), *King Kong* (1933), and *Rodan: The Flying Monster* (1957). Arguably, scenes and characters in *Gorgo* seem inspired by, if not lifted right out of several of these movies.

24. Tom Weaver, "Director of Dinosaurs," *Starlog* (August 1993): pp. 63–68. Following his experiences with *Beast* and *Behemoth*, Lourie was asked by producers Frank

and Maurice King to conceive another dino-monster tale that they could release as a motion picture. In his autobiography *My Work in Films* (San Diego: Harcourt Brace Jovanovich, 1985), Lourie recollected, "I again took the tired dinosaur out of retirement and joyfully destroyed the city of London once more, this time in color and with a wonderful display of spectacular photography" (p. 242). Lourie lent several "novel approaches" to his "tired dinosaur" tale too. For instance, now there were two monsters, although "strikingly different in size." And true to his word, so as not to disappoint his daughter, this time the monsters were not destroyed. Lourie's screenplay originally called for the monsters to be encountered on a Pacific island named "Kuru." But soon they were re-situated to the North Atlantic. Lourie stated cynically, "True to the usual Hollywood practice, the producers commissioned a new team of writers to do a drastic rewrite of the story, changing not only the locale of the story but also adding some violent action and illogical developments.... I was committed to direct, and while directing tried my best to bring some logic to the embarrassing developments of the new story." As related by Mark Berry, *op. cit.*, "the majority of Gorgo's problems are directly related to story tinkering by the producers, expressly against Lourie's wishes ... the military histrionics were added and the principal characters were extensively rewritten, and the humans who populate the finished film are about as unlikeable a bunch as you're likely to encounter ... while the changes forced upon Lourie are irrevocably damaging, and must have been very hard for him to swallow, he kept his chin up and kept plugging" (p. 123–129). Arguably, to me, the novel leaves more impact than film.

25. Bill Warren, *Keep Watching the Skies!*, vol. 2 (Jefferson, NC: McFarland & Co. Publishers, Inc., 1982), pp. 520–528.

26. Jeff Rovin, *The Encyclopedia of Monsters* (New York: Facts On File, 1989), p. 130.

27. Lourie, *op. cit.*

28. Bingham, *op. cit.*, p. 73.

29. There is some confusion regarding the origin of the name "Gorgo." While some believe it pertains to the Cretaceous dinosaur *Gorgosaurus*, another possibility is more likely. As described in the novel, sailing up the Thames, Ryan and Slade spy a banner "Dorkin's London Circus Welcomes Gorgo, the Eighth Wonder of the World!," causing Slade to wonder aloud, "Who the hell is Gorgo?" Dorkin explains they decided to name the creature "Gorgo" based on the mythical Gorgon, "the mere sight of which could turn a man to stone."

30. Bingham, *op. cit.*, pp. 140–141.

31. Daphne Du Maurier, "The Birds," reprinted in *Alfred Hitchcock's Spellbinders in Suspense* (New York: Random House, 1967), pp. 32–64. For the dinosaur-bird evolutionary connection, see Lowell Dingus and Timothy Rowe, *The Mistaken Extinction: Dinosaur Evolution and the Origin of Birds* (New York: W.H. Freeman and Company, 1998).

32. Poul Anderson, "Wildcat," reprinted in *Dinosaurs: Stories by Ray Bradbury, Arthur C. Clarke, Isaac Asimov and Many Others*, ed. Martin H. Greenberg (New York: Donald I. Fine Books, 1996), pp. 138–176.

33. *Ibid.*, p. 156.

34. Geoffrey A. Landis, "Dinosaurs," reprinted in *Dinosaurs!*, ed. Jack Dann and Gardner Dozois (New York: Ace Books, 1990), pp. 195–201. Between 1972 and 1991, the U.S. Department of Defense sponsored a program named "Project Stargate," in which individuals thought to have psychic powers performed "remote viewing" of Soviet military sites.

35. *Ibid.*, pp. 200–201. Landis's intriguing choice of "iridium casings" in this story is a subtle reference to a famous and now proven theory of 1980 in which anomalously high concentrations of the element iridium detected in 65 million-year-old deposits were linked to the collision of a six-mile diameter asteroid (or a ten mile diameter comet) with the Earth. Evidence of the iridium "spike" found globally in deposits dating from this time bore solid indication that the fiery impactor pulverized and spread its iridium-laden contents throughout the atmosphere as fallout debris which became buried in sediments recording this pivotal moment of Earth's history. Alvarez, L. W., Alvarez, W., Asaro, W., and Michel, H. V., "Extraterrestrial cause for the Cretaceous-Tertiary extinction: experimental results and theoretical interpretation." *Science*, vol. 208, pp. 1095–1108; Carl Sagan (1934–1996) considered the extent of a global nuclear holocaust in his "The Nuclear Winter" (1983). After running a baseline model, for a 5,000 megaton war—only accounting for about 10% of the global nuclear arsenal, it was concluded that global temperatures would plunge to minus 13 degrees Fahrenheit for months. Sagan also considers the effect of radioactive fallout which averaged out globally would be one quarter of the dosage equivalent to kill a human. Furthermore, "There are severe and previously unanticipated global consequences of nuclear war—subfreezing temperatures in a twilit radioactive gloom lasting for months or longer.... Many species of plants and animals would become extinct. Vast numbers of surviving humans would starve to death. The delicate ecological relations that bind together organisms on Earth in a fabric of mutual dependency would be torn, perhaps irrevocably. There is little question that our global civilization would be destroyed. The human population would be reduced to prehistoric levels, or less ... there seems to be a real possibility of the extinction of the human species." By contrast, the Hiroshima bomb was only 12 to 15 kilotons. Excerpts from *www.cooperativeindividualism.org/sagan_nuclear_winter.html*. Also see note 40.

36. Dean Owen, *Reptilicus* (Derby, CT: Monarch Books, Inc., 1961). Owen's name was a pseudonym for Dudley Dean McGaughy. For more on this novel, see my article "Alternative Kaiju—Reptilicus (Part 2 of 3)," *G-Fan* no. 70 (Winter 2005): pp. 14–19.

37. Mark Jacobson, *Gojiro* (New York: Grove Press, 1991).

38. *Ibid.*, excerpted from the promotional ad on the back cover of Jacobson's novel.

39. Marc Cerasini, *Godzilla Returns* (New York: Random House, 1996); Marc Cerasini, *Godzilla At World's End* (New York: Random House, 1998).

40. The term "nuclear winter" was coined by physicist Richard Turco in the early 1980s. It was derived from knowledge of how the dinosaur extinctions of sixty-five million years ago would have resulted after photosynthesis would have ceased as an asteroid impact-caused cloud darkened the skies. The hazy gloom would also have lowered worldwide temperatures to below freezing for months.

Chapter 5

1. Allen A. Debus and Diane Debus, *Paleoimagery: The Evolution of Dinosaurs in Art* (Jefferson, NC: McFarland Publishers, 2002), pp. 67–72.

2. To date, only two books have dealt specifically with this theme: *Dinosaur Memories* (2002) by A. Debus and D. Debus, Chapter Twenty; and Jose Luis Sanz' *Starring T. rex!* (2002), Chapter Twelve. Referring to my phrase "poets with brushes" in his 1983 short story "Besides a Dinosaur

Whatta Ya Wanna Be When You Grow Up?," one of Ray Bradbury's characters referred to paleoartist Charles R. Knight by stating, "Man's a poet with a brush." Ray Bradbury, *Dinosaur Tales* (New York: Bantam Books, 1983).

3. Isaac Asimov, "The Ugly Little Boy," in *The Best Science Fiction of Isaac Asimov* (New York: Doubleday, 1986), pp. 274–312; Malcolm Hulke, *Dr. Who and the Dinosaur Invasion* (New York: Pinnacle Books, 1976); Brian Aldiss, "Poor Little Warrior," in *Dinosaurs!*, ed. Jack Dann and Gardner Dozois (New York: Ace Books, 1990), pp. 29–35; Michael Swanwick, "Riding the Giganotosaur," *Asimov's Science Fiction* 23 (October/November 1999): pp. 142–156.

4. H.G. Wells, *The Time Machine*, in *The Science Fiction Hall of Fame*, vol. 2A (New York: Avon Books, 1974), pp. 452–526. For instance, Paul K. Alkon discusses early works dating from the eighteenth century in his *Origins of Futuristic Fiction* (Athens, GA: The University of Georgia Press, 1987).

5. Ray Bradbury, "A Sound of Thunder," *op. cit.*, pp. 51–83. Undoubtedly, as a young man, Bradbury was excited by Wells's *The Time Machine*. And besides the writings of Edgar Rice Burroughs and Jules Verne, who incorporated prehistoric fauna into such novels as, respectfully, *The Land That Time Forgot* (1918) and *Journey to the Center of the Earth* (1864), Bradbury absolutely delighted in dinosaurs, having attended the 1933/34 Chicago World's Fair with his parents, where he saw life-sized mechanical restorations of *Tyrannosaurus*, *Triceratops* and other dino-monsters. At an even younger age he'd feasted his wondering eyes on a silent movie, *The Lost World* (1925), offering "metaphors ... so powerful that they changed my life." So, here, let's probe the unlikely influences behind "A Sound of Thunder," and consider Bradbury's previously unrecognized legacy.

6. Bradbury, *op. cit.*, p. 20. Further insights to Bradbury's inspiration come from this quote, " ...one day ... I said to myself, 'This is the day, I'm going to sit down and write myself a story about dinosaurs.'... let's form a safari.... I've always been interested in people like Frank Buck and Martin Johnson and his wife, when I was a child, and going to Africa. So let's make up a safari in time and send them back to hunt a dinosaur." This quote is excerpted from a website. "A Sound of Thunder" was televised as Episode 24 of *Ray Bradbury Theater*, and first aired on August 11, 1989. Also see Osa Johnson's *I Married Adventure: The Lives of Martin and Osa Johnson* (New York: J.D. Lippincott Company, 1940). Frank Buck (1884–1950) was a wild animal hunter, writer and filmmaker. The Buck/Johnson legacy was the *camera* safari and wildlife conservation, a theme which must have impressed itself on the young Bradbury's fertile mind. See my *Prehistoric Times* article "Time Steps Aside," no. 80, 2007 (in press).

7. H.G. Wells, *The Complete Science Fiction Treasury of H.G. Wells* (New York: Avenel Books, 1978), preface.

8. Isaac Asimov, "The Science Fiction Breakthrough," in *Asimov On Science Fiction* (1981), p. 166; Adrian Desmond, *Huxley: From Devil's Disciple to Evolution's High Priest* (Reading, MA: Perseus Books, 1997), p. 642.

9. Wells's evolutionary interests as well as his obsession with time are reflected in a textbook he coauthored with Huxley's grandson, biologist Julian Huxley, *The Science of Life* (Garden City, NY: Doubleday, Duran & Company, Inc., 1931).

10. Eller Touponce, *Ray Bradbury: The Life of Fiction* (Kent, OH: The Kent State University Press, 2004), p. 91.

11. Touponce, *op. cit.*, p. 127.

12. Asimov, "Ray Bradbury," *op. cit.*, p. 197.

13. Paul J. Nahin, *Time Travel: A writer's guide to the real science of plausible time travel* (Cincinnati, OH: Writer's Digest Books, 1997), pp. 6–7.

14. Nahin, *op. cit.*, pp. 110. Furthermore, because the earth is in rapid motion around the sun and through the galaxy, one would have to *navigate* a time machine in order to remain motionless with respect to the three spatial dimensions. That is, unless the time machine was anchored into stable bedrock substrate, as in Simak's "Small Deer," in *Dinosaurs II*, ed. Jack Dann and Gardner Dozois (New York: Ace Books, 1995), pp. 129–144, and as in Douglas Lebeck's *Memories of a Dinosaur Hunter* (Bloomington, IN: 1st Books Library, 2002).

15. Boitard's novel is discussed on pp. 166–170 of Rudwick's *Scenes From Deep Time* (1992); Charles Hazelius Sternberg, *Hunting Dinosaurs: In the Bad Lands of the Red Deer River, Alberta, Canada* (1917, published by the author; third edition, Edmonton: NeWest Press, 1985); Eric Temple Bell (John Taine, pseud.), *Before the Dawn* (Williams & Wilkins Co., 1934, ; reprinted by Arno Press, 1974); Nahin, *op. cit.*, p. 12, discusses another case of sleeping through time involving dinosaurs awakening in our present day, conceived in N. Loomis' 1950 story, "The Long Dawn." Other low-tech devices and "time machines" used for accessing prehistory include reincarnation, explosions and magic amulets. Examples include Arthur Petticolas' tale of reincarnation, "Dinosaur Destroyer," *Amazing Stories* 23 (January 1949): pp. 13–14; L. Taylor Hansen's "Lords of the Underworld," published in the April 1941 *Amazing Stories*, in which a modern man battles a *T. rex* 20,000 years ago in the prehistoric city of Xibalba; and Robert Moore Williams' novel *The Lost Warship*, discussed previously in chapter three. Glut's 1996 film *Dinosaur Valley Girls* further employed this concept. For more on this movie, see Glut's *Dinosaur Valley Girls—The Book* (McFarland & Company, Inc., Publishers, 1997; Glut's novelization of the movie script is in press). Such tales may also be viewed as alternative lost-world dinosaur adventure stories, or as a variant of the Aldiss' subgenre, "tales of prehistory," although involving creatures misplaced in time. A variation of the theme was broadcast in the televised series *Monsters*, originally aired in 1988, based on a story written by Michael Reaves, titled "Sleeping Dragon," which featured intelligent dinosaurs surviving to the present in time capsules programmed by radioactive isotopes to open after a duration of sixty-five million years. Evidently, the dinosaurs predicted the end of their world and so made a valiant effort to preserve hundreds of their race through suspended animation. However, the dino-monsters die immediately upon exposure to the frigid Arctic environment. (Also see Malcolm Hulke's *Dr. Who and the Cave Monsters*, discussed in the Appendix.)

16. Nahin, *op. cit.*, p. 100.

17. Frederick Pohl, "Let the Ants Try," in *Alternating Currents* (New York: Ballantine Books, 1956), pp. 34–44. Archaeologist P. Schuyler Miller's "The Sands of Time" (1937) also relies on a time machine device and is one of the earliest stories to connect time machines with dinosaurs. Here, a time traveler encounters and photographs dinosaurs in the past. Although he travels into prehistory aiming to kill a dinosaur with a gun, the time travel element is rather simplistic, avoiding paradox. Miller's tale was recently published in *Dawn of Time: Prehistory Through Science Fiction*, ed. M.H. Greenberg, J. Olander, and Robert Silverberg (New York: Elsevier/Nelson Books, 1979), pp. 44–78. Also see note 65.

18. Nahin, *op. cit.*, pp. 170–171, discusses D.R. Daniels's 1935 story, "The Branches of Time," involving parallel worlds. "After Daniels's tale, the splitting time line concept quickly became part of standard science fiction lore, and writers could use it without having to offer a lot of explanation...."

19. Arthur C. Clarke, "Time's Arrow," in *Dinosaurs:*

Stories by Ray Bradbury, Arthur C. Clarke, Isaac Asimov and Many Others, ed. Martin H. Greenberg (New York: Donald I. Fine Books, 1996), pp. 35–51.

20. Clarke's story may have been inspired by a genuine fossil occurrence, a fossilized track way discovered in the bed of the Paluxy River, at Glen Rose, Texas. See Roland T. Bird, "Did Brontosaurus ever walk on land?" *Natural History* 53 (1944): pp. 61–67; Roland T. Bird, "Thunder in His Footsteps," *Natural History* 48 (May 1939): pp. 254–261, 302.

21. Clarke, *op. cit.*, p. 51.

22. Isaac Asimov, "Day of the Hunters," in *Dinosaurs: Stories by Ray Bradbury, Arthur C. Clarke, Isaac Asimov and many others* (New York: Donald I. Fine Books, 1996), pp. 15–25. Quote excerpted from pp. 24–25.

23. For a complete reprint listing of Bradbury's "A Sound of Thunder," see Touponce, *op. cit.*, p. 468.

24. Asimov, 1981, p. 198.

25. Bradbury captured and blended the objectionable theme of extinction of big game fauna with the horror of the hunt as modern "sport." Bradbury set a precedent with his benighted hunters, hell-bent on proving themselves by destroying natural beauty. Another story accentuating the terror of the hunt is Richard Connell's 1924 story "The Most Dangerous Game," reprinted *Alfred Hitchcock's Spellbinders in Suspense* (New York: Random House, 1967), pp. 11–31.

26. Ray Bradbury, "A Sound of Thunder," in *Dinosaur Tales* (New York: Bantam Books, 1983), pp. 51–83. Quote excerpted from p. 53. Elements of my discussion of Bradbury's "A Sound of Thunder" are borrowed, in modified form, from my article, "The Greatest Dino-Time Travel Tales of All Time," *Dino Press* 6 (2002): pp. 65–73 (Japanese; Aurora, Oval, Inc.).

27. Bradbury, *op. cit.*, p. 64.

28. Bradbury, *op. cit.*, p. 73.

29. Bradbury also referred to *T. rex* as the "thunder lizard" in chapter forty-two, pp. 158–159, of his 1962 novel *Something Wicked This Way Comes*.

30. Bradbury, *op. cit.*, pp. 68, 72.

31. Bradbury, *op. cit.*, p. 82. In the early 1990s, Bradbury's classic story was extended through a short series of imaginative novels written by Stephen Leigh. The first two in the series were titled *Ray Bradbury Presents Dinosaur World* (New York: Avon Books, 1992), and *Ray Bradbury Presents Dinosaur Planet* (New York: Avon Books, 1993). The novels pick up where Bradbury's short story ended. Leigh's premise is that after returning from the Cretaceous, Eckels' time safari leader from Bradbury's original 1952 story, Travis, finds himself in an altered Green Town after making a second visit to the past in a hapless effort to reconcile the space-time paradox created by the butterfly's demise. Turns out that Travis' rifle was knocked aside before shooting Eckels, who in turn dove for safety into the time machine. Eckels disappeared into the past, and Travis has commandeered another time machine on a journey through space-time and parallel worlds, in pursuit. Now the space-time pathway extends paradoxically into 1992 Green Town U.S.A., where a dinosaur invasion has begun. Hopping on the "path" found floating in a nearby wood, three teenagers find the blundering, psychotic time-traveler Eckels, and run into a civilization of intelligent, spear-wielding "dinosauroids," known as the "Mutata." Meanwhile, history as we know it is being destroyed by the wavering timestream. Bradbury stated, "Mr. Leigh has taken my tale backwards, forwards, forwards, backwards like the proverbial Lobster Quadrille in *Alice in Wonderland*. He has salted it and basted it, grounded it and flown it in various Time Channels where events and people pass each other like the ricocheting inhabitants of a Mirror Maze" (*Ray Bradbury Presents Dinosaur Planet*, p. 2).

32. Bradbury, *op. cit.*, p. 65. Years later, however, Bradbury had crafted a time travel story where the protagonist meets his younger self, advising him not to make the same mistakes that he did in life. See "A Touch of Petulance," in *The Toynbee Convector* (New York: Alfred A. Knopf, 1988), pp. 201–213.

33. L. Sprague de Camp, "A Gun For Dinosaur," in *Rivers of Time* (Riverdale, NY: Baen Books, 1993), pp. 1–36. Stories related by Reginald Rivers in de Camp's series would date from approximately the 2030s. Quote excerpted from pp. 257–258.

34. De Camp, *op. cit.*, pp. 3–4.

35. De Camp, *op. cit.*, p. 28.

36. De Camp, *op. cit.*, pp. 35–36.

37. Clifford, D. Simak, *Mastodonia* (New York: Ballantine Books, 1978). However, Simak did consider both parallel world possibilities and time travel paradoxes in his novel *Our Children's Children* (New York: G.P. Putnam's Sons, 1974), in which monstrous aliens from our future ultimately escape to the Late Cretaceous where they cause the great dinosaur extinction. Read more about *Mastodonia* in the Appendix.

38. David Drake, *Tyrannosaur* (New York: A Tom Doherty Associates Book, 1993). Parts II and III were published in different form in TIME SAFARI, copyright 1982.

39. Robert Heinlein, "By His Bootstraps," in *The Menace From Earth* (New York: Signet, 1959), pp. 39–87.

40. Michael Swanwick, *Bones of the Earth* (New York: EOS, 2002).

41. Swanwick, *op. cit.*, p. 24; Here, interestingly, a scientific team investigating the Cretaceous dinosaurs speculates that highly adapted dinosaurs who communicated using "infrasound" were deafened by the K-T asteroid impact event sixty-five million years ago, resulting in demise of their fragile ecosystem by "rendering their feeding strategies useless" (p. 288). As opposed to the ideas of modern physics and its implications for time travel, Kurt Vonnegut's concept of time travel is deterministic. In novels such as *Slaughterhouse 5* (1970) and *The Sirens of Titan* (1959), respectively, Vonnegut reflected that "All moments, past, present and future always have existed, always will exist," and "Time can be likened to a fly trapped in amber—we see each moment in time as if it is frozen—it has always occurred and always will occur. All time is all time, it does not change or lend itself to explanations—it simply is. Take it moment by moment and you will find that we are all bugs in amber." Vonnegut quotes from Martin Griffiths' (University of Glamorgan) article, "Deterministic Chronology: Satire, Time & Meaning in the Novels of Kurt Vonnegut" (undated, posted online).

42. Robert J. Sawyer, "Just Like Old Times," in *Dinosaurs: Stories by Ray Bradbury, Arthur C. Clarke, Isaac Asimov and Many Others*, ed. Martin H. Greenberg (New York: Donald I. Fine Books, 1996), pp. 177–191. Quote excerpted from p. 180.

43. Sawyer, *op. cit.*, p. 179.

44. Sawyer, *op. cit.*, p. 185.

45. Sawyer, *op. cit.*, pp. 187–188. Similar conceptually, although not as dark, is Scott Ciencin's *Dinoverse* (1999), involving a mind transfer device capable of whisking an individual's consciousness into primeval organisms. In Ciencin's entry, the minds of several teenagers inadvertently enter a band of Late Cretaceous dinosaurians including a *T. rex*, *Quetzalcoatlus*, *Ankylosaurus* and a *Leptoceratops*. The story, illustrated by Mike Fredericks, is intended for adolescent readers or even to amuse the younger side of older readers, allowing them to enjoy that harmless ultimate fantasy of *being* a dinosaur. Following their remarkable journey as dinosaurs, the teenagers are better equipped to handle adversities in the present because

as a team they've already dealt with harrowing problems in the past. This book spawned a short series of novels.

46. George Gaylord Simpson, *The Dechronization of Sam Magruder* (New York: St. Martin's Griffin,1996). As Stephen Jay Gould proclaimed in his afterword, Simpson was "unquestionably, the greatest vertebrate paleontologist of the twentieth century, perhaps the greatest of all time" (p. 114). Simpson facilitated understanding of how species evolve as populations, and investigated the rate at which evolution occurs. On a firm statistical foundation, Simpson sounded the death knell for the antiquated and erroneous "orthogenetic" evolutionary theory. Simpson's artistry and visual acuity enabled him to graphically project how evolution works through the use of diagrams and pictures. Yet despite these professional successes, Simpson has also been described as a solitary soul, perhaps providing critical inspiration for his novella. Although Simpson's posthumously published work carries a 1996 publication date, it is something of a mystery as to when he actually penned his tale. Magruder's reference to the cold- versus warm-blooded dinosaur debate approximates when Simpson may have written this manuscript, possibly in the mid–1970s.

47. Brian, W. Aldiss, *Cryptozoic* (New York: Avon Books, 1967). Quote excerpted from p. 34. Aldiss further explains that unlocking the secret of temporal mind travel required understanding the human "overmind," an organ evolved to falsely create a perceived state of passing time, or the flow of time from past to future. Although Bush travels from the Devonian, into the Jurassic Period, and later even back into the Precambrian, other than an encounter with a stegosaur herd, he has few perilous encounters with prehistoria. Rather than hunting dinosaurs, Bush is enlisted on a quest, stalking revolutionaries from 2093 who have slipped into time's recesses. In Jack Finney's (1911–1995) 1970 novel *Time and Again*, gifted time travelers "mind" themselves into the recent historic past after contemplating their target period with utmost introspection.

48. Rod Serling, "The Odyssey of Flight 53," in *Time Machines: The Greatest Time Travel Stories Ever Written*, ed. Bill Adler, Jr. (New York: Carroll & Graf Publishers, Inc., 1998), pp. 221–240. Serling's story was originally published in *Twilight Zone Stories* (1962) and aired as an episode of *The Twilight Zone* on CBS on February 24, 1961. Lewis S. Brown, *Yes, Helen, there were Dinosaurs* (Lewis S. Brown, 1982). In Michael Bishop's "Herding with the Hadrosaurs" (1992), "time slips" allow passage into various geological time periods, including the Late Cretaceous. Bishop's tale was reprinted in *Dinosaurs II*, ed. Jack Dann and Gardner Dozois (New York: Ace Books, 1995), pp. 163–184.

49. David Gerrold, *Deathbeast* (New York: Popular Library, 1978). Quote excerpted from p. 200.

50. R. Garcia y Robertson, "The Virgin and the Dinosaur," *Asimov's Science Fiction* 16 (February 1992): pp. 132–168. Also see the Appendix for more on this title.

51. Geoffrey A. Landis, "Embracing the Alien," *Analog Science Fiction* 112 (November 1992): pp. 10–39. Quote excerpted from p. 22.

52. Robert J. Sawyer, *End of An Era* (New York: Ace Books, 1994). Quote excerpted from p. 93.

53. Sawyer, *op. cit.*, p. 221. Modern writers avail themselves of the theoretical "devices & phenomena" of modern physics and astrophysics. Thus, concepts of folded space-time, wormholes, tachyons and faster-than-light "warp-drive" travel, parallel universes, cosmic strings, self-consistency paradoxes, and quantum gravity principles are all fair game to modern writers. Post-Wellsian, modern time travel principles were embraced by Robert Heinlein, as in his short story, "By His Bootstraps" (1941), *op. cit.*,

which didn't involve dinosaurs. Essentially, Heinlein had the ideas filmed in *Back to the Future* and its sequels anticipated by over four decades.

54. Will Hubbell, *Cretaceous Sea* (New York: Ace Books, 2002); Will Hubbell, *Sea of Time* (New York: Ace Books, 2004).

55. Hubbell, *op. cit.*, 2004, pp. 137–139.

56. Bob Buckley, "The Runners," in *Dinosaurs!* ed. Jack Dann and Gardner Dozois (New York: Ace Books, 1990), pp. 76–96. Quote excerpted from p. 95. The supernova theory of mass extinctions was popularized prior to the asteroid impact theory. For more on this historical episode, see Allen A. Debus and Diane Debus, *Dinosaur Memories: Dino-trekking for Beasts of Thunder, Fantastic Saurians, 'Paleo-people,' 'Dinosaurabilia,' and other 'Prehistoria'* (Lincoln, NE: Authors Choice Press, 2002), Chapter Nineteen, "Atomic Age Extinctions," pp. 360–368.

57. L.W. Alvarez, W. Alvarez, F. Asaro, and H.V. Michel, "Extraterrestrial cause for the Cretaceous-Tertiary extinction: experimental results and theoretical interpretation," *Science* 208 (1980): pp. 1095–1108.

58. Mass extinctions theory contributed to the rapidly escalating dinosaur fervor. Perhaps the best science fiction story borrowing from the "Nemesis" star theory and its implications was Robert Silverberg's novel *At Winter's End* (New York: Warner Books, 1988). The story's premise, set many millions of years in the future, is structured around the future of man and his capability of surviving the icy, calamitous episodes (hundreds of thousands of years in duration) wrought by instances of periodically recurring impact cratering on earth. Silverberg's future Earth and evolutionary consequences differ considerably from Wells's perspectives a century earlier.

59. Peter Lerangis, *Last of the Dinosaurs—Time Machine 22* (New York: Bantam Books, 1988). In Lerangis's book, intended for a younger audience, the rules of time travel include, "You must not kill any person or animal," and "You must not attempt to change history."

60. L. Sprague de Camp, "The Big Splash," in *Rivers of Time* (Riverdale, NY: Baen Books, 1993), pp. 183–208.

61. De Camp, *op. cit.*, pp. 203–204.

62. I am indebted to Stan G. Hyde for this information, although to date I haven't been able to trace this particular story. See Hyde's commentary in *Prehistoric Times* 58 (February/March 2003): p. 46. So I wonder whether Hyde may have somehow conflated Miller's 1937 story "The Sands of Time," mentioned here in note 17.

63. Much as later dinosaur movie special effects artists enjoy having their great stop-motion animated carnosaurs scratch an ear, in homage to *King Kong*'s Willis O'Brien (1866–1962).

64. Arthur C. Clarke, *Report on Planet Three and other Speculations* (New York: Berkley Books, 1972), pp. 178–187.

65. Clarke quoted in Nahin, *op. cit.*, p. 78. Coiled spiral time is exactly the gimmick employed by P. Schuyler Miller in his 1937 tale "The Sands of Time," *op. cit.* In one segment the time traveler named Donovan claims, "You can see that the usual paradoxes don't come in at all.... About killing your grandfather, and being in two places at once.... The time screw has a sixty-million-year pitch. You can slide from coil to coil sixty million years at a time, but you can't cover any shorter distance without living it" (pp. 56–57).

66. Utley's "Walking In Circles" was printed in *Asimov's Science Fiction* (January 2002): pp. 62–67, while another of Utley's imaginative tales exploring the same theme—"Treading the Maze"—was published in *Asimov's Science Fiction* (February 2002): pp. 80–85.

67. Nahin, *op. cit.*, pp. 173, 176, 184. For reasons expressed by Utley, both Simak in his *Our Children's Children*

(1974), and Douglas Lebeck, *op. cit.*, viewed time travel to the future as impossible, yet traveling into the past as possible. In Simak's tragic "The World of the Red Sun" (1931), which doesn't involve dinosaurs, one may travel into the far future, but traveling into the past from any temporal point is impossible.

68. Stephen Baxter, *The Time Ships* (New York: Harper-Prism, 1995). See "Book Four—The Palaeocene Sea."

69. A well-done entry is *Journey to the Beginning of Time*, directed by Karel Zeman, released in Czechoslovakia as *Cesta do praveku* in 1955, but re-released in the U.S.A. in 1966. Here four boys take a time journey from their present into the Precambrian along a metaphorical "river of time." Additionally, two films starring Toho's pseudo-dinosaur Godzilla fully employed time travel. These are *Godzilla vs. King Ghidorah* (1991), in which a time machine is used by time travelers to witness Godzilla's pre-atomic theropod form, *Godzillasaurus*; and *Godzilla vs. Megaguirus* (2000), in which a black hole projector transports an infestation of prehistoric dragonflies into modern Japan. *A Sound of Thunder*, a feature film released in August 2005 based loosely on Bradbury's story, proved a disappointment.

70. In his delightful 1993 time travel tale, a lark about evolutionary contingency titled "One Giant Step," John E. Stith offers a peculiar twist on the dinosaur extinction theory. This time, dinosaurs have invented time travel. But upon their arrival sixty-five million years into *their* past, three dinosaurs exit the timeship, one dramatically expressing "That's one small step for a reptile, one giant step for Reptilia." We find that one depressed dinosaur among the trio, named Ektor, has plotted genocide of the Reptilia, intending to destroy the lizard ancestor of all dinosaur species to come, including those evolving heightened intelligence. The perpetrator explains to his astonished, helpless colleagues the necessity of his actions. "Reptiles were not meant to rule the Earth.... Let some other species take over.... In our race for control and self-perpetuation, we have slaughtered how many species? Thousands? Tens of thousands?" Ektor launches three mighty bombs packed with sufficient explosives to cause a nuclear winter and cause viral sterility in any solitary survivors. However, immediately following this catastrophe, another smaller time capsule materializes in the K-T world, although this time piloted by an 80-kilogram cockroach, whose first utterance is, "That's one small step for an insect...." John E. Stith, "One Giant Step," *Dinosaur Fantastic*, ed. Mike Resnick and Martin H. Greenberg (New York: Daw Books, 1993), pp. 78–84.

71. Gould's *Wonderful Life: The Burgess Shale and the Nature of History* (New York: W.W. Norton & Company, 1989) was inspired by the fossil record's theme of contingency. Also see Allen and Diane Debus, *Dinosaur Memories* (2002), Chapter Eighteen, "A Paleontological 'Parallel,'" pp. 341–352.

Chapter 6

1. Stephen Brusatte, *Stately Fossils: A Comprehensive Look at the State Fossils and Other Official Fossils* (Boulder, CO: Fossil News, 2001), p. 109. In James P. Hogan's *The Gentle Giants of Ganymede* (New York: Ballantine Books, 1978), pp. 106–108, a frozen, 25-million-year-old giant rhinocerine, *Baluchitherium*, is discovered onboard a relic alien spacecraft.

2. "Exodinosaur" is a term coined by paleontologist Jose Luis Sanz in his *Starring T. Rex!: Dinosaur Mythology and Popular Culture* (Bloomington: Indiana University Press,

2002), pp. 69–72. Here, I will further establish and expand significantly on his term, merging the concept of "dinosauroids" with exodinosaurs as well.

3. For in-depth discussion of dinosaur *movie* titles, see Mark F. Berry's *The Dinosaur Filmography* (Jefferson, NC: McFarland & Company, Inc., 2002). For others listed in this paragraph, see listings in Bill Warren's *Keep Watching the Skies!* (Jefferson, NC: McFarland & Company, Inc., Volume 1, 1982; Volume 2, 1986. *Planet of Dinosaurs*—which has ties to David Gerrold's *Deathbeast*, discussed both in Chapter Five and the Appendix—was a case of benighted human space travelers crashing down on a planet conveniently mired in its "dinosaur age." The exploration team soon confronts a menagerie of stop-motion animated dinosaurs (e.g., a dimply *T. rex*, *Allosaurus*, a "Czerkasaurus"-ceratopsian, *Struthiomimus*, *Polacanthus*, a *Rhedosaurus*, *Brontosaurus*, *Ornitholestes*, a herd of *Stegosaurus*, and a giant spider thrown in for good measure) that steal many scenes in non-stop fashion. Of this 1978 release, Mark Berry offers the following observations: "Fantasy films ... have often been accused of 'wasting' excellent special effects in the service of otherwise dreadful pictures. On this charge, *Planet of Dinosaurs* is grievously guilty. But its dinosaurs are so very, very good that 'Planet' is also a dinosaur fan's ultimate guilty pleasure" (p. 316). Predictably, after the dinosaurs are conquered, the stranded survivors civilize the infant world. Kudos, however, to sculptor Stephen Czerkas for creating the primeval exo-fauna.

4. Even the Mother Alien from the film *Aliens* (1986) resembles the skeleton of a theropod dinosaur, and in Marc Cerasini's 2004 novel *AVP: Alien vs. Predator* (pp. 197, 236), the Predator species are viewed as "reptilian humanoids," with bony heads that seem dinosaurian.

5. Frank R. Paul, *Fantastic Adventures* 7, no. 5 (December 1945)—back cover painting titled "Stories of the Stars ... Aldebaran."

6. Alexander Blade, *ibid.*, p. 178. The quote is excerpted from the author's copy of the issue.

7. Gustavus W. Pope, *Romances of the Planets: N. 1, Journey to Mars* (G.W. Dillingham, 1894), p. 324.

8. Harry Lange, *Space Journal: Dedicated to the Astro-Sciences* 1, no. 5 (March–May, Winter 1959), front and back cover painting by Harry Lange, titled "Project Star—Landing on Planet One Hundred Million Years Younger than Earth." More recently, Lange's painting was reproduced as two small black and white images in "Exodinosaurs Attack!" (Part 1) by Allen A. Debus, *Prehistoric Times*, no. 61 (August/September 2003): p. 18.

9. Helmut Hoeppner and B. Spencer Isbell, "Project Star," *ibid.*, p. 50.

10. Philip N. Shockey, "The ultimate necessity of space travel," *ibid.*, p. 8.

11. In a more recent example artist Ron Miller illustrated Venus as being (currently) in its Carboniferous age, even spotting a giant dragonfly (*Meganeura*) prominently in the depiction. This was republished on the July 6, 1979 cover of *Science*. The caption reads, "Artist's view of Venus based on ideas of some scientists in the first half of the 20th century.... High mountains, swamps, vast oceans, and dense water clouds were postulated. Venus was widely thought to be similar in development to Earth in the Paleozoic era." Author Ray Bradbury's short story "The Long Rain" (1950) in *The Illustrated Man* (Bantam Books) projects the horror of Venus's alleged swampy environment, although without an overtly stated prehistoric element.

12. Joseph Harold Rush, *The Dawn of Life* (Garden City, NY: Hanover House, 1957), pp. 202–203.

13. Isaac Asimov, ed. *Before the Golden Age: A Science Fiction Anthology of the 1930s* (Garden City, NY: Doubleday & Co., Inc., 1974), p. 605.

14. Donald F. Glut, *The Dinosaur Scrapbook: The Dinosaur in Amusement Parks, Comic Books, Fiction, History, Magazines, Movies, Museums, Television* (Secaucus, NJ: Citadel Press, 1980). The painting is also reprinted on the acknowledgments page, yet was only briefly described in *The Dinosaur Scrapbook*. In 2003, Don himself couldn't recall too many details about the story other than he'd borrowed the issue from Forrest J. Ackerman. Of the *TWS* image, Don had written in 1980, "Cover artwork by Howard V. Brown showing a scene familiar to moviegoers of the 1950s, 1960s and 1970s." Unfortunately, *The Dinosaur Scrapbook* gave no indication which story title was associated with Brown's artistry, or who the author was, or even what the story was really about. So for years I had only wondered about the story, until the summer of 2003, when I decided to read it. First, relying on the Internet, I learned more about Howard Vachel Brown (1878–1945), who had done this "smashing" illustration. Brown, trained at the Chicago Art Institute, had illustrated covers for magazines such as *TWS, Astounding Stories, Scientific American, Argosy,* and *Science and Invention*. A second Google search revealed a scan of the April 1940 *TWS*, with its vivid coloration. Weeks passed before I could get my hands on an original issue of the magazine. These old pulps are rare and becoming expensive, so count your lucky stars if you can find them!

15. Henry Kuttner, "Beauty and the Beast," *Thrilling Wonder Stories* 16, no. 1 (April 1940): pp. 67–76. All quotes from the story are excerpted from my copy of the magazine. To my knowledge the story hasn't been reprinted since its original publication in *TWS*.

16. John Wyndham, *The Day of the Triffids* (New York: Ballantine Books, 1951. Henry Slesar's *20 Million Miles to Earth* (Amazing Stories Science Fiction Novels), adapted from the screenplay by Bob Williams and Christopher Knopf, was published in 1957.

17. Sir Arthur Conan Doyle usually receives credit for having invented the idea of the "dino-monster menacing Metropolis" theme. For in Conan Doyle's 1912 novel *The Lost World*, Professor Challenger releases a pterodactyl from a cage, and it escapes through a window into London's night sky. Sight of this winged demon silences his detractors. But in the 1925 silent movie, producers incorporated a more dramatic conclusion: instead of a pterodactyl, it is Challenger's captured "brontosaur" which escapes into London's streets, knocking buildings aside before swimming up the Thames river. The 1925 movie advertisement poster is reproduced in Berry, *op. cit.* This eye-catching poster art for First National's 1925 production *The Lost World* featured an oversized tyrannosaurid on the outskirts of a city clutching a passenger train car with its foot; streetlights can be discerned in the background.

18. Camille Flammarion, *Le Monde avant creation de l'homme origines de la terre, origines de la vie de l'humanite* (Paris: C. Marpon and E. Flammarion, 1886).

19. Martin. J.S. Rudwick, *Scenes From Deep Time: Early Pictorial Representations of the Prehistoric World* (Chicago: The University of Chicago Press, 1992), pp. 216–217.

20. For instance, there is the 1925 poster for First National's *The Lost World* to ponder, even though such a scene never appeared in the novel or film. (See note 17.) For more on the archetypical connections to *Gojira*, see my article "Godzilla's Roots: The Earliest Stego-Tyrannosaur 'Hybrid,'" *G-Fan* no. 67 (Spring 2004): pp. 12–14.

21. Astor died aboard the *Titanic*. In his novel we find interesting passages like this. "If Jupiter is passing through its Jurassic or Mesozoic period, there must be any amount of some kind of game." Then later, "Clumps of huge ferns were scattered about and the ground was covered with curious tracks. 'Jupiter is evidently passing through a Car-

boniferous or Devonian period such as existed on earth, though, if consistent with its size, it should be on a vastly larger scale.'... here they came upon a number of huge bones, evidently the remains of some saurian, and many times the size of a grown crocodile." Later they encounter a *Mastodon*, reptilian birds and pterodactyls. Astor refers to the Jovian fauna as a "neat illustration of the 'survival of the fittest.'" *A Journey in Other Worlds: A Romance of the Future* has been posted online and may be readily found via a search engine under its title.

22. Robert Silverberg, "Heart of Stone," *Asimov's Science Fiction* 27, no. 12 (December 2004): p. 9.

23. Arthur K. Barnes, "The Hothouse Planet," *Thrilling Wonder Stories* 10, no. 2 (October 1937): pp. 12–29.

24. Glut's *Dinosaur Scrapbook*, p. 78, indicates that Barnes's story was also printed in the September 1937 issue of *Startling Stories*. Here the "Whip" featured in a front cover painting appears a bit more tyrannosaurian than in Brown's *TWS* painting.

25. This cover was reprinted in Sanz' popular book, *op. cit.* Although said Centosaurs do appear to be exodinosaurian in the 1940 cover illustration, Sanz included no commentary about them in his book.

26. G.H. Irwin, "Lair of the Grimalkin," *Fantastic Adventures* 10, no. 4 (April 1948): pp. 8–53. To my knowledge this story hasn't been reprinted.

27. One of Malcolm Smith's illustrations of the Grimalkin was more recently reproduced on page 135 of Jeff Rovin's *The Encyclopedia of Monsters* (New York: Facts On File, Inc., 1989).

28. Although from Irwin's description, it seems as if Grimalkin may not have originated on Venus. "It was like a Cerberus, guarding the gates of Hell, terrible and knowing and waiting. It was like chaos before life, the time-aura that hung stinking about it. This thing had winged across worlds before man crawled from the sea, one would think. It was like a Harpy, sleeping and dreaming of blood and the shedding of blood and the drinking. It was like the sea bottom, aged and ageless, barnacled and hoary and littered with bones about it. It was terror incarnate...." (p. 31)

29. Besides Grimalkin, dinosaurian-like "Felars" dwell in the great swamp (p. 19) as do smaller pterodactyl-like "featherless flying reptiles."

30. Anne McCaffrey, *Dinosaur Planet* (New York: Ballantine Books, 1978)—with a terrific cover painting by Darrell Sweet; Donald F. Glut; *Spawn* (New York: Laser Books 43, 1976)—featuring cover art by Kelly Freas. Cathy Hill's painting of this world was printed as the frontispiece to Glut's *Dinosaur Scrapbook* (1980); O'Neil De Noux, "Tyrannous and Strong," *Asimov's Science Fiction* 24, no. 2 (February 2000): pp. 66–81; Robert Silverberg, "Our Lady of the Sauropods," in *Dinosaurs*, ed. Martin H. Greenberg (New York: Donald I. Fine Books, 1996), pp. 267–285.

31. Sanz, *op. cit.*, p. 69.

32. McCaffrey, *op. cit.*, pp. 169–163.

33. In McCaffrey's 1984 sequel *Dinosaur Planet—Survivors* (New York: Ballantine Books), it is finally divulged that "This planet's a zoo.... A sanctuary for the dinosaurs. The Thek have been stocking it for millennia—even before the cataclysm ... the critters are from Mesozoic Terra ... the Thek surveyed Old Terra eons ago and were entranced by the dinosaurs. Long before the animals were threatened with extinction by a climatic cataclysm, they had imported them to Ireta which they knew would permanently provide the proper environment.... Dinosaurs are Thek pets" (p. 289).

34. Glut, *op. cit.*, p. 16.

35. *Ibid.*, p. 17.

36. Hypnotic powers wielded by victims of Erigon's car-

nivorous dinosaurs recalls how Burroughs' Mahars devour entranced victims in subterranean Pellucidar, and the alien virus idea was later used by Robert J. Sawyer in *End of An Era* (see Appendix to this volume). After hurtling through "Cth space" to Earth aboard the *J-17*, Bishop remains intrigued by Leea's profound fear of the dinosaur hatchlings. They've already discounted the possibility that the odd behavior of Erigon's dinosaurs has anything to with the system's twin suns (obviously a non-terrestrial condition). But they never realized that Erigon's exodinosaurs are infested with an intelligent alien organism which has subjugated the dinosaurian bodies and minds. Since Erigon's dinosaurs are on the inevitable path to extinction, traveling aboard the *J-17* to Earth as symbionts within the eggs samples presents an ideal opportunity for them to proliferate on a more fertile world! All this becomes revealed in the climax when Bishop becomes hypnotized by a menacing tyrannosaur encountered in Dino-World. "As waves of horror swept over his mind and threatened to drive him mad, he knew he was now locked inside the skull of the saurian. Gene Bishop *was Oedipus rex*!" (My italics: "was") While Erigon was a world formerly dominated by nature red-in-tooth-and-claw, "a world of ancient heedless cruelty—a violent world, where life and death are but a jaw's width apart, a world of jaws and hungry bellies that clamor to be filled, a world that continually resounds with the squeaks and bellows of the dying," by the time of the *J-17's* arrival, exodinosaur species are languishing, their populations cut down by adverse, gradually cooling environmental conditions and a virus prevalent throughout Erigon's atmosphere. Yet the sentient aliens remain imprisoned within the bodies of the exodinosaurian races. So their only chance is to proliferate on a virus-free world where they can rule in their dinosaur bodies once more. So it's Earth versus exodinosaurs once more; their invasion is thwarted at the last minute.

37. Arthur C. Clarke, *2001: A Space Odyssey* (New York: A Signet Book, 1968). Furthermore, as aptly noted by Thomas D. Clareson, "...even after the American continent had been spanned, the frontier kept its hold on American imagination. Increasingly in popular fiction since World War Two the yearning for that new land has taken the form of exploring either the far reaches of the galaxy or the depths of the 'inner space' of the human psyche ... was not all civilization a prison?" (From Clareson's Introduction to *Kioga of the Unknown Land* (New York: Daw Books, Inc., 1978), p. 6.

38. Charles DePaolo, "Arthur C. Clarke's *2001: A Space Odyssey*: the promise of humanity," Chapter Eight in *Human Prehistory in Fiction* (Jefferson: NC: McFarland & Company, Inc., 2003), pp. 79–93.

39. James P. Hogan, *Inherit the Stars* (New York: Ballantine Books, 1977). Books such as Hogan's coupled the romance of the space race with far-out human paleoanthropology.

40. John D. Barrow and Frank J. Tipler, *The Anthropic Cosmological Principle* (Oxford University Press, 1986), pp. 586–590.

41. Dale A. Russell, "Models and Paintings of North American Dinosaurs," in *Dinosaurs Past and Present*, vol. 1, ed. S.J. Czerkas and E.C. Olson (Natural History of Los Angeles County in association with University of Washington Press, 1987), p. 125.

42. Allen A. Debus and Diane Debus, "A Paleontological Parallel," Chapter Eighteen of *Dinosaur Memories: Dino-Trekking for Beasts of Thunder, Fantastic Saurians, "Paleopeople," "Dinosaurabilia," and other "Prehistoria"* (Lincoln, NE: Authors Choice Press, 2002), pp. 341–352.

43. Frederick D. Gottfried, "Hermes to the Ages," in *The Science Fictional Dinosaur*, ed. Robert Silverberg,

Charles G. Wauch and Martin Harry Greenberg (New York: Avon Books,1982), pp. 111–146.

44. *Ibid.*, p. 133.

45. *Ibid.*, p. 144

46. S.D. Howe, "Wrench and Claw," *Analog* 68, no. 11 (November 1998): pp. 60–91. In Michael Carroll's "The Terrible Lizards of Luna," *Asimov's Science Fiction* 24, no. 6 (June 2000): pp. 54–62, scientists investigating a lunar crater discover 100-million-year-old three-toed footprints and a map of Earth in the Jurassic carved into a cave wall alongside alien "glyphs."

47. In Howe's story, as of sixty-five million years ago dinosaurs had "conquered" the moon and nearby planets. Mirroring Poul Anderson's theme in "Wildcat," a dino-scientist occupying a Lunar Observation Post asserts, "The idea of colonization, I thought, was to end ... wars by fighting against the challenges of space—of conquering new land." But the rival Martian cultist colony is intent on halting that worthy goal. For a warring faction of dino-extremists situated on the Martian colony have harnessed nuclear energy. Meanwhile, the lunar base allied to Earth's political faction is attacked by Martian loyalists. Lunar scientist survivors realize that even though the Martian dinosaurs have nuclear capability, they wouldn't bomb the Earth because "that would be nuts. They'd leave the whole planet uninhabitable. They couldn't return if they wanted to." Their premise turns out to be correct because, instead, the Martian dinos are using their nuclear devices as engines, towing a ten-mile-diameter asteroid to Earth with inevitable consequences. While Earth's ecology is literally sent into the dark ages, somewhere on the moon relics await discovery, remains of warriors and ancient technology, testimony which might endure for a billion years or more, eons beyond mankind's short reign in space-time.

48. Personal correspondence received from Dr. Hopp, dated April 2, 2001; Thomas P. Hopp, *Dinosaur Wars* (Lincoln, NE: Authors Choice Press, 2000). Conceptually, Hopp's novel is analogous to Barry B. Longyear's *The Homecoming* (New York: Walker and Company, 1989), to be discussed here in Chapter Eight. The theme of Longyear's premise poses a fitting conclusion to the Quintaglio odyssey, discussed later in this chapter.

49. Thomas P. Hopp, *Dinosaur Wars: Counterattack* (iUniverse, 2002).

50. My term "intelligent design" is not to be equated to an identical term recently surfacing with respect to the teaching of evolution in American biology classes. Instead, here, I simply mean that the course of evolution in a promising species has somehow been guided or directed along some set pathway leading to heightened intelligence—more or less like Moon-Watcher's was by the *2001* monolith—by an advanced celestial entity which may indeed seem god-like. For more on "intelligent design" as it pertains to present controversy within the American school system, see Richard Dawkins and Jerry Coyne, "In science, fact, not faith, measures ideas' validity," *Chicago Tribune*, September 18, 2005, section 2, pp. 1, 4. The Quintaglio trilogy comprises Robert J. Sawyer's *Far-Seer* (New York: Ace Books, 1992); *Fossil Hunter* (New York: Tor Books, 1993); and *Foreigner* (New York: Ace Books, 1994).

51. That is, the satellite "Land" is tidally locked, or for the astronomers reading this, within its "Roche Limit."

52. As the Watcher muses, "...the dinosaurs I had favored most, partly because they'd already had a long and successful history as a group, were tyrannosaurs: large, slope-backed carnivores with great heads and giant teeth. Only one problem: for almost the entire lifetime of this group, their forelimbs had been diminishing until now they were withered and all but useless, with just two clawed fingers on the end of each hand. The Jijaki read

the genetic code of these creatures and found the instructions that had originally produced a third and fourth finger, instructions that now were turned off in the early stages of embryonic development. On some of the individuals being transplanted, the *Jijaki* edited out the termination sequence" (*Fossil Hunter*, p. 199). Thus *Jijaki* engineered the five-fingered hands of the Quintaglio, contributing to their evolutionary success.

53. Or as Sawyer states, the *Jijaki* are "...extinct beings evolved from transplanted *Opabinia*, with six legs, five phosphorescent eyes each on a long stalk, plus a long flexible trunk ending in a pair of cup-shaped manipulators. The first intelligent form to emerge in this universe, used by the Watcher to transplant life from the Crucible" (*Foreigner*, p. 262). Sawyer, who once aspired to become a paleontologist, based *Jijaki* on the Cambrian genus *Opabinia*, a fossil invertebrate known exclusively from British Columbia's Burgess Shale deposits.

54. Sawyer, *op. cit.*, p. 121.

55. James Patrick Kelly, "Think Like a Dinosaur," *Asimov's Science Fiction* 19, no. 7 (June 1995): pp. 10–32. Kelly's exodinosaurs are highly selective as to which "sapients get to join the galactic club," because first "they must prove total commitment to preserving harmony." There must be no paradoxes, such as individuals *duplicated* by the transportation process. So when a girl is accidentally replicated (with her "twin" transported to her destination and the original still alive on the transporter), the protagonist becomes a cold-blooded killer, as he shoves her into an airlock which is then depressurized into space. "I don't know how long it took. The *thumping* slowed. Stopped. And then I was a hero. I had preserved harmony, kept our link to the stars open. I chuckled with pride; I could think like a dinosaur" (pp. 24, 31). Kelly's classic tale recalls another, although not involving a transporter: Tom Godwin's "The Cold Equations" (1954), republished in *The Science Fiction Hall of Fame* (New York: Avon Books, 1970).

56. Kelly's tale merits a short digression into exodinosaurs wielding fantastic technologies—transporter devices! One wouldn't associate exodinosaurs with transporter devices, like in *Star Trek*, but years before Captain Kirk made a habit of "beaming down," famed sci-fi author A.E. Van Vogt (1912–2000) wrote about alien dinosaurs invading a spaceship in *The Voyage of the Space Beagle* (New York: Collier Books, 1950): "...these monstrous things had been transported alive across light-centuries. It was like a dream, too fantastic to have happened at all.... Smith turned from the monster he had been studying. He said slowly, "Earth could have produced something like their type during the dinosaur age" (pp. 190–191).

57. While the scientists initially perceived that a six-mile-diameter asteroid or perhaps a ten-mile-diameter comet could have exterminated the dinosaurs, various astrophysical mechanisms conceived over the past quarter century have relied on either comets vs. asteroids. Science fiction writers find themselves picking their poison, so to speak.

58. Geoffrey A. Landis, "Embracing the Alien," *Analog* 62, no. 13 (November 1992): pp. 10–39. Landis' story seems an updated retelling of Fredric Brown's (1906–1972) "Arena" (1944), a classic tale that inspired *Star Trek*'s "Gorn" reptiloid race: Fredric Brown, "Arena," in *The Science Fiction Hall of Fame* (New York: Avon Books 1970), pp. 291–309. Brown's Arena planetoid was even inhabited by strange, sentient lizards—which, at a stretch, could be taken as little exodinosaurs.

59. Landis pays homage to Bradbury where, after they realize they've returned to Mesozoic Earth, one character orders, "*Don't* harm any animals you encounter! A change in history at this point could have severe consequences

millions of years hence." Then, as another crew member "gently brushed the insect off [his] shoulder," they all "put away their weapons" (p. 22).

60. Meanwhile, prior to impact, the *Outsider* rescued specimens of the Mesozoic species most likely to evolve into intelligent exodinosauroids which may evolve in seclusion on some as yet uncharted planet elsewhere in the Milky Way galaxy. Someday, once more, it will be time to embrace the "alien"—a remnant out of our shadowy past.

61. Recently, certain "pure" science fiction writers have disparaged space romances such as the *Star Trek* and *Star Wars* series of "formulaic" novels because they lure readers from other notable, perhaps more serious literature. But before we dismiss *Star Trek*, let's recognize that the classic television series was voted the number one science fiction series of all time, as noted in John Java's *The Best of Science Fiction TV* (New York: Harmony Books, 1987). And—hey!—I happened to love this particular novel. The *Star Trek* romance is at least a first-rate scientific romance, no less so than Gustavus Pope's or Astor's early entries—or even Edgar Rice Burroughs' when considered under contemporary standards. Furthermore, lest we forget—a Ph.D. paleontologist created *First Frontier*. Well done!

62. Importantly, on page 318 of *Star Trek—First Frontier*, we learn that Mesozoic ancestors (i.e. *Troodon*) of Clan-Ru were deliberately "seeded" on their world in our proper universe by an extinct species known as the Preservers. As I said, *First Frontier*'s plot *is* "complexly woven." And for purposes of discussion, I must qualify and clarify the term "dinosauroid," used here in referring to intelligent dinosaurs belonging to parallel universes (be they space-faring or not). Intelligent dinosaurs developed from genuine dinosaur stock within our "proper" universe, even in another galactic sector—such as the Clan-Ru—may be loosely regarded as "dinosauroids" (not because of their *appearance*) if they've mastered *technology*. So while Quintaglio and Clan-Ru have mastered technology and are dinosauroid-like, they're still not classical dinosauroids. However, the dinosauroids of Landis's story and those foreseen in a parallel universe by the *Enterprise* crew—as witnessed through the Guardian of Forever—*are* classical dinosauroids, based on late–1970s speculations of Dale Russell and, independently, Carl Sagan. Author Harry Harrison conceived another group of true dinosauroids— the *Yilane*—which, because of their non-space-faring nature, will be discussed in the next chapter instead of herein. In *Star Trek—First Frontier*, the dinosaur genus *Troodon* is an intelligent (non-dinosauroid) species having powers of intraspecies verbal communication.

63. During the mid–1970s, author Harlan Ellison proposed a story idea highly analogous to *Star Trek—First Frontier* for the first *Star Trek* film. This is mentioned by Stephen King, *Danse Macabre* (New York: Berkey Books, 1981), pp. 370–372. As described by Ellison, "...the story ... involved going to the end of the known universe to slip back through time to the Pleistocene period before Man first emerged. I postulated a parallel development of reptile life that might have developed into the dominant species on Earth had not mammals prevailed. I postulated an alien intelligence from a far galaxy where the snakes *had* become the dominant life form, and a snake-creature who had come to Earth in the *Star Trek* future, had seen its ancestors wiped out, and who had gone back into the far past of Earth to set up distortions in the time-flow so the reptiles could beat the humans. The *Enterprise* goes back to set time right, finds the snake-alien, and the human crew is confronted with the moral dilemma of whether it had the right to wipe out an entire life form just to insure its own territorial imperative in our present and future." Still, no asteroid, and no dinosaurs, per se.

64. Also, how curious that the Guardian of Forever's revelation of Earth's geological history recalls Axel's "waking dream" in Jules Verne's *Journey*.

65. And in a fitting conclusion on p. 383, Spock wrestles with a space-time paradox that even *he* is baffled by: "...the paradox of time travel is troubling me.... Since the Clan-Ru exists here and now, and we know they went back in time to stop the asteroid, then *you* must have been in the past also to keep them from stopping it. The circularity of time suggests that time cannot actually be changed. However, since we have been in the changed time, and we have experienced this kind of anomaly before, we know that it can be. Therefore, is the Guardian of Forever a danger, or is it part of the pattern of time itself...?" Kirk cuts him off, claiming he's giving him a headache. Warp factor five. Steady as she goes.

66. Carl Sagan, *Cosmos* (New York: Ballantine Books, 1980).

Chapter 7

1. James Gleick, *Chaos: Making A New Science* (New York: Viking Penguin, Inc., 1987); Stephen Jay Gould, *Wonderful Life: The Burgess Shale and the Nature of History* (New York: W.W. Norton & Company, 1989).

2. Robert Bakker, in *Earth–Special Supplement. The Dinosaurs of Jurassic Park: How They Really Lived* (1994), p. 19.

3. Michael Crichton, *Jurassic Park* (New York: Ballantine Books, 1990), p. 313.

4. David E. Fastovsky and David B. Weishampel, *The Evolution and Extinction of the Dinosaurs*, 2nd ed. (Cambridge: Cambridge University Press, 2005), p. 289.

5. Michael Crichton, *The Lost World* (New York: Alfred A. Knopf, 1995). According to Crichton, "The first book was, to me, about microsubjects and DNA technology, while the second one [i.e., *The Lost World*] is about macrosubjects. It's about populations, longterm trends and extinction." Crichton quoted in Bill Warren's article "Champion of the Prehistoric," *Dinosaur: Jurassic Park The Complete Saga* (Starlog Movie Series, 1997), p. 33.

6. Allen A. Debus and Diane E. Debus, "Tickled By Feathers," Chapter Twenty in *Paleoimagery: The Evolution of Dinosaurs In Art* (2002).

7. Max Begouen, *Quand le mammouth ressuscita* (Paris: Hacchette, 1928), p. 104. This quote is excerpted from pp. 13–14 of Claudine Cohen's *The Fate of the Mammoth: Fossils, Myth and History* (The University of Chicago Press, 2002).

8. Piers Anthony, *Balook* (New York: Ace Books, 1990).

9. *Ibid.*, p. 223.

10. *Ibid.*, p. 224.

11. *Ibid.*, pp. 28–29.

12. This quote is excerpted from Allen A. Debus and Diane Debus, *Dinosaur Memories* (2002), pp. 469–470.

13. Harry Adam Knight (pseudonym for John Brosnan), *Carnosaur* (London: A Star Book, 1984), p. 3. In 1985, Knight also wrote another experimental DNA-out-of-control thriller for Star Books titled *The Fungus*.

14. *Ibid.*, p. 100.

15. *Ibid.*, p. 108.

16. *Ibid.*, p. 110.

17. *Ibid.*, p. 212.

18. Harry Harrison, *West of Eden* (New York: Bantam Books, 1984), p. 318.

19. "Trembling Earth" was recently republished in *Dinosaurs II*, ed. Jack Dann and Gardner Dozois (New York: Ace Books, 1995), pp. 197–253. It originally appeared in *Isaac Asimov's Science Fiction Magazine* 14, nos. 11 & 12 (November 1990): pp. 52–93.

20. Gottfried's story was republished in *The Science Fictional Dinosaur*, ed. Robert Silverberg, Charles G. Waugh and Martin Harry Greenberg (New York: Avon Flare Book, 1982), pp. 111–146.

21. Olsen's story appeared in *Dawn of Time: Prehistory Through Science Fiction*, ed. Martin H. Greenberg, Joseph Olander and Robert Silverberg (Elsevier/Nelson Books: New York, 1979), pp. 79–89..

22. Robert Silverberg, "Our Lady of the Sauropods," in *Dinosaurs*, ed. Martin H. Greenberg (New York: Donald I. Fine Books, 1996), p. 273.

23. *Ibid.*, p. 285.

24. John H. Ostrom, "The Supporting Chain," *Discovery—Magazine of the Peabody Museum of Natural History* 5, no. 1 (Fall 1969): p. 10.

25. John H. Ostrom, "Osteology of *Deinonychus antirhopus*, an Unusual Theropod from the Lower Cretaceous of Montana," *Bulletin 30*, Peabody Museum of Natural History (July 1969). See their frontispiece and p. 142.

26. *Ibid.*, pp. 143–144.

27. *Life Before Man: The Emergence of Man*, by the Editors of Time-Life Books (New York: Time-Life Books, 1972), p. 89.

28. Adrian J. Desmond, *The Hot-Blooded Dinosaurs: A Revolution In Palaeontology* (New York: Warner Books, 1975), p. 108.

29. Allen A. Debus and Diane E. Debus, "A Paleontological Parallel," Chapter Eighteen in *Dinosaur Memories*, p. 345.

30. During this period two artists produced striking feathery impressions of raptors. Otter Zell's sculpture of a feathered *Deinonychus* (1984), Wayne Barlowe's painting of a *Velociraptor* enjoying a twilight vigil (1992), and Louis P. Jonas' circa-1970s *Deinonychus* sculpture are three of my favorites.

31. William Stout, *The Dinosaurs: A Fantastic New View of a Lost Era*, ed. Byron Preiss, narrated by William Service (New York: Mallard Press, 1981).

32. Sylvia J. Czerkas and Everett C. Olson, eds. *Dinosaurs Past and Present*, vol. 1 (Seattle: Natural History Museum of Los Angeles County in assoc. with University of Washington Press, 1987), p. 16.

33. Other images of contemporary "raptor" dinosaurs include Ely Kish's *Dromaeosaurus* and *Drocomeiomimus*, published on pp. 182 and 132, respectively of Edwin H. Colbert's *Dinosaurs: An Illustrated History* (Maplewood, NJ: Hammond Inc., 1983). *Sauronithoides* figured in Carl Sagan's "Tales of Dim Eden," the pivotal Chapter Six in *The Dragons of Eden* (New York: Ballantine Books, 1977).

34. Based on George Langelaan's "The Fly," published in *Playboy*, June 1957. Interestingly, Goldblum would later star as *Jurassic Park*'s Ian Malcolm.

35. S. Paabo, "Molecular cloning of Ancient Egyptian Mummy DNA," *Nature* 314 (1985): pp. 644–645.

36. Charles R. Pellegrino, "Dinosaur Capsule," *Omni* 7, no. 4 (January 1985): p. 40. George Poinar and Roberta Hess' preliminary examination of a forty-million-year-old fossil fly led the researchers to the conclusion that insect organelles are preserved in some amber specimens. Poinar and Hess, "Ultrastructure of 40-Million-Year-Old Insect Tissue," *Science* 215 (March 5, 1982): pp. 1241–1242.

37. Pellegrino, *op. cit.*, p. 115.

38. Michael Benton, "To clone a dinosaur," *New Scientist* (January 17, 1985): pp. 41–43.

39. Edward M. Golenberg, et. al., "Chloroplast DNA sequence from a Miocene *Magnolia* species," *Nature* 344 (April 12, 1990): pp. 656–658.

40. Rob DeSalle, et. al., "DNA Sequences from a Fossil Termite in Oligo-Miocene Amber and Their Phyloge-

netic Implications," *Science* 257 (September 25, 1992): pp. 1860–1862; Raul J. Cano, et. al., "Amplification and sequencing of DNA from a 120 to 135-million-year-old weevil," *Nature* 363 (June 10, 1993): pp. 536–538.

41. Cano quoted in *Chicago Tribune*, June 10, 1993.

42. Scott R. Woodward, et. al., "DNA Sequence from Cretaceous Period Bone Fragments," *Science* 266 (November 18, 1994): pp. 1229–1232.

43. "'No Go' for *Jurassic Park*–Style Dinos," *Science* 276 (April 18, 1997): p. 36. In particular, extractions of material from amber-preserved thirty-million-year-old termite and 125-million-year-old weevil experiments proved not to be repeatable, casting doubt on prior assertions that fossil DNA had been recovered.

44. Michael Crichton, *Jurassic Park*, p. 5.

45. *Ibid.*, pp. 146–147.

46. *Ibid.*, p. 306.

47. *Ibid.*, pp. 108–109.

48. *Ibid.*, p. 159.

49. *Ibid.*, p. 305.

50. *Ibid.*, p. 306.

51. *Ibid.*, p. 394.

52. John O'Neill, "Dinosaurs–R–Us: The (Un)Natural History of *Jurassic Park*," in *Monster Theory: Reading Culture*, ed. Jeffrey Jerome Cohen (Minneapolis: University of Minnesota Press, 1996), p. 296. In Crichton's *The Lost World*, zoologist Sarah Harding becomes an *Alien* sort of "Ripley" heroine.

53. *Ibid.*, p. 302.

54. Mary Shelley, *Frankenstein* (1831; reprint, New York: Pyramid Books, 1964). All quotes from *Frankenstein* excerpted from my paperback copy. For more on Shelley's inspirations for *Frankenstein*, see Radu Florescu's *In Search of Frankenstein* (Boston: New York Graphic Society, 1975).

55. Shelley, *ibid.*, introduction to 1831 ed., pp. 7–8.

56. Allen G. Debus also considers "palingenesis" as an early form of revivification of former organisms, perhaps even conceptually anticipating the genetic restorations attempted in 1980s dino-fiction. Palingenesis was allegedly achieved by liquefying an organic entity such as a plant or bird in a glass vial. Later an image of the organisms could be spied inside the vial when heated from below by a candle. Allen G. Debus, "A Further Note on Palingenesis: The Account of Ebenezer Sibly in the *Illustration of Astrology* (1792)," *Isis* 64 (1973): pp. 226–230. If only this could be done with fossil matter as well.

57. Paul Semonin, *American Monster* (New York: New York University Press, 2000).

58. Of course, because both the monster and his bride are wholly human, genetically, their progeny would be ordinary humans, not supermen or even monsters, although we can't fault Mary Shelley for not knowing this. This discussion also recalls that of the female Mahars' "Great Secret" for controlling overpopulation in Burroughs's *At the Earth's Core* series. See Chapter Two.

59. *Jurassic Park's* premise, that unpredictable, catastrophic chaos can arise from complicated ordered systems (related to the natural extinction of dinosaurs in Crichton's sequel, *The Lost World*), may seem tired or even flawed in its presentation. For Ian Malcolm, a mathematical chaotician, cautions that dinosaurs shouldn't be cloned from ancient DNA, although by then it is too late. According to paleontologist Stephen Jay Gould, Steven Spielberg's "...Malcolm ... preaches the opposite of chaos theory," and is given "the oldest diatribe ... and predictable staple of every Hollywood film since Frankenstein: man ... must not disturb the proper and given course of nature; man must not tinker in God's realm." Stephen Jay Gould, "Dinomania," in *The New York Review*, August 12, 1993. Yet Gould was mistaken in tracing the origins of this time-honored theme to Hollywood. For a century earlier, in 1831, Mary Shelley penned these words following a terrifying nightmare in which she "saw the pale student of unhallowed arts kneeling beside the thing he had put together. I saw the hideous phantasm of a man stretched out, and then, on the working of some powerful engine, show signs of life and stir with an uneasy, half vital motion. Frightful must it be for supremely frightful would be the effect of any human endeavor to mock the stupendous mechanism of the Creator of the world" (Shelley, *ibid.*, p. 8). The chaos which follows the unleashing of Frankenstein's monster on the world in Shelley's novel certainly rivals the chaotic impact of Crichton's dinosaurs.

60. Dennis R. Dean, *Gideon Mantell and the Discovery of Dinosaurs* (Cambridge: Cambridge University Press, 1999), p. 131.

61. Victor Appleton, *Tom Swift No. 4: The DNA Disaster* (New York: Pocket Books, 1991); Ian McDowell, "Bernie," *Asimov's Science Fiction* 18, no. 9 (August 1994): pp. 64–80; Frank M. Robinson, "The Greatest Dying," in *Dinosaur Fantastic*, ed. Mike Resnick and Martin H. Greenberg (New York: Daw Books, Inc., 1993), pp. 54–66; Penelope Banka Kreps, *Carnivores* (New York: Zebra Books, 1993).

62. Thomas Hopp, *Dinosaur Wars* (New York: Authors Choice Press, 2000); Hopp, *Dinosaur Wars: Counterattack* (iUniverse, 2002).

63. Bill Johnson's "Vaults of Permian Love," *Analog* (May 1999), pp. 72–85, ties retro-evolution to lesbianism. Lori Selke's "The Dodo Factory," *Asimov's Science Fiction* (March 2005): pp. 60–81, uses *Jurassic Park*–like technology to recreate the extinct dodo bird.

64. Rob DeSalle and David Lindley, *The Science of Jurassic Park and the Lost World* (New York: BasicBooks, 1997). For reflections on mammoth DNA restorations, see Robert Silverberg's editorial, "Pleistocene Park," *Asimov's Science Fiction* (September 2000): pp. 4–7.

65. Debus and Debus, "Just Like the Dinosaurs: Deep-Freeze Mammoths," Chapter Ten in *Dinosaur Memories*, pp. 177–190.

66. Allen A. Debus, "'A Look Bakk'- Robert Bakker: Revolutionary Paleontologist" (Part 3 of 3), *Prehistoric Times*, no. 71 (April/May 2005), p. 50.

67. Jeff Kurtti, *Dinosaur: The Evolution of an Animated Feature* (New York: Disney Editions, 2000).

68. *Anonymous Rex* (SciFi Pictures, 2005) was based on an acclaimed series of novels by Eric Garcia. According to a plot summary posted at SciFi.com, "Comprising a small percentage of the world's population, the dinosaurs' descendants have infiltrated every sector of life as doctors and lawyers, housewives and actors ... keen private eye Vincent Rubio is an evolved *Velociraptor*.... Ultimately, "Rex" is a reflection of culture—our foibles and addictions, our dreams and loves—as illustrated by the experiences of a dinosaur living among us." Garcia's novels will be discussed in Chapter Eight.

69. Craig Johnson, et. al., "Preservation of biomolecules in cancellous bone of *Tyrannosaurus rex*," *Journal of Vertebrate Paleontology* 17, no. 2 (June 1997): pp. 330–348. Researchers including John Horner concluded that heme, which is the molecular iron-containing portion of myoglobin (a muscle protein), and hemoglobin (the component of red blood cells assisting in the transfer of oxygen to cellular tissues and transport of waste carbon dioxide), as well as proteins associated with indigenous *T. rex* hemoglobin and possibly myoglobin, were positively detected in their experiments. Instrumentation designed to spectroscopically examine or separate extracted components detected molecules in the fossil bone that could also be extracted from ostrich, human or pigeon blood.

70. Mary H. Schweitzer, et. al., "Soft-tissue Vessels and

Cellular Preservation in *Tyrannosaurus rex*," *Science* 307 (March 25, 2005): pp. 1952–1955. This was a different bone specimen than that referenced in note 67.

71. Aldous Huxley, *Brave New World* (1946; reprint, New York: Perennial Library, 1978), pp. x–xiv.

72. Harrison, *op. cit.*, p. 468.

73. Crichton, *op. cit.*, p. 284.

74. Patrick Cox, "Jurassic Park a Luddite Monster," *Wall Street Journal*, July 9, 1993, p. 1.

75. Allen A. Debus, "It!'s Origins: Genesis of a Monster—the Controversy of Ideas," *Filmfax*, no. 104 (October/December 2004): p. 132.

Chapter 8

1. Allen A. Debus, "Decade of the Dinosaur," *Fossil News: Journal of Avocational Paleontology* 11, no. 5 (May 2005): pp. 7–16. For an in-depth look at the popular dinosaur collectibles available during the period and those who avidly collected, see "Mom, don't throw those dinosaurs away. They may be collectibles someday!," Chapter 34 in the author's *Dinosaur Memories: Dino-Trekking for Beasts of Thunder, Fantastic Saurians, 'Paleo-people,' 'Dinosaurabilia,' and other 'Prehistoria'* (Lincoln, NE: Authors Choice Press, 2002).

2. Jack Dann and Gardner Dozois, "A Change in the Weather," reprinted in *Dinosaurs!*, ed. Dann and Dozois (New York: Ace Books, 1990).

3. Allen A. Debus and Diane E. Debus, "Why Not the Mammals?," Chapter Five in *Dinosaur Memories: Dino-Trekking for Beasts of Thunder*, etc., pp. 85–110; Robert T. Bakker, "The Superiority of Dinosaurs," *Discovery: Magazine of the Peabody Museum of Natural History, Yale University* 3, no. 2 (Spring 1968): pp. 11–22.

4. Stephen Jay Gould, "The Dinosaur Rip-off," in *Bully For Brontosaurus* (New York: W.W. Norton & Company, 1991), pp. 94–106; W.J.T. Mitchell, *The Last Dinosaur Book: The Life and Times of a Cultural Icon* (Chicago: The University of Chicago Press, 1998).

5. H.P. Lovecraft, "The Shadow Over Innsmouth," reprinted in *The Dunwich Horror and Others* (Sauk City, WI: Arkham House Publishers, Inc., 1963), pp. 303–367.

6. Malcolm Hulke, *Doctor Who and the Cave-Monsters* (London: A Target Book, 1984); James Blish with Gene L. Coon, *Star Trek 2* (New York: Bantam Books, 1968), "Arena," pp. 1–12.

7. And many children have been raised with books and televised programs featuring talking anthropomorphic dinosaurs, such as the purple dinosaur Barney," the *Dinosaurs* 1990s television show, Syd Hoff's *Danny and the Dinosaur* (1958), etc. .

8. Italo Calvino, *Cosmicomics* (New York: Harcourt, Brace & World, Inc., 1968). For further scholarly discussion concerning Calvino's story, see W.J.T. Mitchell, *op. cit.*, 1998, pp. 41–46. Calvino's work anticipates Eric Garcia's, to be discussed later in this chapter.

9. Dale A. Russell, "Models and Paintings of North American Dinosaurs," in *Dinosaurs Past and Present*, vol. 1, ed. Sylvia J. Czerkas and Everett C. Olson (Seattle and London: Natural History Museum of Los Angeles County in association with University of Washington Press, 1986), p. 130.

10. Steven Utley, "Getting Away," reprinted in *Dinosaurs!*, ed. Dann and Dozois (New York: Ace Books, 1990).

11. Utley, *ibid.*, p. 75.

12. Nixon quoted on the back cover of Rachel Carson's *Silent Spring* (Greenwich, CT: A Fawcett Crest Book, 1970).

13. Adrian J. Desmond, *The Hot-Blooded Dinosaurs: A Revolution in Palaeontology* (New York: Warner Books, 1975), pp. 281–283.

14. Leigh Clark, *Carnivore* (Book Margins, Inc., 1997); K. Robert Andreassi, *Gargantua* (New York: Tor Books, 1998). For more on *Gargantua*, see my article "Alternative Kaiju–Part 3: Gargantua," *G-Fan* no. 71 (Spring 2005): pp. 70–75.

15. Arthur N. Strahler and Alan H. Strahler, *Environmental Geoscience: Interaction Between Natural Systems and Man* (Santa Barbara, CA: Hamilton Publishing Company, 1973), p. 498.

16. Clifford D. Simak, *Mastodonia* (New York: Ballantine Books, 1978). Also see note 37 to Chapter Five and the Appendix.

17. Sharon Farber, "The Last Thunder Horse West of the Mississippi," reprinted in *Dinosaurs!*, ed. Dann and Dozois (New York: Ace Books, 1990).

18. Harry Turtledove, "The Green Buffalo," in *The Ultimate Dinosaur*. ed. Robert Silverberg (New York: iBooks, Inc., 2000), pp. 390–401.

19. James Gurney, *Dinotopia: A Land Apart From Time* (Atlanta: Turner Publishing, Inc., 1992); James Gurney, *Dinotopia: The World Beneath* (Atlanta: Turner Publishing, Inc., 1995).

20. James Gurney, interviewed by Allen A. Debus for *Dinosaur World* 1, no. 3 (October 1997): pp. 21–24.

21. Gurney, *op. cit.*, 1992, p. 77.

22. Gurney, *op. cit.*, 1997.

23. *Ibid.*, p. 132.

24. Alan Dean Foster, *Dinotopia Lost* (Atlanta: Turner Publishing Company, 1996). A dozen children's books on the *Dinotopia* theme were published as well. One example is Donald F. Glut's *Dinotopia: Chomper* (Atlanta: Turner Publishing Co., 2000).

25. Gurney, *op. cit.*, 1997.

26. James Patrick Kelly, "Mr. Boy," *Asimov's Science Fiction* 14, no. 6 (June 1990): pp. 118–174. A similar idea is explored in Pat Cadigan's "Dino Trend" (1993), published in *Dinosaur Fantastic*. Here people transform themselves into trendy dinosaurs utilizing nanotechnology. Another means for dinosaurs to assimilate themselves into human society is for them to become household *pets*, as in David Gerrold's 1993 short story, "Rex," concerning a genetically engineered tyrannosaur, or Kevin O'Donnell Jr.'s "Saur Spot" (1993), about a DNA-regenerated *Coelophysis* with a taste for roaches, both published in *Dinosaur Fantastic*. An alternative to house pets is dinosaurs as zoo animals, as explored in Gene Wolf's 1997 story, "Petting Zoo," published in *Return of the Dinosaurs*.

27. Mark Jacobson, *Gojiro* (New York: Grove Press, 1991).

28. Eric Garcia, *Anonymous Rex* (New York: Villard Books, 1999); Eric Garcia, *Casual Rex* (New York: Villard Books, 2001).

29. Garcia, *op. cit.*, p. 78.

30. *Ibid.*, p. 92.

31. *Ibid.*, p. 261.

32. *Ibid.*, p. 262.

33. Barry B. Longyear, *The Homecoming* (New York: Walker and Company, 1989), p. 119. Longyear's book is expertly illustrated by Alan M. Clark. In particular, the concept of jokes and humor is foreign to the Nitolans.

34. Ray Bradbury, *The Martian Chronicles* (New York: Bantam Books, 1972), p. 181.

35. John Noble Wilford, *The Riddle of the Dinosaur* (New York: Alfred A. Knopf, 1985), p. 272.

Select Bibliography

Several of the references cited in chapter footnotes have been omitted from this bibliography presenting mainstream documents, all of which should be more readily available through university or public library systems. Here, I have been highly selective about listing fanzine periodicals and society journals which ordinarily aren't archived in libraries (e.g., microfilm, microfiche, or hard copy form). However, I have incorporated science fiction magazine references cited in this volume which are ordinarily maintained within and are accessible through library systems. I have focused here on mainstream documentation bearing most directly on chapter subjects. Other information may be found under individual chapter footnotes.

Aldinger, Harley S. "The Way of a Dinosaur." *Amazing Stories* 3, no.1 (April 1928): pp. 35–37.

Adler, Jr., Bill, ed. *Time Machines: The Greatest Time Travel Stories Ever Written.* New York: Carroll & Graf Publishers, Inc., 1998.

Aldiss, Brian W. *The Best Science Fiction Stories of Brian W. Aldiss: Man In His Time.* New York: Collier Books, 1988.

_____. *Cryptozoic.* New York: Avon Books, 1967.

Aldiss, Brian W., with David Wingrove. *Trillion Year Spree* New York: Avon Books, 1986.

Alkion, Paul K. *Origins of Futuristic Fiction.* Athens, GA: The University of Georgia Press, 1987.

Alvarez, L.W., W. Alvarez, F. Asaro, and H.V. Michel. "Extraterrestrial cause for the Cretaceous-Tertiary extinction: experimental results and theoretical interpretation." *Science* 208 (1980): pp. 1095–1108.

Andreassi, K. Robert. *Gargantua.* New York: Tor Books, 1998.

Appleton, Victor. *Tom Swift No. 4: The DNA Disaster.* New York: Archway, 1991.

Asimov, Isaac, ed. *Before the Golden Age: A Science Fiction Anthology of the 1930s.* Garden City, NY: Doubleday & Co., Inc., 1974.

_____. *The Best Science Fiction of Isaac Asimov.* New York: Doubleday, 1986.

Asimov, Isaac, Martin H. Greenberg, and Charles G. Waugh, eds. *The Birth of Science in Fiction.* New York: Knightsbridge Publishing Company, 1981.

Bakker, Robert T. *Raptor Red.* New York: Bantam Books, 1995.

_____. "The Superiority of Dinosaurs." *Discovery: Magazine of the Peabody Museum of Natural History, Yale University* 3, no. 2 (Spring 1968): pp. 11–22.

Ballard, J.G. *The Drowned World.* New York: Berkley Books, 1966.

Barnes, Arthur K. "The Hothouse Planet." *Thrilling Wonder Stories* 10, no. 2 (October 1937): pp. 12–29.

Batory, Dana Martin, and William A.S. Sarjeant. "The Terror of Blue John Gap—A Geological and Literary Study." *ACD—The Journal of the Arthur Conan Doyle Society* 5 (1994): pp. 108–125.

Baxter, Stephen. *The Time Ships.* New York: HarperPrism, 1995.

_____. *Evolution.* New York: Ballantine Books, 2000.

Bear, Greg. *Dinosaur Summer.* New York: Warner Books, 1998.

Beecham, John Charles. "Out of the Miocene" (Parts 1–2). *The Popular Magazine* 33 (August 23, 1914): pp. 88–107; (September 7, 1914): pp. 141–166.

Benton, Michael. "To clone a dinosaur." *New Scientist* (January 17, 1985): pp. 41–43.

Berry, Mark F.*The Dinosaur Filmography*. Jefferson, NC: McFarland & Company, Inc., 2002.

Berry, Mark F."Joe DeVito: A Mighty Interview" (Parts 1–2) *Prehistoric Times* no. 73 (August/ September 2005): pp. 28–31, 47; no. 74 (October/November 2005): pp. 28–31, 45.

Bierce, Ambrose. *The Collected Works of Ambrose Bierce*. Vol. 1. New York: Neale Publishing Co., 1909.

Bingham, Carson. *Gorgo*. Derby, CT: Monarch Books, Inc., 1960.

Bird, Roland T. "Did Brontosaurus Ever Walk on Land?" *Natural History* 53 (1944): pp. 61–67.

_____. "Thunder in His Footsteps." *Natural History* 48 (May 1939): pp. 254–261, 302.

Blade, Alexander. "Stories of the Stars ... Aldebaran, in Taurus." *Fantastic Adventures* 7, no. 5 (December 1945): p. 178, back cover.

Bradbury, Ray. "The Beast From 20,000 Fathoms." *The Saturday Evening Post* (June 23, 1951): pp. 28–29, 117–118.

_____. *Dinosaur Tales*. New York: Bantam Books, 1983.

_____. *The Martian Chronicles*. New York: Bantam Books, 1972.

Breyer, John, and William Butcher. "Nothing New under the Earth: The Geology of Jules Verne's *Journey to the Center of the Earth*." *Earth Sciences History* 22, no. 1 (2003): pp. 36–54.

Brown, Lewis S. *Yes, Helen, There Were Dinosaurs*. N.p.; self-published, 1982.

Brusatte, Stephen. *Stately Fossils: A Comprehensive Look at the State Fossils and Other Official Fossils*. Boulder, CO: Fossil News, 2001.

Burroughs, Edgar Rice. *At the Earth's Core*. 1914. Reprint, New York: Ace Books, 1978.

_____.*Back to the Stone Age*. 1936, 1937. Reprint, New York: Ace Books, 1978.

_____.*The Land That Time Forgot*. 1918. New York: Ace Books, 1963.

_____.*Out of Time's Abyss*. 1918. Reprint, New York: Ace Books, 1979.

_____. *Pellucidar*. 1923. 1921, New York: Ace Books, 1963.

_____. *The People That Time Forgot*. 1918. Reprint, New York: Ace Books, 1979.

_____. *Tarzan the Terrible*. 1921. Reprint, New York: Ballantine Books, 1963.

_____. *Tanar of Pellucidar*. 1929. Reprint, New York: Ace Books, 1978.

_____. *Tarzan at the Earth's Core*. 1930. Reprint, New York: Ballantine Books, 1964.

_____. *Tarzan of the Apes*. 1912. Reprint, New York: Ballantine Books, 1982.

Cabot, John York "Blitzkrieg in the Past." *Amazing Stories* 16, no. 7 (July 1942): pp. 8–47.

Capek, Karel. *War With the Newts*. 1936. Reprint, trans. Ewald Osers, Highland Park, NJ: Catbird Press, 1985.

Carey, Diane, and James I. Kirkland. *Star Trek: First Frontier*. New York: Pocket Books, 1995.

Carson, Rachel. *Silent Spring*. 1962. Reprint, Greenwich, CT: A Fawcett Crest Book, 1970.

Cerasini, Marc. *AVP: Alien vs. Predator*. New York: HarperEntertainment, 2004.

Chester, William L. *Kioga of the Unknown Land*. 1938. Reprint, New York: Daw Books, 1978.

Ciencin, Scott. *Dinoverse*. New York: Random House, 1999.

Clark, Leigh. *Carnivore*. Fort Washington, PA: Book Margins, Inc., 1997.

Clarke, Arthur C. *The Hammer of God*. New York: Bantam Books, 1993.

_____. *Report on Planet Three and Other Speculations*. New York: Berkley Books, 1972.

_____. *2001: A Space Odyssey*. New York: A Signet Book, 1968.

Cohen, Claudine. *The Fate of the Mammoth: Fossils, Myth and History*. Chicago: The University of Chicago Press, 2002.

Cohen, Jeffrey Jerome, ed. *Monster Theory: Reading Culture*. Minneapolis: University of Minnesota Press, 1996.

Costello, Peter. *Jules Verne: Inventor of Science Fiction*. NewYork: Charles Scribner's Sons, 1978.

Crichton, Michael. *Jurassic Park*. New York: Ballantine Books, 1990.

_____. *The Lost World*. New York: Alfred A. Knopf, 1995.

Czerkas, Sylvia M., and Donald F. Glut. *Dinosaurs, Mammoths, and Cavemen: The Art of Charles R. Knight*. Syracuse, NY: E.P. Dutton, Inc., 1982.

Czerkas, S.J., and E.C. Olson, eds. *Dinosaurs Past and Present*. Vol. 1. Natural History of Los Angeles County in association with University of Washington Press, 1987.

Dann, Jack, and Gardner Dozois, eds. *Dinosaurs!* New York: Ace Books, 1990.

_____. *Dinosaurs II*. New York: Ace Books, 1995.

Darwin, Charles. *The Origin of Species: By Means of Natural Selection Or the Preservation of Favoured Races in the Struggle for Life*. 6th ed.1872. Reprint, with a foreword by George Gaylord Simpson, New York: Collier Books, 1905.

Debus, Allen A. "Decade of the Dinosaur." *Fossil News: Journal of Avocational Paleontology* 11, no. 5 (May 2005): pp. 7–16.

_____. "The Great and Terrybubble." *The Baum Bugle* 48, no. 2 (Autumn 2004): pp. 20–23.

_____. "Humphry Davy's *Consolations*" (Parts 1–2). *Journal of Avocational Paleontology* 12 (May 2006): pp. 14–17; (June 2006): pp. 14–17.

_____. "Reframing the Science in Jules Verne's *Journey*." *Science Fiction Studies* (in press, Vol. 33, November 2006, no. 100).

_____. "Sorting Fossil Vertebrate Iconography in Paleoart." *Bulletin of the South Texas Geological Society* 44, no.1 (September 2003): pp. 5, 10–24.

Debus, Allen A., and Diane E. Debus. *Dinosaur Memories: Dino-trekking for Beasts of Thunder, Fantastic Saurians, 'Paleo-people,' 'Dinosaurabilia,' and other 'Prehistoria.'* Lincoln, NE: Authors Choice Books, 2002.

_____. *Paleoimagery: The Evolution of Dinosaurs in Art.* Jefferson, NC: McFarland & Company, Inc., 2002.

De Camp, L. Sprague. *Rivers of Time.* Riverdale, NY: Baen Books, 1993.

De Camp, L. Sprague, and Catherine Crook De Camp. *The Day of the Dinosaur.* 1968. Reprint, Garden City, NY: Doubleday, 1985.

De Noux, O'Neil. "Tyrannous and Strong." *Asimov's Science Fiction* 24, no. 2 (February 2000): pp. 66–81.

DePaolo, Charles. *Human Prehistory in Fiction.* Jefferson, NC: McFarland & Company, Inc., 2003.

Desalle, Rob, and David Lindley. *The Science of Jurassic Park.* New York: Basic Books, 1997.

Desmond, Adrian J. *The Hot-Blooded Dinosaurs: A Revolution in Palaeontology.* New York: Warner Books, 1975.

DeVito, Joe, and Brad Strickland. *Merian C. Cooper's King Kong.* New York: St. Martin's Griffin, 2005.

Dingus, Lowell, and Timothy Rowe. *The Mistaken Extinction: Dinosaur Evolution and the Origin of Birds.* New York: W.H. Freeman and Company, 1998.

Dixon, Dougal. *The New Dinosaurs: An Alternative Evolution.* Topsfield, MA: Salem House Publishers, 1988.

Doyle, Arthur Conan. *The Lost World.* In *The Strand Magazine* 43 to 45 (April to November 1912).

_____. *The Lost World of Arthur Conan Doyle.* 1912. Reprint, Collector's Anniversary Edition, ed. John R. Lavas, New Zealand, 2002.

_____. "The Terror of Blue John Gap." *The Strand Magazine* 40 (September 1910).

Drake, David. *Tyrannosaur.* New York: Tor Books, 1993.

Evans, Arthur B. "The Illustrators of Jules Verne's *Voyages Extraordiniaires.*" *Science Fiction Studies* (July 1998): pp. 241–270.

_____. "Literary Intertexts in Jules Verne's *Voyages Extraordinaires.*" *Science Fiction Studies* 23, no. 2 (July 1996): pp.172–173.

Farlow, James O., Michael Brett-Surman, and Robert Walters. *The Complete Dinosaur.* Bloomington: Indiana University Press, 1997.

Figuier, Louis. *The World Before the Deluge.* London: Cassell & Company, 1867.

Finney, Jack. *Time and Again.* New York: Simon and Schuster, 1970.

Fitting, Peter, ed. *Subterranean Worlds: A Critical Anthology.* Middletown, CT: Wesleyan University Press, 2004.

Flammarion, Camille. *Le monde avant la creation de l'homme. Origines de la terre. Origines de la vie. Origines de l'humanité.* Paris: C. Marpon and E. Flammarion, 1886.

Foster, Alan Dean. *Dinotopia Lost.* Atlanta: Turner Publishing Company, 1996.

Garcia, Eric. *Anonymous Rex.* New York: Villard Books, 2000.

_____. *Casual Rex.* New York: Villard Books, 2001.

Gerrold, David. *Deathbeast.* New York: Popular Library, 1978.

Glut, Donald F. *The Dinosaur Scrapbook.* Secaucus, NJ: Citadel Press, 1980.

_____. *Dinosaur Valley Girls.* Rockville, MD: Sense of Wonder Press (in press), 2006.

_____. *Frankenstein in the Lost World.* Castle of Frankenstein, Tome 6. 1971. Reprint, Highwood, IL: Druktenis Publishing, 2002.

_____. *Spawn.* New York: Laser Books, 1976.

Goetzmann, William. *New Lands, New Men.* New York: Viking Penguin, Inc., 1986.

Golden, Christopher. *King Kong.* New York: Pocket Star Books, 2005.

Gould, Stephen Jay. *Bully for Brontosaurus.* New York: W.W. Norton & Company, 1991.

_____. *Wonderful Life: The Burgess Shale and the Nature of History.* New York: W.W. Norton & Company, 1989.

Greenberg, Martin H., ed. *Dinosaurs.* New York: Donald I. Fine Books, 1996.

Griffiths, Martin. "Deterministic Chronology: Satire, Time & Meaning in the Novels of Kurt Vonnegut." Undated, posted online.

Gurney, James. *Dinotopia: A Land Apart from Time.* Atlanta, GA: Turner Publishing, Inc., 1992.

_____. *Dinotopia: The World Beneath.* Atlanta, GA: Turner Publishing, Inc., 1995.

Hachya, Michihiko. *Hiroshima Diary.* New York: Avon Books, 1955.

Hanson, L. Taylor. "Lords of the Underworld." *Amazing Stories* 15 (April 1941): pp. 8–47.

Harrison, Harry. *Return to Eden.* New York: Bantam Books, 1988.

_____. *West of Eden.* New York: Bantam Books, 1984.

_____. *Winter In Eden.* New York: Bantam Books, 1986.

Heilmann, Gerhard. *The Origin of Birds.* London: Witherby, 1926.

Hering, Henry A. "Silas P. Cornu's Divining Rod." *Cassell's Family Magazine* (June 1899): pp. 65–71.

Hitchcock, Alfred, ed. *Spellbinders In Suspense.* New York: Random House, 1967.

Hogan, James P. *Inherit the Stars.* New York: Ballantine Books, 1977.

Holmes, John Eric. *Mahars of Pellucidar.* New York: Ace Books, 1976.

Holtzmark, Erling B. *Edgar Rice Burroughs.* Boston: Twayne Publishers, 1986.

Hopp, Thomas P. *Dinosaur Wars.* Lincoln, NE: Authors Choice Press, 2000.

_____. *Dinosaur Wars: Counterattack.* iUniverse, 2002.

Howe, S.D. "Wrench and Claw." *Analog* 68, no. 11 (November 1998): pp. 60–91.

Hubbell, Will. *Cretaceous Sea.* New York: Ace Books, 2002.

_____. *Sea of Time.* New York: Avon Books, 2004.

Hulke, Malcolm. *Dr. Who and the Dinosaur Invasion.* London: A Target Book, 1976.

_____. *Dr. Who and the Cave-Monsters.* London: A Target Book, 1983.

Huxley, Aldous. *Brave New World.* 1946. Reprint, New York: Perennial Library, 1978.

Hyne, C.J. Cutcliffe. *The Lost Continent.* 1899. Reprint, New York: Ballantine Books, 1972.

Irwin, G.H. "Lair of the Grimalkin." *Fantastic Adventures* 10, no. 4 (April 1948): pp. 8–53.

Jacobson, Mark. *Gojiro.* New York: Grove Press, 1991.

Johnson, Bill. "Vaults of Permian Love." *Analog* 119, no. 5 (May 1999): pp. 72–85.

Johnson, Craig. "Preservation of biomolecules in cancellous bone of *Tyrannosaurus rex.*" *Journal of Vertebrate Paleontology* 17, no. 2 (June 1997): pp. 330–348.

Johnson, Osa. *I Married Adventure: The Lives of Martin and Osa Johnson.* New York: J.D. Lippincott Company, 1940.

Kelly, James Patrick. "Mr. Boy." *Asimov's Science Fiction* 14, no. 6 (June 1990): pp. 118–174.

_____. "Think Like A Dinosaur." *Asimov's Science Fiction* 19, no. 7 (June 1995): pp. 10–32.

King, Stephen. *Danse Macabre.* New York: Berkley Books, 1981.

Knight, Harry Adam. *Carnosaur.* London: A Star Book, 1984.

Knipe, Henry Robert. *Nebula to Man.* New York: J.M. Dent & Company, 1905.

Kreps, Penelope Banka. *Carnivores.* New York: Kensington Publishing, 1993.

Kuttner, Henry. "Beauty and the Beast." *Thrilling Wonder Stories* 16, no. 1 (April 1940): pp. 67–76.

Landis, Geoffrey A. "Embracing the Alien." *Asimov's Science Fiction* 62 (November1992): pp. 132–168.

Lankester, E. Ray. *Extinct Animals.* London: Archibald Constable, 1905.

Laudan, Rachel. *From Mineralogy to Geology: The Foundations of a Science 1650-1830.* Chicago: The University of Chicago Press, 1987.

Lebeck, Douglas. *Memories of A Dinosaur Hunter.* Bloomington, IN: 1st Books Library, 2002.

Lees, J.D., and Marc Cerasini, eds. *The Official Godzilla Compendium.* New York: Random House, 1998.

Leigh, Stephen. *Ray Bradbury Presents Dinosaur World.* New York: Avon Books, 1992.

_____. *Ray Bradbury Presents Dinosaur Planet.* New York: Avon Books, 1993.

Lerangis, Peter. *Time Machine 22: Last of the Dinosaurs.* New York: Bantam Books, 1988.

Lessem, Don. *Raptors: The Nastiest Dinosaurs.* New York: Little, Brown and Co., 1996.

Levine, Joseph M. *Dr. Woodward's Shield: History, Science, and Satire in Augustan England.* Berkeley, CA: University of California Press, 1977.

London, Jack. *Before Adam.* New York: The Macmillan Co., 1907.

Longyear, Barry B. *The Homecoming.* New York: Walker and Company, 1989.

Lourie, Eugene. *My Work in Films.* San Diego: Harcourt Brace Jovanovich, 1985.

Lovecraft, H.P. *The Dunwich Horror and Others.* Sauk City, WI: Arkham House, 1963.

Lovelace, Delos W. *King Kong.* New York: Grossett and Dunlap, 1932.

Mackal, Roy P. *A Living Dinosaur?* Leiden, The Netherlands: E.J. Brill, 1987.

Marche II, Jordan D. "Edward Hitchcock's Poem: The Sandstone Bird (1836)." *Earth Sciences History* 10, no. 1 (1991): pp. 5–8.

Mayor, Adrienne. *The First Fossil Hunters.* Princeton: Princeton University Press, 2000.

_____. *Fossil Legends of the First Americans.* Princeton: Princeton University Press, 2005.

McCaffrey, Anne. *DinosaurPlanet.* New York: Ballantine Books, 1978.

_____. *Dinosaur Planet–Survivors.* New York: Ballantine Books, 1984.

McGowan, Christopher. *The Dragon Seekers: How an Extraordinary Circle of Fossilists Discovered the Dinosaurs and Paved the Way for Darwin.* Cambridge, MA: Perseus Publishing, 2001.

Meritt, Abraham. *The Face in the Abyss.* New York: Liveright, 1931.

Milner, Richard. *The Encyclopedia of Evolution.* New York: Facts On File, 1990.

Mitchell, W.J.T. *The Last Dinosaur Book: The Life and Times of a Cultural Icon.* Chicago: The University of Chicago Press, 1998.

Moore, James, R., ed. *History, Humanity and Evolution: Essays for John C. Greene.* Cambridge: Cambridge University Press, 1989.

Moser, Stephanie. *Ancestral Images: The Iconography of Human Origins.* Ithaca, NY: Cornell University Press. 1998.

Moskowitz, Sam, ed. *Science Fiction by Gaslight.* Cleveland and New York: The World Publishing Company, 1968.

Nahin, Paul J. *Time Travel: A writer's guide to the real science of plausible time travel.* Cincinnati, OH: Writer's Digest Books, 1997.

Nye, Nicholas. *Return to the Lost World.* Upton upon Severn, Worcestershire, England: The Self-Publishing Association, Ltd., 1991.

Obruchev, Vladimir. *Plutonia.* 1924. Reprint, Moscow: Raduga Publishers, 1988.

Ostrom, John H. "Osteology of *Deinonychus antirrhopus*, an Unusual Theropod from the Lower Cretaceous of Montana." *Bulletin 30* (Peabody Museum of Natural History, July 1969).

_____. "The Supporting Chain." *Discovery—Magazine of the Peabody Museum of Natural History* 5, no. 1 (Fall 1969).

Owen, Dean. *Reptilicus.* Derby, CT: Monarch Books, 1961.

Pellegrino, Charles R. "Dinosaur Capsule." *Omni* 7, no. 4 (January 1985): pp.38–40, 11–115.

Petticolas, Arthur. "Dinosaur Destroyer." *Amazing Stories* 23 (January 1949): pp.8–71.

Piers, Anthony. *Balook.* New York: Ace Books, 1990.

Pohl, Frederick. *Alternating Currents.* New York: Ballantine Books, 1956.

Poinar, George, and R. Hess. "Ultrastructure of 40-million-year-old Insect Tissue." *Science* 215 (March 5, 1982): pp. 1241–1242.

Pope, Gustavius W. *Romances of the Planets: N. 1 Journey to Mars.* G.W. Dillingham, 1894.

Preston, Douglas. *Tyrannosaur Canyon.* New York: Forge, 2005.

Price, Robert M., ed. *The Antarktos Cycle: At the Mountains of Madness and Other Chilling Tales.* Oakland, CA: A Chaosium Book, 1999.

Rainger, Ronald. *An Agenda for Antiquity: Henry Fairfield Osborn and Vertebrate Paleontology at the American Museum of Natural History, 1890-1935.* Tuscaloosa: The University of Alabama Press, 1991.

Reid, Constance. *The Search for E. T. Bell: Also Known as John Taine.* Washington, D.C.: The Mathematical Association of America, 1993.

Resnick, Michael, and Martin H. Greenberg, eds. *Dinosaur Fantastic.* New York: Daw Books, Inc., 1993.

_____. *Return of the Dinosaurs.* New York: Daw Books, Inc., 1997.

Rivkin, J.F. *Age of Dinosaurs No. 1: Tyrannosaurus rex.* New York: Roc, 1992.

Roberts, Charles G.D. *In the Morning of Time.* London: Hutchinson & Company, 1919.

Robertson, Garcia y. "The Virgin and the Dinosaur." *Asimov's Science Fiction* 16 (February 1992): pp. 132–168.

Robeson, Kenneth. *The Land of Terror.* 1933. Reprint, New York: Bantam Books, 1965.

Rovin, Jeff. *The Encyclopedia of Monsters.* New York: Facts On File, 1989.

_____. *Fatalis.* New York: St. Martin's Paperbacks, 2000.

Rudwick, Martin J.S. "Caricature as a Source for the History of Science: De la Beche's Anti-Lyellian Sketches of 1831." *Isis* 66 (1975): pp.534–560.

_____. "The Emergence of a Visual Language for Geological Science." *History of Science 1760-1840* 14 (1976): pp. 149–195.

_____. *Scenes from Deep Time: Early Pictorial Representations of the Prehistoric World.* Chicago: The University of Chicago Press, 1992.

Rush, Joseph Harold. *The Dawn of Life.* Garden City, NY: Hanover House, 1957.

Russett, Cynthia Eagle. *Darwin In America: The Intellectual Response 1865-1912.* San Francisco: W.H. Freeman and Company, 1976.

Sagan, Carl. *The Dragons of Eden.* New York: Ballantine Books, 1977.

Sand, George. *Laura: A Journey Into the Crystal.* London: Pushkin Press 2004.

Sanz, Jose Luis. *Starring T. Rex!: Dinosaur Mythology and Popular Culture.* Bloomington: Indiana University Press, 2002.

Savile, Frank. *Beyond the Great South Wall.* New York: Grosset and Dunlap, 1901.

Sawyer, Robert J. *End of an Era.* New York: Ace Books, 1994.

_____. *Far-Seer*. New York: Ace Books, 1992.

_____. *Foreigner*. New York: Ace Books, 1994.

_____. *Fossil Hunter*. New York: Tor Books, 1993.

Schweitzer, Mary H. "Soft-tissue Vessels and Cellular Preservation in *Tyrannosaurus rex*." *Science* 307 (March 25, 2005): pp. 1952–1955.

Selke, Lori. "The Dodo Factory." *Asimov's Science Fiction* 29, no. 3 (March 2005): pp. 60–81.

Semonin, Paul. *American Monster: How the Nation's First Prehistoric Creature Became a Symbol of National Identity*. New York: New York University Press, 2000.

Shelley, Mary. *Frankenstein*. 1831. Reprint, New York: Pyramid Books, 1964.

Silverberg, Robert. *At Winter's End*. New York: Warner Books, 1988.

_____. "Heart of Stone." *Asimov's Science Fiction* 27, no. 12 (December 2004): pp. 4–9.

_____, ed. *The Ultimate Dinosaur*. New York: iBooks, 2000.

Silverberg, Robert, Charles G. Waugh, and Martin H. Greenberg, eds. *The Science Fictional Dinosaur*. New York: Avon Books, 1982.

Simak, Clifford D. *Mastodonia*. New York: Ballantine Books, 1978.

_____. *Our Children's Children*. New York: G.P. Putnam's Sons, 1974.

Simpson, George Gaylord. *The Dechronization of Sam Magruder*. New York: St. Martin's Griffin, 1996.

Sommer, Marianne. "The Romantic Cave? The Scientific and Poetic Quests for Subterranean Spaces in Britain." *Earth Sciences History* 22, no. 2 (2003): pp. 172–208.

Sternberg, Charles Hazelius. *Hunting Dinosaurs: In the Bad Lands of the Red Deer River, Alberta Canada*. 1917. Reprint, with an introduction by David A.E. Spalding, Edmonton: NeWest Press, 1985.

Strickland, Brad, with John Michlig. *Kong: King of Skull Island, Created and illustrated by Joe DeVito*. Milwaukie, OR: DH Press, 2004.

Swanwick, Michael. *Bones of the Earth*. New York: EOS, 2002.

_____. "Riding the Giganotosaur." *Asimov's Science Fiction* 23 (October/November 1999): pp.142–156.

Taine, John. *Before the Dawn*. 1934. Reprint, New York: Arno Press, 1974.

_____. *The Iron Star*. 1930. Reprint, Westport, CT: Hyperion Press, 1976.

Taliaferro, John. *Tarzan Forever: The Life of Edgar Rice Burroughs, Creator of Tarzan*. New York: Scribner, 1999.

Thompson, Ruth Plumly. *Speedy in Oz*. Chicago: The Reilly & Lee Co., 1934.

Time-Life Books. *Life Before Man: The Emergence of Man*. New York: Time-Life Books, 1972.

Trinkaus, Erik, and Pat Shipman. *The Neandertals: Changing the Image of Mankind*. New York: Alfred A. Knopf, 1993.

Tsutsui, William. *Godzilla on My Mind*. New York: Palgrave Macmillan, 2004.

Twain, Mark. *Letters From the Earth*. Ed. B. DeVoto. New York: Harper & Row, 1938.

Utley, Steven. "Treading the Maze." *Asimov's Science Fiction* 26 (February 2002): pp. 80–85.

_____. "Walking in Circles." *Asimov's Science Fiction* 26 (January 2002): pp. 62–67.

Verne, Jules. *Backwards to Britain*. New York: Chambers, 1992.

_____. *Journey to the Center of the Earth*. 1867. Reprint, trans. William Butcher, Oxford: Oxford University Press, 1998.

_____. *The Village in the Treetops*. 1902. New York: Ace Books, 1964.

Vernier, J.P. "The SF of J.H. Rosny the Elder." *Science Fiction Studies* 6 (July 1975): pp. 156–163.

Warren, Bill. *Keep Watching the Skies!* Vol. 2. Jefferson, NC: McFarland & Company, Inc., 1982.

Weart, Spencer. "From the Nuclear Frying Pan Into the Global Fire." *The Bulletin of the Atomic Scientists* (June 1992): pp.19–27.

Weist, Jerry. *Bradbury: An Illustrated Life*. New York: William Morrow, 2002.

Wells, H.G. *The Complete Science Fiction Treasury of H.G. Wells*. New York: Avenel Books, 1978.

_____. *Mr. Blettsworthy on Rampole Island*. Garden City, NY: Doubleday, Doran & Co., Inc., 1928.

_____. *The Time Machine*. In *The Science Fiction Hall of Fame*. Vol. IIA. Ed. Ben Bova. New York: Avon Books, 1973, pp. 452–526.

Wells, H.G., Julian Huxley, and G.P. Wells. *The Science of Life*. Garden City, NY: Doubleday, Doran & Co., 1935.

Wendt, Herbert. *Before the Deluge*. New York: Doubleday & Company, Inc., 1968.

Wilford, John Noble. *The Riddle of the Dinosaur*. New York: Alfred A. Knopf, 1985.

Williams, Robert Moore. "Jongor of Lost Land." *Fantastic Adventures* 2, no. 8 (October 1940): pp. 10–57, 133.

_____. "The Lost Warship." *Amazing Stories* 17, no. 1 (January 1943): pp.8–56.

Winslow, J.H., and A. Meyer. "The Perpetrators of Piltdown." *Science 83* (September 1983): pp. 32–43.

Wollheim, Donald, ed. *Flight Into Space: Great Science-Fiction Stories of Interplanetary Travel*. New York: Frederick Fell, Inc., 1950.

Woodward, John. *Essay Toward a Natural History of the Earth*. London, 1723.

Index